GENRE and TELEVISION

GENRE and TELEVISION

From Cop Shows to Cartoons
in American Culture

Jason Mittell

ROUTLEDGE
NEW YORK AND LONDON

Published in 2004 by
Routledge
29 W 35th Street
New York, NY 10001
www.routledge-ny.com

Published in Great Britain by
Routledge
11 New Fetter Lane
London EC4P 4EE
www.routledge.co.uk

RoutledgeFalmer is an imprint of the Taylor & Francis Group.
Printed in the United States of America on acid-free paper.

10 9 8 7 6 5 4 3 2 1

Library of Congress Cataloging-in-Publication Data
Mittell, Jason.
    Genre and television: from cop shows to cartoons in American culture / by Jason Mittell.
        p. cm.
Includes bibliographical references.
    ISBN 0-415-96902-6 (alk. paper) ISBN 0-415-96903-4 (pbk.: alk.paper)
1.   Television serials—United States. 2.   Television program genres—United States. I. Title.
PN1992.3.U5 M55 2004
791.45'6—dc22   2003027169

Portions of this book have appeared in earlier versions in the following publications:

Chapter 1, "A Cultural Approach to Television Genre Theory," *Cinema Journal*, 40:3, Spring 2001, 3-24.

Chapter 2, "Before the Scandals: The Radio Precedents of the Quiz Show Genre," in *The Radio Reader: Essays in the Cultural History of US Radio Broadcasting*, edited by Michele Hilmes and Jason Loviglio (New York: Routledge, 2002), 319-42.

Chapter 3, "The Great Saturday Morning Exile: Scheduling Cartoons on Television's Periphery in the 1960s," in *Prime Time Animation: Television Animation and American Culture*, edited by Carol Stabile and Mark Harrison (New York: Routledge, 2003), 33-54.

Chapter 4, "Audiences Talking Genre: Television Talk Shows and Cultural Hierarchies," *Journal of Popular Film and Television*, 31:1, Spring 2003, 36-46.

Chapter 6, "Cartoon Realism: Genre Mixing and the Cultural Life of *The Simpsons*," *The Velvet Light Trap* #47, Spring 2001, 15-28.

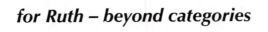

for Ruth – beyond categories

Contents

Acknowledgments

Acknowledgment pages in academic books are practically genres unto themselves, with their own particular textual conventions — like noting the collaborative nature of scholarship — and associated reading practices — such as flipping first to the acknowledgments to see who is thanked or snubbed. But while they might be formulaic and routine, they can also be quite sincere. As this project is the culmination of a decade of study, I have numerous people to thank for their support, input, and participation in my work.

This project originated at University of Wisconsin–Madison, and Julie D'Acci offered engaged direction and feedback from its inception to final draft, providing invaluable guidance from the theoretical to the pragmatic, and always offering more respect and encouragement than I could ever need. John Fiske taught me how to read and teach theory, and Michele Hilmes made me (finally!) appreciate the value of history — both with remarkable collegiality, friendship, and optimism. Many other faculty offered key insights and inspiration along the way, including Don Crafton, Vance Kepley, Jo Ellen Fair, Paul Boyer, David Weberman, Ron Radano, and especially David Bordwell. My first-class peers, with whom I shared, debated, discovered, and developed ideas throughout my years in Madison, added immeasurably to this project, with particular thanks to Daniel Marcus, Kevin Glynn, Tasha Oren, Derek Kompare, Chris Smith, Dorinda Hartmann, Donald Meckiffe, Jennifer Wang, Bill Kirkpatrick, Philip Sewell, Christine Becker, Jennifer Fay, Sally Ross, and Scott Higgins. Four peers were especially generous with their friendship and intellectual engagement, deserving of more thanks than can be expressed here: Michael Kackman, Elana Levine, Ron Becker, and Paul Ramaeker.

As my geographic range widened, more guidance, advice, and support came from Henry Jenkins, Joshua Meyrowitz, Michael Curtin, Allison McCracken, Susannah Stern, Kathy Battles, Sue Murray, Annette Hill, and Brian Rose, all adding to the scholarly soup along the way. At Georgia State University, a number of colleagues provided sympathetic input and encouragement, including David Cheshier, Sujatha Sosale, Carol Winkler, Allaine Cerwonka, and most notably Greg Smith and Ted Friedman. Finally at Middlebury College, I have benefited tremendously from a vibrant community allowing me to finish the manuscript with support and intellectual engagement. Special thanks to Brett Millier, Michael Newbury, Holly Allen, Will Nash, Deb Evans, Tim Spears,

John McWilliams, Leger Grindon, and especially Chris Keathley, who all provided feedback, encouragement, and camaraderie in the final innings. Matt Byrnie's editorial work is most responsible for shepherding this novice author into print, and I cannot thank him enough for his continued commitment to this project.

I was fortunate to be able to interview industrial personnel — thanks to Susan Harris and Paul Witt for taking time to talk with me about *Soap* and especially Linda Simensky for providing invaluable insight about Cartoon Network and modeling an exemplary bridge between scholarship and practice. The staffs of a variety of libraries and archives were helpful in my research, including the National Archives in College Park, Maryland; University of California, Los Angeles; Museum of Television and Radio in Los Angeles; and especially the great staffs of the University of Wisconsin Memorial Library, Wisconsin Center for Film and Theater Research, and Wisconsin State Historical Society Archives. Michael Pogorzelski and Lars Negstad provided great hospitality during research trips, and Kelly Cole was the perfect advance scout for my foray into the FCC collection. Crucial financial support was provided by the Ruth McCarty Dissertation Research Grant (Department of Communication Arts, University of Wisconsin), University of Wisconsin Graduate School Dissertation Fellowship, and Summer Research Funding (Department of Communication, Georgia State University).

My family has been more supportive of my eclectic career choice than I could hope for, always providing encouragement and excitement, as well as some bewilderment over the idea of writing about cartoons and *Dragnet*. My two daughters, Greta and Anya, were born during the marathon of seeing this book into print, and they continue to prove perspective on what really matters. But all of these previous thanks combined could not match the importance of my partner's contributions to this project. Ruth Hardy has provided love, support (in every meaning of the term), patience, intellectual engagement, and P.F.W. way above and beyond the realm of spousal expectations. Without her participation and partnership, neither this project nor I could be what we are today, and for that (and so much more) I dedicate this book to her with love.

The ideas explored in this book are intended to create a dialogue and spur new ideas, but books are a hopelessly one-way form of communication. To avoid these pages representing the "final word" on the topic, I invite you to continue the discussion online at http://community.middlebury.edu/~jmittell, where I encourage dialogue, feedback, debate, questions, comments, corrections, and further explorations into genre and television.

Introduction: Genres That Matter

In the early 1990s — before I discovered the field of media studies — I had a close encounter with television genres. As a regular weekly ritual, I would gather with friends to watch one of our favorite television programs, *Northern Exposure* (1990–95). One friend, Wendy, called *Northern Exposure* her favorite sitcom. As was typical of our friendship, this set off a heated yet friendly debate. I argued that *Northern Exposure* was a drama, not a sitcom; Wendy stood pat. I marshaled a range of evidence for my case — *Northern Exposure* was an hour-long show, not like half-hour sitcoms. *Northern Exposure* had no laugh track, featured ongoing dramatic story arcs, and was filmed in a cinematic style typical of dramas. *Northern Exposure* won Emmys and Golden Globes for Outstanding Drama Series, not Comedy. I even showed her copies of reviews that called the show a drama to prove my case, but Wendy would not relent — she argued that because the show made her laugh, it was a sitcom. This argument ended, as they usually did, in a stalemate. In retrospect, what does this generic dispute tell us about television genres? Certainly not that either of us was correct or incorrect — much more interesting is that *Northern Exposure*'s genre seemed to matter so much to us as television viewers, while at the same time generic categorizations were not simple and clear-cut. Why would such a trivial thing as a television show's generic classification matter?

This book argues that television genres do matter a great deal, but not in the ways in which scholars have generally used them. Television genres matter as *cultural categories*, an argument the rest of this book develops. Genres work within nearly every facet of television — corporate organizations, policy decisions, critical discourses, audience practices, production techniques, textual aesthetics, and historical trends. Most texts have some generic identity, fitting into well-entrenched generic categories or incorporating genre mixing like dramedies such as *Ally McBeal* (1997–2002) or blends like *Make Me Laugh* (1979), a comedy/game show. Industries use genres to produce programs, to define brands and identities (channels such as ESPN or Cartoon Network), and to target audiences through scheduling (locating genres within timeslots, as in daytime soap operas). Genres help audiences organize fan practices (generically determined clubs, conferences, and Web sites), guide personal preferences, and frame everyday conversations and viewing practices, like my debate with Wendy. Academics use generic distinctions to delineate research projects and organize teaching, while journalistic critics rely upon genres to locate programs within a common framework. Even going to the video store or skimming through *TV Guide* reveals genre as the primary framework to sort out television's vast array of programmatic options. Despite these multiple ways in which television genres matter, little scholarly work has been aimed at explaining how and why they do.[1]

This book offers a television-specific genre theory and argues for the continued importance of genre in organizing televisual practices. Specifically, I contend that television genre is best understood as a process of categorization that is not found within media texts, but operates across the cultural realms of media industries, audiences, policy, critics, and historical contexts. I draw this theoretical position from a cultural studies perspective that focuses on a circuit of cultural practice operative in multiple sites, instead of a singular realm of textual criticism or institutional analysis. Thus, genres can be seen as key ways that our media experiences are classified and organized into categories that have specific links to particular concepts like cultural value, assumed audience, and social function. By considering genre an ongoing multifaceted practice rather than a textual component, we can see how genre categorization points to much more than just whether *Northern Exposure* is a comedy or a drama, providing greater insight into the specific ways in which our most widespread cultural medium shapes our social world through categorical differences and hierarchies. This theory of genre situates genre distinctions and categories as active processes embedded within and constitutive of cultural politics, pointing to how media engage with and shape our culture, and how underexamined facets of media, like genres, matter.

But why genre? Don't other categorical axes — like racial identity, gender, class, or age — matter more in today's post-Fordist economic model, which has supplanted genre with other modes of categorization such as market segment, target audience, or network identity? Likewise, many critics have argued that television programming in the postmodern era is marked by such genre hybridity that the notion of pure generic forms is outdated.[2] Although genre is certainly not the only mode of televisual categorization active today, and "pure" generic examples are comparatively rare today, neither of these critiques invalidates the importance of genre. For every industrial practice defined primarily by market segment (like Lifetime's definition as a "women's channel"),[3] there are equivalent uses of generic categories for similar ends (like Sci-Fi Channel). Additionally, even if genres exist today only in blended form, they are still significant in how they operate within mixtures — *Buffy the Vampire Slayer* (1997–2003) mixes horror and teen drama, but both of these genres (and others) matter explicitly within the text and in discourses surrounding the show's production and reception. As I discuss in Chapter 6, cases of mixture often foreground generic conventions even more than "core" examples of a genre, as often unstated generic assumptions rise to the surface through textual juxtapositions, production decisions, and reception controversies. Thus we cannot jettison genre analysis simply because the cases are not "pure," but must look instead to the multiplicity of genres evoked in any instance. Through the prevalence of generic mixing and niche segmentation, genres may be even more important today than in previous television eras.

Even if genre is still a relevant and operative notion in today's televisual practices, why must we look to the specificities of television genre? Film and literary genre theorists have addressed many of the points I explore in this book, often proposing solutions that may seem adequate to understanding the way television genres work as well — why not simply apply these theories to television? While not ignoring the contributions of literary and film genre analysis for television, many specifics of television cannot be addressed through the lens of film and literary studies, as some specific attributes of television question the fundamental thrust of these traditional approaches. Unlike literature or film, television rarely has pretensions toward high aesthetic value, making it problematic to consider television using the same aesthetic tools designed for high literature or visual arts, because this simply dooms television to evaluative failure and misrepresents the way the majority of television viewers and producers engage with the medium. Similarly, television resists clear authorial definition, with an episodic style of programming and production practices that are even more collaborative than for film, problematizing the authorship models that are evoked in film and literary genre studies.

Besides their aesthetic ties, literary and film genre studies have focused primarily on cases of fictional narrative, with many genre theories grounded upon narrative analysis as the primary constitutive element of genres.[4] While this might be acceptable in literature, which makes a clear distinction between fiction and nonfiction as an object of study, and somewhat acceptable for film, where non-narrative forms like documentary or avant-garde styles are clearly separate from mainstream film production, television regularly mixes narrative and nonnarrative formats. From prime-time's mix of news magazines and sitcoms to daytime's blend of soap operas and talk shows, as well as the ubiquity of commercials that blur the narrative/nonnarrative lines even further, the logic of the television schedule and the average viewer's experiences of watching television schedules resist the easy equation between narrative and genres. Furthermore, many popular programming formats actively flout narrative/nonnarrative distinctions — professional wrestling, dramatized true-story crime shows such as *Unsolved Mysteries* (1988–97), staged courtroom programs like *Judge Judy* (1996–), and nearly all "reality shows" mix narrative norms and documentary forms. Thus, unless we impose a narrative framework upon nonfiction programs (which seems quite far-fetched for home shopping or sports highlight shows), television genre theory cannot rely on narration as its core constitutive aspect.

Additionally, film and literature genre theories simply cannot account for some of the industrial practices specific to television programming. While some film genre theorists have looked to Hollywood's practices as partially constitutive of genre definitions, there are specifics of the television industry that have no precedents or parallels in film paradigms.[5] For instance, scheduling practices are a central mechanism for television programmers to distinguish between shows, creating distinctions that have clear genre repercussions (like the importance of daytime programming in defining the soap opera), but no real parallels in other media.[6] The television industry contributes to the creation and maintenance of genre definitions through other practices such as genre-specific channels (like Game Show Network, Sci-Fi Channel, and ESPN), target marketing (for example, CBS's strategic redefinition of the sitcom audience from rural to urban in the early 1970s), and alliances with other industries (such as different generically segmented facets of the music industry within channels such as MTV, Country Music Television, and Black Entertainment Television). None of these practices — discussed more in Chapter 3 — could be accounted for within a theory of genre designed for literary or film texts.

To understand how television genres operate with both medium specificity and accounting for generic practices beyond media texts, we need a theoretical account of genres as cultural categories. In Chapter 1, I offer a detailed theoretical approach to television genres, examining how genre categories operate throughout the range of spheres that constitute television as a medium — industries, texts, audiences, policies, critics, and historical contexts. Rather than emerging from texts as has traditionally been argued, genres work to categorize texts and link them into clusters of cultural assumptions through discourses of definition, interpretation, and evaluation. These discursive utterances may seem to reflect on an already established genre, but they are themselves constitutive of that genre; they are the practices that define genres, delimit their meanings, and posit their cultural value. Genres operate in an ongoing historical process of category formation — genres are constantly in flux, and thus their analysis must be historically situated. By examining television genres as historically contextualized practices, we can better explore how the use of genre categories is shaped by — and shapes — cultural power relations that form the critical agenda of much contemporary media scholarship. In laying out a detailed theoretical model, I highlight a number of issues and concerns that encourage genre scholars to adapt our approach to be more consistent with contemporary media studies.

As cultural studies rightly insist that theory be grounded in historical instances, the bulk of this book explores television genres in specific cases. While no one case study provides an account of any genre in its entirety (if such a thing is even possible), each places a specific instance within a larger historical and cultural context, while illuminating particular attributes about television genres. The selected genres present a wide range of television offerings, including nonnarrative, narrative, hybrid, controversial, and underexamined genres, as well as looking at specific moments that span from television's radio and film origins to contemporary incarnations. Despite offering a range of specific genre analyses, this book is explicitly not claiming to be a television genre handbook.[7] I make no claims for comprehensive coverage of all television genres — news, sports, advertising, medical dramas, educational television, and science fiction are among the important genres that receive only passing mentions.[8] The goal of this book is to illuminate and exemplify a theoretical approach to genre that may be used to study any genre or historical moment, not to offer brief overviews on every television genre. The specific analyses do not claim to be comprehensive accounts of their genres, as there is much more to say about all of the genres explored here; rather, by focusing on specific issues and historical moments, we can see how genres work at the micro-level of media practice.

While ranging across genres and historical moments, the case studies are all centered upon television as practiced within the United States. Although my theoretical approach to genre certainly could be applied to broader global examples, I focus solely on American examples within this project for continuity and focus. The histories of particular genres would be quite different across different national and international contexts — for instance, the industrial history of television animation in Chapter 3 would change radically if considering the cultural operation of cartoons in Japan. Likewise, the talk show audiences in Chapter 4 specifically address American talk shows, although the assumed hierarchies and values certainly would be made richer through an international comparative approach. By limiting myself to American television genres, I hope not to limit the possibilities of applying this approach to a range of media practices throughout the world, as the field of media studies is fortunately turning more to international and comparative approaches in recent years.

Chapter 2 addresses media historiography in relation to cultural policy issues, exemplifying a model of generic genealogy. Using the quiz show scandals of the late 1950s as a point of departure, I trace the history of the quiz show backwards to explore how this canonized event in television history can be better understood using the tools of genre study. The core conflict surrounding the scandals — the public's shock upon realizing that quiz shows were staged — drew upon central generic assumptions. According to various histories of this incident, the audience was scandalized by the violation of what they had taken to be a core generic convention — quiz shows televise unrehearsed "fair" competition. Yet this assumption was not an uncontested and uniform attribute of the quiz show, especially in the genre's emergence on radio through a number of less notorious scandals, which culminated in an attempted FCC ban of quiz shows in 1948. By focusing on the conflicting discourses of the quiz show genre before the television scandals, as circulating among media audiences, industries, regulators, critics, and texts, the scandals appear less as a unique violation of media norms than as a continuation of a series of controversies surrounding the genre's definition, cultural value, and role in American society. The genre's history on radio demonstrates the use of genre categories in cultural policy-making and regulation, with a complex series of negotiations between governmental regulators, the broadcasting industry, and radio's national audience over generic norms and assumptions. This analysis demonstrates the importance of a model of genre history that looks beyond texts by including the areas of industrial and audience practice, facets which the next two chapters explore in further depth.

Television-specific industrial practices work to constitute genres, as exemplified by two moments in the history of the cartoon — the creation of the Saturday morning animated programming block in the early 1960s and the emergence of Cartoon Network in the 1990s. Through this industrial history in Chapter 3, I examine how scheduling practices shifted the genre, from general audiences watching cartoons as theatrical shorts in the 1950s, toward a redefinition of the cartoon as a children's-only (and thus childish) genre, exploring the cultural implications of this shift for media constructions of the child audience and new cultural hierarchies of taste. Thirty years later, Cartoon Network's scheduling and marketing practices worked to redefine the genre's audience and cultural assumptions of value and taste beyond the child-centered paradigm forged in the 1960s, even though many of the specific texts involved in both moments are identical. In both instances, I situate these generic practices within the context of larger industrial trends, such as 1960s generic cycles and 1990s market segmentation. By considering the television industry as a vital realm of genre formation, we can uncover the industry's power to define genre as a production and distribution strategy and further particular cultural assumptions as linked to generic categories.

Although the television industry wields great power in creating and controlling genres, audiences engage in their own practices, which often run counter to industrial norms. To explore the realm of media audience practice, Chapter 4 turns to the contemporary genre of the talk show to consider how viewers use and make sense of wide-ranging generic labels. Through an original audience research study exploring the discourses of distinction that audience members use concerning the talk show genre, we can see how television genres play a crucial role in forming and maintaining cultural hierarchies and categories of social identity, such as gender, age, and racial difference. Thus, within the intrageneric categorization of talk shows, audience members link cultural validity to the assumed audience identity of programs ranging from *Larry King Live* (1985–) to *The Jerry Springer Show* (1991–). In this audience analysis, I foreground how genres are not homogenous sites of cultural consensus, but rather function as sites of struggle over contesting assumptions, pointing toward the contradictions, conflicts, and controversies that typify audience discourses surrounding this contentious genre. Following Pierre Bourdieu's framework for studying cultural taste, I ground these hierarchies within the specificities of the cultural debates concerning talk shows in the 1990s.[9] Through this analysis, I highlight how audiences use generic categories differently than industries, critics, and academics, questioning the assumptions that media scholars often make in studying the cultural operation of genre categories.

After exploring the operations of genre at the level of industries and audiences, I turn to the more traditional site of generic analysis: the text. While maintaining that genres are not derived from texts, Chapter 5 explores how textual analysis might be reconfigured within my cultural approach to genre by examining the stylistic and ideological elements of the police genre within the landmark (yet underexplored) program *Dragnet* (1951–59; 1967–70) in its multiple historical eras. In its original 1950s context, *Dragnet* offered a uniquely stylized program, with textual elements adapted from semidocumentary and *film noir* cinema undergirding its discursive links to authenticity and ideology. I explore how the show linked these elements to television genre categories and helped set vital precedents tying the television police show to dominant meanings of law, criminality, and social order. When *Dragnet* returned to the air in 1967, it attempted to deal with the changing times by addressing contemporary issues like drug use and hippie subculture, all within a highly structured 1950s ideological mindset that ignored key generic shifts within the police show throughout the 1960s. By examining *Dragnet*'s revised context — and mostly unchanged text — of the 1960s, I explore the relationship of a text and genre to its historical context, arguing how we might look at a genre's history across eras as part of a larger process of cultural history and generic circulation.

Chapter 6 considers the key issue of genre mixing through a mode of programming in which generic codes are made especially manifest: parody. Using both *Soap* (1977–82) and *The Simpsons* (1989–) as examples, I examine genre parody as a textual and industrial strategy and explore how critics and audiences engage with these parodic practices of genre, often resulting in cultural controversies. *Soap* debuted to boycotts, protests, and inflammatory rhetoric due to its overtly sexual content; by examining the wealth of discourses surrounding this controversy, I argue that *Soap*'s use of genre parody fueled its transgression of hierarchical norms and categories (including daytime/prime-time, humorous/serious, and adult/family targeted), fanning the flames of controversy. Although less controversial, *The Simpsons* similarly fostered debates through its violation of clear-cut categories, particularly by bringing an adult satiric sensibility to both a family-friendly genre (domestic sitcom) and child-centered format (cartoon). Rather than following some critics who suggest that postmodern hybridity and parody indicate the decline or growing irrelevance of genres, I ultimately argue that genre mixing and parody point to the continued importance of genre as an organizing principle, bringing the conventions, codes, and assumptions of genres to the surface of texts and surrounding industry and audience discourses.

The book concludes with some brief reflections on the newest genre category to emerge: reality television. By exploring some of the potential ways of thinking about reality television as a cultural category, we can see both the possibilities and limitations of my approach to television genres as cultural categories. At its most provocative level, this book argues for a reconceptualization of genre studies, contending that projects which have followed the traditional approach to genre study — analyzing a set of texts grouped by a genre category — do not actually study genres. Rather, I contend that analyzing genres must consider the processes and practices of categorization itself, not just the elements which fall under a categorical rubric. The analysis of texts categorized by a genre is certainly a worthy endeavor, but not equivalent to the study of that genre — to understand reality television as a genre, we need to look at more than reality shows. By focusing on genres as cultural categories, we can better understand this key aspect of media practice that does matter to audiences, critics, industries, and producers — by returning the issue of genre to the agenda of television studies, I want to suggest how genres should matter for scholars as well.

1
Television Genres as Cultural Categories

In one of the most famous instances of genre analysis in action, U.S. Supreme Court Justice Potter Stewart wrote that, while he couldn't define pornography, "I know it when I see it."[1] This famous phrase highlights two key points for understanding media genres: genre definitions often have palpable "real world" impact (even with admittedly weak rationales), and genre practices emerge in a wide range of sites, including legal and policy decisions. The "I know it when I see it" mode of genre definition is not limited to jurists, however, as it describes the way most people experience their own ubiquitous categorization of media. Genres are so common throughout various arenas of cultural practice that their definitions can often seem like givens — we all agree upon a basic understanding of what a sitcom is, so no further elaboration is needed.

However, one of the great lessons of poststructuralism is to question the categories that seem to be natural and assumed. Genre definitions are no more natural than the texts that they seem to categorize. Genres are cultural products, constituted by media practices and subject to ongoing change and redefinition. To better understand what genres are and how they operate in cultural practice, we need genre theory to ground our understanding of how they work within various cultural realms. But the turn toward genre theory is not an easy move for television scholars. The vast body of genre theory, as produced within literary and film studies, has trouble accounting for many of the specific industry and audience practices unique to television (such as scheduling decisions, commonplace serialization, habitual viewing, and channel segmentation), as well as for the mixture of fictional and nonfictional programming that constitutes the lineup on nearly every TV channel. Importing genre theories from other media into television studies cannot

1

address key specificities of the television medium, which are formative of the genre categories we may wish to analyze.[2]

Beyond the issue of medium specificity, television genre theory needs to work against some of the core assumptions of traditional approaches to genre. Most genre theory has focused on issues that may seem outdated to some media scholars. Formal and aesthetic approaches to texts, or structuralist theories of generic meanings, for example, may seem incompatible with contemporary methods of cultural analysis. In particular, the central questions motivating many media scholars today — how do television programs fit into historically specific systems of cultural power and politics? — appear distant from those that typify genre theory.[3] Thus a return to genre theory might imply theoretical backtracking, either to structuralism, aesthetics, or ritual theories, all of which take a backseat to current cultural studies paradigms within television studies. Even the most influential discussion of television genre theory, Jane Feuer's essay in *Channels of Discourse*, ultimately concludes that genre analysis, as a paradigm, does not work as well for television as it has for film or literature.[4] Yet genres remain central to both television industries and audiences, begging the question of how television genre studies might move theoretically forward.

The answers to this question thus far have not been fully satisfying. Many television genre studies seem to be content in taking genres at face value, using the categorical labels that are culturally commonplace without much consideration of the meanings or usefulness of those selfsame labels. Television scholars who do engage in theoretical issues have been quick to employ film and literary theories, often (though not always) with brief disclaimers noting the flaws inherent in these paradigms, while signaling the now ubiquitous "more work in this area is needed." This book offers "more work in this area," proposing an alternative approach to television genre theory that might account for the cultural practices of television genre better than traditional paradigms. At its core, this approach argues for a reconceptualization of what has been typically placed under the rubric of genre analysis, an argument not easily made in abstract theoretical terms. Thus, while this chapter offers most of the theoretical "heavy lifting," the rest of the book engages with the specific nuances of television genres in cultural practice, using detailed historical and critical analyses to put my theoretical approach to work.

Traditional Genre Analysis and the Textualist Assumption

Traditional approaches to studying television genres have posed a number of central questions about what genres are and how they work. The first major approach to genre — dating back to Aristotle himself — poses *questions of definition*. The core question that an analysis of genre definition seeks to answer is "what makes a given genre distinct?" Definitional approaches seek to identify the core elements that constitute a given genre, looking inward at texts to explain and delimit the formal mechanisms constituting the essence of any given genre. Clearly, this approach is tied to aesthetic and formalist paradigms, looking at texts in and of themselves to understand their internal operations and the "proper" taxonomy of a genre. Definitional approaches to genre have a long history in literature and film studies, although few scholars have taken up this approach to understanding television genres.[5] The reasons for this lack are somewhat obvious — few scholars are willing to defend television as primarily an aesthetic medium, especially when it comes to nonnarrative genres that seem resistant to traditional aesthetic theories.[6]

However, is a central goal of definition and formal understanding necessarily incompatible with television? Certainly the majority of television genre analyses do provide a brief account of what definitions of the genre are being used, drawing somewhat upon formalist genre theory; often these definitions may seem careless or inconsistent, prompting a call toward greater rigor and precision in formal analysis. Certainly I would not suggest that we dispense with the tools of formal analysis, as much can be gained through careful examinations of textual mechanics — I employ formal analysis in considering *Dragnet* and the police genre in Chapter 5. Despite the strengths of what may be understood through aesthetic paradigms, definitional approaches and formal analyses have distinct limitations. One such limitation of formal analysis is that examining the mechanics of a text cannot generally explain how that text functions within larger cultural contexts, which I would contend is the main goal motivating cultural media studies — and certainly is the central goal of my project. Imagine studying the mechanical composition and structure of an automobile engine — you can discover why a car runs, but you won't find out any answers as to why people like to drive it. Noël Carroll's formal analysis of the horror film, probably the most rigorous definitional account of a media genre, succeeds most when he explains the formal operations and definition of the horror genre. But Carroll tries to discern why audiences like horror films using the same methodology he uses to explain the genre's narrative structure — looking "under the hood" of the text. The incompatibility between Carroll's textual method and his question about reception leads to the most unsatisfying conclusion in his book — that audiences enjoy horror films *in spite of* the fear they produce, as they willingly pay the price of horror to enjoy narrative pleasures. While this might be a reason some audiences (including, I suspect, Carroll himself) enjoy horror films, it certainly contradicts the pleasures experienced by the majority of viewers who go to horror movies precisely *to be scared*. To avoid dubious assertions about audiences, we must look beyond the text itself — to understand how genres work beyond mere textual mechanics, we need to look behind the wheel as well as under the hood.

The goals of a cultural approach to media necessitate that we look beyond questions of definition to understand the cultural operation of genres. This is not to suggest that we jettison notions of definition altogether — genre definitions are crucial to how genres operate within larger cultural systems. But definitional approaches to genre studies are not generally interested in fitting these definitions into larger contexts. Carroll's study of the horror film arrives at a precise and rigorous definition of the genre, but it is contrary to how the genre is defined and conceived of in more common everyday use. This is particularly notable as his definition of the genre — centering on a monster which is an unnatural being inexplicable by science — explicitly excludes *Psycho*, a film that for most critics, audience members, and industrial personnel is one of the most important horror films of all time. The problem with this account is not simply an inadequate definition that needs to be refined — we might be able to accept Carroll's definition, even excluding *Psycho*, as more convincing and thus analytically "correct" than the commonsense definitions we all hold.[7] Definitional critics like Carroll are less interested in how genres are *actually* defined in cultural practice than in identifying the abstract theoretical "essence" of a genre in an idealized form, a model that seems unsuitable for cultural scholars. Definitional accounts certainly may be useful as "practical theory" designed to help teach artists how to effectively create, as Aristotle's urtext *Poetics* was designed. But if we are to understand how genre definitions impact media more broadly than artistic design, we need to approach definitions not as abstract essences but as realized practices, asking how genres are defined in broader cultural circulation.

The second mode of genre analysis, probably the most widespread and influential approach, poses *questions of interpretation*. As many media scholars are interested in the relationship between media texts and cultural politics, most work explores this relationship by interpreting the textual meanings of genres and situating them within their social contexts. Within this larger approach of studying generic meanings, a number of specific (although often overlapping) theoretical orientations have emerged — ritual, ideological, structuralist, psychoanalytic, and some cultural studies approaches, just to name the central paradigms.[8] Despite the core differences between these paradigms, there are key continuities within these approaches. Although their political goals and theoretical assumptions may all differ greatly, each of these paradigms approaches texts and genres as collections of meanings to be decoded, analyzed, and potentially critiqued.[9]

While interpretive genre studies have been quite influential and successful — having effectively formed the field of media genre analysis and offered dozens of crucial analyses — there are some crucial limitations to using an interpretive model for cultural genre analysis. The particular applications of this approach have led to some of these shortcomings. While there is nothing inherent in the practice of generic interpretation that requires critics to de-emphasize historical specificities in favor of sweeping generalizations, most generic interpretations do follow this latter model. Interpretive genre analyses might offer a broad range of core meanings — for instance, the soap opera has been read both as patriarchal, ideological propaganda, and as inherently feminine and resistant of dominant masculine ideologies.[10] In the face of contradicting genre analyses like these, we cannot necessarily determine which is a more "valid" account of the genre's meaning, because most genres are textually open and heterogeneous enough to allow for such diverse interpretations. A particular genre might culturally activate either or both of these interpretations, but the text alone cannot determine its cultural meanings. Interpretive critics posit a meaning of a genre that does not necessarily cohere with the ways in which the genre is actually culturally experienced. The texts of a given genre are much more broad ranging and diverse than can be summed up by typical claims of political re- or progressivity.

Interpretive analyses tend to treat genres as ahistorical and static, ignoring the ways genres shift and evolve in relation to their cultural contexts.[11] Attempts to provide the inherent meaning of a genre such as the sitcom, which has had a widely varying history for over fifty years, seem automatically doomed to oversimplification and partiality. Accounts of genre interpretation must correspond with the ways in which genres are actually experienced, whether by focusing on specific historical shifts or examining the meanings that culturally circulate around a given genre. Just as audiences and industries use genre definitions to make sense of media, people interpret genres and associate them with certain meanings on a daily basis. This is the question that interpretive genre criticism might shift toward, asking how a given genre has accrued particular meanings in a historically specific instance.

Thus, instead of reading outwards from a textual interpretation to posit how people make sense of a genre, we should look at the meanings people make in their interactions with media genres to understand the genre's meanings. Robert Allen has provided such an analysis with soap operas, looking at the meanings that scholars, producers, and audiences have associated with the term "soap opera" in order to understand the genre.[12] Allen's account is, unfortunately, an exception to the lack of specificity found within interpretive studies of television genres. Instead of asking what a genre means (the typical interpretive question), we need to ask what a genre means *for specific groups in a particular cultural instance*. Since this approach to generic meanings in action is quite different than traditional interpretive models, it requires a new conception of genres and an appropriate method to study them, an approach that I will discuss more below.

Some genre critics have looked beyond the limitations of definitional and interpretive approaches. *Questions of history* have been posed, emphasizing the changing dynamics of genres that other approaches usually ignore. Additionally, historical approaches often consider the influence of forces outside generic texts, looking at how changing cultural circumstances, industrial motivations, and audience practices all work to bring about generic shifts. Finally, a historical examination necessitates an analysis of the actual cultural life of a genre, not as it is abstractly defined or interpreted to be. Thus, historically centered generic analysis is more applicable to understanding genres in cultural practice than the two other reigning approaches. But historical work, at least as it has been executed if not conceptualized, still succumbs to a number of central shortcomings.

Feuer offers a historical take on the sitcom genre to contrast her accounts of aesthetic, ritual, and ideological paradigms; given the influence of her work on television genres, her brief account of the historical approach stands as the most prominent example of this type of television genre analysis.[13] Historical accounts of genres, as with previous examples, often efface specific instances in favor of overarching generalizations — a widespread syndrome for genre studies. Although historical work usually does not engage in such theoretical abstraction or interpretive idealism, many genre historians still posit large-scale shifts or master narratives of a genre. While major generic shifts may be relevant, histories that offer an account of the genre's large-scale transformations — such as Feuer's account of the sitcom's shift from politicization in the 1970s to its depoliticization of the 1980s — cannot account for the breadth of texts categorized by a genre at a given time. While Feuer's history accounts for canonized sitcoms like *All in the Family* (1971–79) and *The Mary Tyler Moore Show* (1970–77), it has little to say about equally popular contemporaneous shows like *Here's Lucy* (1968–74) and *Happy Days* (1974–84). The simultaneous success of these latter more "escapist" programs and the former "socially relevant" sitcoms forces us to question the usefulness of large-scale characterizations of a genre's historical meaning. Histories written to provide broad-based accounts seem inadequate to understand the ways genres work at any specific moment.

Feuer's historical approach raises another issue common to various generic paradigms. She charts the genre's evolution by looking at major transformations in the 1970s and 1980s, relating them to specific industrial and cultural shifts. But she specifically divides these elements between developments "internal to the genre," namely textual form and content, and those that are "external," such as cultural and industrial changes.[14] While this division may seem useful, this internal/external binary obscures how genres culturally operate. Under Feuer's model of genre history, the genre is a collection of texts that all bear "internal" markings of the sitcom; "external forces" are useful in understanding the meanings and changes in these texts at any time, but they are not a component of the genre itself. The model of genre history exemplified by Feuer does not offer a history of genres as categories but, rather, charts the history of generic texts, a distinction that is crucial to understanding how genres operate culturally. This "history of texts" approach, as well as definitional and interpretive approaches, depends on an assumption that genre is primarily a textual feature. While this position is not often questioned within genre studies, we need to step back and examine the basis of a textual theory of genre.

We might characterize this central notion about genres as the "textualist assumption." This position takes many forms; some scholars, more typical of literary theory, make explicit claims that genre is an intrinsic property of texts.[15] Media scholars more frequently *imply* genre as a textual component through a number of practices — situating genre within larger discussions of texts (as opposed to industries, audiences, or culture),[16] mapping an internal/external distinction onto texts versus "other factors,"[17] and methodologically examining genres primarily through textual analysis.[18] Thus media studies has regularly posited genre as a component of media texts. This textualist assumption seems to have contributed to the decline in genre analysis; as cultural media scholars have moved away from textual analysis as primary critical practice, genre has been left behind with concerns like narrative and stylistic analysis as perceived relics of extinct methodologies.

So what is wrong with this textualist assumption? Aren't genres just categories of texts? Certainly genres do primarily categorize texts. In some cases genres may categorize industrial practices (such as Sci-Fi Channel) or audience members (such as sci-fi fans) as well, but in these instances the textual category of "science fiction" precedes the industry's and audience's use of the term — science fiction programs are the implied unifying factor within both the industry and audience categories. Hence, I agree that genres are primarily categories of texts. But there is a crucial difference between conceiving genre as a textual *category* and treating it like a textual *component*, a distinction that most genre studies elide.

The members of any given category do not create, define, or constitute the category itself. Categories link a number of discreet elements together under a label for cultural convenience. While the members constituting a category might all possess some inherent trait binding them into the category (perhaps all horror texts do have monsters), there is nothing intrinsic about the category itself. Think of our contemporary understanding of racial difference — while all people who are categorized as "black" might have dark skin (although certainly this is not always true), there is nothing inherent about dark skin that makes it a racial category. Eye color or hair color have no categorical equivalents to skin color; while these are all differing physical components of human bodies, only some are considered culturally salient categories. We can accept the distinction between a biological trait (like skin color) and the cultural category that activates it into a system of differentiation (namely race) — these are related, but not identical, physical and conceptual elements. If we shifted the same biological bodies into another cultural system of difference, other physical traits could become activated into operative categories of differentiation (such as height). The physical elements do not change, but their categorization does, suggesting that the category itself emerges from the relationship between the elements it groups together and the cultural context in which it operates.

The same type of distinction holds for media texts. We do not generally differentiate between shows that take place in Boston and those that take place in Chicago, but we do differentiate between programs set in a hospital and those set in a police station. Texts have many different components, but only some are activated into defining generic properties. As many genre scholars have noted, there are no uniform criteria for genre delimitation — some are defined by setting (like westerns), some by profession (like legal dramas), some by audience affect (like comedy), and some by narrative form (like mysteries).[19] This diversity of definitional criteria suggests that there is nothing internal to texts mandating how they are to be generically categorized — in some instances, the same text becomes "regenrified" as cultural contexts shift.[20] If the same text is flexible enough to be categorized into various genres, it follows that the confines of the text cannot be the sole repository for generic definitions.

Genres are not found within one isolated text. *Wheel of Fortune* (1975–) is not a genre in and of itself, but rather a member of the generic category "game show." Genres only emerge from the intertextual relations between multiple texts, resulting in a common category. But how do these texts interrelate to form a genre? Texts do not interact on their own; they come together only through cultural practices such as production and reception. Audiences link programs together all the time — "*Family Guy* (1999–2002) is just a rip-off of *The Simpsons*" — as do industrial personnel — "*Roswell* (1999–2002) is *Dawson's Creek* (1998–2003) meets *The X-Files* (1993–2002)." Texts themselves do not actively link together without this type of cultural activity. Even when one text explicitly references another (such as in the case of allusions, parodies, spin-offs, or crossovers), these instances become activated only through processes of production or reception. If we watch *The Jeffersons* (1975–85) without the knowledge that it spun off from *All in the Family*, as many viewers surely have, then can we claim that intertextuality is relevant or active at that moment of reception? Thus, if genres are dependent on *intertextuality*, they cannot be an inherently *textual* component.

Most analyses of genres have analyzed texts because they are the most imminent and material objects of media. This analytic mode is seemingly logical as well — following from traditions of biological taxonomy, to understand the taxonomic family of frogs, we need to look at the members of that category (i.e., frogs). Traditionally, we do the same for genres — if you want to understand music videos, watch as many as you can.[21] But unlike frogs, music videos do not reproduce on their own. We cannot understand why *Unsolved Mysteries* followed *America's Most Wanted* (1988–) just by watching the shows — there is no causal mechanism or active process of generic continuity in the programs themselves. Processes of genre reproduction, such as creating new sitcoms and news magazines, only occur through the actions of industries and audiences, not texts themselves.[22] Likewise, no inherent genetic code forbids cross-genre mating. Although a biological imperative maintains a natural distinction between frogs and tulips, nothing genetic stopped the creation of the generically mixed music video/police drama, *Cop Rock* (1990). But the creation of *Cop Rock* did not stem from texts themselves — *Hill St. Blues* (1981–87) and Madonna's music video *Like a Virgin* (1984) did not create their own sordid offspring. Genre mixing, as explored more in Chapter 6, is a cultural process, enacted by industrial personnel, often in response to audience viewing practices. While we may study frogs to understand their biological category, texts themselves are insufficient to understand how genres are created, merge, evolve, or disappear. We need to look outside of texts to locate the range of sites in which genres operate, change, proliferate, and die out.

Instead of biological taxonomy, a better parallel for media genres might be brands of automobiles. Most people would locate the difference between Chevrolets and Toyotas within the internal mechanics of the two brands, noting different designs, machinery, and engine systems. While this may be an important site of differentiation, it is not necessarily the primary way the two brands differ. Many differences in automobile brands are established through industrial practices — manufacturing styles, labels, marketing, corporate reputation and nationality — and cultural circulation — driver preferences, press accounts, consumer ratings, and advertising. In some extreme cases, the two brands might contain identical parts, be assembled in the same plant, and utilize indistinguishable internal mechanics; as car experts Tom and Ray Magliozzi of NPR's *Car Talk* wrote in 1993, "Chevy and Toyota build a car together in California. At Toyota dealers, they call it a Corolla, and at Chevy dealers, it's called the Geo Prizm. Except for minor details, the Corolla and Prizm are the same exact car."[23] In this instance the differences are completely cultural, not mechanical, but cars are always cultural products, accruing meanings and associations through their widespread circulation, links that are not guaranteed by their mechanical essence or internal design. Automobiles are also clearly historical — few would argue that the essence of a Chevy is the same today as it was in 1920. Mechanical designs, corporate structure, consumer usage, and cultural associations have all shifted dramatically. Yet many scholars treat genres as timeless essences defined by an inner core rather than constituted by changing cultural practices, using taxonomic biological parallels that are less apt than those of cultural technologies like automobiles.

Genres are not intrinsic to texts — they are constituted by the processes that some scholars have labeled "external" elements, such as industrial and audience practices. We need to look beyond the text as the locus for genre, locating genres within the complex interrelations between texts, industries, audiences, and historical contexts.[24] Genres transect the boundaries between text and context, with production, distribution, promotion, exhibition, criticism, and reception practices all working to categorize media texts into genres. But by decentering the text as the site of generic essence, a potential problem emerges — if genres are categories that do not emerge from intrinsic textual features, then isn't any system of categorization potentially a genre? Traditionally, film studies has tied generic categories to narrative structure to avoid this potential abundance of genres, but given television's frequent nonnarrative programming, narrative content cannot be the anchor for generic categorization. Nevertheless, it is not enough to say that any categorical system can be a genre — a category like "8:30 p.m. programs" seems quite different from typical generic categories, despite the time label's usefulness and cultural operation. Genres are more than just any category. They must be culturally operative within a number of spheres of media practice, employed by critics, industries, and audiences. Thus a term like "soap opera" would not have become a genre had it not transcended its original usage as trade journal shorthand and been picked up by the industry and audiences at large, much like film terms like "oaters" which do not become generic labels.[25]

But the use of genres is further tied to the assumption that they refer to core aspects of generic texts, not more arbitrary industrial or critical decisions — the music video genre is predicated on a perceived textual attribute linking popular music to visual accompaniment, even though I would argue that this defining attribute is not the "core" defining attribute of the genre. Even though genres do not emerge from core textual essences or structures, the use of generic categories is predicated on a cultural assumption that genres *do* in fact refer to internal textual features. Like with racial categories, genres are not bound by their categorized attributes, but they culturally function *as if* they emerged from intrinsic textual features, seemingly flowing from that which they categorize. The sitcom does not boil down to core textual features, such as repeated situations and laugh-tracks, but the cultural use of the term operates as if the genre were primarily defined by these recognizable elements. When genres are culturally used, they act as shorthand for textual definitions, even though they are not dependent on textual properties. A categorical term like "8:30 program" or "NBC show" so clearly foregrounds its industrial origins over its textual attributes, that it would not circulate culturally as a genre.[26]

Just as nontextually referential categories like timeslots and networks problematize our notions of genres, the frequent nesting of subgenres complicates simplistic categorical schemas. One traditional occupation of genre critics has been defining what constitutes a genre — is the "backstage musical" a genre itself or a subset of the musical genre?[27] For television, we might look at a series of potentially

nested genres — from dramas to crime dramas to police dramas to police procedurals — and try to identify which categorical level is most "generic." Although we
need to recognize the relevant differences between genres and any other category,
answering questions of subgenre categorization should not focus on textual structure and form (as has been the traditional path), but instead look at a category's
operative coherence. Does a given category circulate within the cultural spheres of
audiences, press accounts, and industrial discourses? Is there a general consensus
over what the category refers to in a given moment? Do so-called "subgenres" play
a useful and widespread role in classifying, interpreting, or evaluating programs?
If these questions can be answered positively (such as for "police drama"), then the
category operates as a genre; if not (as for "police procedural"), then the category
does not have enough cultural relevance to work as a genre, at least during that
particular historical moment. This subgeneric litmus test is useful for discerning
how genres work, but it is ultimately a critical dead end to try to hierarchize and
clearly draw lines between genres and subgenres. Genres do not operate by following these clear nesting categorizations, but rather through cycles of evolution
and redefinition. Boundaries between genres and subgenres are too contingent
and fluid to carry across differing historical or cultural moments — what is a subgenre today might easily become tomorrow's genre through more widespread cultural circulation (like teen drama's evolution out of family dramas) or a forgotten
category relegated to television's archives through the waning of a generic cycle
(like the distinctions between quiz shows and stunt shows discussed in Chapter 2).

To sum up my argument thus far, genres have traditionally been treated as textual components. Although genres are categories of texts, texts themselves do not
determine, contain, or produce their own categorization. Generic categories are
intertextual and, hence, operate more broadly than within the bounded realm of a
media text. Even though texts certainly bear marks that are typical of genres, these
textual conventions are not what define the genre. Genres exist only through the
creation, circulation, and consumption of texts within cultural contexts. Textual
analysis cannot examine media genres as they operate at a categorical level — there
are texts that are categorized by genres, but their textual sum does not equal the
whole of the genre. Instead, we must distinguish between the common practice of
analyzing generically labeled texts and specific analysis of genres as cultural categories. Analyzing generic texts is certainly worthwhile, but they cannot explain
how genres themselves operate as categories. We thus need to rethink genre analysis using different methods. But what is this new approach to genre?

Discursive Practices and Generic Clusters

A potential approach to understanding genres as cultural categories was offered
by a prescient early essay by Andrew Tudor.[28] Although his argument was not as
influential in the 1970s as it deserved to be, Tudor's analysis of genre criticism
highlighted what he called "the empiricist dilemma" — genre critics isolate a

group of texts to establish a genre's definitional criteria but, by doing so, merely reproduce the initial assumptions that led to establishing their primary sample of films. Thus in the case of Carroll's work on horror, Tudor would note that Carroll's assumption that monsters are necessary to horror is formative of his exclusion of *Psycho* from the genre, thus leading to a definition that reinforces and justifies this exclusion. Tudor proposes a rough vision of what might replace this circular mode of genre criticism, namely an account of how genres operate in the "interplay between culture, audience, films, and filmmakers".[8] Years before American media studies turned toward cultural methods and theories, Tudor argued that genres "are sets of cultural conventions," suggesting that "genre is what we collectively believe it to be".[7] While Tudor does not offer a fully realized model for this approach, he keenly points out that analyzing generic texts is not an effective way to examine genres themselves, but rather just another mode of textual analysis.[29] Tudor's critique may be extended into a more realized method of genre analysis by exploring the categorical aspects of genres over their textual attributes.

Decentering texts within genre analysis might cause some methodological hesitation. When genres are viewed as components of texts, there is a clear site of analysis upon which to focus our critical attention. But if genres are not textual properties, where exactly might we go to analyze them? To understand how genre categories become culturally salient, we can examine genres as *discursive practices*. By regarding genre as a property and function of discourse, we can examine the ways in which various forms of communication work to constitute generic definitions, meanings, and values within particular historical contexts.

This discursive approach emerges out of contemporary poststructuralist theories, as genre seems to fit well into Michel Foucault's accounts of discursive formations.[30] This move might seem odd at first — after all, Foucault wrote almost nothing on either mass media or genres. Yet Foucault's diverse projects all work to historicize and analyze concepts that appear intrinsic and natural, pointing toward the cultural construction of a wide range of notions, from madness to sexuality, punishment to subjectivity. I am conceiving of genre as a conceptual category formed by cultural practices and not inherent to the objects that they seem to describe, a position parallel with (and drawn from) Foucault's various analytical projects. I wish to extrapolate from his approach and insights, posing an understanding of genre that becomes more robust and rich through continuities with Foucault's work and theoretical legacy.

Foucault's conception of discursive formations seems particularly apt to generic analysis. Foucault analyzes broad discursive formations such as sexuality, insanity, and criminality, arguing that they are historically specific systems of thought, conceptual categories that work to define a culture's experiences within a larger system of power. These discursive formations emerge not from a centralized structure or single site of power, but are built bottom-up from disparate micro-instances. Even though discursive formations are often marked by discontinuities, they do follow overall regularities, fitting into a society's larger "regime of truth." Finally, discursive formations often appear to be "natural" or internal properties of beings, such as humans, but are actually culturally constituted and variable. All of these features of Foucault's broad social discursive formations seem to hold for the more limited (and admittedly less socially powerful) categorical system of genres as well.

To examine generic discourses, the site of genre analysis must shift from isolated texts precategorized by their genre to culturally circulating generic practices that categorize texts. Discursive formations do not adhere to seemingly clear boundaries, such as between texts and audiences. Foucault emphasizes that discourse is a practice, and as such, we must analyze discourses in action as they are culturally operative, not in abstract isolation. Thus for genres, we must look at how they transect boundaries that have inadequately located genre primarily within the bounds of the text. Genres do run through texts, but also operate within the practices of critics, audiences, and industries — anyone who uses generic terms is participating the constitution of genre categories. Thus we might look at what audiences and industries say about genres, what terms and definitions circulate around any given generic instance, and how specific cultural assumptions are linked to particular genres. These discursive practices concerning genres should not be used as a "check" against textual genre features, as traditional scholars have used "commonsense" cultural genre definitions to verify their own textual definition.[31] Rather, the discourses surrounding and running through a given genre are *themselves* constitutive of that generic category; they are the practices that define genres and delimit their meanings, not media texts themselves. Since genres are formed through intertextual relationships between texts, then the discursive enunciations that link texts under a categorical rubric become the site and material for genre analysis.

Following Foucault's historical model of genealogy, discursive formations of genres should be studied not through interpretive readings or deep structural analysis, but in their surface manifestations and common articulations. To understand the cultural history of a genre, we must examine generic discourses as they are culturally operative, without attempting to isolate genres from their applied contexts or to read deeper meanings into the discursive utterances of genres. We should not attempt to interpret generic discourses by suggesting what statements "really mean" or how they express meanings beneath the cultural surface — a critic's condemnation of a genre should not be the object of analysis for hidden subtexts or unconscious assumptions. Instead of interpreting either discourses or texts in depth, we must focus on the breadth of discursive enunciations around any given instance, mapping out as many positions articulating generic knowledge as possible and situating them within larger cultural contexts and relations of power. For example, to examine the quiz show

genre in Chapter 2, I look beyond single sites such as texts or production practices, gathering as many diverse enunciations of the genre from the widest
possible range of sources, including corporate documents, press commentaries,
trade journal accounts, regulatory policies, audience responses, filmic representations, promotional materials, and the texts themselves. By exploring the
broad variety of generic discourses around any given instance, we can understand the more elaborated workings of generic discursive formations. Linking
together these numerous generic discourses will begin to suggest more large-
scale patterns of generic definitions, meanings, and hierarchies, but we should
arrive at these macro-features through an analysis of micro-instances. While
discontinuities and ruptures among generic assumptions may emerge, generic
discourses follow an operative coherence to provide a genre's appearance of
stability.

Our goal in analyzing generic discourses is not to arrive at a genre's "proper"
definition, interpretation, or evaluation, but to explore the material ways in
which genres are culturally operative. By shifting focus away from projects that
attempt to provide the definitive definition or most nuanced interpretation of
a genre, we can look toward the ways in which genre definitions, interpretations, and evaluations are part of the larger cultural operations of genre. Instead
of guiding questions such as "What do police dramas mean?" or "How do we
define quiz shows?" we might look toward widespread cultural practices of
genre interpretation and definition, leading to questions such as "What do talk
shows mean for a specific community?" or "How is the definition of animation
strategically articulated by socially-situated groups?" This approach requires
much more specific and detailed research into a genre at a given historical
instance, suggesting that sweeping generic accounts are too partial and incomplete. This is not to say that genres do not have large-scale diachronic and
cross-media histories — these larger trends are valid objects of study, but the
abstract and generalized mode of media history most common to generic historiography tends to efface specific instances in the name of macro-patterns.
We can begin to build a more satisfying macro-account of a genre's history from
the bottom up, by collecting micro-instances of generic discourses in historically specific moments and examining the resulting large-scale patterns and
trajectories. This bottom-up approach reflects how genres actually form and
change over time — out of the specific cultural practices of industries and audiences, not out of macro-structures.[32]

This discursive approach to genre necessitates that we decenter the text as the
primary site of genre, but not to the extent that we ignore television texts —
media texts function as important locales of generic discourses and must be
examined on par with other sites, such as audience and industrial practices.
Instead of examining texts as bounded and stable objects of analysis, texts
should be viewed as sites of discursive practice in which genre categories may

be articulated. Television programs explicitly cite generic categories, and advertising, promotions, parodies, and intertextual references within shows are all vital sites of generic practice, aspects of genre explored in depth in Chapters 5 and 6. In decentering the text from genre analysis, we cannot jettison the text as a site of discursive generic operation; rather we should acknowledge that an isolated text does not comprise a genre on its own.

Foucault's work offers another important concept for analyzing genres. In one of his more famous essays, he proposes a particular mode of discourse called the "author function."[33] Instead of regarding texts as the products of authors, Foucault reverses this binary by arguing that certain texts or discourses have an active author function that indicates its authored status but does not carry a direct linkage to the "real individual" who created the discourse. Authorship is not the process of individuals creating texts, but a culturally activated function of texts that links them to a particular figure and system of knowledge named "the author" via broader contextual circulation. Tony Bennett and Janet Woollacott productively extend Foucault's discussion of authorship into the realm of media texts, identifying three cultural facets of the author function: as a *system of classification*, a site of *interpretive consistency*, and a marker of *cultural value*.[34] Not surprisingly, these features are not unique to authorship — we may extend this notion of textual function to other aspects of media, such as genre.[35]

How might "generic function" operate like Foucault's author function? Certainly all three attributes of authorship Bennett and Woollacott discuss apply to genre as well. Genres obviously primarily work to classify texts together, much like authorship — for film studies, genre and authorship have been the two most prominent modes of scholarly classification. Genres also serve as sites of interpretive consistency, as generic interpretations posit core meanings for any given genre — police dramas as conservative rituals of assurance, horror as a mean to cope with social anxieties. Additionally, interpretation and classification often merge in practice, with central meanings serving as definitional attributes for most genre analysts — the western can be defined by its meaningful opposition between nature and civilization. Finally genres are activated in systems of cultural value, with nearly every genre located on the highbrow/lowbrow axis — medical dramas are positioned as more socially valued and intrinsically "better" than soap operas by nearly anyone expressing an opinion. While few would contest the centrality of definitions, interpretations, and evaluations in genre criticism, Foucault's approach reminds us that these are not innate properties of a textual genre, but rather the cultural operations that themselves form genre categories. Just as Foucault's relocated the site of authorship — from individual subject to discursive practices — my analysis of "generic function" suggests that genres do not emerge from their assumed central site of origin, the text, but rather are formed by the cultural practices of generic discourses.

Following Foucault, Bennett, and Woollacott, we can break down the discursive practices that constitute genres into three basic types: *definition* ("this show is a sitcom because it has a laugh track"), *interpretation* ("sitcoms reflect and reinforce family values"), and *evaluation* ("sitcoms are better entertainment than soap operas"). These discursive utterances, which may seem to reflect on an already established genre, are *themselves* constitutive of that genre — they are the practices that define genres, delimit their meanings, and posit their cultural value. Cultural practices of *definition, interpretation,* and *evaluation* are the three primary ways genres circulate and become culturally manifest; thus these practices should be the central objects of study for genre analysis. In the specific analyses that constitute the rest of this project, I focus on how discourses of generic definition, interpretation, and evaluation operate within specific spheres of media practice and raise issues for genre analysis, such as the role of genre mixing and practice of generic historiography. This trio of generic discursive types comprises the "raw material" for my analyses of television genres in cultural practice.

Since genre discourses do not stem solely from a central source — be it industrial or ideological — genre history should be viewed as a fluid and active process, not a teleological tale of textual rise and fall. Thus, instead of typical questions of definition or interpretation, we should foreground *questions of cultural process* to analyze media genres. The notion of genre as a discursive process has been explored by a number of scholars, although it is still developing as a more fully realized approach.[36] The key work in this area is Rick Altman's *Film/Genre*, certainly one of the most important works of genre theory in many years.[37] While providing many compelling and convincing arguments for a process-based approach to genre that I adapt for television, Altman's book ultimately argues for augmenting his influential textualist semantic/syntactic theory of genre with an account of pragmatic aspects of genre. While I agree with the importance of pragmatics, his structuralist account of texts is ultimately incompatible with his poststructuralist account of generic processes and pragmatics. Despite Altman's foregrounding of cultural processes, textual structure still remains the centerpiece of his approach, making it difficult to provide an account of how genre categories operate outside the bounds of the text.

I contend that we should examine the cultural processes of generic discourses *prior to* examining the generic texts that have been traditionally viewed as identical to the genre itself. Specifically, genre theory should account for how generic processes operate within cultural contexts, how industry and audience practices constitute genres, and how genres can both be fluid over time yet fairly coherent in any given moment. We should also examine the specificities of the medium — Altman convincingly argues that the film industry promotes multiple genres around any single movie to maximize audience appeals. Even though we might find similar trends for television, we cannot simply import such an argument into a distinct medium with vitally different industrial structures and audience practices. We should carefully adapt the theoretical advances offered within film studies to the particularities of television genres, while allowing insights to emerge from the detailed analysis of television genres.

By approaching genres as discursive practices, we must balance notions of genre as both active process and stable formation. Although genres are constantly in flux and under definitional negotiation, generic terms are still sufficiently salient that most people would agree on a similar working definition for any genre. Even if we cannot provide an essential definition of a genre's core identity, most of us still know a sitcom when we see one. Discourse theory offers a model for such stability in flux — genres work as *discursive clusters*, with certain definitions, interpretations, and evaluations coming together at any given time to suggest a coherent and clear genre.[38] However, these clusters are contingent and transitory, shifting over time and taking on new definitions, meanings, and values within differing contexts. At any given time, a generic cluster functions as a stable cultural convenience, a shorthand label for a set of linked assumptions and categorized texts, yet these discourses (and associated texts) are bound to shift meanings and definitions as a genre's history transpires.

Central to this metaphor is that these generic clusters are hollow, formed from the outside but lacking an internal essence; the clustering of meanings creates the appearance of a generic core, but this center is just as contingent and fluid as the more "fringe" discourses. At any given moment, a genre might appear quite stable, static, and bounded; however the same genre might operate differently in another historic or cultural contexts. For example, cartoons were once presumed to be essentially defined by their childish appeal and fantastic narrative worlds, but Chapters 3 and 6 point to how these assumed "core" values have emerged and transformed throughout the genre's history. Generic clusters can work simultaneously as fluid and static, an active process and a stable product. Thus, to understand a genre's history, Chapter 2 offers a model to account for this type of categorical flux, tracing a genealogy of discursive shifts and rearticulations to account for a genre's evolution and redefinition, not just a chronology of changing textual examples.

The cultural approach to genre that I am advocating is thus of a somewhat different order than the traditional methods of genre analysis. Typical approaches to genres all engage in *textual generic criticism*, looking at genre texts to uncover and identify definitions, meanings, and historical changes. There are some other important, though less common, approaches to genre that look at different questions of genre. One such approach might be termed *theoretical genre creation*. This approach follows literary critic Tzvetan Todorov's distinction between "historical" genres — those that are found in cultural practice — and "theoretical" genres — those that form ideal categories for scholars, positing their own genre categories by strategically recategorizing specific texts under the rubric of a new generic term.[39] These theoretical genres become culturally relevant if they are adapted within larger cultural practices outside the academy, such as critics and industries. The most discussed theoretical media genre is *film noir*; Altman discusses the scholarly creation of another theoretical genre, the woman's film.[40] Such theoretical genre creation has been less common for television studies, with no examples that seem to take hold as widespread generic terms.[41]

Another less-common approach to media genres is *psychological genre examination*. This approach primarily asks why people enjoy and regularly consume genres, despite their formulaic and repetitive qualities. A variety of paradigms have explored audience pleasures, including the aforementioned ritual and cultural studies models, but the two primary paradigms looking to this question are psychoanalysis and cognitive psychology.[42] Though the differences between cognitivism and psychoanalysis are great (as the heated debates between their supporters suggest), the basic approach that each takes in analyzing film genres is similar — begin with a theoretical model of human psychology and apply it to a series of texts to deduce what audience pleasures drive the given genre. Thus, while the guiding *questions of pleasure* are different from typical textualist approaches, psychological methods still foreground the text as the primary site of genre analysis.

The approach to *cultural genre analysis* I have outlined is quite different in scope from each of these approaches, looking to sites outside the text as much (if not more) than the texts themselves to explore genres. Both psychological and textual approaches assume that genre categories are already given (per Tudor's argument), using the specific delimitations of the generic category to isolate particular texts to be analyzed. Even though theoretical genre creation does engage with genres as categories, it does so in a way that purposely runs counter to the operation of generic terms in everyday life, trying to redefine the categories that are culturally commonplace. Most genre critics realize the importance of categorical analysis to understand genres — as Steve Neale suggests, "a genre's history is as much the history of a [generic] term as it is of the films to which the term has been applied."[43] But only cultural genre analysis as an approach, following the work of Tudor, Altman, Allen, and others, analyzes how genres work as *cultural categories*, not textual properties.

While we might accept all of these methodological options in the name of theoretical pluralism — and I certainly do not dismiss the usefulness of these other approaches for gaining insights into media practices — there is a logical disjunction in the field: if genres are understood as cultural categories rather than textual components, then most typical textual approaches do not actually analyze *genres* per se. Rather, they use generic categories to delimit textual projects, not engaging in the level of categorical analysis that an account of genre necessitates. Thus, per Tudor, it is "putting the cart before the horse" to analyze the texts of a given genre in the name of analyzing the genre itself — we must explore the categorical operation of a genre if we want to understand the genre in cultural practice. Once we chart out how genres are culturally constituted, defined, interpreted, and evaluated, we might use other methods to analyze common textual forms, psychological pleasures, or structuring principles, but we must first understand how genres are formed and operate culturally if we wish to avoid Tudor's empiricist dilemma.

We might return to one of the key terminological distinctions in film genre studies to help clarify this difference in scope — Thomas Schatz's delineation of *film genres* versus *genre films*. For Schatz, a film genre is a broader system, while a genre film is a specific iteration of the system.[44] While I do not wish to follow Schatz's structuralist and textualist leanings, reframing this distinction for television genres may be useful. Under my approach, a *television genre* is a cultural category, constituted by the generic discourses that posit definitions, interpretations, and evaluations. Television genres function as cultural shorthand that link together a range of cultural assumptions to a shifting corpus of texts, or *genre television*. Unlike Schatz and other textualist approaches, I contend we cannot understand *television genre* categories by analyzing the grammar, content, or history of *genre television* texts. Rather, I argue that to understand television texts — which arguably are nearly universal in their categorization into one or more genres — we need to first understand how television genre categories work to form a set of assumptions which individual programs draw upon and respond to.

Exemplifying Genre Analysis with Michael Jackson's Music Videos

If genres are categorical clusters of discursive processes transecting texts via their cultural interactions with industries, audiences, and broader contexts, where do we start to analyze a genre? We might begin a genre analysis with a textual example, an industrial practice, a historical shift, or an audience controversy, but our study of generic processes needs to account for how all of these realms work in interactive tandem. As a brief example of how this approach differs from traditional genre criticism, how might Michael Jackson's trio of successful music videos from 1983, *Billie Jean*, *Beat It*, and *Thriller*, be analyzed within the context of the music video genre?

How might traditional textual methods of genre analysis approach this case study? A hypothetical definitional approach might isolate the core elements constituting the genre, positing that the genre is defined by the musical song, with the video elements taking a secondary role. These videos would represent a spectrum from core (*Billie Jean* as prototypical dance/performance piece) to periphery (*Thriller* as a generic exception, with fourteen minutes of narrative mixed with song and dance), to *Beat It*, on the genre's fringe (with its integration of narrative and a brief nonmusical segment). An interpretive approach might relate these videos to their social situations by showing how each is symptomatic of cultural anxieties or concerns. Thus, these videos might be read as embodying rebellion as a countercultural urge (*Beat It's* gang fight, *Thriller's* monsters), while acknowledging that they recuperate the status quo in the end in the name of dominant ideology.[45] A typical historical approach might chart the shift from performance-centered videos like *Billie Jean* to the narrative model of *Beat It*, with *Thriller* representing the extreme possibilities of a narrative music video that would rarely be matched. This approach might situate the videos within the context of industrial practices and cultural contexts, but would look primarily to the videos themselves for the site of genre definition and meaning.

All of these approaches might offer valuable insights about genre television texts, but some questions cannot be adequately addressed using these approaches: how did MTV's practices help constitute the genre category? How did audiences use genre distinctions within this instance? How did the broader cultural circulation of these videos draw upon generic categories? How did other systems of cultural differentiation, such as race, impact the genre? How did categories of musical genre operate in this case study? To exemplify this approach, I will offer a brief analysis of these videos, an account intentionally narrow in scope, focused solely on the industrial practices involving these music videos, especially MTV's role in defining the genre. Since my approach looks at microinstances in practice, as opposed to broader accounts of the genre as a whole, this analysis does not offer the same scope as the hypothetical examinations above. Instead, I will briefly explore how the music video operated as a cultural category via MTV at the particular historical moment of this trio of videos. By emphasizing the realm of industrial practice, I will not address how audiences, critics, artists, or texts contributed to the generic cluster at this historical moment — an entire chapter (at least) would be necessary to adequately address these topics. However, this case study does exemplify how generic categories operate in specific instances and how industrial practices work to define genres, linking them to cultural hierarchies and systems of difference.

In 1983, MTV was a comparatively new entity, still establishing its industrial practices and constructing an audience.[46] While the channel was known for featuring the newly emergent music video genre, MTV used a particularly narrow generic definition to reach its target audience — the channel notoriously excluded black artists in the name of featuring only "rock" videos.[47] MTV's industrial practice is not separable from an abstract notion of the genre's definition — MTV had the institutional power to dictate the mainstream definition of the music video through its choice of what to program and what to exclude. This is not to say that, if MTV excluded a video, it would be unrecognizable as a music video, but rather that the common sense definitions of the genre as circulating within American culture were expressly tied to (and constituted by) MTV's industrial practices — MTV defined the *dominant* conception of the genre. Press accounts of music videos in the early 1980s mention white artists like MTV staples Duran Duran, Culture Club, and the Stray Cats as typical music video stars, while few articles name any black artists before Jackson's breakthrough in 1983 (except explicitly as artists that MTV would not feature). While there were other outlets for music video exhibition, they either directly followed MTV's white-centric lead (like NBC's *Friday Night Videos*) or offered explicit counterprogramming (newly formed BET's *Video Soul*), thereby allowing MTV to define the mainstream generic terms. Prior to Jackson's videos and subsequent crossover success, MTV delimited the boundaries of the music video genre, using its narrow notions of target audience (white suburban youth) and musical style (new wave, heavy metal, classic rock, and white pop).[48]

MTV drew upon previously held generic discourses constituted within the popular music and radio industries, using a definition of "rock" music to definitionally exclude black audiences and artists, a move effacing the racially hybridized origins of rock as a musical style.[49] Through their industrial practices, MTV actively linked a number of discourses to the generic cluster of the music video: commodified rock rebellion, segregated suburban culture, "rock" performance style specifically embodying a straight white male identity, and a posture of cutting-edge newness and anticommercial style. MTV's practices constructed a particularly narrow target audience of young white suburban straight boys, although the crossover appeals to female and gay tastes were far less resisted than those across racial lines, as many early MTV stars like Cyndi Lauper and Culture Club transgressed gender and sexuality boundaries.[50]

Whereas genre scholars have traditionally explored how industrial practices constitute genres, this case study highlights some of the specifics of television that film models cannot address. Examining production cannot explain MTV's genre practices, as the channel did not produce any of the music videos that they aired (or excluded). Yet MTV's practices of selecting videos, highlighting particular artists and musical styles, framing videos through VJ introductions, and bringing generic texts to cable-wired households all shaped the genre's definitions, meanings, and cultural values. An analysis of the television industry's generic practices must look beyond production to note how exhibition, advertising, and textual framing all work to constitute television genres, as explored more fully in Chapter 3.

Into this context of MTV's white-only programming came the release of what would become the best selling musical album of all time, Michael Jackson's *Thriller*.[51] MTV maintained its controversial policy by initially refusing to play the first two videos from *Thriller*, *Billie Jean* and *Beat It*. Jackson's label, CBS Records, saw the crossover potential of Jackson's album and pressured MTV to program

Jackson's videos in their lineup, allegedly threatening to withdraw all CBS artists from MTV if Jackson continued to be excluded. Facing this pressure (as well as Jackson's tremendous success in record sales), MTV yielded and added *Billie Jean* to their playlist, eliciting tremendous audience response. *Beat It* followed soon thereafter, with both videos in heavy rotation on MTV by March 1983.[52] The third video from the album, title track *Thriller*, was even more unusual for MTV — a 14-minute big-budget narrative film integrating the song into a larger horror story, as directed by top Hollywood director John Landis. MTV gladly accepted this video, given Jackson's overwhelming commercial success, as the network featured *Thriller* in December 1983 with heavy promotion and fanfare. The success of Jackson's videos helped change MTV's racially segregated programming policies, bringing in additional black artists like Prince and Tina Turner, and adding legitimacy to the emerging music video format.

But MTV's industrial practices alone did not define the generic terrain of the music video in 1983 — active audience voices countered MTV's policies. These voices are less accessible to media historians, except when they come from sites of high cultural capital and access to major media. We can see counter-MTV practices in select press accounts and critiques of MTV's segregation policies, protests by outspoken artists like Rick James and David Bowie, the actions of BET and CBS Records, and the staggering sales of Jackson's album and *Making of Thriller* video. These discursive practices criticized MTV's conception of the genre by positing different links within the generic cluster — calling attention to the implicit racism in MTV's "rock-only" policy, opening up the music video to a wider range of audiences, and highlighting the crossover appeal of black artists like Jackson. MTV altered their policies in reaction to these voices, not just because the "marketplace" demanded change (as they alleged), but due to industrial threats from CBS and high-profile white artists like Bowie. While the music video genre is not simply a top-down practice, with the industry mandating public tastes, the industrial discourses point to the power of intra-industry practices to shift generic definitions, interpretations, and evaluations.

While MTV justified their racial ban primarily in terms of musical genre (rock instead of R&B or soul) and target audience, the channel also referenced the textual form of *Beat It's* opening shot — a 20-second prologue without musical accompaniment. MTV claimed that this was not truly a music video and would only play the video by editing out this nonmusical beginning.[53] While this policy was not upheld for long, as later videos regularly incorporated nonmusical segments (although few to the degree of *Thriller*), this moment serves as a micro-instance of the how the processes of generic differentiation may be activated in a public cultural forum. MTV, the most powerful player in the music video business, made a brief claim for the genre's proper formal definition, using form as an excuse to maintain a controversial policy. Generic practices like this occur often, whether a network forces a program to "genre" itself more explicitly — like ABC imposing a laugh-track on *Sports Night* (1998–2000) — or public controversies ensue over a genre's appropriate content — like adult themes in cartoons *Beavis & Butthead* (1993–97) and *South Park* (1997–). Previous models of genre analysis have trouble accounting for these cultural practices, as they occur outside the boundaries of the text. Examining genres as constituted by discursive processes allows us to analyze the ways genre definitions, interpretations, and evaluations all intermingle with cultural power relations.

In the case of Michael Jackson, we see the music video genre as the nexus point of a number of crucial cultural practices — race-based distinctions and hierarchies, industrial debates over the genre's proper target audience, assumptions of the genre's textual "essence," Jackson's growing star persona, and public protests over MTV's exclusionary policies. No single one of these elements defined the genre in full — we must rather look at the conjuncture of these various discourses into a generic cluster. I have tried to isolate the most relevant institutional discourses to understand how the genre operates in this specific instance, but surely other cases would necessitate considering many more cultural, industrial, and audience practices as formative of the genre's meanings, definitions, and cultural values at a given moment.

This brief example shows the necessity of exploring media genres in detailed specificity, not overarching generalities. We can never know a genre's meaning in its entirety or arrive at its ultimate definition, because this is not the way genres operate — the music video is a wide-ranging ever-changing cluster of discourses, not a uniform transhistorical essence. Genres are always partial and contingent, emerging out of specific cultural relations, rather than abstract textual ideals. We need to examine how genres operate as conceptual frameworks, situating media texts within larger contexts of understanding. The goal of studying media genres is not to make broad assertions about the genre as a whole, but to understand how genres work within specific instances and how they fit into larger systems of cultural power. This approach to television genre analysis can better our understanding of how media are imbricated within their contexts of production and reception, and how media work to constitute our vision of the world. I conclude this chapter by highlighting five core points to clarify some of the specific facets of this approach to television genre analysis that I follow throughout the rest of this project.

Genre Analyses Should Account for the Particular
Attributes of the Medium

We cannot simply superimpose genre definitions from film or literature onto television. Certainly, medium distinctions are becoming increasingly blurred with the rise of technologies such as home video and integrated digital media, and thus we cannot regard "medium" as an absolute fixed category, any more than genre. But the lessons of film genre studies cannot account for many of television's specific practices — television's constant integration of fiction and nonfiction, narrative and nonnarrative, especially confounds the dependence on narrative structure typical of most film genre criticism. Similarly, film has few equivalents to genre-defined channels or genre-delimited scheduling practices that are commonplace for television, as addressed more in Chapter 3.[54] Audience practices of genre consumption and identification also differ for television, featuring more active practices of fan involvement with ongoing series, especially serials.[55] While not essentializing television's medium-defining practices, we must account for the specific ways in which a medium operates in a particular moment — including understanding how multiple media can work together in specific instances, such as television's intersections with music (as addressed above), radio (see Chapters 2 and 5), and film (see Chapters 3 and 5).

Genre Studies Should Negotiate between Specificity and Generality

Obviously, genre is a categorical concept and therefore somewhat transcends specific instances. But traditional genre analysis has tended to avoid detailed specificities in lieu of sweeping generalizations. A more nuanced approach can account for this tension more effectively. We might approach genre analyses from two general directions. First, we might start with a genre and analyze one specific element of it. This could mean focusing on a historic turning point (like the quiz show scandals), isolating a core social issue (representations of minorities on sitcoms), or tracing a genre's origins (the prehistory of music videos). By narrowing our focus to a specific aspect of a genre's definition, meaning, history, or cultural value, we can avoid the problems of overgeneralization that have been typical of more traditional genre studies, as well as acknowledging that genres are too multifaceted and broad to be understood in their totality. In the next three chapters, I begin with the particular genres of quiz shows, cartoons, and talk shows, narrowing my focus to examine particular historical moments and sites of generic articulation.

The second way to approach genre analysis would start with a specific media case study and analyze how genre processes operate within this specific instance, much like the case of Michael Jackson's music videos. Such projects might isolate a variety of starting points — an industrial formation (like Cartoon Network), audience practices (science fiction fan conventions), a textual instance (genre parody in *The Simpsons*), a policy decision (educational programming mandates), or a moment in social history (the coverage of civil rights struggles in news and documentaries). These specific topics each may serve as the nexus point of analysis, but we cannot let them dictate the methodological terrain of the entire study. We can start with isolated instances from a specific sphere of media practice, but analyses of genre must incorporate the interrelated operations of genre weaving through the multiple realms of media. In my final chapters, I turn to the specific textual instances of *Dragnet*, *Soap*, and *The*

Simpsons, focusing on how genre categories operate within their particular cultural histories.

Genre Histories Should Be Written Using Discursive Genealogies

Genre histories have traditionally chronicled generic texts, often drawing upon both definitional and interpretive approaches. To understand genres as cultural categories, we need different historiographic methods, avoiding the trap of interpreting genre practices — generic discourses are not deep repositories of hidden meanings, formal structures, or subtextual insights. Rather, we should follow the model of Foucauldian genealogy, emphasizing breadth of utterances over interpretive depth to collect many discursive instances surrounding a given instance of generic process. By viewing the discourses of genre clusters, larger scale patterns and meanings will emerge, but we should resist plugging these findings into old systems of macro-structures or interpretive generalizations. Insights into television genres can best emerge out of detailed research and specific cultural articulations of definition, interpretation, and evaluation, rather than decontextualized analyses of form or text. To accommodate this attention to discursive process, genre analysis should gather instances of genre activity in interrelated sites of audience, industrial, and cultural practices.

In calling for "breadth over depth," I am not suggesting studying genres in broad generalities. Rather, we must take a broad look at the various *sites* of genre operation, even as we limit our object of analysis to one historical moment or facet of a genre. Genre operates in various cultural sites, encompassing the broad range of media practices available to be studied. Industrial practices using genre range widely, including production techniques, corporate structures, niche marketing, star personae, choices in sponsorship, marketing techniques, scheduling decisions, press releases, trade press accounts, interviews, behind-the-scenes documentaries, rejected programming, and network or channel identity. Textual features include traditionally studied generic aspects like thematic content, narrative, and setting, but should also include specific televisual techniques like visual style, mode of production, recording format, audio conventions, editing techniques, and programmatic flow. The coverage of television in the press is a central realm of generic operation, with *TV Guide* categorization as America's primary circulator of genre labels. Other press sites should include newspaper and magazine reviews, fanzines, "behind-the-scene" features, schedule listings, interviews, editorials and commentaries, rating reports, and niche periodicals focused on genres (like *Soap Opera Digest*). Audience voices are often difficult to access, but there are numerous sites in which these audiences publicly use and constitute generic categories — Web pages, fan conventions, chat rooms, letters to the editor, personal conversations, fan fictions and other creative endeavors, clubs and discussion groups, interviews within articles, and letters found in corporate archives. Finally, there are sites of generic operation that defy categorization — video store shelves are dependent on genres, yet they are generally not part of the "industry" per se (unless referring to studio-owned Blockbuster). Likewise, the genre categories used on program guides via digital cable or TiVo have direct material impact on viewer practices, and thus should be included within the scope of genre studies. Certainly other sites of genre articulation exist — it is up to the genre critic to hunt these out and incorporate an array of these sites to create a broad and rich genealogy of generic operation around any specific example.

Genres Should Be Understood in Cultural Practice

Feuer discusses Todorov's distinction between theoretical and historical genres, suggesting that television studies is too new to have established theoretical genres, but that a goal of "television genre criticism is to develop more theoretical models for these historical genres, not necessarily remaining satisfied with industrial or commonsense usage."[56] I contend that "industrial or commonsense usage" is exactly the site where genres are operative and constituted. Attempts to establish theoretical models of a genre's formal mechanics or deep structures of meaning cannot tell us how genres work within a historical context, how they evolve and emerge, or how they fit into larger relations of power. If our goal is to understand genres as cultural categories, we should first examine the discourses that constitute the *television genre* category before examining the *genre television* texts that seem delimited by the genre. While certain instances might dictate the proposal of new categories, it seems that analyzing the operation of historical genres and their relation to cultural power is a more pressing concern for media scholars.[57]

Genres Should Be Situated within Larger Systems of Cultural Hierarchies and Power Relations

A central goal of much media scholarship is to understand the media, not in isolation, but as a component of social contexts and power relations. One of the reasons that genre studies have been marginal within cultural media studies is that genre has been traditionally conceived as a formal textual element and thus less conducive to the study of cultural politics. Even when scholars do approach genre by foregrounding power relations, such as in traditions of ideological and structuralist criticism, they tend to analyze genres at a level of abstraction ill-suited to understanding the specifics of cultural practice. By looking at genre as a contextual discursive process, we can situate genres within larger regimes of power and better understand their cultural operation. Since genres are systems of categorization and differentiation, linking genre distinctions to other systems of difference can point to the workings of cultural power.

The ways these linkages might play out are limitless. While there is certainly a strong tradition linking genre analysis and gender differences (down to their etymological roots), we can broaden this approach to include other axes of identity differentiation as well, such as race, age, sexuality, class, nationality, etc. We might also look at how genre differences are imbricated within hierarchies of cultural value, both between genres and within one specific genre; the common process of generic evaluation locates genres within social hierarchies and is one of the crucial ways in which genres are culturally constituted. Drawing on the influential studies of cultural distinctions by Pierre Bourdieu, we could map a genre like the talk show onto larger distinctions such as aesthetic value, audience identity, and hierarchies of taste, a project I undertake in Chapter 4.[58] This analysis produces a spectrum of generic conventions and assumptions (such as "tabloid" versus "hard" news) that are explicitly tied to greater systems of cultural power and differentiation. This approach to genre distinction avoids the tradition of text-centered analysis, accounting for the ways in which cultural agents articulate genre differentiation as constitutive of genre definitions, meanings, and values.

By grounding genre categories in cultural contexts, their links to power relations often emerge in unexpected ways. Genres are not neutral categories, but are situated within larger systems of power and, thus, often come "fully loaded" with political implications. If we accept that genres are constituted by cultural discourses, we need to acknowledge that those enunciations are always situated within larger systems of power that cannot be effaced from our analyses of generic processes. As addressed in Chapter 3, the importation of film cartoons to television might seem most relevant as part of an industrial history, but we should be attuned to the political implications of this industrial shift — the scheduling of cartoons on Saturday mornings effectively created a marginalized location for the genre that redefined films designed for mass audiences in movie houses into "kid-only" fare. This generic redefinition linked a number of hierarchies of cultural value, assumptions of "proper" content (such as controversies over violence and the excision of racial stereotypes), and limited visions of children's entertainment to the discursive cluster of the cartoon genre. Even in cases where politics might appear secondary, foregrounding how specific articulations of genres emerge out of power relations can point toward some important insights concerning both genres and broader cultural issues.

My approach to television genre analysis — examining genres as cultural categories, constituted by clusters of discursive processes operative within texts, audiences, industries, and cultural contexts — attempts to place genre analysis back onto the agenda of critical media studies. The traditional scholarly practices of analyzing generic texts will not — and should not — simply disappear. Much has been gained by all of the methodological and theoretical approaches discussed in this chapter, ranging from more careful formal understandings of horror narratives to critiques of the structures underlying the typical western film. But we need to question the "given" in these approaches — that there is an already established generic category that can serve as the foundation of a genre analysis. By first examining genres as cultural categories, unpacking the processes of definition, interpretation, and evaluation that constitute these categories in our everyday experiences with media, we can have a more satisfying account of the categorical assumptions operative within media genres. Hopefully through application of this mode of generic analysis, the resulting projects will elucidate both the specificities of television genres that have been under-analyzed and the ways in which cultural processes such as genre are formative of larger and more powerful systems of cultural relations and difference.

As suggested throughout this chapter, my mode of cultural genre analysis is better suited for practical application than abstract theorization. The rest of this project explores the conceptual arguments of this chapter through a number of specific analyses, each accomplishing a number of goals. Each chapter provides an example of cultural television genre analysis, hopefully offering supporting evidence for the usefulness of this theoretical approach. Additionally, each chapter highlights a particular aspect of genre in more depth, focusing on five facets of genre analysis: genre historiography, industrial practices of genre constitution, audience use of genres and structures of taste, generic textual analysis, and generic mixing. Finally, each case study stands alone as a piece of cultural analysis, exploring the relationship between television and cultural power that motivates me as a media scholar. Hopefully it is clear that each analysis would not be possible without the approach to genre study outlined here, as the ultimate goal of each case study and this project as a whole is to arrive at a clearer understanding of how genres work to shape our media experiences and how media work to shape our social realities. Since all of my examples — and my theoretical approach to genre itself — treat genre as a historical phenomenon, I will first turn to the issue of generic historiography, examining the crucial issues underlying the practice of writing genre histories.

2

Before the Scandals — Genre Historiography and the Cultural History of the Quiz Show

By reconceiving television genres as cultural categories, we must also redefine how we write genre histories. Media studies, as a field, has turned toward history in recent years, augmenting more generalized theories with examinations of historically specific instances. Genre scholars have only partially embraced this shift, as historical approaches to genres have been limited both in theory and practice, as discussed in Chapter 1. Far less common than interpretive or definitional studies, genre histories have typically followed the model of the textual chronicle, charting out a succession of generic programs with only brief nods toward the importance of industries, audiences, and contexts.[1] This model of history explains generic evolution using programs as documents of larger historical changes. Textual histories are unsuited for the cultural approach to genre I have outlined — if genres do not reside within television programs, then programs are inadequate evidence to write a genre's history. This chapter expands the model of genre historiography outlined in Chapter 1, locating generic history in the development and change of the category itself, using the quiz show genre as an example of genre genealogy in practice.

Media historians always engage in a process of historical selection that constitutes the parameters of our historical objects. This is especially pertinent for genre studies. Since genre analysis explores the processes of cultural categorization, the act of writing generic histories can be viewed as a definitional practice for genre categories. The history of any given genre is a subjective articulation of that genre's definition, meaning, and cultural value — writing a genre's history always stakes a claim that helps constitute the genre itself. Not only do genre histories help define the composition of their particular genre, but they also offer a particular vision of what genres are. As discussed in Chapter 1, most generic historians assume that the objects of their studies are a collection of texts that they view as the contents of the given genre. This reduces a given genre to a somewhat restrictive corpus — for instance, David Marc's influential history of the sitcom is equated with a list of the shows he views as most exemplary.[2] More centrally, these genre histories further the notion that genres are reducible to lists of texts.

What might we view as an alternative object of genre history? Genre histories should posit the *category itself* as the object of genre historiography. The history of the sitcom should not chronicle the various programs that may (or may not) fall under the generic rubric, but rather trace out the various assumptions that have been actively tied to the categorical cluster of the sitcom. The history of a genre would thus explore how particular definitions, interpretations, and evaluations became associated or disassociated with the cultural category and trace out how these discursive practices play out within the various realms of industry, audience, text, critics, policy makers, and broader social context. This mode of generic history locates its object of analysis as the operation of generic categories, and thus looks to the cultural circulation of *television genres* rather than *genre television* to understand how genres evolve, change, and disappear. Since generic categories are composed of discursive practices, Foucault's approach to discursive history as a genealogy is most useful.[3] Generic genealogies chart out the discursive regularities and discontinuities constituting any given genre, tying these practices to contextual power relations and larger discursive regimes, as the object of generic history becomes the wide variety of discursive practices constituting a genre as a cultural category in any given historical moment or shift.

In writing this history of a genre category, we must be wary of the pitfalls of historical writing. The most common approach to mediating histories in written form (as well as other media) is through *narrative*, structuring the retelling of the past as a story.[4] Using typical narrational strategies, like plot structure, engaging characterizations, and focusing on particularly momentous moments, historians narrate the past via their historical writing. For genre histories, the practices of historical narration have resulted in an overly simplistic plot formula applied to most genres — the genre emerges out of a particular innovative instance, matures when the formula reflects dominant social anxieties, and eventually disappears through parody and increasing self-consciousness.[5] While this oft-told tale makes a good read, it rarely represents the actual histories of media genres. Rick Altman offers a revised account of film genre history, suggesting that genres follow far less defined teleologies than those typically told by media historians.[6] Instead, we must look at genres through micro-histories of specific instances, building up an account of larger generic patterns through the collection of particular moments. This type of micro-history runs counter to the narrative template traditionally employed in genre histories — this is not to say that we must eschew narrative as a mode of telling genre history, but that we must recognize narrative form as but one option for writing histories, an option that may or may not be appropriate for any given case study.

Another pitfall of generic history is an overreliance on media texts as historical evidence. As dictated by the traditional textualist assumption, genres are seen as residing in the texts that they seem to categorize — thus genre historians have primarily examined the accessible, bounded, and pleasurable evidence to be found in media texts to support their historical claims. Yet if we view genre categories as primarily operating within the contextual circulation of industrial, audience, and critical practices, the site of historical evidence must shift. Depending on the specific era, topic, and events within a generic history, historians should look beyond media texts to explore how genres operate in sites such as trade press coverage, popular press coverage, critical reviews, promotional material, other cultural representations and commodities (like merchandise, media tie-ins, and parodies), corporate and personal documents, production manuals, legal and governmental materials, audience remnants, and oral histories. In my historical account of quiz shows, I draw from almost all of these types of sources, pointing to the breadth of potential sites of generic historiography and research — no one site of generic practice could account for the wide-ranging operation of genre categories within any specific historical moment. To create a rich and detailed account of media genre history, we must include as many of these types of sources as feasible and appropriate in any given project.

Although this historiographic model — charting the micro-historical operation of genre categories drawing from a broad array of sites of evidence from media industries, audiences, critics, and historical contexts — can be brought to bear on potentially any genre history, the specific issues raised by writing cultural genre histories are best explored in practice. The rest of this chapter examines the quiz show genre to exemplify how a genre history might be written following a cultural approach to genre genealogy. By foregrounding the processes of historiography that often go unsaid in media histories, this example can point to more than just the specific history of an under-examined genre; it can illuminate both the pitfalls and potentials of doing cultural histories of television genre categories.

Genre History and the Discursive Practices of Quiz Shows

The quiz show occupies an unusual place within media history. For the most part, it is a neglected genre, consigned to the historical margins along with other predominantly daytime genres, such as cooking programs, magazine shows, and children's programs, in favor of more legitimized evening genres, like sitcoms, news, and primetime dramas. Occasionally, the genre is thrust into the mainstream, such as the boom in primetime quiz shows the late 1990s, led by the breakout transnational success of *Who Wants to Be a Millionaire* (1999–). By far the most hailed example of the genre's popularity was in the late 1950s, when the genre occupied a central place within American culture at the locus of the so-called "quiz show scandals." Media historians have focused on this crucial moment in the genre's history, looking at the "big money" primetime quizzes, which were revealed to be rigged, to the virtual exclusion of other periods or incarnations of the genre. Of course, I would not argue that the scandals of the late 1950s were unimportant — in terms of larger cultural and industrial impact, the scandals were certainly the most significant contribution of the quiz show genre to media history. Yet the scandals are more often than not examined in a generic vacuum, based on the assumption that the genre emerged out of nowhere to both captivate and disillusion the American viewing public.

In this chapter I gaze backward from the quiz show scandals to consider the genre before the scandals. By looking at the quiz show genre prior to the scandals, I am not attempting to reconstruct the succession of texts that eventually led to *Twenty-One* (1956–58) and *The $64,000 Question* (1955–58). Rather I trace out how the genre, as a cluster of definitions, interpretations, and evaluations, helped set the stage for the scandals. As presented in traditional accounts of the scandals, television audiences assumed certain generic conventions — such as "televised fair play" and "spontaneous unrehearsed competition" — as definitional elements of the genre; when the programs' actual production practices were revealed to contradict these conventions, the 1950s scandals ensued. But how did these conventions become associated with the quiz show? What other associations did the genre hold that may have helped lead to the scandals? To answer these questions, we need to look backward to the quiz show as it emerged and became popular as a genre on radio — the radio era established the quiz show genre's clustered definitions, interpretations, and evaluations that helped foster the scandals, including setting the vital precedent that the quiz show belonged at the center of highly publicized controversies.[7] The important events and impacts of the television scandals would be difficult to imagine without the vital precedents established on the radio era, a facet of the genre's history that has been mostly overlooked by media historians.

Most histories of the quiz show scandals insufficiently address the genre's previous radio incarnation. Kent Anderson's detailed history of the scandals dispenses with the radio era in three pages, while prosecuting District Attorney Joseph Stone's account only mentions radio quiz shows as previous credits for relevant television producers.[8] The most comprehensive history of quiz shows is Thomas DeLong's *Quiz Craze*, which accounts for the genre from its radio inception to its post-scandal reformulation as daytime game shows.[9] While DeLong's book provides much valuable information (and is certainly an enjoyable read), he exemplifies the model of textual chronicle that has often typified popular generic histories — successions of texts described and discussed in relation to their producers and level of popularity, but with little critical analysis or argumentation. Other radio histories discuss quiz shows only in passing, if at all.[10] Clearly, this genre and the relationship between the television scandals and the radio era has been neglected within media history.

Despite this lack of examination, the links between the television quiz show scandals and the genre's history on radio are both vital and complex. The quiz show emerged on radio in the earliest days of the medium's commercialization, with local stations broadcasting programs like WJZ-New York's *The Pop Question Game* in 1923.[11] Unlike most radio genres, the quiz show did not emerge as an adaptation of literary, cinematic, or theatrical entertainment. DeLong suggests a number of antecedents, specifically newspaper puzzles, parlor games, spelling bees, and gambling, while the memoirs of TV quiz show producer Norm Blumenthal mentions carnival games and movie-house contests like "Screeno."[12] Quiz programs continued on local stations throughout the 1920s, but the networks generally avoided the genre in this era, fearful of FRC (Federal Radio Commission, later Federal Communications Commission) policies against on-air lotteries and threats that this genre did not operate "in the public interest," per FRC mandate.[13]

The first major shift in this practice came in 1934, when Major Edward Bowes and his program *The Original Amateur Hour* (1935–45) became the most popular host and show on the airwaves.[14] This program, awarding cash prizes to amateur performers selected by audience phone-in voting, brought many of the quiz show's textual conventions to network radio: listener participation by phone, live competition, and monetary rewards.[15] Bowes' success prompted numerous successful imitators — as one popular press article assessed the genre in 1937, "The amateur hour long has wiggled and wobbled as the No. 1 radio craze of the nation." In attempting to discern what generic development may follow, the unnamed author shrewdly predicted that "the new question- and spelling-bees [could] now make a bid for nationwide popularity."[16] While *Professor Quiz* (1936–41) was not the first national quiz show, it was the first major success, prompting the first wave of successful quiz shows in the late 1930s, including hits like *Ask-It-Basket* (1938–40), *Battle of the Sexes* (1938–42), *Dr. IQ* (1939–48), *Information Please!* (1938–45), and *Quiz Kids* (1940–50).

The first anti-quiz-show backlash followed quickly, as NBC's *Pot o' Gold* (1939–41) debuted with a new gimmick: calling random people chosen from phone books and awarding them $1,000 just for answering their phone, interspersed with musical numbers by host and bandleader Horace Heidt. The show simultaneously became tremendously popular and controversial, as the FCC asked the Department of Justice to prosecute the show as a lottery; although Justice declined to press charges, NBC was cautious enough to pull the hit after only two seasons. The other networks followed, retooling quiz shows to be certain that they did not violate lottery laws and FCC sentiments.[17] Quiz shows continued throughout the war years, drawing solid audiences but evoking little controversy for the first half of the 1940s. A number of new spins on the genre emerged, most notably stunt shows like *Truth or Consequences* (1940–49) and *People Are Funny* (1942–50); these programs used the question and prize format as an excuse to force contestants to perform "zany" and "daffy" stunts in order to win increasingly lavish prizes.[18]

The late 1940s marked the second explosion in radio quiz show popularity, as programs raised the stakes of extravagant prize packages and cash jackpots of thousands of dollars. *Truth or Consequences* ran the "Mr. Hush" contest to identify a mystery voice for $13,500 in prizes in 1946, leading to a flood of big-money giveaways.[19] *Stop the Music!* (1948–51) and *Sing It Again* (1948–51) returned to *Pot o' Gold* territory in 1948 by soliciting its contestants via random phone calls, while shows like *Queen for a Day* (1945–56) dispensed with questions altogether, awarding bounty based on which contestant could evoke the most pity from studio audiences. Ratings soared again, with upstart *Stop the Music!* beating longtime radio favorite Fred Allen in his timeslot, leading Allen to publicly denounce quiz shows. As the upsurge peaked in 1948, critical backlash arose from both outside and inside the radio industry, and in August the FCC threatened to deny license renewals to any station broadcasting giveaway shows, which they had ruled to be lotteries.[20] As I discuss more below, networks protested and sued — by the time the courts decided in 1954 that giveaways were not lotteries, quiz shows had lost popularity and lowered their jackpots, but the number of programs remained high as they migrated to fill the emerging television schedule.[21] The quiz show would not experience another peak in popularity until the rise of big-money television quizzes and their subsequent scandals in the late 1950s, by which time the genre had practically vanished from the radio dial.

This brief chronicle of the cyclical life of the radio quiz show suggests that this genre had two of the features often cited as unique to the television quiz show scandals: vast popularity and publicized controversy. The genre's radio incarnation, through the cultural assumptions articulated to the quiz show genre, also set the stage for many of the other issues evoked in the late 1950s crisis. The television scandals were predicated on assumptions of what were normal and proper aspects of quiz shows. The radio quiz show helped form this generic terrain with direct linkages to how the television scandals played out, especially in establishing the hierarchies that served as the cultural scaffolding supporting the genre throughout its scandalized history. Looking at the discursive circulation of the generic category in the radio era, we can trace specific linkages that had profound impact upon television quiz shows and their controversial history, yet have been mostly overlooked in the historical accounts of the scandals. The rest of this chapter charts out the definitions, interpretations, and evaluations operative in press coverage, corporate and legal archives, references in popular culture, and a variety of other sources. I conclude by looking more closely at the most controversial moment of radio quiz show history, surrounding the FCC's attempts to remove quiz shows from the air for violating lottery laws, pointing to how genre studies might be applicable to the growing area of cultural policy studies.

Before looking to the specific articulations of the quiz show genre, I should clarify the use of *quiz show* as the defining generic term. Terminology is a central issue in genre study, because genres operate primarily by allowing one general term to stand in for many cultural assumptions and categorized texts. As such, the choice of term is quite significant — the relevant assumptions operative within one given genre could be quite different, depending on whether it were labeled *police show*, *crime show*, *detective show*, or *law show*. In each instance, we might find differing assumptions of definition, interpretation, and evaluation tied to the genre's name. Similarly, a number of terms circulated around the genre that I label the *quiz show — giveaway*, *question-and-answer*, *contest*, *cash-and-query*, *question-bee*, and *gift shows* are all terms I found mentioned in my research, while *amateur*, *audience participation*, *talent*, and *stunt shows* all share enough significant generic assumptions with the quiz show to warrant analysis.[22] I use the term *quiz show* to signify the broad genre category to remain consistent with the narrative of the television quiz show scandals, and to follow the language of press discourses, which use *quiz show* more than any other term.

The typical history of the quiz show scandals paints a particularly narrow definition of the television genre — high-minded contestants answer intellectual questions in an allegedly "honest" competition for a large prize of cash and merchandize. While this definition fits the scandalized programs like *The $64,000 Question* and *Twenty-One*, other popular television quiz shows of the 1950s such as *You Bet Your Life* (1950–61) and *I've Got a Secret* (1952–67) followed different definitional rules, featuring humorous banter and celebrity panels with low-stakes prizes. This divergence points to a typical trap of generic analysis — generalizing an entire genre based upon a limited corpus of texts. Generic texts of any one era tend to be much more wide-ranging and divergent than genre histories acknowledge; thus we must be wary of claims of a genre's uniform definition in any historical moment. But despite this warning of generic diversity, discourses of definition constituting the television quiz show as a cultural category did cohere in particularly salient ways during the 1950s. Especially surrounding the scandals, the category of "quiz show" came to mean something more specific than the broad array of programs that might fall under its categorical rubric. For the 1950s television genre, quiz shows were culturally understood more narrowly as intellectually rigorous, high-stakes, allegedly honest competitions typified by the later-scandalized programs. Despite the actual range of 1950s television quiz shows surpassing this narrow genre definition, the categorical set of assumptions tied to the quiz show label was more focused, leading to key material effects at the center of the scandals.

How are we to understand this simultaneous diversity in programs categorized by a generic label, and the clear cultural primacy given to one central incarnation of the genre? It is useful here to draw upon the notion of a generic *dominant*, a term adapted from Russian formalist approaches to textual analysis.[23] Much like a generic cycle, a dominant refers to the prevailing incarnation of a genre at any given time; the historical change within a genre stems from a cascading series of successive dominants, generally defined by textual strategies. This concept can apply to genres as cultural categories as well — in any given moment, a particular set of assumptions may emerge as the foremost incarnation of the genre in cultural circulation. While there will probably be contradictory texts and discontinuous discourses active in the generic cluster, a generic dominant functions as the primary connotative implication of generic terminology. Thus in 1956, when the term *quiz show* was used, it was generally understood across cultural spheres to refer to big-money, question-centered programs like *Twenty-One*, as well as the genre's associated assumptions of cultural legitimacy and honest competition. Other textual examples contradicting the dominant were not viewed as outside the genre — *You Bet Your Life* was still categorized as a quiz show — but in the genre's role as cultural shorthand for a set of assumptions, the dominant was more limited than the entire quiz show category. This notion of generic dominants is useful in exploring how genre categories can change over time, yet still encompass similar categorical scope across different eras.

Quiz shows were markedly diverse in both textual conventions and cultural assumptions throughout their multi-decade run on radio, yet the genre had specific dominants at particular historical moments. These dominants, like genres, often refer to textual elements, but are clusters of cultural assumptions, fostered by discourses of definition, interpretation, and evaluation. In the cultural history of radio quiz shows, three specific dominants helped link certain assumptions and conventions to the generic cluster of the quiz show — the *question-centered quiz*, the *stunt show*, and the *giveaway*. These three dominants each included particular cultural assumptions, a series of discursive articulations that were drawn upon as the genre shifted to television and led to the well-known climax of the quiz show scandals.

The genre's initial incarnation, following from the popularity of amateur shows, focused primarily upon the intellectual challenge of contestants competing for modest prizes, typified by *Professor Quiz* and *Dr. IQ*. This was the dominant incarnation of the quiz show — the question-centered quiz — which producer Dan Golenpaul was reacting against through his innovation of *Information Please!* in 1938. By reversing the typical procedures of the quiz show, audience members mailed the program questions to pose to a panel of experts.[24] Another adaptation in the format of these question-centered quiz shows shifted focus onto children contestants, most notably on *Quiz Kids* in 1940. All of these popular programs typified the dominant features of the early quiz show: questions of intellectual knowledge, small prizes, and highbrow educational overtones. As Herta Herzog suggests in her landmark audience study of *Professor Quiz*, listeners valued the educational merits as well as the competitive participation of the genre's programs.[25] Contestants were seen as highly-educated elites, able to match wits with the erudite panelists of *Information Please!* or *Quiz Kids*, and the genre was understood as a legitimate and culturally valued form of broadcasting.

This dominant understanding of the quiz show was affirmed by its positive placement in hierarchies of social value. The popular press featured parents and teachers praising the educational value of *Quiz Kids*.[26] Similarly, an on-air promo highlighted the show's educational aspect: "Boys and girls everywhere are taking new interest in their school work and their studies — and, believe it or not, they are finding it fun.... Teachers and principles have worked a long time to accomplish what you Quiz Kids have done in just six months — that is, you've actually succeeded in making education popular."[27] *Information Please!* was also accorded favorable cultural value, as *The Saturday Review of Literature* gave the show an award for "Distinguished Service to American Literature" in 1940, working against the clear hierarchy that valued literature and publishing over broadcasting.[28] The educational value of quiz shows was reiterated throughout many audience letters as well, confirming that, for at least some listeners, educational factors were an important component of the genre's appeal; as one letter asserts, "My husband, children and myself have gained more general knowledge from quiz shows than we learned in school."[29] Thus, the question-centered quiz show dominant explicitly linked intellectual competition with positive social values and education.

Tied to this genre dominant was a significant underlying assumption under debate: quiz shows were spontaneous, ad-libbed, and featured unrehearsed, fair competition. Although these genre conventions were violated in television's quiz show scandals to great public dismay, the way these elements were articulated around these earlier radio programs forces us to question the myth of the innocent television public of the late 1950s. Few public accounts directly suggest that programs were not spontaneous. The description of the local Baltimore program *Quiz the Scientist* (1941) in a popular magazine stands as an exception, as the show allowed listeners to query a panel of expert scientists for a $1 reward, but admitted that the answers were scripted to assure scientific accuracy and educational value.[30] A similarly extreme example in the popular press told the "story about an emcee who wanted a certain contestant to win, and he told her the correct answer before they went on the air. When he threw the question at her, the lady's mind went blank. 'I can't remember,' she moaned into the mike, 'what you told me to say.'"[31] Despite these exceptions, most popular accounts of quiz shows reiterated the program's authenticity in featuring unstaged competition in the face of debate.

Skepticism about the genre's veracity was fairly common among commentators and audience members. One magazine writer suspected that a local program called *Meet the Experts* was fixed, because the show featured station employees like the receptionist and sales manager answering difficult questions on British royalty, furthering the assumption that quiz show contestants were not the typical working American.[32] Audience letters, as found in both the NBC corporate collection and the FCC archives, indicated that a number of listeners doubted the programs' authenticity. One anonymous letter to the FCC, allegedly from a former quiz show writer, claimed that some shows use "stooges" or hired contestants, and that any pretense of randomly selecting contestants was fraudulent.[33] Skepticism concerning the genre's authenticity was further indicated by the number of press accounts that reiteratively insisted that quiz shows were in fact unrehearsed and fair.[34] Just as Foucault suggests that the degree to which the Victorian era denied sexuality provided evidence of the cultural centrality of sex, it would seem that the regular reiteration of the genre's authenticity had to be in response to skepticism which was more widespread than documented.[35]

This skepticism and affirmation played out quite clearly in the case of *Quiz Kids*. Listeners regarded the erudition of the young contestants with suspicion, writing to NBC and the press with their concerns. One listener complained to NBC about perceived dishonesty within *Quiz Kids*, citing suspicions that a 7-year-old contestant could answer questions so quickly and correctly, noting "the recitation manner of his delivery, the committing to memory of a certain definition and telling the same in school room fashion." She went on to discuss the evidence that confirmed her suspicions at length:

> When Mr. Kelly, at the close of the program, engaging in ad-lib conversation with this child about the turtle question, he ruined forever your *Quiz Kids* program, for this same Girard answered him with "And besides I know the man who sent in the question." The prolonged laughter and applause by the studio audience seemed to come from pent up feelings of doubt and unbelief that had been eagerly awaiting the bomb which your Girard released on your show to convince them that the whole thing is a hoax and a deception. This sort of program

should not be permitted to be aired in the name of an unrehearsed program, because every response from this child Girard has been drilled into him and has come forth in labored, recitation form.

The writer concluded by arguing, "This could have been such an interesting and instructive program if it had been kept honest, but I don't believe anything you could do now would reinstate it in public favor."[36] While NBC officials wrote back to assure her that there were no unfair elements in the program's competition, it would appear that some viewers felt betrayed by the program's perceived violation of the implied generic norms.

Quiz Kids prompted more claims of both doubt and authenticity; writers in the popular press reported listener skepticism that children could be so erudite and quick with their answers, while assuring readers of the show's spontaneity.[37] One magazine article suggested extreme public uproar in reaction to a detailed recitation of Greek mythology by one Quiz Kid:

> Bitter letters poured in, charging that the whole thing was a fake, that the children were given the questions ahead of time and rehearsed, which is not true. Topping the protests was a formal document from a reading society in Roxbury, Mass., signed by the president, the secretary, and the "technical adviser." "Imagine," it demanded, indicating that such radio charlatans should be thrown in jail, "a seven-year-old boy well acquainted and well founded on Greek mythology!"[38]

The writer assured readers that many people had researched the matter and proven that the show was authentically spontaneous. Despite this assurance, these instances suggest that claims of the public's naïve and innocent belief in the authenticity of quizzes in the late 1950s are not as clear-cut as historians have asserted, as suspicions of the genre's use of scripted answers and planned outcome had distinct precedence on the radio.

While spontaneity was a central though disputed generic assumption, many articles in the popular press pointed to how the shows were carefully planned, despite their impromptu results. An article on *Information Please!* suggested that the show was "unrehearsed, but that doesn't mean that it is not carefully planned or, as radio lingo puts it, 'programmed.'" Producer Dan Golenpaul originally intended for listeners to ask their own questions on the air, but one person changed his query for the live broadcast: "After the show, the iconoclast explained that he regarded the whole thing as staged, and proposed, in fact, to stump the experts."[39] Thus, Golenpaul countered accusations of inauthenticity by exerting more control and planning. One article quoted a writer on another show discussing his ability to control when contestants hit the jackpot: "You can't make a person win, but you can be reasonably sure of making him miss.

No one can answer a question if you don't want him to. With a week's preparation, I can stump anybody." He vaguely added that when it was time for the jackpot to be won, "We lay it in their laps."[40] Another article assured audiences that while "their programs sound as if all the words were made up on the spur of the moment. . . each show is carefully rehearsed for hours, with scripts that are blank in the spots in which the names of winners or losers are used."[41] While spontaneity was asserted as a core generic assumption, the quiz show was also described as highly controlled, with scripts and planning serving to balance the illusion of completely ad-libbed programming, suggesting that the tension between spontaneity and planning was a part of the genre long before the 1950s scandals.

Thus, the dominant conception of the quiz show genre in the early 1940s clustered a number of central assumptions and conventions. Programs focused on contestants competing to win prizes via intellectual questioning. The genre was socially validated as providing educational and cultural uplift, focusing on legitimated realms of knowledge via asking questions of fact and objective knowledge. While the competition was generally regarded as unstaged and "fair," currents of doubt ran through the cultural circulation of quiz shows, articulated in audience letters, press commentaries, and industrial defenses of the genre's authenticity. Even as the genre was primarily understood as spontaneous, notions of staged entertainment were part of the generic cluster, as producers publicly acknowledged their ability to control the seemingly ad-lib format. This dominant cluster of generic assumptions formed the baseline foundation of the quiz show genre, the core set of definitions, interpretations, and evaluations that future innovations and generic shifts would be compared to. Two other emerging dominants proved to be important steps in the genre's road toward eventual scandal.

As Rick Altman has argued (and I consider more in Chapter 6), genre mixing is a primary way that genres evolve and change throughout their history — by drawing upon the conventions and assumptions of other genres, new subgenres and fully distinct genres can emerge.[42] Quiz programs were subject to frequent genre-mixing on radio, often combining with other established program styles to create new variations. For example, 1940s radio featured comedy stunt/audience participation programs (*Truth or Consequences*), comedy quiz programs (*You Bet Your Life*), quiz parodies (*It Pays to be Ignorant*), mystery-quizzes (*$1000 Reward*), and many musical quiz shows (*Pot o' Gold*). Through genre mixing in the early 1940s, two new dominant incarnations of the quiz show emerged that would help lead the genre to its 1950s scandalized destiny: the stunt show and the giveaway show.

The stunt show emerged in the early 1940s alongside the rise of the standard question-centered quiz show, but it reversed many of the definitional elements and cultural assumptions that had constituted the earlier dominant generic cluster. While standard quiz shows featured intellectual questions, fair competition, and modest prizes, stunt programs downplayed the role of the question and answer format in the name of highly staged contests and lavish prizes. The primary innovator and smash hit of this variation of the quiz show was *Truth or Consequences*, "the one audience-participation program where the disappointed contestants are those who answer their questions correctly."[43] On this popular program, host and creator Ralph Edwards brought members from the studio audience and asked them a "Truth," or standard quiz show question. While the Truth paid $15 for a correct answer, most contestants failed to answer it properly:

> The questions are ridiculous twisters, to start with; they must be answered in twenty seconds, and Edwards jams eighteen of those twenty seconds with other questions like 'Is your work going well?' and 'Are you happy being here?' No one minds the obvious fraud. Most contestants prefer to accept an alternative reward of five dollars and whatever Consequences Edwards has cooked up.[44]

Other magazine articles suggested that contestants purposely answered the Truth incorrectly to participate in the Consequence — a direct inversion of assumed quiz show norms.[45] Edwards claimed he devised the show to avoid the humiliation he thought failed quiz show contestants must have felt, giving them something fun to do instead of simply proving their intelligence.[46]

Even though *Truth or Consequences* still used quiz questions as a framing device, the role of the question as the central entertainment of the quiz show was replaced by the "stunt" in this particular subgenre, often labeled *crackpot shows, zany audience-participation shows*, or just *stunt shows*. These stunts or "Consequences" ranged in degrees of complexity and excess; for example Edwards once solicited listeners to send a contestant pennies, resulting in over 300,000 cents arriving within a few weeks.[47] Another more elaborate stunt ran over a number of months and sent the contestant, Mr. Rudolph Wickel, on a wild hunt through a number of states for the ultimate reward of $1,000.[48] Another particularly elegant stunt offered a contestant $1,000 if he could simply fall asleep over the course of that evening's program — onstage in front of the studio audience. Edwards' prime stunt competitor was Art Linkletter's *People Are Funny*, whose more notable stunts included making a woman not speak for one week to win $1,000, and giving a family an airplane for answering the question "What is your name?"[49] Along with downplaying the intellectual question, the stunt quiz shows raised the stakes of the jackpots awarded to the "winners," focusing on the lavish merchandise and cash prizes featured on the programs, such as Linkletter's proud offer of "the first complete prize in radio history — a home, garage, lot, car, and a lifetime job in Southern California."[50]

As this new dominant form of the quiz show emerged in the early 1940s, a number of complaints followed within the popular press. The general dumbing down of questions became a topic of consternation among many writers, as caricatured by this hypothetical quiz show host's patter: "Who wrote *Hamlet?* His first name is William. No coaching, please. Don't *shake*, Mrs. Stupidovitch; I'm not going to stick you with a *spear.*"[51] One article celebrated intellectual throwback *Twenty Questions* because, "unlike most radio quizzes, no one wins $5,000,000 for knowing who was President during the Wilson Administration, or gets smacked with a bag full of wet cement if he fails to get the correct answer."[52] The most scathing lament of the intellectual question's demise was Edwin O'Connor's highbrow critique of the genre in *Atlantic Monthly.* O'Connor suggested that originally, quiz shows "stipulated that the contestant should answer that question in order to win the attached award. Moreover. . . they held that the answer must come from the contestant himself, with no outside assistance." As the genre grew older, it changed: "Although it still asks questions, it regards the unaided answer as an irrelevancy. . . . The time has come to abandon all the hocus-pocus of the question program, which really is looking for no answers at all."[53] Thus the decline of the intellectual question was culturally activated as a sign of generic devaluation and derision, as the remaining "real" quiz shows like *Information Please!* were celebrated within intrageneric hierarchies as more legitimate than stunt shows like *Truth or Consequences.*

The competing cultural conceptions of dual dominants in the early 1940s — question-centered quiz versus stunt show — drew upon the cultural understanding of quiz shows as both educational and entertaining. Despite the presence of educational discourses in constituting the question-centered dominant of the genre, all quiz shows were associated with entertainment far more than education. Even *Information Please!* the program often held up as the most purely intellectual quiz show, was celebrated for its entertainment value as well. One *New York Times* writer noted that the show improved on its early efforts as it "increased its entertainment value by stressing the personalities on its board of experts. They don't just answer questions now, as they did at first. They put on a show."[54] Likewise, a magazine writer contrasted the numerous educational accolades the program received to the "fortunate" fact that the experts "still think they're playing a game, having a lot of fun, and are not educating the populace."[55] As one article summed up, "Quiz shows are conceived as entertainment. Their primary object is to amuse."[56] Other pleasures notwithstanding, the entertainment function of quiz shows was rarely contested, even by a highbrow magazine writer who condemned the genre as "an attempt. . . to entertain its listeners by the simple device of proving to them that their fellow citizens were not quite bright."[57] As a radio production manual asserted, the quiz show's "purpose is almost invariably entertainment, though occasionally it might have educational or instructional overtones."[58]

Even though both dominants were acknowledged to primarily feature entertainment, the specific form of entertainment provided by quiz shows was a common topic of discussion in the press. For instance, the shift away from "hard knowledge" programs such as *Professor Quiz* and toward more comedic shows like *How'm I Doin'?* and *Take It or Leave It* (1940–46) was characterized by "less difficult questions. . . [and hosts] given to extended wisecracking; equipped also with music, their programs have a distinct touch of the variety show." Likewise on *Truth or Consequences*, "the questions are incidental to the slapstick comedy involved in the goofy consequences; it is as much vaudeville as radio."[59] By the mid 1940s, humor became central, surpassing competition: "Today a quiz program is mainly designed to exhibit slices of life, to present a cross section of strange, wonderful, bizarre and queer specimens of humanity. Frequently the dumber a contestant is, the funnier he sounds on the air."[60] This shift, tied to the rise of the stunt dominant, formed the grounds for many condemnations of the genre, suggesting nostalgia for an earlier quiz show incarnation, as expressed by "professional contestant" Louis Fehr in 1946:

> Outside of *Professor Quiz*, none of the emcees is running a genuine quiz program. They run circuses. They purposely needle and ride the contestant in order to upset him, so he will make a fool of himself and the show will make people laugh. They don't want the cool, composed type or the intelligent, well-informed citizen. They want the boobs.[61]

Similarly, in the underrated 1950 film *Champagne for Caesar*, the character of "know-it-all" Beauregard Bottomley (Ronald Colman) decries the degradation of knowledge promoted by quiz shows. While watching a quiz show for the first time, he contends that if knowing facts like "2 + 2 = 4" were rewarded upon these shows, the average intelligence of the American public would sink to this level. When other "common" audience members tell him that they found the show entertaining and the host (played by *People Are Funny* host Art Linkletter) funny, he dismissed them (and the genre) as lowbrow and unrefined — until he realizes that he can put his knowledge to economic gain by outwitting the program.[62] Although the rise of the comedic quiz show gave ammunition to highbrow critiques of the genre, the primacy of entertainment has always been a central assumption of the quiz show genre. But the distinction between legitimated educational and intellectual pleasures of the genre and its less respected entertaining functions played an important role leading to the television scandals.

While both educational and entertainment discourses were central in the distinction between question-centered and stunt dominants, other pleasures were activated within this generic dichotomy. One distinct generic pleasure was "what quiz-industry tycoons call 'the unrehearsed, unwritten ending.' The biggest ratings in radio and TV, they point out, invariably go to special events whose outcomes are in doubt and whose scripts are unprepared."[63] Tied to the convention of spontaneity, quiz shows presented situations that invited audiences to believe that anything could happen, even when audiences and producers both knew that the overall results were quite controlled to follow the patterns of previous programs. But within specific moments of the program, audiences could wonder whether a given question would be answered correctly, whether a given contestant would succeed or fail. Both forms of the genre tapped into this general pleasure of competition and limited unpredictability, as listeners rooted for or against contestants and competed vicariously at home, believing that results would not be predetermined.

Among the quiz show's primary appeals was the pleasure of vicarious competition. Producer Mark Goodson wrote that the quiz show "permits listeners to compete in the game... and most quiz shows are listened to, not passively the way people listen to drama or music, but actively as a game in which the listener participates."[64] One *New York Times* writer cited the "listener's vicarious involvement in conflict... he gets almost as much enjoyment out of the game as the real player and, what's more, can't lose," and a production manual agreed, "The charm and audience interest in a quiz program is vicarious participation."[65] An article in *Parents' Magazine* described the experience of listening to *Quiz Kids*: "You find yourself sitting on the very edge of your chair in your own desire to participate in the questions that are being asked, and you may be mortified when you realize you do not know the answer."[66] Fans of *Information Please!* gathered each week to compete against the experts on the radio, literally involving themselves in the program's competition.[67] Producers recognized the importance of sustaining vicarious dramatic interest — despite the ad-libbed format, a production manual insisted that the quiz show "must follow out the basic tenets of good showmanship and contain conflict, rising interest, a climax, and a dénouement."[68] Thus, as the competitive framework of the quiz show, established in the radio era, formed one of the prime pleasures for the audience, the outrage of the television scandals resulted partially from the realization that this competition was overly controlled, relying more upon structuring the drama than allowing the contests to generate their own excitement.

While competitive and dramatic pleasures have always been central to the genre, the rise of the stunt show dominant altered the ways in which competition and vicarious participation factored into the genre. *Truth or Consequences* and its aforementioned lengthy "wild goose chase" with Mr. Wickel exemplified to commentators of the day that the show's pleasures were not in winning contests, but in delaying people's gratification, especially considering that the audience was practically assured that contestants would win their prizes.[69] Even though the stunt shows in the 1940s downplayed intellectual competition, the potential for participation remained a vital pleasure associated with the genre.

Many of the stunts featured on these programs involved the home audience's participation, as the unpredictable path of the contestants might involve a national treasure hunt or mail-in element that could involve listeners directly. But it was the rise of the third dominant of the radio quiz show, the giveaway program, that both thrust listener participation into the foreground of the genre's constitutive assumptions and set the wheels in motion that most directly led television quizzes down the path toward scandal.

Giveaway programs first achieved public infamy in 1939 with NBC's *Pot o' Gold*. Much more of a musical program than quiz show, the program featured one contest per show embedded within ten musical numbers by Horace Heidt and his Musical Knights.[70] As fictionalized in the 1941 film *Pot o' Gold*, the show was primarily a musical program that "accidentally" stumbled upon the giveaway gimmick as a successful marketing move.[71] The actual origins of the program were far less accidental (or driven by a typical romance plot), but strategically devised as a gimmick to make Heidt stand out among the glut of broadcast big bands.[72] The giveaway format of *Pot o' Gold* featured no question and answer component — contestants won $1,000 simply for answering their phones when randomly called. The FCC interpreted this format as violating lottery laws, requesting that the Justice Department prosecute *Pot o' Gold* as illegal. Despite Justice's inaction, *Pot o' Gold* left the air in 1941, following these accusations, as other shows avoided giveaways to avoid FCC prosecution.

The second (and more successful) rise of giveaways grew out of stunt programs. In 1946, Ralph Edwards started a contest called "Mr. Hush" on *Truth or Consequences* — each week a mystery voice read a riddle and series of clues. Edwards would then phone a random number, asking whomever answered to identify the mysterious "Mr. Hush"; after weeks of trying, eventually the listener giving the correct answer of Jack Dempsey won an enormous jackpot of sponsor-provided merchandise. Subsequent contests, such as "Walking Man" and "Mrs. Hush," were expanded to allow listeners to submit their phone numbers, encouraging regular listening and active participation. These telephone contests became a national sensation, with winners making headlines, ongoing speculations in gossip columns discussing the potential answers, and publicity boosting the show's ratings to record levels.

Edwards's contests reinvigorated the giveaway format, leading to programs based solely upon the giveaway gimmick. The most successful giveaway show was *Stop the Music!*, which rode its high-stakes contest, asking listeners to name mystery songs, to both ratings success and regulatory disapproval. As I discuss below, the rise of the giveaway as a dominant led to a cultural crisis that presaged many of the issues arising in the more notorious television scandals. The various definitions, interpretations, and evaluations that constituted all three dominants of the radio quiz show would reappear within both the late 1940s radio scandals and the 1950s television version. While traditional approaches to generic analysis tend to paint genres in broad strokes, positing generic norms as clear, bounded, and fairly static, I contend that genres are commonly sites of cultural struggles and dissent rather than clearly established consensus and regularity. Media genre analysis needs to recognize the role of contradiction and struggle within generic processes, looking to how generic categories operate primarily through the tensions arising from the cultural debates around genres and their role within media and society. To demonstrate this further, I now turn to a micro-analysis of this third dominant of the radio quiz show, focusing on a particularly contentious moment in the history of the genre — the FCC's attempted ban of quiz shows in the late 1940s.

Regulating Genre Categories and Crisis Historiography

Media historians have assumed that the television quiz show scandals of the late 1950s were an anomaly in the history of the genre, but I wish to argue that these scandals were unique more as a matter of *degree*, rather than *kind* of controversy. The radio era set the generic stage for the television scandals in a number of key ways: focusing on one particular dominant of the genre, the big-money question-driven program; building upon nascent audience skepticism of the genre's construction of authenticity; and relying upon the primacy of entertainment in manipulating dramatic intrigue and vicarious audience pleasures. But another association was fostered in the radio era that has not been explored sufficiently by media historians — the radio quiz show was established as a common site of well-publicized controversy, scandal, and cultural policy regulation.

Traditional approaches to genre rarely consider policy making as a site of generic practice. Yet, to understand how genre operates as a cultural site in a wide range of spheres, we must look at regulatory practices and policies. Following recent developments in cultural policy studies as a realm of media analysis, we must regard the practices of regulation as constitutive of cultural knowledge — in the case of genre, regulators are a facet of the institutional apparatus of media that can exert powerful discourses that shape genre categories.[73] While certainly not as directly influential in programming as in other countries with public service television models, American television regulation frequently impacts genre categories — public television actively participates in defining the boundaries of educational and children's television; congressional hearings on television violence in the 1960s linked particular assumptions of value and meaning to crime and action genres.[74] Policy practices will serve as a site of generic practice in a number of this book's case studies, from censorship cries concerning *Soap* and talk shows, to governmental cooperation in producing *Dragnet*'s representations of the police. For quiz shows, a central generic assumption throughout the genre's history across media is the legitimization of the genre as a valid site of cultural policy and regulation.

Generally, the agency charged with regulating American broadcasting takes little interest in programming formats, as the FCC is explicitly forbidden to censor programming or mandate particular programming practices.[75] Yet the FCC does have both the authority and duty to enforce a number of programming guidelines, as stipulated within the Communications Act of 1934; among these policies was a regulation outlawing lotteries using the airwaves.[76] In 1948, the FCC issued an official statement positing an interpretation of the quiz show genre that defined the programs as lotteries, and threatened to deny license renewals to any station broadcasting giveaways, effectively outlawing the genre. While the FCC's ban was eventually dismissed by the U.S. Supreme Court and never fully enforced, this moment of generic regulation stands as an important turning point in the genre's history, establishing important precedents that impacted the more notorious scandals of the late 1950s.

The FCC's actions concerning quiz shows in the late 1940s were not without precedent. Throughout the 1930s and 1940s, the FCC refused to advise broadcasters whether planned programs would violate the lottery section of the Communications Act, as the Commission did not have the authority to judge programming before airing.[77] The FCC did assert, however, that they could, per federal mandate, prosecute broadcasters for actually airing lotteries and deny them license renewals after the fact; in 1940 the Commission attempted to follow through with this threat. The FCC recommended a number of mostly local programs for prosecution to the Department of Justice, for alleged violation of Section 316 of the Communications Act; the only high-profile program in this group was NBC's hit *Pot o' Gold*. FCC Chairman James Lawrence Fly argued that giveaway contests violated the public interest, "placing radio in the position of 'buying' its audience."[78] Thus, the FCC generically linked giveaways to lotteries, associating the genre with "illegitimate" broadcasting rather than "proper" entertainment.

While the Justice Department refused to prosecute the broadcasters for violating lottery laws in 1940, the genre's cultural understanding and programmatic practices were effectively changed by this action; as one article asserted, "The radio industry got a big scare, [and] quickly began revamping the shows FCC objected to."[79] The link between quiz shows and lottery laws became the topic of public debate and press coverage, establishing the genre as a site of regulatory concern. As fictionalized in the 1941 film *Pot o' Gold*, the mechanism for the quiz show had to be carefully designed to operate legally in the public interest. When Jimmy Stewart's character tried to devise a way to legally give away $1,000 randomly on the air, a government representative was brought in to oversee the construction of the gimmick in accordance with the lottery laws. While this type of regulatory oversight was exactly what the FCC was forbidden to do — the Commission was required to only *react* to programming, unable to advise broadcasters on program preparation lest it be accused of censorship — the fictional recreation of *Pot o' Gold*'s origins posited that the program was designed to operate in the public interest and conform with the letter of the law, furthering a discursive association between the quiz show genre and legal concerns.

By the late 1940s, the genre had transformed significantly. Stunt programs had raised the monetary stakes for prizes and replaced intellectual competition with behavioral spectacles and long-running contests. The home listener give-away format, which had waned after the 1940 investigation, returned to the airwaves via ongoing contests featured on stunt programs, garnering more publicity with larger jackpots — although not all hype was positive, as both press coverage and a feature film, 1950's *The Jackpot*, noted how prize winners might view the ensuing tax burden and publicity tied to winning as more of a curse than blessing.[80] The lightening rod program was ABC's *Stop the Music!* which debuted in early 1948 and quickly rose to the #2 slot of the weekly radio ratings. The show's structure was simple — host Bert Parks would call a randomly selected phone number and offer a high-stakes jackpot if the listener could name the Mystery Melody featured in an ongoing contest. The program's success was met with controversies, within both the industry and more widespread circulation: the National Association of Broadcasters (NAB) publicly distanced themselves from giveaways, pronouncing that they were committed to entertaining over "buying" audiences; critics decried the decline of the genre's intellectual and entertainment content; audience members flooded networks and the FCC with letters weighing in on the controversy; and stars like Fred Allen lambasted giveaways in the press. Throughout this generic controversy, we can see a number of specific articulations of the genre's definition, interpretation, and evaluation that set vital precedents for how the genre would operate as a site of cultural policy making during the scandals of the television era.

Just as the quiz show genre had changed by the late 1940s, the regulatory context of the era had shifted from when the FCC had previously attempted to prosecute *Pot o' Gold*. Following World War II, the FCC began examining public service practices and failures of radio broadcasters, resulting in a 1946 report famously known as the Blue Book.[81] The FCC criticized broadcasting practices that seemed to focus on advertising, ratings gimmicks, and popular sponsored programs over locally produced shows, public affairs coverage, and nonsponsored sustaining programs. While the FCC never followed through with their threats in denying license renewals over Blue Book accusations, the atmosphere had shifted due to the agency's revised rhetorical stance concerning programming content. The NAB loudly protested the FCC's regulatory threats and lobbied Congress to keep the agency's power in check. Thus in the late 1940s, the regulatory environment had shifted toward a more activist mode, with the FCC weighing in on programming issues, an area of broadcasting that had been largely unregulated for the previous two decades. The FCC ruling against giveaways in 1948 emerged out of this context, with the agency establishing itself as more of a watchdog over commercial interests in the name of the public interest.

As the FCC threatened to drive giveaway programs from the air, much press coverage of the issue highlighted the questionable entertainment value of the genre, interpreting the giveaway as explicitly "buying an audience." One article described a potential shift "toward entertainment programs, away from prize questions, prize songs, prize telephone calls. . . . A mild revolution in radio thus is about to take place. Program appeal once more will depend on entertainment instead of the lure of easy money."[82] Fred Allen reinforced this distinction, praising the FCC: "It's about time radio was taken away from the scavengers and given back to the entertainers."[83] A local Florida station decided to cancel three local giveaway programs prior to binding FCC action because "the audience would rather have good entertainment."[84] NBC similarly eschewed the giveaway format using these terms: "We will have no part of it. It isn't entertainment. Instead of a script and actors, all they use is a lot of refrigerators and an announcer who can talk fast."[85] The FCC defined the giveaway in similar terms — as Commissioner James Fly wrote, "listeners are attracted not by the quality of the program but simply by the hope of being awarded a valuable prize simply by listening to a particular program. This is not good broadcasting."[86] Within these generic discourses, giveaway shows were positioned in opposition to "honest" quality entertainment formats like drama, music, and comedy, working against the central linkages between quiz shows and entertainment established throughout the genre's history on radio.

Not all discussions around the FCC action suggested that the quiz show had no entertainment value. Many voices distinguished between the "properly" entertaining quiz and the giveaway which tried to buy its audience; a spokesperson for New York station WOR offered this dichotomy: "The giveaway craze and large prizes have begun to overshadow the entertainment value of [quiz] programs. Such overemphasis is not healthy for radio."[87] Other industry players insisted that the giveaway was no different in entertainment value from the genre as a whole, such as ABC's claim that their quiz shows "were all purely entertainment."[88] Likewise *Stop the Music!* producer Louis Cowan filed a brief with the FCC insisting on the entertainment value of his program and the giveaway format, highlighting the vicarious pleasures, community-building participation, "everyman" appeals, and dramatic structure of giveaways.[89] Despite protests by ABC and Cowan, this dichotomy between "entertaining" intellectual quizzes and audience-buying giveaways was reinforced by the networks' actions: pulling most of the controversial home giveaways off the air, while favoring quiz shows in which only in-studio contestants won prizes.

While this opposition did win out, eventually structuring the genre for the 1950s and television, it was not without controversy, as illustrated by debates featured in the press. A former contestant on *Winner Take All* (1946–51) complained, "it's a shame the FCC should be so nasty as to try to stop all this nice entertainment."[90] Magazine writer and quiz show fan Jerome Beatty defended giveaways: "In spite of what some people say, each of these shows is entertaining — the music is good, the questions are interesting, and the breathless masters of ceremonies make them as exciting as a horse race."[91] *New York Times* radio critic Jack Gould summarized proponents' argument: "There may be more drama in a housewife's groping for an answer to a $15,000 question than in a Broadway play. The public, in short, finds many things 'entertaining' outside the world of professional entertainment."[92] Thus many voices questioned the legitimacy of the distinction between proper entertainment and giveaway pleasures, problematizing what the FCC claimed to be not in the public interest.

The public at large voiced its opinions concerning the FCC's actions through a deluge of letters to the Commission. While, according to one trade article the letters were 60% in favor of the ban, my examination of the hundreds of letters stored at the National Archives suggests a range of positions concerning the FCC's policy.[93] Some letters did address the FCC's specific accusation against giveaways — that they were lotteries in violation of Communications Act and U.S. Criminal Code stipulations. Yet most letter writers were not interested in debating the legal interpretations of lotteries; rather they were concerned with more evaluative judgments as to the genre's social role and appeals to the radio audience. Letters in support of the FCC's action labeled quiz shows "junk," "cheap," morally destructive, and promoting gambling. Many letters decried the genre's promise of easy riches, suggesting that "numerous addicts are neglecting family duties endeavoring to win something."[94] Another letter highlighted the detrimental effects the genre might have had on listeners, writing that such programs "engender envy, jealousy, unrest, and discontent."[95] Numerous letters argued that giving away money and prizes in exchange for answering the phone or listening to the radio ran counter to American values of hard work, explicitly drawing links between quiz shows, gambling, runaway inflation, and Communism.[96] Listeners condemning giveaways linked the genre to lowbrow forms, antisocial behavior, un-American morals, and lack of quality in order to support the FCC's ban.

The letters to the FCC endorsing giveaways posit quite different discursive links. Supportive listeners highlighted the genre's entertainment value, the educational merits of quiz shows, and the belief that giveaways offer hope to average Americans. Quiz shows were held up as a legitimate "vice," especially when compared to other bad habits; one listener suggested that quiz shows saved her marriage, as the hope of winning kept her husband home instead of in taverns.[97] The genre was explicitly labeled as "wholesome" entertainment in the face of the FCC's accusation of violating lottery laws. Many letters expressed disbelief in the Commission's generic interpretation as illegal lotteries, as they could not understand how programs could be viewed as gambling; as one listener wrote, "there is no gambling on these programs; those who fail to win never lose anything, for nothing is risked."[98] Listeners employed intergeneric hierarchies to justify the pleasures of quiz shows, citing "inferior" genres such as romances, violent detective shows, tired comedies, recorded music, and most colorfully, "soap operas, singing commercials, blood & thunder murders, hammy & the most banal performers."[99] Evaluative comparisons between genres furthered existing hierarchies, such as the cultural stigmas attached to soap operas and recorded programming, boosting the comparative value of quiz shows.[100] Thus, the quiz show became a site of struggle over competing interpretations concerning the genre's value and legitimacy — the FCC and some listeners found the programs in poor taste and violating the edicts of anti-gambling statutes, while producers and other audience members found this interpretation far-fetched and ill-defined, attempting to regulate what seemed to be primarily a matter of taste.

This debate played out in the legal arena as well. The FCC's case interpreting giveaways as lotteries rested upon the legal definition of lottery; to violate lottery laws, contests were required to draw upon the three aspects of "prize, chance, and consideration."[101] While "prize" was clearly part of all giveaways, and "chance" was usually used at least to select contestants, "consideration" was at the crux of the legal debate, referring to what the contestant must furnish in order to win. Traditionally this aspect of the lottery law protected entrants from spending money or purchasing products in hope of winning a contest; the FCC offered an extremely broad legal interpretation in defining consideration. In addition to the typical requirement "to furnish any money or thing of value," the FCC's expansive definition of consideration included requiring winners to be listening to the program or station, to answer a question whose answer has been given previously on the program or station, or to answer the phone or write a letter to be broadcast or read over the air. The rationale for this broad definition of consideration rested upon the "unique nature of the medium of radio" — since radio was available to listeners free of charge, the "thing of value" furnished by listeners was listening itself. The system of commercial broadcasting sells listeners to advertisers; thus the FCC defined the time spent listening to "free" programming of sufficient value to legally qualify as consideration.[102] As they presented in their brief to the U.S. Supreme Court, consideration needed to be redefined for radio: "The classic lottery looked to advance cash payments by the participants as the source of profit; the radio give-away looks to the equally material benefits to stations and advertisers from an increased radio audience to be exposed to advertising."[103]

Legally this was a stretch at best — as former FCC counsel Leonard Marks argued in a law review essay, the Commission's definition of consideration was the weak link in their argumentative chain. Identifying the primary rationale behind the FCC's attempted ban of giveaways was in response to violations of the "public interest, convenience, and necessity," which the Commission is mandated to uphold, Marks argued that this would have been a stronger legal basis for their argument.[104] Numerous legal briefs from various networks and local stations decried the FCC's interpretation of consideration, as well as their general assertion that the genre was not in the public interest, given the overwhelming popularity of the programs — since the television industry and FCC have both traditionally defined the public interest as that which interests the public as measured by popular response. The FCC's policy also offered overly broad rules, potentially outlawing the entire genre of the quiz show, including programs giving prizes only to in-studio contestants based on knowledge and skill more than chance.[105] While the FCC claimed that these broad definitions of the genre would not be enforced, as the policy was designed only to restrict giveaway programs like *Stop the Music!*, this instance exemplifies the distinct material effects of cultural processes of generic definition and interpretation.

ABC led a lawsuit against the FCC's rules, effectively enjoining the policy until it reached the U.S. Supreme Court in 1954. The Court ruled 8–0 (with one absence) in favor of ABC, striking down the FCC's proposed rules. Basing their decision upon the Commission's inadequate definition of consideration, the Court wrote that "it would be stretching the [lottery] statute to the breaking point to give it an interpretation that would make such programs a crime."[106] The decision, as written by Chief Justice Warren, highlighted that the FCC cannot administer rules based upon their evaluation of the genre's legitimacy: "Regardless of the doubts held by the Commission and others as to the social value of the programs here under consideration, such administrative expansion of §1304 does not provide the remedy."[107] Thus, while the Supreme Court's decision did not offer its own generic definition or evaluation — Warren specifically noted that the debate was not about the value of the programs, but the FCC's jurisdiction in outlawing them — this decision clearly highlights how the cultural processes of genre definition and evaluation can operate within the realm of public policy and legal decisions.

Even though the FCC's policy was struck down by the courts, the desired effect was achieved. The giveaway format died out on radio in the early 1950s, as ratings fell and programs designed to clone the success of *Stop the Music!* left the airwaves. As early as 1949, press accounts signaled the decline of the giveaway format:

> Nowhere was there a specific cause for the giveaways' decline. Perhaps it had been hastened by publicized difficulties of jackpot winners in their struggles to rid themselves of windfalls which nevertheless subjected them to stiff taxation. Perhaps the novelty had worn off the trick. And perhaps it was simply that the same people who had let dust gather on their mah-jongg tiles from sheer ennui finally had tired of the giveaway.[108]

While giveaways did not completely disappear from radio (and some made the transition to television in the early 1950s), the FCC's attempts to ban giveaways effectively stigmatized this generic dominant. The discursive circulation of the quiz show, as transferred to television in the early 1950s, clearly linked cultural legitimacy with the question-centered and stunt dominants rather than big-money giveaways.

Due to the anti-giveaway backlash, the quiz show genre that transferred to television primarily featured contestants selected from a studio audience or who auditioned to appear in the studio. As the giveaway controversy of the late 1940s posited an opposition between entertaining and buying an audience, the quiz shows of the 1950s explicitly foregrounded their entertainment value. By highlighting the legal and cultural problems with giving away prizes directly to listeners, the FCC and other critics helped shift genre conventions and assumptions of the quiz show in the 1950s, foregrounding entertainment and "legitimate" knowledge. Thus, the late 1940s giveaway controversy set two vital precedents for the more well-known television scandals: quiz shows were established as sites for public controversy and policy debate, and quiz shows that emphasized intellectual drama and competitive entertainment were legitimated over giving away prizes to home listeners. While there may be no direct causal linkages, it seems clear that as the cultural assumptions of the quiz show shifted toward valuing entertainment and drama, producers worked to highlight these aspects in their televised quiz shows. To regain cultural legitimacy, producers turned toward the question-centered dominant that had remained comparatively untainted by the FCC's actions of the late 1940s. Foregrounding entertainment pleasures, contestants were featured as characters in the ongoing drama of the quiz; like actors, they often received direction from the programs' producers, worked on reciting their lines, and took their places within an increasingly staged and controlled form of entertainment. While the FCC certainly did not urge producers to "fix" quiz programs, the meanings of the genre that the FCC did encourage — entertainment and competitive drama — pushed the quiz show toward the direction that would eventually result in its most infamous role in media history.

In charting out the various discourses constituting the quiz show genre in the radio era, certain assumptions clearly became linked to the genre with significant effects for the television scandals. These linkages are not explicitly causal and direct, yet traditional historical analyses of the scandals have been lacking, in part because they have neglected to account for the genre's radio history. By charting out how the quiz show genre operated as a cultural category leading up to the scandals, the actions of the television industry and American audience in the 1950s become clearer, as certain generic definitions, interpretations, and evaluations had become naturalized and foregrounded prior to the scandals. Particularly, we can see that the genre had been established as a site of controversy by the FCC's actions, norms of entertainment and dramatic action had been identified as valued aspects of quiz shows, and the assumption of fair play was regularly both challenged and reiterated throughout the radio era. These linkages are not evident through a historical approach offering primarily a textual chronicle, as we must explore the cultural operation of generic categories within a variety of media sites to understand how the quiz show category came to cluster this particular set of assumptions and practices that became more notoriously manifest in the late 1950s.

The three dominant modes of the quiz show in the radio era were all important precedents for the 1950s television quiz show scandals. The initial question-centered quiz show dominant provided the baseline for the genre throughout its history on both radio and television; for the television quizzes of the 1950s, producers drew upon the cultural assumptions of legitimated social value and entertainment through educational and intellectual competition. Both the stunt and giveaway dominants provided the 1950s programs clear identities to oppose, defined in contrast to these more devalued populist forms. Yet the programs of the 1950s drew upon giveaway and stunt dominants both for textual conventions — lavish prize packages, contestants returning through multiple episodes — and cultural assumptions — publicized debates over the genre's value and a tendency toward controversial and regulatory responses. To understand the quiz show scandals more fully, we need to acknowledge these linkages, exploring how the scandals did not emerge in a generic vacuum. Likewise, we can understand the recent boom in primetime quiz shows as continuing certain assumptions established in the radio era, with *Who Wants To Be a Millionaire* drawing from both the legitimated intellectual competition of early quizzes and the "everyman" contestant, huge jackpot, and telephone participation of the giveaway form. Trying to understand a particular moment of any genre's development requires a historical perspective to chart the continuities of precedents and cultural assumptions that have constituted the genre's longitudinal arc.

While sketching out the vital assumptions tied to the radio quiz show at large, I have focused particularly on the FCC's attempted ban. There are a number of reasons for this concentration: first, it could certainly be argued that this was the most crucial moment in radio quiz show history, especially concerning the impact these generic precedents would have upon the television scandals. Additionally, since this moment has a clear boundary, centered on distinctive legal and policy practices, it provides a justified specific instance to examine the genre in micro-operation rather than macro-tendencies. While both of these rationales are legitimate, I believe that this type of convenience and prioritization of seminal events can be problematic for generic historians. By focusing only on high-profile examples, we can end up with a highly skewed picture of the genre, considering the exceptions to the norms more than everyday examples. If generic categories operate primarily by regularizing a set of norms and shared assumptions, looking at the ruptures in this regularity does not represent how genres work most of the time.

Yet I do believe that there is another distinct advantage to this mode of "crisis historiography." While certainly genres operate at the level of regularity and continuity most of the time, the normal processes of generic consensus leave far fewer evidentiary traces than moments of generic crisis. When generic categories are uncontroversial, the majority of the historical remnants are media texts themselves; it takes a moment of crisis to generate the amount of audience letters, press accounts, and institutional documentation that I have utilized in this chapter. While we cannot mistake these moments of controversy as typical, it often takes a generic crisis to make the traces of the genre's everyday categorical operation manifest and accessible to historians. Since genres function at a level of cultural convenience, a mode of shorthand linking a number of unsaid assumptions under a single categorical rubric, it takes a crisis to make the unsaid audible.

Crisis historiography is one of the crucial tools available to the generic historian to access the underlying cultural assumptions constituting generic categories; I return to it in Chapter 6 in examining generic parody. We cannot rely solely on these moments of crisis to examine genres — media genres are operative in moments of stability just as much as in moments of rupture — yet we cannot overlook the potential bounty of source material that can emerge in these crisis points. Ideally, generic histories should aim for a balance between the operation of generic categories as points of consensus and sites of crisis, looking to both to understand the range of roles that genres play in organizing media practices. I have tried to strike such a balance through my examination of the quiz show, looking at how norms were both established and debated, how assumptions became activated and contested. Hopefully this approach to generic historiography both provides a model for future genre historians and allows us to better understand the quiz show scandals in greater historical depth, looking at how one of the crucial turning points in media history should be reappraised in the historical light of the quiz show genre as a cultural category. We can also examine how genres operate by focusing more in depth on particular spheres of media practice — I now turn to an examination of the specific ways genres work within media industries.

3
From Saturday Morning to Around the Clock — The Industrial Practices of Television Cartoons

Genres traditionally have been primarily conceived of and studied as textual systems, subjected to scholarly definition and interpretation. Despite the ubiquity of this textualist assumption within film and television studies, many scholars have acknowledged the role of media industries in creating genres, incorporating industrial practices into their accounts of textual genres. This chapter examines the industrial facet of genres in depth, addressing specific attributes of the television medium. While most accounts of industrial practices frame the industry as a producer of genres through the creation of *generic texts*, I wish to look at the industry's productive role in constituting genres through the circulation of *generic discourses*. The role of the industry in generic processes supercedes the traditional confines of production as the primary industrial practice, especially for the television medium, as exemplified by two moments in the history of the cartoon genre.

Most scholarly accounts of media industries posit genres as a useful tool for industries to systematize similarity and differences, maintaining efficiency both for production and audience reception practices. Yet nearly all accounts of the industry's role in constituting genres have been solely focused on the process of textual production as the primary way by which industries constitute genres, implying that genres are encoded into texts through production — the author (whether individual or institutional) draws upon some facets of a given genre category, and encodes that particular genre definition into the text itself. This production-centered model has been most prevalent within film genre studies.

Thomas Schatz highlights the role of the Hollywood studio system in utilizing genres as part of a factory-like mode of production.[1] Other specific genre studies highlight the role of individual *auteurs*,[2] studios,[3] or even nations[4] in the production practices of genres. While certainly these are important considerations toward understanding the industry's role in film genres, scholars rarely consider how nonproduction practices of industrial organizations and personnel also constitute genres. How do industries "produce" film genres through techniques such as marketing (advertising campaigns, trailers, posters, press releases, star publicity, internet presence, merchandizing), distribution (packaging, saturation versus rollout, targeting markets, international sales, rereleases), exhibition (placement in film bill, location of theaters, show times, ratings, theatrical technologies), and nontheatrical practices (availability and location within video stores, sales to television, editing for new markets)?[5] For most film genre analyses, examination of "industry" is equated with the study of "production."

This elision is even more troubling for television, because the industrial practices of television are far less production-centered than for the film industry. The predominance of ongoing series as the primary textual form on television leads to greater ambivalence as to when exactly is the "moment of production" — if a program lasts for many years, can we identify exactly what notion of genre was operative within the production process? For instance, the sitcom genre shifted significantly throughout *All in the Family*'s run. In 1971, the show was rebelling against a conservative and predictable genre, while in its later years the program shifted toward restoring notions of family and tradition to the genre that it had been instrumental in reconstructing. In this case, is there a singular "moment of production" to be studied? Production is an ongoing process in the majority of television, revising notions of genre throughout the run of a series as producers respond to the ongoing cultural circulation of programs; our analytic accounts of television industries must account for these ongoing processes.[6]

The predominance of previously produced programs within any channel's schedule is another aspect lessening the importance of production for television. From television's early reliance on repackaged film westerns to the emergence of reruns in the 1960s, from pay cable channels playing feature-length films to contemporary channels like TV Land, featuring only "classic" programming, the term production is inadequate to describe how many channels air programs. While reusing or repurposing footage is a rarity for the film industry — generally used as a gimmick as in *Dead Men Don't Wear Plaid* (1982) — it is common enough within television to be more than just a marginal exception. Additionally, many major players in the television industry are not primarily producers, ranging from networks who purchase most of their programs (especially primetime entertainment shows) from film studios or independent producers, to cable channels like MTV whose primary programming was (at least initially) provided by music labels. Nevertheless, as argued concerning

Michael Jackson's videos in Chapter 1, industrial institutions like MTV or ABC are directly constitutive of television genres even when they are not "producers" per se.

How might we examine the industry's role in constituting television genres without focusing solely on textual production? A variety of industrial practices work to articulate discourses within a larger generic cluster. Advertising, trade press accounts, and target audiences all foster generic definitions and meanings within both film and television. In addition to the cinematic practices mentioned above that are also applicable to television, we need to consider specific practices that are unique to television. Although generating a comprehensive list of industrial sites where genre operates is nearly impossible, some important practices include sponsorship decisions (how do sponsors use genres to target customers and "purchase" appropriate audiences?), corporate synergy (how do conglomerates employ specific genres to further profits and cross-promotions?), regulations and policies (how do both self-regulation and governmental policy utilize generic distinctions in defining their regulatory scope?), technological shifts (how might technical developments favor or discourage certain genres?), and intermedia relations (how do institutions transfer genres across media, such as film adaptations of television, or shifting radio programs to television?). A specific case study might dictate other important ways in which industrial practices utilize, and are constitutive of, genres as cultural categories.

Two specific types of television's industrial practices seem particularly relevant for understanding television genres: program scheduling and channel identity.[7] Scheduling practices organize programs for audiences and often communicate generic assumptions (like daytime versus late-night talk shows). Both placing programs within larger temporal blocks (Saturday morning, late-night, "family hour") and stringing together programs in a block (ABC's TGIF line-up, UPN's night of African-American sitcoms) use genres to reach specific audiences, working to constitute the genre by linking it with particular assumptions. Scheduling is probably more important for networks and affiliates attempting to reach mass audiences, rather than niche-defined cable channels; the latter tend toward 24-hour generic consistency instead of compartmentalizing different timeslots for various audiences. Nevertheless in all instances, scheduling practices are one of the primary ways the television industry provides generic frameworks to situate program.

The identity of the channel or network carrying a program also can activate genres explicitly (Comedy Central) or implicitly (NBC's reputation for urban white sitcoms in the 1990s). This is clearly more prevalent in recent years, given the outgrowth of cable/satellite channels with explicit generic names (SoapNet and Game Show Network) or generic acronyms (CNN's Cable News Network and A&E's Arts and Entertainment). Generically loaded channel identity has historical precedents as well — CBS's switch from rural sitcoms in the 1960s to urban shows in the 1970s is probably the most famous example. Channel identity can operate on a more local level as well. Boston's two main UHF stations in the 1980s had different generic reputations for their programming of syndicated reruns and films — WSBK-38 played reruns of "highbrow" sitcoms, like *M*A*S*H* and *The Bob Newhart Show*, and classic Hollywood films on *The Movie Loft*, while WLVI-56 featured more kid-friendly shows like *Happy Days* and *The Flintstones*, low-budget kung-fu films, and Saturday afternoon's *Creature Double Feature* of 1950s horror movies. Of course, both stations were less culturally valued than the more reputable network affiliates and their full range of generic offerings. Any channel develops its identity by accumulating assumptions from programming decisions and promotional strategies, forming a framework for audience comprehension often linked to genre categories.

Both scheduling and channel identity can articulate genres to particular target audiences and cultural hierarchies. For instance, daytime soap operas are linked to female audiences and lowbrow cultural tastes through their scheduling, while generic differences between different networks' offerings form important distinctions for fans. For instance, NBC soaps are often seen as pandering to a young audience, while CBS offers more traditional soap operas for older, longtime fans. Even though channel identity and scheduling frame the ways audiences interact with television, they are by no means determinate of audience pleasures, nor are they necessarily imposed from the top down. Audiences often use time-shifting technologies, such as VCRs and Digital Video Recorders, to work against industrial scheduling practices and partially disconnect a show from its industrial matrix.[8] Additionally, channel identity can emerge out of audience practices as well, such as when a station gains a reputation counter to its explicit definition (like E!'s growing reputation for shameless sensationalism instead of their nominal "Entertainment Television" label). But even if some audiences counter industrial practices, industries still construct the framework for most people's interactions with media.

These two industrial practices of scheduling and channel identity forge discursive associations within a genre, activating cultural hierarchies and values, mobilizing certain assumptions of "proper" audience identity and pleasures, and policing the boundary of what texts are legitimate components of the genre. Sometimes a single text can be recategorized via shifts in scheduling and channel identity — Susan Murray offers a fascinating example of how *American High*'s (2000–01) shift from Fox to PBS triggered a host of new genre associations without changing the program itself.[9] I illustrate the importance of both scheduling practices and channel identity in genre formation by examining two distinct moments in the history of the cartoon genre, highlighting the need to move beyond production as the primary industrial practice. Many television cartoons that are popular to this day were produced for theatrical film distribution in the 1930s and 1940s, prior to television's rise. Despite the cinematic origins of these animated shorts, they acquired different definitions, interpretations, and valuations through their television circulation. Examining production practices cannot account for the changing generic implications linked to Warner Brothers' short *Hair-Raising Hare* from its theatrical premiere in 1946, to its appearance on ABC's Saturday morning *Bugs Bunny Show* in 1965, to being featured on *Cartoon Network's Greatest 50 Cartoons* in 1999. Despite the stability of the film text itself, its generic implications have shifted between these historical moments, from mass-audience film short to kid-only television filler to classic of American culture. To account for these generic shifts, we need to examine the industrial practices that have worked to constitute and transform definitions, interpretations, and evaluations of the cartoon genre on television.

Although I am focusing on industrial practices and their role in generic processes for cartoons, it is important to remember that the industry is not separable from the larger circulation of media texts and audience practices within historical contexts. The industry is not a self-sufficient and isolated sphere of media practice; thus my analysis foregrounds the linkages between the industry and other aspects of media operation. This is how television works — in interactive tandem through all realms of media practice. Additionally, it is inadequate to conceive of categories like "industry" as discrete and clear. For instance, where might we place the generic practices found within the covers of *TV Guide*? While, traditionally, we might consider the magazine part of the popular (not trade) press and within the sphere of reception, the magazine is both owned by a major media conglomerate (News Corporation, which also owns Fox television and cable channels), and offers enough of an "insider" perspective that it clearly resides partially inside the industrial sphere. Additionally, the generic labeling found in *TV Guide*'s listings are sanctioned by industrial press releases and promotional documents, suggesting that we cannot rest upon the clear boundary between industrial trade press and mass-market popular press. *TV Guide* exemplifies the fluid boundary between the spheres of industry, audience, and broader cultural circulation. In this case study, while I foreground the industry as a powerful and productive site of genre practice, the ways the cartoon genre operates within these historical moments always exceeds the somewhat arbitrary limits of our conception of industry. By looking at industrial practices through trade and popular press accounts, archival documents, and personal interviews, we can understand how industrial practices operate in tandem with other spheres of media practice to constitute genres as cultural categories.

Saturday Morning Genres: Scheduling Cartoons on Television's Periphery

Nearly everyone can agree on a textual definition of the cartoon genre — if it's animated, it's a cartoon.[10] But genres are more than just bottom-line delineations of a category; the genre is formed by a broad array of cultural assumptions of meaning, value, and social function exceeding any textual definition. Even if we all agree what texts should be labeled as cartoons, there is no consensus as to the implications of that label. While Bugs Bunny shorts have been consistently labeled as cartoons since their creation in the 1930s and 1940s, what this generic label means has changed over time. This is the job of the genre analyst and historian: to trace out the changing ways in which generic categories operate culturally. We can see these shifts in the two major transformations within the cartoon genre on American television, focusing primarily on how the television industry was an active creator of this generic category outside the process of production itself. I am focusing specifically on cartoons within the United States — the history of animation in other countries, such as Japan, would tell a very different tale of the category, furthering the point that we must examine generic histories within culturally specific confines.

There is no "canonical" history of television animation, as animation has been a marginal topic within film studies — and within the small body of animation scholarship, television has been viewed primarily as "the cartoon's graveyard."[11] Television scholars have mostly ignored animation, and those that have examined the genre tend to focus more on recent works than on televised animation from the 1950s and 1960s.[12] Yet this early period was the formative era for television cartoons, establishing most of the assumptions that the genre would adhere to until the 1990s — especially for industrial practices, as television networks linked the genre explicitly with a scheduling timeslot that would come to define the cultural category with a three-word phrase: Saturday morning cartoons.

The cartoon genre's shift during this era is striking. In 1957, ABC had no Saturday morning programming at all, while CBS and NBC featured a variety of live-action children's shows, adventure programs, and one cartoon each — *The Mighty Mouse Playhouse* (1955–66) and *Gumby* (1957), respectively.[13] Cartoons were scattered throughout television schedules in the late 1950s, with occasional network primetime entries, like CBS's *Gerald McBoing Boing Show* (1956–58), and a vast number of syndicated afternoon and evening showings of *Popeye*, *Looney Tunes*, and *Krazy Kat*. Most televised cartoons in this era were recycled film shorts, often presented by a live-action clown or cowboy host to serve as a framing device. Cartoons, especially as syndicated programs, garnered quite high ratings with both children and adults and often won their timeslots against live-action original programming. As a cultural form, cartoons were still known as they were in the era of the studio system: as entertainment for mass audiences, but with particular appeal to children.

A decade later in 1967, the picture had drastically changed. All three networks now featured full schedules of Saturday morning programming from 9:00 a.m. to 12:30 p.m., showing nothing but animated programs such as *Space Ghost and Dino Boy* (1966–68) and *George of the Jungle* (1967–70). Nearly all of these cartoons were produced originally for television, with the notable exception of Saturday morning stalwart *The Bugs Bunny Show* (1960–2000). Cartoons had virtually disappeared from other parts of the network time schedule, with the era of primetime cartoon experimentation ending by the mid-1960s. Syndicated cartoons still persisted across the schedule, but ratings were far weaker, especially among adults. Most importantly, cartoons were now culturally defined as a genre whose primary audience was children, and not legitimate entertainment for adults as part of a mass audience.

How did the cartoon genre undergo these transformations? Various industrial practices undertaken by television producers, programmers, networks, sponsors, and syndicators during this time period worked to redefine the cluster of generic discourses constituting the cartoon genre. Production is not the primary motivating factor in this case — many of the cartoons themselves were produced many years before their television appearance, designed for a different medium and exhibition context altogether. Rather it is the ways in which these texts, both recycled and original, were situated through scheduling and cultural circulation that linked the genre to a set of shared assumptions that have remained associated with the cartoon genre to this day. Specifically, the transformation of what was once a mass-market genre with so-called "kidult" appeal into the kid-only Saturday morning margins led to some key shifts in our cultural understanding of the genre.

There is no single causal factor for this generic shift. As in most historical examinations, there are a variety of causes needed to understand this cultural phenomenon. A number of large-scale factors were partially formative of this shift, providing cultural and industrial contexts for this transformation from 1957's broad distribution of cartoons to the emergence of 1967's Saturday morning enclave. In examining the story of the cartoon's move to Saturday morning in the early 1960s in greater detail, I map out the stimuli leading to the genre's redefinition. This shift was not culturally "neutral," but rather loaded with a number of assumptions in terms of cultural value, constructions of children's tastes, and industrial commercialization.

One crucial contextual development for the rise of television animation stemmed from the transformation of cinematic animation units. Throughout the 1930s and 1940s, animated film shorts were featured on most film bills, with studios providing their own shorts (notably Warner Brothers and MGM) or distributing cartoons from independent producers (like Disney or Walter Lantz). This system flourished due to the vertical integration of the studio system, guaranteeing exhibition of animated shorts in studio-owned theater chains or through block-booking practices including cartoons within packages of feature films. Although cartoons were not profitable themselves, they were part of the whole package that film studios offered to moviegoers to fend off independent competitors. This situation was disrupted by the Paramount case of the late 1940s, ending vertical integration and guaranteed exhibition of studio products. Studios reallocated their priorities toward large-budget A pictures throughout the 1950s, attempting to draw audiences to floundering theaters through spectacle and gimmickry.[14]

The demise of cinematic cartoon units was a gradual but direct reaction to the Paramount decision. Since cartoons had traditionally not been a source of direct studio income, they were one of the primary areas that studios could downsize to remain economically viable. Independent exhibitors would not pay much for cartoons, as they did not seem to lead to greater box office numbers, so studios could earn little via theatrical distribution of these comparatively expensive short products.[15] As the theatrical market for cartoons declined, many studios dismantled their animation divisions: MGM in 1957, Warner Brothers in 1963, even Disney all but ceased short production in the 1960s. Independent animators were similarly withdrawing from the theatrical market, with Terrytoons selling out to CBS in 1955 and Famous Studios ceasing production of its popular *Popeye* series in 1957.[16] Not only did these shutdowns make film animation scarce, but they also resulted in a number of out-of-work animators seeking employment through the new avenue of television production.

One of the few profitable activities of animation studios in the 1950s was selling shorts to television. Disney pioneered the use of animation on television through its primetime hit *Disneyland* (1954–61). The show mixed older cartoon shorts with new live-action segments, all framed within a promotional pitch for the company's forthcoming theme park.[17] Other cartoon studios followed suit by selling their pre-1948 libraries to television in the mid-1950s, including Terrytoons, Warner Brothers, Columbia, and Paramount's *Popeye* series. These shorts were primarily distributed via syndicators like Associated Artists Productions (A.A.P.), a subsidiary of United Artists that owned *Popeye* and *Looney Tunes* libraries. These syndicated shorts soon entered daytime and early evening lineups on stations across the country, gaining favor with programmers as top-rated programs with no production costs. Animation studios realized that their most profitable assets were not new shorts produced for theatrical release, but old libraries made available for endless repetition on television, shifting the primary site of the animation genre to the television screen.[18]

Although the move from theaters to televisions did not necessarily alter the cartoons themselves, there were a number of textual transformations that helped redefine the genre for its new medium. Cartoons were rarely programmed on their own — since shorts were typically six to seven minutes, they needed to be combined to fit into the half-hour matrix of the television schedule. Stringing together three or four cartoons in a half-hour block significantly changed the way audiences experienced the shorts — instead of working as an amusing break before or between features, cartoons became the feature themselves, attracting audiences who found cartoons enough of a draw for their viewing time. As I discuss below, this meant primarily (but not exclusively) children. Additionally, most of the recycled cartoons were presented within a live-action frame. These programmatic contexts ranged from a host simply introducing the cartoons (such as a clownish Dick Van Dyke on 1956's *CBS Cartoon Theater* during primetime) to a larger program with characters and live-action narratives, like the single cartoon within *Captain Kangaroo* (1955–84) episodes.[19] While the cartoon itself may have remained the same from the film era, the way cartoons were presented on television altered their textual flow and relocated the texts within the realm of children's programming.

Not all cartoons migrated to television unchanged, however. In addition to the selection process instigated by industrial maneuvers (like the union-mandated cutoff date of 1948 for television releases),[20] cartoon libraries were culled and edited for social reasons as well. While the visual style and humor of cartoons was celebrated for not aging, some content was deemed troubling for recirculation. Most notably, a number of shorts with explicit racial stereotyping, such as Warner Brothers' *Coal Black and De Sebben Dwarfs* (1943), never made it to television due to concerns about their appropriateness a decade later, especially for children. While it is nearly impossible to identify exactly what cartoons were not imported to television, reminiscences of animators suggest that television sponsors and programmers were fearful of featuring any representations of black cartoon characters, whether explicitly racist or not.[21] Other cartoons produced during World War II were not shown on television, due to both their racist anti-Japanese content (like *Bugs Bunny Nips the Nips*, 1944) and their dated (and often brutal) references to wartime current events.

Some cartoons were edited to pare down or change questionable material as well. *Tom & Jerry* cartoons were regularly changed for television, transforming the character of a black maid, Mammy Two Shoes, into an Irish maid by redubbing her voice and recoloring her legs and arms (all that was seen of the character) white.[22] Numerous racially suspect scenes, as well as images of violence deemed excessive, characters smoking or drinking, and representations of guns, were all edited from Disney, Warner Brothers, and MGM shorts when appearing on television.[24] While not implying that the changing or censoring of racist or other images was inappropriate, it is important to note the cultural effects of such practices. By eliminating references to blacks and other nonwhite human characters out of fear of complaints of racism, television programmers effectively created a white-only genre of programming. This policy was consistent with network live-action practices of the 1950s and 1960s — both to avoid accusations of racist representations and to placate racist viewers who did not want to see "positive" images of blacks, television presented mostly white characters.[24] The elimination of racist representations from cartoons was performed under the common rubric of "protecting children," working to make cartoons a space free from controversial images (although the genre would come under fire in the late 1960s for its violent and commercial content). Finally, by eliminating racist (though highly sophisticated and topical) cartoons like *Coal Black*, programmers shifted the genre's content away from the cultural references that typically entertained adult audiences in theaters, and more toward repetitive visual humor and slapstick violence. The censorious practices of the television industry helped redefine the cultural content and associations of the preexisting film cartoon genre.[25]

The reorganization of the film industry helped bring archived theatrical animation to television, albeit in somewhat altered form, but it was not the only reason for the rise of televised cartoons. A number of animators began experimenting with original animation for television in the 1950s, an option that had been viewed as economically unfeasible. The production costs for typical animation were far too exorbitant to be justified for the still uncertain television market — a typical MGM seven-minute animated short in the 1950s cost between $40,000 and $60,000, while half-hour live-action telefilms could be made for only $15,000.[26] The 1950s saw the rise of a new technique, called "limited animation," which minimized movement and repeated cels to decrease both the number of drawings used and time required to animate segments, therefore reducing costs.[27] This technique was most heralded in the work of theatrical animation studio UPA and their 1951 short, *Gerald McBoing Boing*, which used limited animation primarily for aesthetic variation. The earliest pioneer of limited animation for television was Jay Ward, who created *Crusader Rabbit* for syndication in 1949 (reemerging in a more sophisticated form in 1957). *Crusader* was an extreme example of bargain basement production, as it reduced motion to an average of only one movement per four seconds (compared to the 10–20 moves per second of traditional animation), and cost only $2,500 per 20-minute episode.[28] More typical was Hanna-Barbera's debut program in 1957, NBC's first Saturday morning cartoon *Ruff and Ready* (1957–64), which cost $3,000 per 5-minute segment.[29] Both *Crusader Rabbit* and *Ruff and Ready* exemplify a number of shifts in animated form that would become typical on television: minimal visual variety, emphasis on dialogue and verbal humor, and repetitive situations and narratives.[30]

By 1957, there were two distinct forms of televised cartoons: endlessly rerun Hollywood shorts and low-budget original programs. Both modes of animation were primarily used to reach the children's audience — while the animated shorts of the theatrical era were regarded as mass entertainment, they were definitely skewed more toward children. As Warner Brothers producer Leon Schlesinger remarked in 1939, "we cannot forget that while the cartoon today is excellent entertainment for young and old, it is primarily the favorite motion picture fare of children."[31] Likewise, while the television cartoon genre had not yet been designated as *just* for children, the industry did conceive of children as the *primary* audience for cartoons in the 1950s. Whereas other television generic offerings in the 1950s were invested in promoting associations with quality, prestige, and sophistication to promote the nascent medium, cartoons were mostly seen as low-budget filler.

An exception to the cartoon's low cultural locale in the late 1950s was *The Gerald McBoing Boing Show*. CBS jumped on the limited animation bandwagon in 1956 by contracting UPA to produce a primetime program, consisting of both recycled *McBoing Boing* theatrical shorts and original material. The program tapped into the prestige of UPA's *McBoing Boing* series, which had been hailed as the savior of theatrical animation. UPA's graphic style was explicitly linked to modernist aesthetics and design, with the Dr. Seuss scripted premiere short winning an upstart Academy Award in 1951 over the traditional powerhouses of MGM, Disney, and Warner Brothers. The television show combined UPA's high cultural legitimacy with educational segments like "Meet the Inventor," all under the auspices of low-budget animation techniques that held particular appeal to CBS. While critics and parents hailed the show as educational, cultured, and even "avant-garde" entertainment, the show never met CBS's expectations to compete against *Disneyland* in the ratings.[32] While primetime cartoons would get additional chances in the 1960s, television animation and cultural legitimacy seemed incongruous bedfellows from the beginning.

The genre's low cultural value partly stemmed from the industry's initial disinterest in reaching children's audiences. While television featured many programs for children, they were seen as a necessary component to serve a mass audience rather than a desirable separate advertising niche. Television's industrial predecessor of radio reached out to children as a part of the mass audience, primarily with kid-friendly family programming. As NBC executive Fred Wile Jr. wrote in a 1954 memo concerning children's programming on Saturday morning, "all our experience in radio indicates that the Saturday morning audience is not exclusively a kiddy audience. If you recall, the highest ratings on Saturday morning used to be the all-family appeal show." He suggests "what we should strive for are all-family appeal shows with an emphasis on the young-sters."[33] Nevertheless, networks were reaching out to sponsors to target children, such as in a 1954 NBC promotional piece highlighting the captive audience of "15,000,000 kids every Saturday morning." Featuring a boy holding a toy sword and the caption "the generals have gone AWOL," the brochure calls for sponsors to "give him his marching orders on NBC television."[34] However, NBC's mid-1950s lineup of clowns and puppet shows failed to make much of an impact on either sponsors or Saturday morning audiences.

The industrial appeal of a predominantly children's audience grew during this time, as a number of sponsors began targeting children as primary consumers. In the early 1950s and before, toy manufacturers generally thought toys were not viable objects of advertising, as children were not active consumers. Some toy companies incorporated live advertisements into local children's shows, but in general there was little market for sponsors aiming directly at children. But in 1955, just as upstart ABC had successfully ridden *Disneyland* toward legitimacy as a network, a small toy company named Mattel decided to invest its entire corporate value in advertising by sponsoring ABC's new *The Mickey Mouse Club* (1955–59) children's program for a full year. The risk paid off, as Mattel's Burp Gun became the first nationwide toy sensation in 1955. Mattel broadened its customer base to girls in 1959, by using television advertising to promote their new doll Barbie, whose success is obvious. Through the phenomenal success of these two campaigns, the toy industry and other companies wanting to target children, such as cereal manufacturers, dedicated themselves to reaching the sizable baby-boom children's audiences via television.[35]

By the late 1950s, the networks were primed to deliver children to eager sponsors, but the only surefire method was through the Disney name. CBS attempted to counter Disney by purchasing Terrytoons' studio and holdings, leading to a primetime anthology of shorts, *CBS Cartoon Theater*, and two Saturday morning cartoon retreads, *The Mighty Mouse Playhouse* and *The Heckle & Jeckle Show* (1956–60).[36] While both Saturday morning programs were popular enough to enjoy long runs and solid ratings for sponsor General Foods, the Terrytoons material failed to produce the cultural excitement of ABC's two Disney programs. NBC was unsuccessful in finding an established animation studio to team with except for Columbia/Screen Gems, whose "cartoons were among the least appealing short subjects ever released."[37] So in 1957 NBC took the risky step of ordering original animation production for the still undefined slot of Saturday morning, purchasing *Ruff and Ready* from the new animation studio Hanna-Barbera. *Ruff and Ready* was a hit, although NBC was not willing to jump aboard an animation bandwagon, maintaining their Saturday morning mix of cartoons with puppet shows, adventures serials, and educational programming.

This moment in 1957 was the calm before the televised cartoon storm. While still few cartoon programs aired on Saturday morning, a number of central cultural assumptions had been linked to the cluster of the cartoon genre. Television cartoons were still associated with their theatrical antecedents, as most televised animation were recycled or adapted from film sources. As such, the programs were still tied to notions of a mass family audience with primary appeal toward children. Cartoons were considered "filler" and culturally devalued, often shoehorned into live-action programs or relegated to the syndicated margins of the television schedule. The few cartoons that were able to gain cultural legitimacy borrowed their prestige from the cinematic reputation of their producer (Disney) or character (Gerald McBoing Boing). Yet the late 1950s would witness a transformation of the set of cultural assumptions included in the cartoon genre, as sponsors looked to target children and producers brought more original animation to television. But how did the industry construct the newly desirable target audience of children?

As sponsors became more interested in reaching the children's audience, the television industry attempted to understand what this audience wanted to see and how best to sell them to sponsors. But as Ien Ang has argued, the television industry never merely accesses or targets preconstituted audiences, but works to construct audience categories through their programming, marketing, sales, and measuring practices.[38] The television industry constituted the children's audience during this era by linking together a number of associations under the rubric of what the trade press often called "kidvid" or the "moppet market." One notable assumption was that children did not mind the repetition of shorts found in recycled film cartoons like *Bugs Bunny* or *Popeye*. The President of A.A.P. suggested that children actually preferred repeated over fresh material as they relished the familiarity.[39] An NBC executive questioned the discerning taste of children when noting that syndicated shows of old recycled film shorts were doubling the ratings of NBC's stalwart *Howdy Doody* (1947–60).[40] The success of recycled film shorts, the industrial profitability of such textual reuse, and the assumption that children could not tell the difference all led *Variety* to predict in 1957 that original animation would never fly on television.[41]

Another vital assumption about children was that they could not discern levels of "quality" (which are usually held up as self-evident by adult reviewers). In discussing Walter Lantz's unpolished performance as host of *The Woody Woodpecker Show* (1957–58), a *Variety* reviewer asked, "since when do kids need the kind of polish adults demand in adults?"[42] Another reviewer suggested, "where the moppets are fixated by virtually anything on the TV screen, adult audiences are at least one notch more discriminating."[43] Assumptions about children's lack of taste carried over to the rise of limited animation. While adult reviewers noted that the visuals in original television animation were far less sophisticated and nuanced than in classic theatrical shorts, the industry clearly believed that children could not discern (or simply did not care about) the difference between the two styles.[44] Elements of animation that critics assumed would appeal to children included "noise and fast action" and unrealistic violence.[45] As original television animation emerged in the late 1950s, the industry's construction of the children's audience was a key component of the generic cluster containing the cartoon. The subsequent rise of Hanna-Barbera and their model of television animation drew upon and revised these notions of the children's audience, adult appeals, and cultural status of the cartoon genre.

The emergence of Hanna-Barbera was the catalyst that would eventually lead to the institution of Saturday morning cartoons, traveling through the unlikely detour of primetime. Bill Hanna and Joseph Barbera were former MGM animators who had popularized the *Tom & Jerry* series in the 1940s, but found themselves out of work following MGM's animation shutdown in 1957. Seeing the potential of animation for the television market, they pitched their services by adapting UPA's style of limited animation. However, instead of

UPA's modernist graphic style, Hanna-Barbera offered a pared-down visual style, emphasizing dialogue, sound-effects, and repeated motion. They followed *Ruff and Ready* in 1958 with a syndicated program owned by Kellogg's, *Huckleberry Hound* (1958–62). While Kellogg's was certainly aiming at a children's audience in lucrative late-afternoon timeslots, the show transcended its targeted audience. One report suggested that over 40% of *Huckleberry*'s audience were adults, while another article described daily *Huckleberry Hound* watching rituals in a Seattle bar.[46] Hanna-Barbera's next syndicated program was equally popular with adults, satirizing popular westerns with *Quick Draw McGraw* (1959–62). The breakout success of these programs led to the biggest boom of cartoons in television history.

The immediate success of Hanna-Barbera's original television animation led to an overhaul of what animation would look and sound like for years to come. Today, most animation scholars and fans assume that this shift was for the worst — the limited animation style of television "killed off" the classic animation of Warner Brothers and MGM, with only Disney carrying the torch into their feature film work. We can see this hierarchy at work in interviews with canonized cartoon directors like Chuck Jones, who called Saturday morning cartoons "crap" and termed them "illustrated radio," dominated by dialog without any visual vibrancy.[47] Likewise cartoon voice artist Mel Blanc claimed that television animation "kill[ed] the cartoon industry."[48] Academics have reproduced this hierarchy by valorizing classic full animation from Disney, Warner, and Tex Avery's MGM work through detailed analysis, while only mentioning Hanna-Barbera as the nadir of the form.[49] Implicit in this hierarchy is that the classic animation of the studio era was better suited to a discerning mass audience, able to amuse and amaze all ages through its superior humor and vibrant visuals, while the television material of the 1960s was low-budget and low-brow filler, suited only to the unrefined taste of children.

While this argument might be defensible on aesthetic grounds, the history of the reception of these early television cartoons suggests that they were not objects of adult derision upon their emergence. Rather, the early Hanna-Barbera programs were held up as valued advances in animation that were more entertaining for adults and children than the studio shorts that we now regard as "classic." Critics hailed characters like Huckleberry Hound, Quick Draw McGraw, and Yogi Bear (who was featured on *Huckleberry Hound* before getting his own syndicated spin-off in 1961) for their adult wit and satirical content. The puns, malapropisms, and old jokes that may seem stale today, made Hanna-Barbera cartoons appear groundbreaking in their intergenerational appeal. This goal of reaching the "kidult" audience was achieved not through creating unified cartoons with universal appeals, but by specifically aiming the visuals and "wacky" sound effects at the "moppets," and the dialog at adults.[50] As *Howdy Doody*'s Bob Smith suggested in 1961, "Hanna and Barbera are creating children's visual shows and adult audio shows. Turn off the sound and children will enjoy what they see. Turn off the picture, and adults will enjoy what they hear."[51] A *TV Guide* reviewer similarly summed up the different appeals of *Huckleberry Hound*: "Children like the show because of the action and the animals. . . . Adults like the show for its subtleties, its commentary on human foibles, its ineffable humor."[52] These programs that have long been condemned for dumbing down animation were viewed at the time as actually broadening the genre's appeal through intelligence and sophistication.

Some critics explicitly compared Hanna-Barbera shorts with classic studio material. A *Parent's* magazine writer called the cartoons of 1962 "as far removed from the old animated cartoons of pre-World War II vintage as today's car is from a Model T."[53] One of the grounds for comparison was violence, a common object of discussion concerning animation. This same writer praised Hanna-Barbera's material for relying upon character "rather than sadistic action," noting the violent content of most studio shorts seen on television — as is typical in violence debates, a strain of selective myopia emerges, as she hailed Hanna and Barbera's early work on *Tom & Jerry* as being appropriate for "family audiences," overlooking that *Tom & Jerry* was quite possibly the most excessively violent of all studio series. Despite this article, few accounts during this era castigated cartoons for their violent content, explicitly noting the difference between real violence and the fantasy actions in animation, a distinction that seems to have been lost in most discussions of television violence today. By this point in the early 1960s, cartoons were well ensconced within what James Snead calls animation's "rhetoric of harmlessness," with cartoons regarded as culturally marginal enough to exist only in the world of innocuous fantasy, without "real-life" effects.[54] Interestingly, although children's televisual tastes and practices were a site of parental and cultural activism in postwar America, cartoons' assumptions of harmlessness exempted the genre from much of the anxiety that dominated this historical moment's construction of childhood.[55]

While the Hanna-Barbera material was the most popular original television animation and certainly led the animation boom of the early 1960s, another producer made a series of important cartoons that fit a similar pattern of "kidult" appeal: Jay Ward. Whereas Hanna and Barbera were established studio animators who immediately created a popular formula for television, Ward was an industry outsider whose style never achieved mass appeal. *Rocky and his Friends* (1959–61) played during early evening hours, reaching a solid family audience despite little network support. Ward's style matched the basic model of Hanna-Barbera, with bare-bones visuals, broad characterization, and pointed satirical references to contemporary America, especially Cold War politics. *Rocky* and its later incarnation of *The Bullwinkle Show* (1961–64) form the primary exception to today's critical disdain for early television animation. However, in the late 1950s, Ward's shows were far less successful than

Hanna-Barbera's cartoons, even though most critics at the time regarded the work of both producers as equal in adult appeal.

Entering the 1960 season, the generic cluster of television cartoons had a number of new facets: animation had established itself as having legitimate "kidult" appeal within syndicated late-afternoon and early-evening timeslots. Cost-cutting techniques of limited animation had reduced production costs sufficiently to warrant network experimentation with original animated programming. Additionally, the success of studio shorts in syndicated reruns suggested that the market for animated properties on television was potentially eternal; as one *Broadcasting* article suggested, "they never grow old, never depreciate."[56] Advertisers had begun showing interest in reaching young audiences, while animation had gained enough legitimacy to be viewed as more than just "kid's stuff." In 1960, ABC took a risk by programming three animated programs in their primetime lineup, including an original animated sitcom aimed primarily at an adult audience, *The Flintstones* (1960–66).[57] Although ABC's innovation would be a huge popular success, leading to television's biggest boom in primetime animation, the end result of *The Flintstones'* success would be to drive cartoons out of primetime for a generation.

ABC was not on equal footing with NBC and CBS in 1960. Always the upstart, ABC was at a disadvantage in shifting from radio to television, lacking the name programs and talent of NBC and CBS. Deficient in capital and market penetration, ABC established itself in the mid 1950s by taking innovative programming risks, reaching out to audiences and producers that the other networks ignored. ABC reached the Nielsen Top Twenty for the first time in 1954 through a partnership to create *Disneyland*, and similarly forged a successful alliance with Warner Brothers to produce a string of hit westerns in the late 1950s.[58] Like Fox in the early 1990s, ABC's marginal status enabled — and forced — the network to follow less traditional paths, withstanding many failed experiments in the hope of one breakout success. Its animation experiment of 1960 was, thus, not an anomalous move for ABC, but the outcome was certainly not what the network anticipated.

Two of ABC's three primetime cartoon entries in 1960 fit into established practices of television animation. *Matty's Funday Funnies* (1959–61) originally aired late Sunday afternoons, but was moved to Friday night in 1960 to reach a broader audience. The show consisted primarily of old shorts from the Harvey/Paramount studios, such as the Casper the Friendly Ghost and Baby Huey series, framed by new animated characters Matty Mattel and Sister Belle, designed by sponsor Mattel for merchandising purposes.[59] ABC's second primetime cartoon was *The Bugs Bunny Show*, featuring both recycled and new animation from Warner Brothers. Since Warner's pre-1948 shorts had been saturated in syndication by A.A.P., ABC capitalized with its strong relationship with the studio to highlight Warner's post-1948 material on *The Bugs Bunny*

Show. This program made television regulars out of classic cartoons from directors Chuck Jones and Friz Freleng, featuring newer characters Pepe LePew, Foghorn Leghorn, the Tasmanian Devil, and the duo of Road Runner and Coyote. Warner also contributed original animated bumpers and framing narratives to the program, sustaining the market for the studio's animation unit. *The Bugs Bunny Show*, moving to Saturday morning in 1962, provided exposure to Warner Brothers animation for multiple generations to come and soon became synonymous with classic television cartooning.

The biggest surprise of the entire 1960 season was certainly *The Flintstones*, a Hanna-Barbera cartoon that defied nearly all established conventions of animated television. The show was formally structured like a sitcom, complete with single half-hour narrative episodes, suburban setting, domestic plots, and even a laugh track, deriving primary character and situational inspiration from *The Honeymooners* (1952–57). Hanna-Barbera was attempting to capitalize on the adult audiences for their syndicated programs, and ABC primarily targeted an adult audience as well — the show's initial sponsors were Miles Labs and R. J. Reynolds, until parental protests that the show was selling cigarettes to children forced the latter to withdraw in 1961. The 8:30 p.m. Eastern timeslot was later than typical for children's programs, and the trade press clearly indicated that ABC and Hanna-Barbera were primarily aiming at adults with the show.[60] The show was a breakout success, finishing the season at #18 in the overall Nielsen ratings and giving ABC a still comparatively rare non-western hit.

Critics gave the program mixed reviews. Some enjoyed the show's satirical jabs at suburbia and the sitcom format, while others found the humor obvious and the situations contrived. Surprisingly, no reviewer that I found questioned the appropriateness of animation for an adult audience, suggesting that the genre had yet to develop a "kids only" stigma.[61] Ironically, reviewers of *The Bugs Bunny Show* assumed the show was solely aimed at a children's audience, even though the shorts featured on the program had been created for mass consumption in movie theaters. *The Flintstones* was viewed as more adult oriented, primarily because it drew upon the cultural assumptions of the more adult, family-friendly genre of the sitcom. Through genre mixing, *The Flintstones* was able to establish more cachet and legitimacy than cartoon shorts.[62] Yet today our critical hierarchies have been inverted — the Warner shorts are seen as "classics," worthy of academic study and cultish devotion, while Hanna-Barbera programs like *The Flintstones* are blamed for the death of classic animation and viewed as childish Saturday morning filler.

The success of *The Flintstones* led to television's first animation boom, bringing a variety of subject matters and settings to both primetime and Saturday morning cartoons. ABC tried to strike gold again with two primetime animated sitcoms during its next season, Hanna-Barbera's *Top Cat* (1961–62) and *Calvin and the Colonel* (1961–62). The latter program is an interesting footnote in media history, starring the voices of Freeman Gosden and Charles Correll in an adaptation of their characters of Amos and Andy that had made them one of radio's biggest success stories. Since *Amos 'n' Andy*'s (1951–53) television incarnation had been cancelled under fire, Gosden and Correll had been unable to translate their radio hit to the television screen. After their radio show ended its three-decade run in 1960, they tried their hand at television once more, literally exemplifying Chuck Jones' pejorative phrase "illustrated radio." Gosden and Correll revisited some of their classic radio scripts with few changes in content, while animating their blackface characters as a wily fox and dumb bear (without losing their stereotypical black dialects and malapropisms) from the South who moved up North to predictably "wacky" results. While animation studios were pressured to excise egregious racial representations from their television libraries, ABC felt comfortable recasting well-known racist caricatures as animated animals within *Calvin and the Colonel*. The show was cancelled from primetime within a season due to poor ratings, although the show survived in syndication throughout the 1960s, seemingly free of controversy.

The other networks tried their hand at primetime animation in 1961 as well. NBC signed *The Bullwinkle Show* after ABC had given up on moose and squirrel, placing it on Sunday evenings as a lead-in to *Walt Disney's Wonderful World of Color* (1961–81), which they had also lured away from ABC. CBS offered *The Alvin Show* (1961–62), based upon the 1958 hit novelty record by Alvin and the Chipmunks, on Wednesday evenings. ABC kept both *Bugs Bunny* and *The Flintstones* in primetime, renaming *Matty's Funday Funnies* in winter 1962 to *The Beany and Cecil Show* (1962–63) and retooling the program to focus on the show's most popular animated segment. Thus, in the 1961–62 season, networks programmed seven animated series in primetime, a record showing for the cartoon genre. This boom is in keeping with a programming trend of the 1960s — as networks gradually wrested control of programming away from sponsors in the late 1950s and early 1960s, they developed strategies for using genre cycles and formulas to spread success throughout their lineups. This led to the cycle of "innovation–imitation–saturation," whereby one successful groundbreaker begets clones that eventually clutter the schedule to such a degree that the formula quickly dies through overexposure.[63] This pattern of generic cycling is still common in television programming, but was central to this era, with similar cycles of westerns in the late 1950s, documentaries in the early 1960s, and spy programs and fantasy sitcoms in the mid 1960s.[64]

The saturation phase of the cartoon boom was surprisingly quick in coming — the only primetime cartoon from 1961 which would last through 1963 was *The Flintstones*, which reputedly survived primarily because of a dedicated following amongst teenagers.[65] Other cartoons attempted to take hold in primetime in subsequent seasons, including Hanna-Barbera's *The Jetsons* (1962–63) and *The Adventures of Jonny Quest* (1964–65), as well as UPA's *The Famous*

Adventures of Mr. Magoo (1964–65), but none lasted more than one season in primetime. All of these cartoons were met with the critical scorn typical for derivative clones of previous successes in all genres; as one *Variety* reviewer suggested, "with cartoon shows in boomsville, subject matter is getting harder to find."[66] Importantly, reviewers suggested that the only way these shows would succeed was "in attracting the less critical moppet audiences," although success with children was not enough to sustain a program in the primetime lineup.[67] *The Flintstones* lasted in primetime until 1966, marking the last network primetime cartoon until *The Simpsons* emerged in 1990. Cartoons disappeared from primetime because of their perceived inability to reach adult audiences; although certainly the boom waned because of the typical effects of generic saturation, the industry took the failure to mean that the genre was inappropriate for adults. This assumption about the audience appeals of animation became one of the vital meanings that entered into the generic cluster of the cartoon in the 1960s, helping to form the shape of genre for decades to come.

The post-bust residue of other generic booms in the 1960s disappeared from the airwaves — the documentaries, westerns, spy shows, and fantasy sitcoms that lasted only one season generally were not to be aired again, at least until the rise of cable. This was not true for cartoons, however. Since the industry believed that the "uncritical moppets" would watch any cartoon that moved, they looked for a way to capitalize on their expensive investment in primetime animation. CBS found the answer in spring 1962 — *The Alvin Show* had been a primetime bomb, but CBS had already paid the producers for a season of product (a typical arrangement for animation because of the extended production time needed to animate a program). Instead of merely cutting their losses in primetime as with other genres, CBS moved the program to Saturday mornings. In doing so, the network drew upon two assumptions from the cartoon generic cluster — children did not mind watching repeats and recycled material, and children were uncritical viewers who would accept programs of any quality. CBS's move was considered a ratings success and other networks would follow suit, with nearly every primetime animated failure finding a new home on Saturday morning in the 1960s.

Prior to this shift, Saturday mornings had featured a mix of live-action programming and cartoons, with the latter mostly composed of recycled film shorts like *Mighty Mouse* and *Heckle and Jeckle*. Networks were generally reluctant to invest the money necessary to create original Saturday morning cartoons, as sponsors wishing to reach children were still most interested in late-afternoon and early-evening timeslots with their superior overall ratings. NBC had programmed a few original Saturday morning cartoons, such as Hanna-Barbera's *Ruff and Ready* and *King Leonardo and his Short Subjects* (1960–63), but still scheduled these programs among educational programs, sitcom reruns, clown and puppet shows, and other live-action children's fare. ABC followed *Alvin*'s lead, moving *Bugs Bunny* and *Top Cat* from primetime to Saturday morning in fall 1962. CBS pushed Saturday morning animation further, creating the first cartoon-dominated lineup in 1963, programming *The Alvin Show, Mighty Mouse Playhouse, Quick Draw McGraw*, and the original *Tennessee Tuxedo and His Tales* (1963–66) in a highly rated two-hour block, appealing to kid-seeking sponsors such as General Mills and Kellogg's.[68]

The success of this block demonstrated the importance of niche marketing within television programming. Saturday mornings did not have strong overall ratings, especially compared with the late-afternoon slots that sponsors had been using to reach children audiences. The central difference, as illustrated by NBC's internal study of audience potential for different timeslots in 1962, concerned not the number of children watching, but the relative density of age groups.[69] The weekday 5:00–7:30 p.m. timeslot reached 41 million viewers, double the reach of Saturday morning's 20.5 million. The late-afternoon slot reached more children in all age groups than Saturday morning, including children under 6 (6.4 to 5.7 million), 6–12 years (10.0 to 8.5 million), and teenagers (4.7 to 2.1 million). Yet television stations and networks sold slots to advertisers, especially in the early years of demographic targeting, based primarily on total ratings points and shares. Since adults were much more of a component of the late afternoon slot than on Saturday morning (19.9 to 4.2 million), advertisers who were aiming primarily at children would have to pay higher rates for the late-afternoon slots because of the high numbers of total viewers. While there were more children 12 and under among the late-afternoon audience than on Saturday morning, proportionally they made up only 40% of the late-afternoon audience as compared to 69% of Saturday mornings. Advertisers targeting children could spend less on Saturday morning ads, but reach a higher proportion of their target audience per dollar, making it a successful mode of niche marketing. This practice presaged the logic of narrowcasting that would dominate in the 1990s, as market segments were constituted both by appealing to core groups of children and by driving away undesirable adult audiences.[70]

The industrial logic of Saturday morning cartoons was motivated by this early example of television narrowcasting. CBS's lineup in 1963 was highly successful in drawing both children viewers and child-hungry sponsors. More primetime rejects found themselves on Saturday morning schedules, including *Bullwinkle, The Jetsons, Beany and Cecil*, and eventually *The Flintstones*. As the genre continued to be dominated by theatrical retreads and primetime failures, production costs were negligible for most Saturday morning cartoons — networks and producers could maximize returns on their productions by endlessly rerunning one season of a program like *Top Cat* or *The Alvin Show*, making the generic timeslot a comparatively low-risk venture with high potential for long-term profits.[71] Saturation hit Saturday morning quickly, but it did not result in the typical generic decline; instead networks saw the timeslot as a cash cow for toy and food sponsors looking to reach the "kidvid" audience and decided to raise the stakes by including more original Saturday morning cartoons. In 1965, the two biggest cartoon hits were ABC's *The Beatles* (1965–69) and NBC's *Underdog* (1964–66), as well as other modest successes like *Atom Ant* (1965–67). Many of these subsequent original cartoons followed the structure of *The Flintstones*, featuring half-hour stories per episode rather than the compilation of shorts typical of older animation. Thus, cartoons were further defined by the industrial imperatives of network schedulers, abandoning the traditional model of the seven minute short that predominated in the film era. New production continued through the 1960s, leading to the spate of superhero programs that triggered controversies concerning both cartoon violence and merchandizing, and firmly establishing Saturday morning as the primary home for television animation.[72]

The boom in Saturday morning cartoons in the mid 1960s also stemmed from the pendulum swing within this era's regulatory climate. Newton Minow made a historic splash in 1961, introducing his tenure as FCC Chairman by chiding broadcasters for their banal television programming. He specifically noted a number of offending genres in his "vast wasteland" speech, including game shows, westerns, sitcoms, and repeatedly cartoons.[73] Minow, claiming that cartoons "drowned out" quality children's programming, challenged broadcasters to improve children's broadcasting by eliminating "time waster" shows and move toward more educational and "uplifting" programming. Networks responded by making modest offerings to appease Minow's calls for transformation, bringing educational children's programs to the air, such as *Discovery* (1962–71), *Exploring* (1962–66), and *1, 2, 3 — Go!* (1961–62), even though sponsors were less than eager about these offerings. But when Minow left the FCC in 1963 and Lyndon Johnson encouraged a hands-off policy for the FCC, the networks quickly swung back toward their profit-maximization practices, encouraging the booming expansion of cartoons on Saturday morning and shuttling less lucrative live-action educational programs to even more marginal Sunday mornings.[74]

As Saturday morning cartoons rose in popularity, the syndicated market for animation dried up in these years as well. Networks bought up some of the most popular syndicated programs for Saturday morning filler, including *Quick Draw McGraw* and *Yogi Bear* (1961–63). Additionally, the rise of color television in the 1960s made black-and-white reruns less desirable; monochrome animation such as *Popeye* and early *Looney Tunes* was viewed as comparatively inferior to the all-color output of Hanna-Barbera and newer Warner Brothers material on Saturday morning.[75] Finally, and perhaps most importantly, the late-afternoon slots were less effective at drawing only children, leading to comparatively inflated advertising rates because of more adult viewers, whom cereal and toy companies wanted to avoid. Syndicated animation shifted primarily to fringe UHF stations, a televisual site even more marginalized than Saturday mornings.

While certainly Saturday morning cartoons were successful at drawing the children's audience, we need to look for generic appeals outside the texts themselves. Many of the programs that helped create the Saturday morning cartoon boom of the mid 1960s were originally designed for mass audience appeal, either in primetime television or theatrical run — or both, in the case of *Bugs Bunny*. While certainly the bulk of the original animation created for Saturday morning was designed with kids in mind, most of the assumptions constituting the television cartoon genre were already established before the boom of original animation in the mid-1960s. The generic label "Saturday morning cartoons" was primarily the result of numerous industrial practices, including sponsor narrowcasting, the rise of limited animation techniques, and the reorganization of the film industry. Additionally, the industry, as part of a larger cultural context, drew upon and furthered cultural assumptions linked to the cartoon genre — that kids will gladly watch recycled and repeated programs, that kids cannot discern quality of animation, that cartoons should not address "adult" subject matter, and that cartoons are "harmless" entertainment. All of these factors coalesced in the 1960s to constitute the generic cluster identified by the category "Saturday morning cartoons."

The main effect of establishing Saturday morning cartoons as a cultural category was filing the entire genre under a "kid-only" label. This was accomplished less by shifting cartoons toward a children's audience and more by moving away from the adult audience. Cartoons had been on Saturday mornings since the mid 1950s, but it was only in the mid-1960s that they became difficult to find anywhere else in television schedules. Likewise, sponsors embraced Saturday mornings not because they could reach *more children* in that timeslot, but because they could actually reach *fewer adults*, thus raising the percentage of children per rating point and advertising dollar. The cartoon's appeal to children was always considered a default — in the mid-1960s what changed was the assumption that adults could like cartoons too. Following their Saturday morning exile, cartoons became stigmatized as a genre *only* appropriate for children, removing the traditional affiliations with a mass audience. This was accomplished partially by networks latching onto an existing phenomenon — adults watched the least amount of television on Saturday mornings. But the industry furthered this association by marketing Saturday morning cartoons solely to children, by ignoring the visual complexity and adult humor that marked earlier animation, by sponsors only advertising to children during the timeslot, and by isolating cartoons from all other genres and timeslots to maintain tight associations between all texts within the generic category. The marginalization of cartoons also furthered its appeal among its target audience — one of the joys of Saturday morning cartoons for children was the very fact that adults were not watching the programs (and ads) aimed primarily at kids. Parents accepted the generic timeslot's role as "babysitter" and yielded media control to children, furthering the industrial commitment to defining the genre narrowly.

The rise of the Saturday morning cartoon paradigm is deeply rooted in its 1960s context, both emerging out of and impacting American culture during this era. Central to this context are changing notions of childhood; recent scholarship in cultural studies has examined childhood as a social construction, considering how cultural practices and media constitute the shifting meanings and boundaries of youth.[76] Changes in the cartoon genre were dependent on the growing acceptability of targeting children as a consumer market — and the success of these efforts on television certainly encouraged both greater marketing to children and the subsequent backlash over these practices in the 1970s. The size of the baby boom generation focused greater attention on 1960s children as a desirable marketing demographic, as programming strategies successfully created Saturday morning as a kids-only island in the weekly schedule, further reinforcing the boundaries of this market niche. As this generation of children was defined as a discrete segment of society — along with the simultaneous delineation of teenagers as a distinct social group and market — Saturday morning cartoons helped to further fracture American society into market niches that were both created by industries and lived within families. Even if sponsors and networks were the primary agents of change for both the cartoon genre and children's consumerism, the practices clustered around these phenomena were adopted into the lived practices of changing family dynamics in the 1960s.

This history of Saturday morning cartoons shows how media industries can define, interpret, and evaluate genre categories outside the realm of the text. Many of the programs labeled cartoons in both the 1940s and 1960s did not change, although their generic definition and assumptions did. This model of genre history does not chronicle the changing texts of a genre — *Crusader Rabbit* begot *The Flintstones* begot *Atom Ant* — but charts the evolution of the category itself. Cartoons shifted from a mass audience theatrical label to a "lowest common denominator" category, implying shoddy production values, formulaic stories and gags, hyper-commercialization, and limited appeals to anyone except children. The effects of this shift helped to define the debates concerning children's television that took hold in the late 1960s and 1970s, with groups condemning the genre's violent content and commercialization. Had cartoons not become isolated in the television schedule and defined as a kid-only genre, these complaints and controversies could not have occurred as they did. The assumptions constituting the cartoon as a cultural category were established in the 1960s through the institution of Saturday morning as a separate realm of programming, impacting the cartoon genre to this day. While many of the categorical assumptions forged in this era still remain operative, cartoons underwent another transformation in the 1990s, one that has worked to redefine the genre and its role in American culture.

Targeting a Taste Culture: Cartoon Network and 1990s Television

"I get it, I get it. I'll never have to change the channel."

— A young Cartoon Network fan[77]

"Saturday morning cartoons" was the reigning generic label through the 1980s. While cartoons still air on Saturday mornings, and the label still has cultural resonance, the generic cluster of the cartoon has broadened significantly in the 1990s and beyond. Cartoons are now seen as more legitimate and respectable programs, as some shows have explicitly adult appeal and primetime success. Networks have moved away from Saturday morning cartoon programming, as both NBC and CBS have yielded the early Saturday morning children's field to Disney-owned ABC and Fox in recent years, counterprogramming with news and sitcoms.[78] Meanwhile cable channels featuring primarily cartoons have reshaped the ways in which audiences interact with animated television. All of these shifts have led to dismantling the enclave of Saturday morning, as the category of the cartoon genre has gained prestige and legitimacy through its expansion beyond the Saturday morning network schedule.

How can we account for this shift? Again, like the creation of Saturday morning, there is no singular cause or motivating mechanism. Rather, the cartoon genre has shifted due to a conjuncture of a number of forces, ranging from macro-industrial changes to the surprise success of a few specific programs.[79] After outlining a number of causes for this shift, I turn to an in-depth analysis of one central site of cartoon genre practice in the 1990s: Cartoon Network. This examination of changes in the cartoon genre and the rise of single-genre cable channels in the 1990s highlights how generic history must look beyond textual chronicles — programs and practices from the 1940s, 1960s, and 1990s are all components of the contemporary generic cluster of cartoons, understandable only through an account of industrial practices.

One important shift contributing to generic redefinition in the 1990s was the rebirth of theatrical animation as a mass-audience phenomenon. Ever since 1937's *Snow White and the Seven Dwarfs*, Disney Studios was known as the preeminent producer of theatrical feature-length animation. The format had dwindled in the 1960s and 1970s, with films like *The Sword and the Stone* (1963) and *The Aristocats* (1970) garnering little critical or audience support. Disney hit its nadir in 1985 with *The Black Cauldron*, an attempt to crossover to a more adult audience that resolutely failed to connect with any audience. Feature-length animation was uncommon and not lucrative in the 1980s, as the format suffered from the generic assumption that cartoons were for kids, as fostered by Saturday morning television.

The success of two Disney films altered these assumptions for both industry and audience, marking the rebirth of theatrical animation. Disney's *Who Framed Roger Rabbit?* (1988), a live-action/animation mix, became a huge box office and critical success. The film played upon nostalgia for the glory days of studio animation, creating an entire world of cartoon production set in 1947 Hollywood, just before the Paramount decision and television's rise dealt death blows to theatrical cartoons. Combining clever adult humor and satire with appearances from classic characters most familiar to younger audiences from Saturday morning television, like Bugs Bunny and Donald Duck, *Roger Rabbit* legitimated cartoon appeal among all audiences, helping to broaden the appeal of marginalized classic animated shorts. Disney's 1989 fully animated film, *The Little Mermaid*, brought the feature-length format back to respectability. Like *Roger Rabbit*, the film received critical praise and box office success from a broad audience of adults and children, capitalizing on its hit soundtrack and sophisticated animated style. Disney parlayed *Mermaid*'s success into a string of animated features, culminating in the first animated film to receive an Academy Award Best Picture nomination — *Beauty and the Beast* in 1991 — and what was then the all-time highest grossing animated film (since surpassed by 2003's *Finding Nemo*) — 1994's *The Lion King*. The success of Disney features with all audiences helped restore the legitimacy and broad appeal of animation, factoring into the genre's transformation on television. Additionally, the growing importation of Japanese animation, both in theatrical releases like *Akira* (1988) and *Princess Mononoke* (1997), and television programs like *Sailor Moon* (1995–2000) and *Dragonball Z* (1996–2003), have fostered a growing cult audience of older viewers to revisit animation beyond the bounds of Saturday morning traditions.[80]

At the same time Disney and anime reached new audiences with theatrical animation in the late 1980s, network primetime television turned to animation for the first time since *The Flintstones* moved to Saturday mornings in 1966. Much like ABC in the 1950s, Fox was a fledgling network in the late-1980s, unable to compete equally with the Big Three; thus Fox was better positioned to take risks, with little to lose from failure. In an attempt to expand upon one of their few successful programs, Fox decided to spin-off the animated bumpers from *The Tracey Ullman Show* (1987–90) into a half-hour animated family sitcom; in January 1990, *The Simpsons* debuted. As I discuss in Chapter 6 in considering genre mixing, the show's immediate success was met with controversy, primarily concerning anxieties over offering adult satirical content to animation's assumed childish audience. Yet *The Simpsons* demonstrated the possibilities of primetime animation to abandon the generic linkages to children and appeal to a broad mass audience, eventually achieving the milestone of the longest running television sitcom, animated or live-action. Much like the success of *The Flintstones* in the early 1960s, *The Simpsons* launched a wave of short-lived primetime animation trying to follow the traditional system of innovation–imitation–saturation. Unlike the 1960s, however, failed shows like *Family Dog* (1993) and *Fish Police* (1992) never made it to Saturday morning reruns, as these programs permanently disappeared from the airwaves quickly. A second wave of primetime animation in the late 1990s was more successful, as *King of the Hill* (1997–), *The PJs* (1999–2001), *Family Guy* (1999–2002), and *Futurama* (1999–2003) all established themselves as at least moderately successful primetime programs, moving the cartoon genre away from Saturday morning as the solitary home for network animation.

The Simpsons and its long-lasting success made primetime animation popular on nonbroadcast channels as well. Both MTV's *Beavis and Butthead* (1992–97) and Comedy Central's *South Park* (1997–) were able to reach teenage and adult audiences, creating merchandizing phenomena and successful feature films capitalizing on the broad appeal of the genre.[81] Even more notably, both programs generated heated cultural controversies following in *The Simpsons'* path; at the center of these controversies was a conflict between their often lewd and satirical content and the generic assumption that cartoons must be primarily for children. These conflicts suggest that, while individual programs and their corresponding industrial and audience practices can redefine the assumptions that are part of a generic cluster, these generic linkages are often sufficiently well rooted and firmly established to resist rapid change. While both *The Simpsons* and *Beavis and Butthead* had fostered nearly identical controversies before them, the conflict over children wearing *South Park* shirts in school demonstrates that the generic linkage between children and animation cannot be easily detached. Yet the success and cultural circulation of these programs have resulted in an overall shift in animation toward acceptability as adult entertainment and a legitimate site of cultural satire.

While the rise of primetime cartoons and rebirth of theatrical animation suggests how new cartoons in the 1990s have moved toward including and addressing adult audiences, it cannot fully account for the changing circulation of animation dating from earlier eras. The 1990s witnessed older cartoons becoming recontextualized in two different directions. The first has been the growth of "classic quality" discourses concerning older animation. Following the ground laid by *Roger Rabbit*, media critics and animation buffs posit a "golden age" of animation in the 1940s and early 1950s, canonizing directors like Tex Avery and Chuck Jones. Via celebratory books, retrospectives, and home video rereleases, the studio animation from Disney, Warner Brothers, and MGM all have become associated with markers of quality that allow them to transcend their Saturday morning confines.[82] Likewise, a new generation of animated programs, like *Tiny Toon Adventures* (1990–92), *Animaniacs* (1993–98), and *Pinky and the Brain* (1995–98), have been positioned as "neo-classical" throwbacks to these traditions, often containing direct references to the "golden age" via character cameos or clever allusions. Thus, according to the classical history of animation, the period from the 1960s to the 1990s is a wasteland of Saturday morning knockoffs (with a few exceptional quality shows like *Bullwinkle*) from which golden age shorts need to be rescued.

Another set of discourses reframes Saturday morning cartoons, not as an object of scorn but as a marker of camp nostalgia. In the irony-saturated 1990s, Saturday morning cartoons gained cultural cachet as a shared set of cultural references, especially among so-called Generation-Xers. Films like *Reality Bites* (1994) and *Slacker* (1991) use ironic readings of cartoons to establish character identification, while popular "alternative rock" bands are featured in recorded compilations covering *Schoolhouse Rock* songs and Saturday morning theme songs. Semi-scholarly books like Timothy and Kevin Burke's *Saturday Morning Fever* openly contest the use of "Saturday morning" as "a shorthand epithet for culture judged to be juvenile, low-quality, moronic, mind-numbing, or cut-rate." The Burkes defend Saturday morning via generational bonding — "a lot of Saturday Morning was crap. But it's *our* crap, and we're tired of smug folks twice our age telling us their crap was better than our crap."[83] Programs like *Speed Racer* (1967) and *The Smurfs* (1981–90) have been reclaimed by adults, not as "quality," but because they contribute to a shared set of childhood memories and identity formation. We can see both of these discourses of quality and nostalgia at work in the industrial formation of Cartoon Network.

The rise of Cartoon Network points toward the central reorganization of the television industry over the last twenty years, as nonnetwork television channels have reached a level of circulation to become vital players in shaping a genre. The rise of cable and satellite in the 1980s and 1990s has remapped the terrain of the television schedule, especially in terms of market segments and genres. In the 1960s, the Big Three networks were able to isolate cartoons on Saturday morning to create a kid-only block to lure specialized sponsors. Similar practices maintained clearly scheduled slots for soap operas, talk shows, game shows, sports, news, situation comedies, and dramas — every genre had its core place in the television schedule, ensuring that at most times, each network would be primarily competing against similar programming for the same audience. Yet as the number of channels has risen, genres can no longer be effectively isolated by timeslot, as entire 24-hour channels exist for news, sports, science-fiction, game shows, music, cooking shows, home improvement programs, and even direct market advertising. The traditional practice of narrowcasting via generic scheduling has given way to channel identity as a prime practice of generic and audience definition.

Like most of the cable channels that emerged in the 1990s, Cartoon Network was born of ownership interests and synergistic possibilities more than of creative pursuits or serving the public interest.[84] Turner Broadcasting purchased the MGM/United Artists library of films in 1985, including A.A.P.'s pre-1948 Warner Brothers and *Popeye* cartoons, to provide programming for its cable superstation WTBS (and later TNT in 1987).[85] Cartoon programs such as *Looney Tunes* and *Tom & Jerry* garnered solid ratings on WTBS, so Ted Turner saw cartoons as an opportunity for expansion. He bought Hanna-Barbera's studio and library in 1992, giving him ownership of the most popular cartoons in television history. Instead of incorporating these cartoons into a larger schedule on WTBS, Turner decided to dedicate an entire channel to reaching cartoon fans, launching Cartoon Network in October 1992.

Cable channels had relied upon cartoons prior to Cartoon Network. Most notably, Nickelodeon had built an audience in the 1980s mixing cartoons with live-action children's programming; the children's channel developed high-profile cartoon offerings with the simultaneous emergence of *Doug* (1991–94), *Rugrats* (1991–), and *The Ren and Stimpy Show* (1991–96). Despite the success of Nickelodeon and their cartoon offerings, they firmly segregated children's programming from their nighttime offerings of rerun sitcoms and dramas known as Nick at Nite. By keeping their cartoons solely in morning and afternoon timeslots, Nickelodeon was relying on the central assumption established by Saturday morning cartoons — television animation is designed for child audiences.[86] This assumption played out on other cable channels as well — both Disney Channel and Family Channel included cartoons in their daytime lineups for kids, but in primetime and late-night, they shifted to live-action "family" programs and movies to draw in mixed audiences.

Cartoon Network drew its scheduling model less from these children's channels and more from the 24-hour single-genre channels that Turner had helped popularize with CNN. While conventional wisdom in the 1970s suggested that the appeals of news, weather, and sports were all too narrow to transcend their well-established places within the television schedule, the success of CNN, The Weather Channel, and ESPN in the 1980s proved that genre narrowcasting could reach sufficient audiences to become profitable. Cartoon Network explicitly defined itself not by audience groups, such as Nickelodeon or Family Channel, but by the singular cartoon genre. Like most startup cable channels, it relied initially on repackaged and rerun programming, milking their self-proclaimed "world's largest cartoon library" of over 8500 programs.[87] Initially, Turner overcame the channel's low penetration on cable systems by luring sponsors through package deals with TNT and WTBS, promising more affordable access to children's audiences than from Nickelodeon.[88]

Cartoon Network grew far more quickly than even Turner's most optimistic predictions. Upon its launch in October 1992, the channel was carried by only 233 cable systems, reaching approximately two million households.[89] Yet the channel garnered high ratings and used the weight of Turner Broadcasting to rapidly expand into more cable systems. By the end of 1994, Cartoon Network was the fifth most popular cable channel in the United States; in the spring of 2001, it ranked second among daily cable ratings.[90] Cartoon Network was bolstered by the 1995 merger of Turner and Time Warner, as the channel was able to add post-1948 Warner Brothers cartoons to its library, as well as newer Warner creations like *Tiny Toons* and *Animaniacs*. The channel's success was conveyed into new program production, transforming Hanna-Barbera into Cartoon Network Studios to produce original cartoons, resulting in popular new programs like *Dexter's Laboratory* (1995–2003), *The Powerpuff Girls* (1998–), *Ed, Edd n Eddy* (1999–2004), and *Samurai Jack* (2001–). Significantly, the channel lacks the demographic uniformity of Nickelodeon or Disney Channel, as over one-third of viewers for Cartoon Network are adults. While the channel does not have the reach of the broadcast networks, they have effectively provided the television cartoon genre with its broadest mass audience since the institution of Saturday morning in the mid-1960s. Cartoon Network's popularity and success in returning cartoons to a mass audience have directly altered and transformed the cartoon genre.

So how has Cartoon Network changed the assumptions constituting the cluster of the cartoon genre in the 1990s? The primary shift is certainly through broadening the genre's assumed target audience. Along with *The Little Mermaid* (and other Disney features) and *The Simpsons* (and the primetime cartoons which followed it), Cartoon Network has worked to disassociate the kids-only stigma from the cartoon genre, which had been predominant since the emergence of Saturday morning. While featuring Saturday morning staples like *The Smurfs* and *Scooby Doo* (1969–76), they also feature many cartoons initially designed for mass audiences, ranging from television productions like *The Flintstones* and *The Jetsons* to theatrical shorts like *Popeye*, *Bugs Bunny*, and Tex Avery's MGM cartoons. While none of these cartoons exclude children, many of them tap into the "classic" discourse surrounding studio animation giving adults a "legitimate" mode of enjoying animation. Notably, Cartoon Network does not play many of Hanna-Barbera's lesser efforts from the late 1960s and 1970s, as these shows would certainly turn off most adult viewers (and probably many children), but instead features the more successful early Hanna-Barbera material under the dual rubrics of quality and campy nostalgia.[91]

According to Linda Simensky, formerly Senior Vice President of Original Animation at Cartoon Network, the channel does not specifically target its programming toward adults or children. She describes the channel's target audience as a "taste culture" or "psychographic" consisting simply of "people who like cartoons," regardless of age.[92] The age breakdowns commonly reported in the trade press — 45% of the audience is aged 2–11, 15% are teenagers, and

40% are adults — suggests that the channel is able to reach a broad audience, yet the programmers are aware that their audience is a niche among the general populace. Compared to other kid-centered cable channels, like Nickelodeon, Disney Channel, and ABC Family, Cartoon Network both reaches a broader audience (in terms of age) and a more narrow one (in terms of taste). This "taste culture" can be sold to advertisers as prepackaged and selected, in keeping with the logic of a post-Fordist media economy.[93]

Cartoon Network constitutes its audience and the corresponding "taste culture" through its promotional activities, use of branding, and trends in original production. The channel promotes itself and its programming through highly kinetic and colorful animated ads, designed to tap into the graphic tastes of cartoon-lovers of all ages. Additionally, the channel uses more "hip" and ironic ads to appeal to adults.[94] In one series, mirroring the celebrated ad campaign for ESPN's *Sportscenter* (1979–), Cartoon Network offices are portrayed as a place where cartoon characters and humans work side-by-side. In one ad, Aquaman from *The Superfriends* (1973–86) proclaims that he likes working at Cartoon Network because it's the only place where "aquatic telepathy is a valuable job skill." Another features a typical Hollywood agent negotiating contracts for his cartoon clients Dexter and Cow & Chicken. These ads directly reach out to adult cartoon fan's knowledge of characters and their imagination of the "behind-the-scenes" world of cartoons portrayed in *Roger Rabbit* as well as classic shorts like Warner Brothers' *You Ought To Be In Pictures* (1940). Additionally, the Aquaman ad taps into nostalgic discourses, as *Superfriends* was a much-revered 1970s Saturday morning staple that has since become a touchstone Gen-X reference point. Cartoon Network uses a similar sensibility in their pre-Super Bowl special, *The Big Game* (2000–01), which features famous sportscasters and stars mocking themselves as they treat cartoons as a major sporting event pitting Bugs versus Daffy, Coyote versus Road Runner, all with parodies of typical Super Bowl hype, half-time shows, and iconic advertisements.

Cartoon Network also uses branding to identify and reach its core audience. Branding has become a vital aspect of 1990s television, working to create channel loyalty through associating a particular channel with a larger lifestyle and set of tastes.[95] Cartoon Network explicitly attempts to brand itself through a variety of techniques, ranging from their ubiquitous logo found in promos and bumpers, to a highly promoted Web site with original "webtoons" and behind-the-scenes material. Some branding efforts tap explicitly into the nostalgic discourses surrounding Saturday morning, as the channel has entered the merchandizing realm with videos of *The Flintstones* and *Jonny Quest* and CDs of cartoon theme songs, while other strategies follow the more typical assault of Disney, as with the ubiquitous *Powerpuff Girl* merchandise appealing to both kid and adult cartoon fans. The specifics of Cartoon Network's brand identity match the defining characteristics of this "taste culture" — people who love cartoons as nostalgia, art, and entertainment. This directly contrasts with the ways other cable channels present cartoons primarily as children's entertainment. Cartoon Network acknowledges that much of their audience is children, refraining from showing more controversial racial representations, war era propaganda shorts, or explicit gun or blood violence, but Simensky suggests that they are less censorious of violence and adult references than Nickelodeon or other outlets for televised cartoons.[96] In 2001, Cartoon Network developed a late-night programming block called Adult Swim, featuring more sophisticated cartoons aimed at an adult audience while advising, "All kids get out of the pool!" As such, Cartoon Network defines itself as a "safe place" for both children and adults to watch cartoons, offering insulation from "questionable" content for kids and enabling adults to acknowledge their animated taste without scorn.

As Cartoon Network developed a strong presence in the cable landscape, it established a distinctive approach to original programming. The earliest series produced by Cartoon Network stretches the definition of the term "original" — *Space Ghost Coast to Coast* (1994–) consisted nearly entirely of recycled animation cels from Hanna-Barbera's archive, originally drawn for their mid 1960s Saturday morning show, *Space Ghost and Dino Boy*. Cartoon Network producers turned the original's bare-bones visuals into an asset by reanimating select cels atop new backgrounds to create a fictional talk show on the moon, hosted by bored hero Space Ghost and his vanquished enemies Zorak and Moltar. The program became a sensation among young adult audiences in its Friday night timeslot as a post-Letterman hyper-ironic deconstruction of the talk show, although Cartoon Network also initially ran the show in the mornings for younger audiences. With a parade of nostalgic has-beens and counter-cultural fringe figures for guests, *Space Ghost* turned Cartoon Network into an original producer for minimal costs, firming the channel's identity as a hip outlet for cartoons that appeal to more than just kids.[97]

Cartoon Network followed the hip cachet of *Space Ghost* by creating a number of truly original cartoons to be featured on 1995's *World Premiere Toons*, a weekly program debuting commissioned shorts from Hanna-Barbera and independent animators. The series was hyped as a throwback to the classic days of studio animation, with full animator control, high budgets, and full animation style. Cartoon Network assessed the long-term potential for each short, signing some animators to create ongoing series out of successful shorts; this testing area brought new cartoons to the air, leading to series like *Dexter's Laboratory*, *The Powerpuff Girls*, and *Johnny Bravo* (1997–). All of these programs fit Cartoon Network's brand identity and taste culture, featuring young characters and animals with outrageous graphics and physical humor for kids, along with sophisticated humor, ironic attitude, and pop culture references for adult fans. Additionally, both the premiere shorts serving as potential series "pilots" and the resulting original series follow the short 7- to 11-minute format that is typical of classic cartoons, tying back to a pretelevision definition of the cartoon genre. The channel promotes the adult appeal of these shows, scheduled mostly in early evening timeslots, through a pseudo-documentary ad campaign showing the exploits of adult fans who try to live their lives following cartoon role models like *Johnny Bravo* and *The Powerpuff Girls*.

While certainly Cartoon Network is committed to the cartoon as a broadly defined genre, it is clear from their programming and ad campaigns that they specialize in a particular type of cartoon, a specific articulation of the genre that the channel works to establish as most legitimate and high quality. Simensky offered a nutshell version of this genre definition by calling Bugs Bunny "the icon of taste" for Cartoon Network, suggesting that if viewers don't appreciate Bugs, they won't enjoy the channel as a whole.[98] This rendering of the cartoon genre replays a dichotomy common to animation studies, positing the binary of Disney's wholesome, family-friendly, artistic, and photorealistic cartoons versus Warner's anarchistic, wacky, sophisticated, and timelessly humorous style.[99] Not surprisingly, considering both Turner's library and its merger with Time Warner, Cartoon Network falls firmly on the latter half of this duality. While the channel offer no explicit definition of the core textual qualities of cartoons, Cartoon Network's industrial practices posit a specific assumed delineation of the cartoon genre, through both its programming of classic cartoons and production of original programs in the Warner mold.

Cartoon Network's generic practices defining the cartoon and evaluating the genre's history become manifest in their marathons of *Cartoon Network's Greatest 50 Cartoons*. First aired in 1998, Cartoon Network offered new iterations of their canon in 1999 and 2001. As genre theorists have discussed, listing texts is a vital way in which critics constitute genres for their further analysis.[100] Creating generic corpuses is not limited to academic critics however, as institutions and audiences participate in the same type of generic analysis through their everyday interactions with genres. The common practice of creating "greatest" or "best" lists of any given category operates as a specific moment in which genre is manifested through defining and evaluative practices. Cartoon Network's 1999 list (see Appendix A) is an example of an evaluative generic discourse that poses a particular definition impacting the cartoon generic cluster. In analyzing the list, I do not mean to suggest that it was necessarily adopted by audiences as definitive statements of value, but certainly the hoopla surrounding releases of most canonized lists (such as AFI's Top 100 Films of the 20th Century list) suggests that audiences do engage with these lists as a touchstone for their own practices of definition and evaluation.[101]

Cartoon Network's list of fifty cartoons from 1999, chosen primarily by the cartoon-fan staff of Cartoon Network, definitely favors the Warner-centric vision of the genre that Simensky suggested. Twenty-one of the shorts were produced by Warner, featuring classic cartoons starring Bugs Bunny, Daffy

Duck, and Porky Pig (with single entries each from Sylvester and Tweety, Foghorn Leghorn, and Road Runner and Coyote). MGM is also well-represented with sixteen cartoons on the list, with the majority directed by the man most credited with developing Warner's anarchistic style, Tex Avery. Avery is certainly the most celebrated director on the list, with fourteen entries beating out Chuck Jones' eleven entries (including Jones filling the top four slots on the list). *Popeye* and *Betty Boop* creator Max Fleischer has five entries on the list, while Hanna-Barbera are represented by two made-for-television shorts and three of their MGM *Tom & Jerry* cartoons. Other major cartoon producers are notably absent, with only one UPA short, and none from either Walter Lantz or Disney. While five made-for-television shorts are included, the list is certainly designed to tap into discourses of quality much more than nostalgia, as it serves to reinforce Cartoon Network as a site for the "best" cartoons on television — as originally seen in cinemas.

The domination of Warner and MGM in the absence of Disney is not surprising, given Cartoon Network's ownership and direct competition with Disney Channel and its subsidiary Toon Disney. Certainly, any viewer with knowledge of the ownership of these subsidiaries might interpret the marathon's selections and omissions with appropriate levels of cynicism, yet certainly a good number of viewers (especially children) would be unaware of these structures. The industrial reasons behind these omissions are not self-evident however — while the cynical viewer might assume that the Turner-owned Cartoon Network is interested only in featuring its own products (as I initially did), the proprietary practices are actually reversed. Cartoon Network, in an effort to make the most comprehensive marathon possible, has tried to feature cartoons from Disney and Nickelodeon in their marathons, but these companies have refused to grant permission for Mickey Mouse or *Ren & Stimpy* to appear on Turner's channel, even as part of a cartoon canon. Clearly, dueling industrial definitions of the cartoon genre are at play, as Disney wishes to maintain control of the specific incarnation of the cartoon that they feature on Disney Channel and Toon Disney, maintaining a separation from their competition at Cartoon Network.

Because of both industrial constraints and certain generic assumptions operative for Cartoon Network, their canon offers a particular vision of the genre. I do not wish to decry any "injustice" or bias in Cartoon Network's self-proclaimed canon — all lists like this are inherently skewed and limited, as well as certainly being driven by particular tastes and contexts. Rather, even if we accept that such a canon is not a "true" selection of the best cartoons ever, it does work to define the genre in a selective fashion that needs to be acknowledged. Because Cartoon Network is one of the primary sites in which the cartoon genre functions as a mass-market format with adult appeal, we need to examine what definition of the genre is being legitimated through its practices and what type of cartoons are being excluded.

One clear way to highlight exclusions is through a comparison with a similar list produced under different contexts. In 1994, animation historian Jerry Beck spearheaded an effort to create a list of *The Fifty Greatest Cartoons* by polling animation professionals and scholars, culminating in a book (published by Turner Publishing) and corresponding 1998 special on Cartoon Network (see Appendix B).[102] Both lists start with the same parameters — ranking cel-animated (apart from claymation or computer animation) short cartoons. Given that Turner's corporation released both the book and television program, we cannot view this list as any more "authentic," unbiased, or outside the industrial mechanisms. Similarly, the goal behind the 1994 list was different than Cartoon Network's 1999 list, as Beck wished to define a canon of classic animation for fans and producers, while Cartoon Network's marathon was clearly a way of self-promotion and celebration of the quality of the channel's library. Despite these contrasting contexts, the differences between the lists point toward the ways Cartoon Network articulates a specific genre definition which is not shared by all cartoon fans or producers.

The 1994 list similarly values the anarchistic Warner style, with four of the top five belonging to Jones' Warner output, ten Jones shorts overall, and seventeen Warner cartoons representing the most from any studio.[103] What is less represented on Beck's list is MGM (seven compared to Cartoon Network's sixteen) and Tex Avery (five to Cartoon Network's fourteen). Also missing from Beck's list are any made-for-television cartoons, which are represented by Cartoon Network through two of their original shorts (*The Chicken from Outer Space* and an episode of *Dexter's Laboratory*), two Hanna-Barbera productions (a Huckleberry Hound short and Pixie & Dixie cartoon), and a Bullwinkle episode. Beck's list fills in these gaps primarily by including Disney shorts, which occupy nine of the slots. I would argue that Disney's exclusion on Cartoon Network is not simply because of ownership, as the brand of humor in the Disney shorts is more subdued and less anarchistic than in Warner or MGM, and not in keeping with Cartoon Network's brand of cartoon. Other inclusions on Beck's list which point toward gaps in Cartoon Network's canon include independent animation (such as Marv Newland's *Bambi Meets Godzilla* and Sally Cruikshank's *Quasi at the Quackadero*), noncomedic shorts (like UPA's adaptation of Poe's *The Tell-Tale Heart* and MGM's anti-war parable *Peace on Earth*), and "controversial" representations (like Warner's *Coal Black and de Sebben Dwarfs* and Disney's *Der Fuehrer's Face*).

Through comparisons with Beck's list, we can see how Cartoon Network's canonizing practices point toward what falls inside and outside the channel's definition of its eponymous "cartoon." Cartoons are primarily comedic (with the sole exception of Fleischer's *Superman*), establishing their multi-generational appeal through the brand of high-energy visual humor typified by Avery and Jones. Simensky suggests that this comedic bias is both because of the limited quality of most noncomedic shorts and because the dark vision of some serious shorts would conflict with Cartoon Network's personality. Cartoon Network's canon are produced primarily by major studios for either theatrical or television exhibition, not by independent animators working outside of the industrial system — again Simensky suggests that the lack of independents is because both their more artistic edge is not appreciated by most Cartoon Network fans and the cost and logistics of securing rights to independents are fraught with numerous difficulties.[104] Cartoon Network generally features a mode of full animation, exemplified by Warner, falling between the heightened realism of Disney and the stripped down abstraction of UPA. And of course, they are mostly owned by the AOL Time Warner Turner conglomerate, an aspect motivated by practicality, cost, external limitations, and self-promotion. All of these features are continually reinforced through Cartoon Network's lineup of recycled theatrical shorts, reruns of Hanna-Barbera television material, and original productions. Cartoon Network defines itself as *the* location for 24-hour cartoons — and simultaneously guarantees the specific definition of the cartoon genre will be featured on the channel.

In recent years, Cartoon Network's brand identity has shifted somewhat, expanding their definition of the cartoon genre. As anime has become a hot commodity — and distribution deals with Japanese companies have become commonplace — Cartoon Network has expanded its lineup of Japanese anime imports. Some programs, like *Dragonball Z*, *Yu-Gi-Oh*, and *Cyborg 009*, air on late-afternoon action block Toonami, whereas others such as *Hamtaro* and *Pokemon* target young children in the early morning; most notably for anime fans, Cartoon Network has brought cult mature anime titles to late-night audiences, including *Cowboy Bebop*, *Trigun*, and *InuYasha*. As befits their Japanese origins, the taste culture of Bugs Bunny is nowhere to be seen in these programs, as they tend toward action, sci-fi, and fantasy narratives more than comedy, while featuring anime's trademark heightened naturalistic graphic style unlike Cartoon Network's norm. Newer original programming from Cartoon Network has also expanded the horizons of its genre norms, as *Justice League* (2001–) offers a serious darker take on the *Superfriends* characters, and *Samurai Jack* mixes the UPA-influenced style of *Dexter's Lab* and *Powerpuff Girls* with Japanese mythology and live-action samurai epics to produce one of the more strikingly original animated television programs ever. Adult Swim mixes the anarchistic adult irony of *Space Ghost* and *Harvey Birdman: Attorney At Law* (2001–) with the subtle humor of *Home Movies* (2001–), producing a lineup most notable for excluding the core cartoon audience of children. None of these programs directly follow the generic norms originally promoted by Cartoon Network, but as its core audience has solidified, the channel has been willing to expand its draw to welcome fans of other animation forms, thereby extending its brand of the cartoon genre. This expansion may cause such generic dilution as to further fracture the channel's taste culture of cartoon fans into isolated sub-markets — it's hard to imagine too many *Tom and Jerry* fans also embracing *Cowboy Bebop* and *Hamtaro* — although it is too soon to tell if the channel's success in broadening its audience will lead to an ultimate weakening of its core identity.

Cartoon Network demonstrates how a channel's industrial practices are constitutive of a genre, through a range of techniques including original production, marketing and advertising, reframing old programs, and establishing a channel identity. The channel is certainly not alone in defining the genre in the 1990s — any attempt at a comprehensive account of the genre would have to account more for changes in feature films, network television, the Internet's fan culture and the rise of online animation, gains in computer animation technology, the animated home video market, and other cable channels. Yet Cartoon Network is a primary site of industrial practice constituting the cartoon genre in the 1990s, directly drawing upon and transforming the larger generic cluster by breaking down the assumptions established by Saturday morning cartoons that animation is primarily a children's form. Cartoon Network mobilizes discourses of nostalgia and classicism to appeal to adults, constituting the unified "psychographic" of "people who like cartoons." Of course, we must keep in mind that this constructed audience is not fans of just any cartoons, with the genre being defined more narrowly toward humorous and visually frenetic mainstream animation in the Warner model.

These two shifts in the history of televised cartoons have had significant generic consequences. The move to Saturday morning in the 1960s severely limited the possibilities of television animation, leading to over-commercialization, a decline in production values, and little acknowledgment of the potential sophistication of the children's (and adult) animation audience. The Saturday morning era represents the nadir of the animation genre, as innovations were foreclosed by the factory-style lowest common denominator approach and kid-only stigma offered by the networks. I regard the shifts in the 1990s to be predominantly positive developments for the genre, working against the genre's stigmas by making cartoons a legitimate form for adult fans via primetime programming, expanded animated feature films, and cable channels, all of which helped bolster the quality of children's animated programming as well — the commercial success of Nickelodeon and Disney have allowed them to invest in noncommercial educational programs for younger children, as well as developing new channels like Noggin. Cartoon Network's practices have helped lead to a cartoon renaissance, both in greater access to cartoon history and in promoting new production featuring full animation, sophisticated content, and a creator-centered approach to production. While acknowledging the limits of the specific articulation of the genre offered by Cartoon Network — personally I would like to see more independent animation and historically suppressed shorts featured on the channel — the industrial practices of Cartoon Network have helped make the cartoon a legitimate genre for mass audiences once again, working to erode the stigmas associated with cartoons since the onset of Saturday morning.

This chapter points to the limitations of texts themselves as evidence for genre analysis; television texts, such as the popular case of Bugs Bunny shorts, cannot tell us how this genre has evolved from its theatrical heyday in the 1930s and 1940s, to the kid-only isolation of Saturday morning in the mid 1960s and 1970s, and now to its rebirth as a mass format via 1990s cable channels. The assumptions constituting the cartoon genre are made up of more than texts, as cultural meanings are actively linked to the generic cluster by press accounts, audience practices, and industrial programming and marketing strategies. These assumptions are not "exterior" to the genre, as practices such as targeting audiences and canon formations are central to the ways in which the cartoon works as a cultural category. Genre critics must account for the specific structures and practices of the television industry, carefully examining how institutions operate for the specific medium of television. While we need to be critical of ownership systems and point out how conglomeration impacts media content (as with Cartoon Network's definition of the genre matching its ownership interests), we cannot simply point to ownership as the ultimate explanatory mechanism for all phenomena (as in political economy's most vulgar form). The history of the cartoon points to the television-specific attributes of scheduling practices and channel identity as constitutive of both media genres and (partially) delimiting the ways in which audiences interact with television. While both Saturday morning cartoons and Cartoon Network were primarily industrial formations, we cannot stop our analysis of these practices at the level of the industry itself — media industries always interrelate within the multiple spheres of texts, audiences, and historical contexts.

Additionally, we can draw a number of conclusions from this case study that pertain to media studies more broadly than the somewhat specialized realm of animation scholarship. As cultural scholars have turned toward examining media constructions of childhood, these genre practices point to how media industries construct child audiences and their tastes. The creation of Saturday morning cartoons worked to posit a particular vision of the child audience as undiscerning, easily satiated by anything animated, and valuable targets of advertising. This formation had substantial impacts, leading to controversies about children's media violence and consumerism in the 1970s.[105] Saturday morning cartoons and Cartoon Network both construct a hypothetical child who needs to be protected from certain content, such as the racial representations in *Coal Black*, but not from other messages, like ads for candy, violent toys, or commercialism itself. These politicized constructions of childhood need to be grappled with if we are to understand how both the cartoon genre and the larger relationship between children and television operate within American society.

The history of the cartoon also provides an insight into the central issue of mass versus niche marketing. The conventional history of television suggests that broadcasters in the 1960s were in the business of reaching mass audiences, caring primarily about numbers of viewers rather than who constituted any audience group. In the age of cable and upstart broadcast networks, this model has been reconceived as narrowcasting, searching for more specific audience segments consistent with a post-Fordist economy. While certainly this overarching pattern has explanatory power, the specific case of the cartoon belies this pattern — Saturday morning cartoons followed narrowcasting practices in the 1960s, with networks attempting to actively exclude adults from their timeslots to provide sponsors with a denser child audience. Conversely, Cartoon Network has explicitly targeted both children and adults in the 1990s, attempting to reach a broader audience than cartoons had traditionally enjoyed on network broadcasts. Certainly Cartoon Network is still a narrowcaster, as "people who like cartoons" is a niche, but the genre's history suggests that the master narrative of "mass to niche marketing" does not apply across all television genres.

A Bugs Bunny short itself has not changed intrinsically from its production in 1946 to its differing television exhibitions in 1965 or 1999. Yet the cartoon genre to which it belongs has undergone a number of crucial transformations that are vital to our understanding of how cartoons operate culturally. Only through analyzing the changing configurations of the cartoon as a cultural category — as constituted by media industries, texts, contexts, and audiences — can we account for how a 50-year-old film can be redefined, reinterpreted, and reevaluated through its various televisual incarnations. By accounting for the cultural operation and evolution of cartoons as tendered by media industries, we are better able to understand the politics and practices that are central to this underexamined genre. But industries are only one site of generic practice — I now turn to an examination of media audiences and how they use generic categories to understand the television talk show.

4

Audiences Talk Genres — Talk Shows and the Intersections of Taste and Identity

In recent years, the audience has emerged as a primary focus in media studies, with dozens of projects exploring, debating, and agonizing over the site of the audience. This turn toward the audience responds to long-held traditions within both film studies and mass communications which locate deterministic power within texts to impact viewers, whether it be through ideological subject positioning or causal media effects models. Within traditional genre studies, the audience seems to function as a given, preconstituted receivers of the formulaic texts traditionally held to be equivalent to a given genre. While many scholars have acknowledged that genres are used by audiences as a shortcut for interpretation or a contract to manage expectations, little work has considered how audiences use genres as cultural categories. This chapter considers how we might try to understand audience practices of genre categories, offering a brief account of how audiences use the contemporary television talk show genre.

Knowing the Viewer: Approaches to Studying Generic Audiences

Even though much media scholarship is undertaken in the name of the audience, there is little uniformity in defining the term "audience" itself. Is the audience only those people who watch a given program? Are people members of an audience even while they are not watching a show? Is studying audiences equivalent to studying media reception or decoding? Can the mass audience be divided up into smaller groups, and how might these groups be studied? Are fans special

94

audiences, or can they stand in for audiences as a whole? Is the audience a collection of individuals or only operative as a collective group? I will not answer these questions definitively (as if I could), but consider them to demonstrate how the object of audience studies is neither stable nor uniform — the assumptions made upon embarking on audience studies construct a specific conception of the audience as an analytic object. Just as Ien Ang argues that television institutions create discursive constructions of television audiences through their industrial practices, media scholars' theoretical assumptions and methodological choices also constitute "the television audience" as a discursive construct.[1] The specific construction of the audience that any scholar examines is necessarily partial, limited, and somewhat disconnected with the lived practices of people who watch television. This is not to dismiss audience studies as a failed project, but we must acknowledge that comprehensive knowledge of the television audience is an impossibility — all we can hope for is to explore narrow pieces of a larger audience pie.

Given the inevitable partiality of any inquiry into audience practices, how might we focus in on how audiences use genres as cultural categories? Following the textualist bias of most genre criticism, many genre analyses have looked at audiences primarily through their hypothetical intersections with media texts. Ranging from psychoanalytic spectatorship models to mass communication media effects paradigms, many scholars have attempted to understand a viewer's relationship to media by decoding what impact texts might have upon audiences. Within genre studies, this model has been most frequently applied to understand ideology at work, suggesting that every genre has dominant pleasures structured into its texts, and that audience pleasures emerge from their enactment of these textual systems through repetitive viewing.[2] Cognitive film studies has similarly posited that analyzing textual systems in conjunction with psychological theories can access spectatorial experiences without undertaking reception research, examining issues such as emotional engagement with film genres often by using the critic's own emotions as a guide to understanding global responses to a film.[3]

While valid insights may be gained through exploring the idealized processes of spectatorial engagement with texts, whether through cognitive psychology or ideological analysis, this text-centered tendency works against an account of genres as changing and historically specific cultural categories. If Bugs Bunny cartoons are categorically redefined by the industry, it would suggest that different audiences would approach these texts with sufficient contextual differences that any attempt to gauge spectatorial experiences from the texts alone would be insufficient. If we are to understand media audiences within a cultural approach to genre, then we need to look beyond the realm of the text, as texts contains neither the audience nor the genre.[4]

Whereas text-centered approaches are predicated on the basic formula of "text plus theory equals audience practice," context-centered approaches to audience analysis look beyond the text. Following Stuart Hall's influential model of polysemic texts and the multiplicity of potential audience readings, a context-centered approach situates texts within historical variables, related discourses, and intertextual relationships to posit potential readings that may be available to actual audiences.[5] If the majority of readings fall into Hall's "negotiated" category, the context-centered approach looks to the various contextual factors that lead to specific negotiations of meaning for particular texts. Thus, Christine Gledhill suggests looking at textual traditions, genres, social movements, and institutional frameworks to uncover the "conditions and possibilities of reading" within a contextualized text.[6] This approach is echoed in Tony Bennett and Janet Woollacott's concept of "reading formations," in which intertextual and historical contexts provide readers with cues that determine potential readings.[7] In these approaches, analyzing relevant historical contexts, including other texts, genres, institutional practices, and social forces, reveal the pressures and limitations that limit the potential polysemy of texts, giving clues to the probable negotiations that actual readers engage in through the process of reception. While acknowledging that contextual analysis can never guarantee the actual meanings that viewers might take away from their media consumption, a contextual approach offers a happy medium between a polysemic free-for-all (as some caricatures of cultural studies have attributed to "straw theorists") and the textual determinism typical of most critical approaches.

For genre analysis, the power of context is crucial, as genre categories work to link assumptions which viewers undoubtedly bring to bear in their interpretive practices. Drawing on Stephen Neale's early work on genre, Bennett and Woollacott view genres "as sets of expectations through which the possibilities of reading are organized," with genres working within broader cultural contexts, outside the traditional realm of texts.[8] Thus, genres often work as a crucial site linking cultural assumptions to specific texts for audiences, as I discuss in Chapter 5 regarding the authenticating meanings activated by *Dragnet*'s incorporation of documentary traditions. The contextual approach is useful in discussing audiences, especially in historical cases where viewer access is quite limited. But in choosing a contemporary genre like the talk show, we do have access to actual viewers and their own generic practices; thus, we can move beyond contextual parameters to hear audiences' own voices.

If any one question has been in the forefront of cultural media studies in the past twenty years, it would be "how can we access actual audiences?" Unsatisfied with merely looking to texts or contexts, media scholars have devised a number of approaches to study viewers, avoiding hypothetical readings in favor of examining empirical audience practices. For historical cases, this approach has been quite limited (and limiting), as addressed in Chapter 2 — using oral histories, archived letters, and other audience remnants is fraught with historiographical landmines.[9] Because of these issues, the bulk of media audience studies have focused on contemporary examples, where access to actual audiences is more viable, if not fraught with different perils. The unifying tenet behind these viewer-centered approaches is that studying the actual practices of audiences can augment, and force us to revise or supplant, the hypothetical readings offered by textual and contextual traditions. While there is an empirical basis in these approaches, valuing the actual words and practices of audiences, viewer-centered studies reject an *empiricist* assumption that evidence received from audiences provides unfettered access to the "truth" of media reception. Ideally, viewer-centered studies strike a balance between allowing audience voices to come forward and speak for themselves, and acknowledging that audience discourses are no less contingent, partial, and socially situated than any other aspect of media (or social) practice.

One of the most productive avenues of audience scholarship has followed from the reader-response literary criticism school most associated with Stanley Fish and the concept of *interpretive communities*.[10] While Fish's own work is more context centered, the notion that specific groups provide their own particular norms, guidelines, and practices of reception has guided a number of viewer-centered studies of interpretive communities.[11] Undoubtedly, the most successful and influential study of an interpretive community is also a genre study (albeit of a literary genre) — Janice Radway's *Reading the Romance*.[12] Radway provides an in-depth look at a group of romance readers via interviews, charting out the specific generic assumptions (or "rules," as she terms them) by which they make sense of the romance genre and directly contrasting the audience's conception of the genre to that of the publishing industry. For genre scholars, Radway's analysis clearly points to the contingency of genres as cultural categories, serving distinctly different purposes for various groups and escaping a top-down definition imposed by either industries or texts.[13]

Radway's work on interpretive communities has been imported into media studies via analyses of a particular type of audience member: the fan. Studies of fan communities were an important development in media studies of the late 1980s and early 1990s, as scholars looked to these often-pathologized groups of viewers as active and engaged sites of analysis.[14] Fans offer particularly fruitful research opportunities, because they are highly visible and accessible — through participation in conventions, online discussion groups, and interpersonal networks — and often produce their own texts as part of their participatory fandom, such as fan fiction, music videos, songs, and Web sites. This latter aspect of fan culture has been particularly inviting to media scholars, as most of us come out of textually centered disciplinary traditions and thus feel most comfortable casting our analytic eyes toward texts, whether they be network television programs or fan-produced fiction. This use of "tertiary texts" as the site of analysis is quite limited, both in centering upon textuality (even if produced by "audiences") and in focusing on the most minute segment of mass audiences who are so moved and involved in media reception as to create their own textual products. This last concern is more generalizable to all fan studies, as often there is a slippage — whether in an analysis itself or its eventual adoption by others — between the practices of these highly self-selected and motivated fan groups and the practices of everyday viewers. By placing so much focus upon fans, cultural media studies has been characterized (or caricatured) as arguing that all audiences actively "poach" and "produce" following the fan model — we must remember that the particular audience constituted by fan studies is much more exceptional than representative of everyday practices. Nevertheless, the analysis of fan practices, especially as active participants in creating generic discourses, provides an important reminder that audiences do engage in media consumption relationally, negotiating with what they are given via texts and industries.

Another issue signaled by the work on fan cultures and interpretive communities concerns methodological access to the audience. While traditional mass communication models have accessed the audience via experimental and quantitative methods designed to scientifically "know" practices of reception and media effects, cultural studies approaches have tended toward an approach to audience research generally termed "ethnographic."[15] Emerging out of Stuart Hall's encoding/decoding model, qualitative approaches to studying decoding practices undertaken by actual audiences were pioneered by David Morley in Britain and taken up by many American media scholars.[16] This work has examined the processes of reception, arguing for the specific impact of contexts, such as race and class, and fostering a greater understanding of the negotiation practices undertaken by audiences. Perhaps most importantly, this viewer-centered methodology has foregrounded the voices and practices of actual audiences, suggesting the limitations of the scholar's own analysis of the text/context conjuncture.

Despite the important insights that have emerged from ethnographic cultural studies, it is by no means a panacea for audience analysis. A number of problems and limitations plague the ethnographic model, both in theory and practice. Treating the "data" of audience voices is perilous, with a pendulum swinging from empiricist use of this data as "self-evident facts,"[17] to the interpretation of audiences simply reproducing the same assumptions and preconceptions typical of textual analysis.[18] The productive middle ground of contextualized analysis can be more difficult than it appears, leading to a paucity of audience research that lives up to its own methodological and analytical promises. Due to limits of resources and access, the most successful ethnographies tend to focus on quite narrow groups, often examining interpretive communities as defined by categories of viewer identity (like the elderly) or generic taste (like science fiction).[19] While this emphasis on specific groups of audiences and their contexts of viewing can be quite productive, especially in discussing how differences in identity (such as race, gender, age, class, etc.)

impact reception, focusing on bounded communities is not indicative of the general ways in which most media audiences behave. Ethnographic methods are excellent for examining particular groups or individuals in depth, but seem less apt for understanding broader everyday audiences that transect axes of differentiation.

Another key limitation of ethnographic models works against exploring genres as broadly circulating cultural categories. Most of the traditions of audience studies have focused on moments of reception and decoding, following Morley's application of Hall's model by foregrounding the meanings that audience members make during their practices of watching television. While interpretation is certainly an important facet of media research, this model posits a particularly limited conception of the audience as "people watching and interpreting television." This construction of the audience both denies the noninterpretive aspects of being an audience member — affective pleasure, cognitive comprehension, evaluation, and technological practices as some instances — and ignores the aspects of being an audience member outside the activity of watching television. Focusing on interpretation is especially problematic for a nonfiction genre like talk shows, as the interpretive practices typical of fictional narratives seem somewhat out of place for understanding how people engage with talk shows.[20]

For a cultural approach to genre, these limitations are particularly problematic, as interpretation is only one of the three core practices that constitute genres — clearly audiences define and evaluate genres as well as interpret them. Additionally, if a genre is not reducible to the texts that it categorizes, do audiences really "watch genres?" Certainly, audiences watch television shows which are categorized by genres (or *genre television*), and the activity of viewing a program may activate, construct, draw upon, or revise generic categories, but I do not believe *television genres* should be viewed as "objects of reception." Thus, audience studies of genres as cultural categories must look beyond the specific moment of television reception. Audiences use and constitute genres outside the moments they watch television — to fully account for audience generic practices, we would need to access everyday conversations ("I don't let my son watch cop shows"), reflections on previous viewing ("Did you see that new reality show?"), applications of genre categories to nontextual objects ("My life is like a soap opera!"), and many other processes that bring genres outside the limited moment of reception. Additionally, genre categories are often used by people who are not members of the viewing audience for the given genre — the derogatory use of genre terms like "soap opera" and "cartoony" often stem from people who reject the genre as an object of media consumption. This applies for the case of talk shows as well, because the genre's "trashy" incarnation has been widely condemned by critics and commentators who refuse to join in the genre's audience. Thus, if ethnography is to explain audience uses of genre categories, we must revise ethnographic models to more broadly construct what audience (and nonaudience) practices might serve as the object of study.[21]

Since genres transcend the bounds of media texts, audience analyses must look more broadly at audience practices as more than just reception. Genres are not just an aspect of textual decoding or interpretation — genres include discourses of definition and evaluation, as well as interpretation. We cannot witness the moment of audiences engaging with a television genre, like we might watch them watching a text, as genres are widespread cultural phenomena that are not discrete or bounded like media texts. We need to explore the use of genres outside moments of reception, as media genres circulate and operate even as audiences are not watching television. While textual and contextual cues provide particular limitations and preferences framing how audiences use generic categories, the cultural lives of audiences can never be reduced to the intersection of social context and texts without exploring the actual practices of real viewers. To explore how we might study actual audiences and their use of genre categories, I turn to an examination of the conjuncture between the talk show genre, taste hierarchies, and issues of social identity.

The primary question I explore is "how do audiences use the generic category of the talk show?" Under that broad goal, a number of more specific questions arise: How do audiences define the talk show genre? What interpretations do they foreground in understanding the talk show? What cultural evaluations and hierarchies do audiences draw upon? What other assumptions and linkages does the generic cluster contain for audiences? How do categories of social identity relate to the talk show genre and its audience? How do audiences view the talk show genre in relation to other genres? What intrageneric divisions, categories, and hierarchies do audiences construct? How do audiences locate particular programs within this generic framework? How do presumptions about the talk show audience itself intersect with these generic assumptions? These questions are certainly too broad and wide ranging to be able to answer comprehensively in a single chapter, but through a brief foray into audience analysis, we can explore a range of audience generic practices concerning this contested genre. Throughout the analysis, I focus on how audience practices work to define, interpret, and evaluate the generic *category* of the talk show, not focusing on audience reception of *programs* that might be categorized as talk shows, as is more typical in the audience research on the genre.[22]

Talk shows are particularly useful to study in this context for two central reasons. First, it is a broadly defined genre, comprising a number of subgenres like the political talk show, celebrity interview show, morning chat program, and, most notoriously, daytime "trash" talk show. Thus, the talk show offers a strong example of intrageneric politics and practices — audiences differentiate within the genre in addition to comparing talk shows to other categories. Secondarily, when this research was first conducted in 1999, talk shows were the most notorious "bad genre" on television, actively vilified across the political spectrum for its low cultural values and deleterious social impacts. As explored in Chapter 2, looking at genres at moments of cultural crisis can elicit more useful discourses to analyze, both in quantity and vehemence. Since this research was conducted, this crisis has passed, as reality television and videogames have emerged as more scorned forms of television — although talk shows have yet to be rehabilitated. Generic crises are cyclical, as quiz shows in the 1940s and 1950s, cartoons in the early 1990s, and various moments in soap opera history clearly demonstrate. However dated the views on talk shows explored here may be, they offer a vital snapshot of a complex genre in cultural practice, with many tendencies and assumptions that can be extended to other "bad" generic categories.

As suggested throughout, genre categories consist of discourses of generic definition, interpretation, and evaluation. This last category seems to be a crucial issue for genre audiences, as hierarchies between programs and genres are one of the primary ways in which television viewers situate themselves in relation to media texts and their own social locations. Generic hierarchies and evaluations are often tied directly to axes of differentiation in terms of cultural identity of viewers — as explored in Chapter 3, the generic shift of cartoons in the 1960s saw a simultaneous shift toward younger audiences and away from discourses of quality. The cultural stigmatization of soap operas — starting with the genre's name itself — has been directly linked to the perception that it is a "woman's genre."[23] Differences in cultural identity have been an important topic of genre studies in recent years — witness the countless books and articles using the etymologically linked dyad "genre and gender." Thus, to explore the connections between cultural identity and genre audiences, I examine how generic hierarchies and evaluations become linked to social differences between audience members, both in viewing practices and perceived assumptions about genre audiences.

Genre hierarchies and evaluations are directly tied to notions of taste. As a number of influential cultural histories have demonstrated, categories of high and low culture are not universally grounded in aesthetics, but have their roots in social power and contingent historical forces.[24] The writings of French sociologist Pierre Bourdieu have been central to questioning and denaturalizing notions of taste and aesthetics within contemporary cultural studies, arguing that taste is not a universal component of aesthetics, but rather a historically grounded cultural practice that both reproduces and produces social systems and hierarchies.[25] Thus, taste is viewed, not just as socially situated (e.g., the educated rich have better taste than the uneducated poor), but as socially situating, a constantly mobile practice that reinscribes and constitutes the very divisions where it seems to be located and natural. An excellent example of this process comes from Radway's study of romance readers — she explores how an interpretive community posits their own specific rules and conventions concerning the genre's definition and evaluation to legitimize their own pleasures within social hierarchies. Her readers specifically dismissed books they deemed pornographic, while valuing historical romances for their educational function. Both the anti-pornographic and pro-education priorities of these audience members work to defend and elevate the worth of romances, opposing the genre's marginalized cultural location, especially in the eyes of the readers' husbands. By valuing books that, even though they are widely disparaged as "trash," can be compared favorably to "more trashy" books (such as pornographic or noneducational ones), readers maintain their own sense of cultural worth in the face of mainstream devaluation of their favorite hobby.[26] This practice of generic evaluation works through an intrageneric hierarchy of taste that reiterates the naturalized (yet historically contingent) dismissal of pornography and celebration of historical fiction.

Bourdieu argues that taste distinctions are also dependent on their contexts, as a given cultural object might be differently located within hierarchies of value depending on the historical moment, the audience's social location, and their way of life, or what he terms the *habitus*.[27] Thus, as discussed in Chapter 3, Warner Brothers cartoons in the early 1960s were culturally regarded as more lowbrow and childish than Hanna-Barbera shows among reviewers and some adult audiences, whereas today animation fans and scholars laud the former and blame the latter for the death of the genre's golden age — a clear case of contingent taste at work. The historical and cultural practices working to constitute genre categories are formative of notions of taste, making hierarchies salient both within and between genres — generic categories are one of the most prevalent means by which audiences discern, discriminate, and distinguish among the vast realm of media products offered by cultural industries.[28] Bourdieu's own empirical analysis of the social distribution and practices of taste within French society suggests that people's tastes — as enacted through the creation and maintenance of categorical distinctions, like genres — are directly correlated with their social identity. For Bourdieu, "classification struggles," whether between axes of social identity or issues of taste, are a primary way people make sense of their own practices and *habitus*, locating themselves via cultural categories. He focuses on two specific axes of differentiation — economic capital (or class) and cultural capital, as specifically tied to level of education. In adapting his model to the contemporary American context, I believe we need to look beyond the dual axes that he uses to map out the entirety of French cultural tastes, especially given the importance of additional axes of differentiation in contemporary American society, such as race, gender, and sexuality. Yet we can import his notion that taste is formed by — and formative of — definitions of cultural identity, as defined by multiple axes, and that categories of identity are imbricated within other cultural categories, such as genres. In examining the talk show, hierarchies and divisions within the genre link directly to notions of viewers' cultural identity, tying practices of televisual taste to generic and identity politics.

The talk show offers a particularly rich case study in linking identity and taste. This very issue became the grist for William Bennett's mill, as Empower America crusaded to "clean up" daytime talk shows in the 1990s — code for shifting the genre to be more in line with a "conservative straight white male" *habitus*.[29] While every genre is constituted by discourses of evaluation concerning quality and taste, the talk show's evaluative discourses actively spilled over into the realm of social values and "bad taste." Thus the genre serves as a ripe site for analyzing evaluative discourses during this cultural moment. These taste discourses are even more filled with cultural meaning through their active articulation to differences in cultural identity, as the daytime issue-oriented talk show was marked as a locale for marginalized voices to express themselves — how might this (alleged) diversity in social representation within talk show texts impact the identity politics of the talk show audience? This particular linkage between generic hierarchies and identity politics is a motivating question for this analysis, looking to explore how representative the accounts of conservative anti-talk-show crusaders were in positing particular generic discourses and locating the genre within a devalued *habitus*.

The talk show genre is a particularly interesting genre to analyze, because it refers to both a shorthand category — daytime issue-oriented programs like *Springer* and *Oprah* — and a broader category of programs distributed throughout the television schedule. I chose to examine the genre broadly, beginning with a generic categorization including any television program that is culturally linked to the genre label "talk show."[30] This decision to look at the genre broadly is partly in response to the scholarly literature on talk shows, which nearly exclusively focuses on the daytime issue-oriented variety of the talk show.[31] Since the term talk show refers to far more than what most academic literature has explored, I wanted to examine how generic definitions, interpretations, and evaluations operate concerning the whole range of television talk shows — do audiences conceive of the category broadly or limited to the daytime incarnation? This broad generic scope also allows me to address intrageneric hierarchies more fully than if with a more narrow definition of the genre. Thus, I look at the genre as inclusively as possible, including all of the types of shows categorized under the generic rubric, from daytime issue-oriented programs like *The Oprah Winfrey Show* (1986–) to late-night celebrity interview shows like *The Late Show with David Letterman* (1982–), from public affairs programs like *Larry King Live* (1985–) to morning "chats" like *Live with Regis and Kathie Lee* (1989–).[32] By conceiving of the genre this broadly, we can see how audiences construct cultural categories out of these diverse programs.

With these goals in mind, how can we best access the cultural practices of audiences surrounding the talk show genre? One viable, and methodologically familiar, option for carrying out this project would be to focus on a particular group via ethnographic methods. Examining how genres operate within specific communities, following the work of Radway, Jenkins, and others, leads to a generic audience portrait favoring depth over breadth, countering my attempt to explore the broad category of talk shows — inclusive definitions of genres work against the exclusive tastes and boundaries typical of generically defined fan cultures.[33] Additionally I was more interested in soliciting a range of opinions from a large cross section of the television audience than looking at in-depth interpretive strategies made accessible by ethnographic studies. If genres are primarily constructed through discursive practices across cultural sites, audience research must gather a broad range of discourses from viewers to see how genre categories are activated and constructed.

To access a broad range of audience discourses, I analyzed talk show audiences via an online survey administered in the fall of 1999. By connecting with my research subjects online, I was able to transcend many of the geographical and temporal boundaries that limit traditional face-to-face ethnography.[34] To generate participation in the survey, I first drew upon the most commonly researched group of social subjects — undergraduate students in introductory courses.[35] This group provided a large number of surveys from a fairly homogenous group — University of Wisconsin students are predominantly white, middle-class, 18 to 22 years old, from the Midwest, and (obviously) share a common educational level.[36] To access a broader range of subjects, I also posted a link to my survey on two USENET newsgroups[37] as well as circulating an e-mail broadly, inviting participation and further distribution via people's e-mail lists. This distribution method took advantage of the "chain-effect" of e-mail, resulting in 76 surveys from both the e-mail and USENET links with more diversity in age, class, region, and education than the student group.[38] Obviously, this sampling did not attempt to achieve a statistically accurate portrait of all talk show audiences, but rather offered sufficient range to suggest some heterogeneity of survey responses, which did certainly emerge.

The sample of audience subjects surveyed was not limited to self-identified talk show viewers. The e-mail solicitation to participants specifically noted, "It doesn't matter whether you watch talk shows or not to participate — I'm just interested in people's perceptions of the genre." This solicitation works against both traditions of media audience studies, with fans and regular viewers as the typical subjects, and common sense — why ask people who don't watch talk shows about the genre? Indeed, as I discuss below, the lack of familiarity with particular programs posed problems for some survey respondents. Yet I purposely chose to survey viewers and nonviewers alike for two main reasons. For one, I wished to disconnect the assumption among viewer-centered studies that *viewing* is the only site of genre audiences — media audiences use generic categories outside the practice of television watching, drawing upon genres in various facets of everyday life, not just in specific reference to viewing a particular text. More importantly, the links between genres and taste are often made most vehemently by people who (actively) do not watch relevant programs within the genre — most of the condemnations of daytime talk shows offered by William Bennett, Empower America, and related commentators were not the taste judgments of regular talk show viewers. Generic categories are often made culturally salient and manifest by people who are not viewers of the genre, but rather use "bad objects" to define their own *habitus* and viewing practices. Evaluative discourses constituting generic categories often come from voices who would be excluded in listening only to actual viewers, and thus an analysis of the genre's cultural circulation would be incomplete without these nonviewers' opinions.

Just as any audience research constitutes a particular understanding of the audience, information-gathering techniques like surveys and interviews directly shape the results that they obtain. While I certainly tried to make my survey as "neutral" as possible, such neutrality is a fiction, as all research methods work to reproduce particular assumptions and tendencies. Thus, in outlining my survey, its limitations are not just caveats impeding desired objectivity, but serve as context for understanding the very specific and unusual discourses that form the "results." The link to the online survey led directly to a consent form. While most of this material simply followed Human Subjects requirements, it also provided a specific framework for subjects to enter into the survey:

> In this research, we are gathering information about peoples' opinions about television talk shows. You will be asked to provide some information about yourself and to answer a series of questions concerning your thoughts about some television talk shows.

By framing the research as interested in "thoughts" and "opinions," the survey directed participants away from factually accurate or "proper" answers, encouraging their more subjective assumptions and ideas. This position was echoed in the next stage of the survey as well: "The following questions are very open-ended — please write anything you think is relevant or comes to mind. We are just interested in your honest opinions — there are no right or wrong answers!" In inviting subjective impressions, I tried to avoid the common conundrum of participants answering what they think the researchers wish to hear, a tendency I especially feared regarding questions of taste and value surrounding a culturally devalued genre.

After providing demographic information, participants were asked a series of questions about the talk show genre in general, such as "What do you think about talk shows?" and "What qualities are typical of most talk shows?" This section of questions — as well as all steps prior to this section — purposely gave no indications as to a particular definition or scope of the talk show genre, whether it be any program involving talk or the more commonly referenced daytime variety. Obscuring leading generic assumptions as much as possible bettered the chances of accessing whatever associations audiences might link to the broad generic label "talk show" without being led by the survey. Of course, survey questions did help mold the responses received, as the next three questions identified three features designed to elicit evaluative discourses — "Do you think talk shows are entertaining?" "Do you think talk shows are educational?" and "Do you think talk shows are good for society?" with each open-ended question also asking "Why or why not?" These three issues of entertainment, education, and social good are evaluative topics that are common to many genres — all three were evoked in discourses concerning quiz shows in Chapter 2. Additionally, these three issues seem particularly active in the discourses circulating around various debates concerning the legitimacy of talk shows, as typified by Empower America's anti-talk-show movement castigating the genre's entertainment and education values, and labeling them bad for society.[39]

The next question, "What type of person watches the typical talk show?" concerns the perceived construction of the genre's audience, as discriminations between programs and genres often construct a hypothetical vision of who likes and dislikes particular cultural objects. This is particularly key for nonviewers of the genre, as the assumed viewership of talk shows connects to the hierarchies used to condemn the genre's value — whom do anti-talk-show activists believe they are protecting by removing these programs from the air? These assumptions of viewership contrast with participants' own tastes, as accessed with their favorite and least favorite talk shows, as well as their perceptions of what talk shows were "most typical" to the genre. Thus, this portion of the survey gathered responses about audiences' views about the talk show genre as a broad category, allowing their own associations that come to mind when they hear or use the term "talk show" to emerge. I specifically tried to trigger their assumptions related to generic evaluation and definition, examining how they might use the category in their own practices of media consumption and everyday life, even through the artificial mechanism of an online survey.

Once completing this portion of the survey, the questions turned to specific programs. Again the survey invited participants to comment about programs whether they watch the shows or not, as "your opinions based on what you've heard or read are important." A series of repeated questions applied identically to five different programs: *The Late Show with David Letterman*, *The Jerry Springer Show* (1991–), *Live with Regis and Kathie Lee*, *Larry King Live*, and *The Oprah Winfrey Show*. *Oprah* and *Springer* were obvious choices of programs, because they were the most popular and talked-about of the daytime issue-oriented programs at the time of the survey. They also inhabited the edges of the genre's evaluative spectrum, with *Oprah* representing all that is good in day-time talk, and *Springer* as "bad object" incarnate. *Letterman* was chosen as a representative of the late-night celebrity talk show, serving an assumed middle-ground between the college-skewing *Late Night with Conan O'Brien* (1993–) and the more conservative *Tonight Show with Jay Leno* (1992–). I included *Regis & Kathie Lee* as a representative of the more celebrity-oriented daytime talk show, like *The View* (1997–) and *The Rosie O'Donnell Show* (1996–2002), specifically choosing *Regis & Kathie Lee* because of its fairly high-profile stars, especially in the light of the success of *Who Wants to Be a Millionaire* in 1999. Finally, *King* is an example both of the public affairs talk show, like *Crossfire* (1982–) and *Meet the Press* (1947–), and a cable-based program; *King* seemed like a good choice because of the cultural recognition of the host. Other choices could have filled other generic niches, like PBS's highbrow *Charlie Rose Show* (1992–), special topic interview shows like Bravo's *Inside the Actor's Studio* (1994–), or E!'s humorous talk show roundup, *Talk Soup* (1991–2002). While these program choices do not represent the entire breadth of the talk show genre, they provide enough of a range to solicit worthwhile comparisons and evaluative practices within the genre.

The six specific questions repeated for each of the five programs followed those concerning the genre as a whole: general thoughts about each program, whether they considered the program to be a talk show, whether each program was entertaining, educational, and good for society, and finally what type of person watches the show. Thus, for each of the five programs selected, I solicited general opinions, generic definitions, specific evaluations, and hypothetical audiences. The survey did not ask respondents to indicate whether they watched the particular show or how often, because I did not want to suggest more interest in the opinions of regular viewers than perceptions about an unfamiliar program; nonetheless, most respondents who did not watch a particular program, indicated as such in the first question of the section and left the rest unanswered.

This survey produced a host of "data" to be analyzed and interpreted in the discussion of generic audiences. These discourses, enunciations about talk shows from a fairly wide range of people, are audience practices, but it is vital to note that these are not the everyday practices of media audiences. They are highly artificial discourses, both in content — few people answer questions like "do you think *Larry King Live* is good for society?" or "what type of person watches the typical talk show?" in everyday life — and context, as the framework of filling out a survey directly impacts how people characterize their own opinions. Nevertheless, these discourses can offer insights into more common practices, because they stemmed from people's everyday opinions and outlooks. In analyzing this "data" qualitatively, we must avoid suggesting that if enough people say something, it must be generalizable truth. Yet these discourses can tell us more than just what specific people said at a specific time on a specific survey —

we can examine patterns and continuities pointing to crucial ways that genre categories, hierarchies of taste, and social identity all work together to constitute the cultural life of talk shows at a historical moment.

Talking Taste: Audience Discourses and the Use of Cultural Categories

Although genres are not defined by textual elements, cultural practices constituting generic categories through definitional discourses typically focus on textual features. Thus, most participants defined talk shows by typical textual conventions: hosts, panels of guests, interviews, "an involved audience," questions and answers, topical issues, celebrities, "outrageous situations," interpersonal conflicts, debates and arguments, unscripted action, monologues, and most basically, "talking (duh)." Many of the identified qualities were more evaluative as well, pointing to aspects like "trash," sensationalism, shock, superficiality, voyeurism, gossip, tabloid, oddities, lowest common denominator appeals, "manufactured excitement," egotistical hosts, hype, and materialism. Although the survey first asked about the genre in broad terms, many respondents pointed to specific types of talk shows, most notably the daytime "trash talk" variety linked to *Jerry Springer*; people using this categorical framework noted fighting, violence, yelling, exploitation, and "staged behavior" as crucial qualities.

In evaluating and defining the genre as a whole, many respondents referenced the identity of people who appear on talk shows: "immature people," "white trash," "horrible use of the English language," under-educated guests, "trailer trash," "an active but remarkably uninformed audience," "dysfunctional families," "bisexuals," "overweight women," lower-class, "mental cases," and broadly "other types of people — strippers, gays, lesbians and others that most people come in contact with every day." Thus, for many participants, talk shows were notably marked by their inclusion of people who were distinctly unlike both the normal American and themselves, placing talk show participants on the low end of numerous evaluative hierarchies. Some respondents did characterize talk shows as featuring people with "positive" characteristics, primarily in referring to "talented" celebrities, "potential heroes," and "intelligent hosts" featured on programs like *Rosie*, *Letterman*, and *Larry King*. A clear hierarchy emerged concerning the identity of talk show participants — programs highlighting "exceptional" people (celebrities, experts) were more valued than those featuring "everyday" people, who often were stigmatized as marginalized "others" to audiences.

This hierarchical vision of identity carried over to perceived audiences as well. Among the surveys that seemed to equate the broad genre with the daytime talk show, participants characterized typical viewers as bored, lonely, passive, and lazy people with extra free time, mostly female and lower class, and not particularly educated. Some of the more evocative phrases used to describe typical viewers included "unemployed drunks," "people who read little," "stay-at-home moms," "people who are isolated," "people who may have questionable lifestyles," "people with limited means and a dearth of imagination," and people "suffering a mental disability they don't want to admit to." One woman's sweeping overall characterization of "underemployed, overweight, lazy, unimaginative, low energy, narrow minded, low income" viewers typified this general placement of talk show viewers on the low end of most imagined social hierarchies. One male respondent contrasted these presumed viewers with "people who have full lives, who think and read, [who] don't have time to spend watching shows of little value." Of course, these characterizations were not universal among respondents, as many noted that a wide range of people watched talk shows and that the genre was so broad that there were no "typical viewers." Although responses were diverse, this construction of the lowbrow and pathological viewer was quite prevalent, both in this survey and in the contextual discourses circulating around the genre, suggesting the broader relevance of this pattern. Given that many of the participants who castigated talk show audiences claim they do not watch the programs, presumably their construction of the genre's ideal audience at least partially stems from these broader discourses that seek to stigmatize talk show viewers.

Evaluative discourses concerning the perceived values of the genre in considering whether talk shows were entertaining, educational, and good for society followed somewhat similar lines. For participants who took a generally negative view of the genre, the pleasures of the talk show were highly questionable and projected onto social others. One male student suggested, "They're only good if you want the uneducated, perverted and interbred part of society revealed." Detractors admitted that the genre might be entertaining, but "only to the lowest common denominator." This denial of audience pleasure was often articulated to gender, as a male student baldly characterized the genre as "sentimental or superficial fluff that is just a waste of time. And only for women." Respondents also linked generic pleasure to class identity, as one male student noted, "they just give the welfare recipients something to watch when they should be working." One female student simultaneously denied the genre's entertainment pleasures and the audience's taste, calling talk shows "like a pathetic circus where people broadcast their serious personal problems to an audience that finds them to be something to joke about." Another female viewer acknowledged that talk shows "are entertaining, but in a sad way."

A few responses reiterated the common assumption that "trash talk" causes social ills — as one female student wrote, "they actually decrease society's existing morals." However, this position was less frequent than I had expected — given the prevalence of discourses castigating talk shows as degrading society, I anticipated seeing this discourse much more often than I did.[40] Most people felt that assessing the genre's social good was either inappropriate — as one man wrote, "do I think Twinkies are good for society?" — or impossible to gauge. Some participants emphasized the comparative impact of talk shows, noting that, while they might be socially detrimental, "guns, cars, shitty schools, tax loopholes for the rich, etc. are all much less good for society." Respondents often noted that they could not answer such a question for the genre as a whole, or that talk shows were no less socially valuable than television in general, which was seen as a detrimental medium for distracting, pacifying, and commercializing audiences. Even some people who generally dismissed the genre acknowledged that talk shows could be socially valuable, as "they do open people's eyes to the issues of racism and homophobia" and expose viewers to diversity. Thus, while many people questioned the social value of talk shows, few reproduced the virulence of the well-publicized discourses condemning the genre as a central societal ill.

Not all participants took a negative view upon the genre, however; many found talk shows pleasurable. One female student admitted that talk shows could be "degrading," but noted that "it's fun to watch and feel sorry or make fun of the guests." Fans clearly were uncomfortable with their own pleasures in the more outrageous programs, noting "it's a sick sort of entertainment" and that they eventually lost interest as "the educated side of me quickly turns away." Many found the "shock value" of daytime shows entertaining, but expressed concerns for whom the genre was appropriate; one female student noted, "I think that an educated individual can safely view talk shows and not be directly affected. However, an uneducated, and impressionable individual my take a harmful message directly to heart." Many viewers claimed that they watched talk shows with a level of ironic detachment, as one male professional noted, "I enjoy *Springer* for the camp and self-reflexivity of the show." Nearly all people who enjoyed the tabloid brand of talk shows emphasized that they were "for entertainment only." One female student noted, "it's like any other sitcom," drawing a generic parallel to the more socially validated, entertainment-centered, and explicitly fictional category. In general, viewers characterized tabloid talk shows as providing entertainment primarily through camp pleasures and detached amusement, rather than offering any deeper emotional, mental, or political engagement, as is often claimed by some of the genre's defenders.

Those viewers who appreciated the genre's "trashiness" for entertainment generally did not claim any educational value, except "perhaps they educate us on how NOT to act," or as one woman noted, "seeing them usually boosts my drive to not be like them." Some fans of the genre noted that the more "sleazy" programs could be educational when they "showcase alternate lifestyles and value systems" and feature diverse voices, because "you get to see an interesting mix of the human population that you otherwise may not see." While a few participants noted that "any show exercising the freedom of speech is good," most talk show viewers who defended talk shows made no claims for the genre's general educational or social values aside from entertainment. Just as participants failed to reproduce the strident anti-talk-show rhetoric offered by Empower America and other highly public voices, the pro-talk show viewers in my survey did not support the scholarly arguments that the genre represents a democratic public sphere or a vital site of diverse representation.[41] Both sides of this critical debate need to take a more careful look at how everyday people actually use the generic category of "talk show," examining what assumptions they bring to their audience practices, before either condemning or celebrating the genre as a whole. From the overall lack of either positive or negative responses to questions of the genre's social good, it seems that most viewers do not use such political frameworks to understand the way they and other audiences engage with talk shows, a response countering many of the claims of cultural studies analysis of media audiences.[42]

In discussing the genre as a broad category, many viewers distinguished between different programs and types of talk shows. The most common distinction was between programs focusing on "public interest" and "important issues," typified by *Oprah* and *The Montel Williams Show* (1991–), and those focusing on more outrageous and "fake" situations, like *Springer* and *Ricki Lake* (1993–). While the latter programs were noted as "just entertainment," respondents suggested that the former shows had educational and social values by bringing up serious issues; this intrageneric distinction often was tied to evaluative terms like "good," "quality," "legitimate," or "informative" shows versus "tabloid trash." Not surprisingly, these hierarchies were often tied to cultural differences, primarily in terms of class and education level — the assumed audience and guests for the tabloid programs were far more uneducated, lower class, and "deviant" than *Oprah*'s audience and guests. As discussed below, the broader assumptions people linked to the talk show genre fractured when confronted with specific programs, offering a vision into the intrageneric landscape of the talk show.

While many participants took the broad category of "talk show" to stand in for a particular type of program, some people explicitly questioned the use of such a sweeping categorical label. In designing the survey, I purposely kept the first portion vague as to what was meant by a "talk show," hoping to bring forth people's own definitions and assumptions associated with the generic term. Many responses noted that there were multiple types of talk shows, denying the vagueness of the generic label by identifying specific subcategories, such as "celebrity," "late-night," "daytime," "issue-oriented," "freak shows," "sensationalistic," "tabloid," "Sunday-morning wonk-fests," "current events," "informative," "entertainment," "comedy," "gossipy," and "confrontational." As a genre, the talk show seems to operate as a less homogenous and uniform cultural category than I presumed before embarking on this project, pointing toward the need to examine generic categories as they are used by audiences, not just by scholars, industries, and critics.

In the second portion of the survey, I wished to fragment any homogenous conception of the talk show category by introducing particular programs spanning the breadth of the genre. While certainly this did "work" for many participants, a large number of responses had previously conceptualized the genre as a fragmented and divided category. But in charting out assumptions tied to particular programs, some broader hierarchies and assumptions emerge as mapped onto the various facets of the talk show generic cluster. The first specific program mentioned was *Letterman* as representative of the late-night talk show, a popular type of program, which is usually absent in the popular (and scholarly) discourses circulating around talk shows. Many respondents did classify the program as a talk show, acknowledging such definitional features such as guests, a host, interviews, conversations about relevant issues, "based around reality," and being "informative and entertaining." Among those who classified it as a talk show, many noted that while it fit the genre, it was different from how they had defined the genre in the first part of the survey, where they based their answers on daytime programs. These respondents differentiated between the typical daytime program and *Letterman* as a "subcategory" of late-night talk shows, which were "classier," less motivated by "spectacle," and more focused on "entertainment" and "Hollywood" than "everyday people." Some respondents claimed that *Letterman* was not a talk show, as it did not air during daytime, did not focus on one particular issue, featured primarily celebrities, did not present people's problems or feature confrontation, or aimed at a different audience than typical talk shows. Some of the alternative generic labels offered by participants included "variety show," "interview show," "entertainment show," "guest star show," and "comedy."

In evaluating *Letterman*, most respondents acknowledged that the show was entertaining, or at least attempted to be. People had generally positive opinions about the show, although a number of respondents noted that it has gone downhill or they have stopped watching it. No distinct patterns emerged as to what type of viewer disliked the program, although some of the older respondents explicitly noted that they hated it. People who found the program entertaining generally thought it was funny, creative, witty, clever, and featured enjoyable guests and musical acts; those who thought it was not entertaining found it boring, repetitive, offensive, annoying, or mean, although no one claimed that the show was not at least attempting to primarily entertain. Almost no one felt that the show was particularly educational, save for some who felt the jokes about the news or keeping people abreast of celebrity projects and gossip could be informative to some audiences, but nearly all respondents answered that the show's primary goal was entertainment. As suggested above, many respondents balked at assessing the genre's social value; in trying to assess whether *Letterman* was good for society, most subjects took a neutral position, as it neither helped nor hurt people, or reiterated that "it's just a TV show" and thus had little social impact. Some participants noted that entertaining people and making them laugh was good for society, encouraging people to "lighten up" about "important" social issues. In noting that the show was not socially detrimental, a number of people mentioned its time slot, as "it's on late enough that children can't watch it," suggesting differing social standards for various schedules and potential audiences.

The survey suggested that people envisioned *Letterman* appealing to a fairly broad audience of adults. Some older respondents specifically felt that the show appealed to a college-aged audience, although some students felt that the show appealed to "old people because [Letterman] is old himself." Many participants felt the show was aimed at a fairly sophisticated audience, middle-class with a college education, and predominantly white — as one "bi-racial" male student wrote, "it's intellectual humor that I feel would turn off minorities." Some respondents suggested that the show appealed to those who could appreciate "a New York dry wit," with the regional locale seemingly indicating a degree of sophistication. A number of surveys suggested that the show appealed particularly to male viewers, although many felt it had cross-gender appeal. In general, the profile of *Letterman* painted by the survey was of a "quality" show that did not fit in with the broader conception of the talk show genre, although typical of its late-night incarnation. This format was primarily based on entertainment, offering a fairly sophisticated and positive program for a broad "quality" audience. This picture contrasted with other programs within the survey.

While most respondents both were familiar with and enjoyed *Letterman*, surveys indicated *Regis & Kathie Lee* as a more marginal program. Many people noted that they were unfamiliar with the show, electing not to answer most of the questions — this unfamiliarity was probably tied to the show's morning timeslot and its incompatibility with the prevalent student and professional schedules of my participants. Most respondents who did know the program thought it was a talk show, with the requisite features of hosts, guests, interviews, live audience, and issue-driven topics; a typical comment noted that "they talk so damn much it has to be a talk show." Even though most people felt it was a talk show, it was rarely mentioned in participants' lists of favorite, least favorite, or typical talk shows. Those who felt it was not a talk show followed the criteria used in defining *Letterman*, as they called it a "celebrity show" or "interview show," or labeled it a "good morning show" along the lines of *The Today Show* (1952–). Most respondents who liked the program were female and older, although a fair number of both college students and men admitted to enjoying the show. Negative opinions about *Regis & Kathie Lee* were more virulent than for *Letterman*, as many surveys called the show boring, grating, cloying, annoying, insipid, intolerable, horrible, and painful. Many participants directed their ire at

the hosts, calling them offensive, loathsome, tedious, obnoxious, "cancer to intelligence," and "two of the most irritating people in the world" — as one colorful cross-generic response suggested, "seeing Kathie Lee's head squashed
between two anvils, Warner Bros. cartoon-style, might be entertaining."

Like with *Letterman*, most participants felt that *Regis & Kathie Lee* was at
least intended primarily to entertain audiences. While many felt the show was
not entertaining because of the hosts, the basic "interview and banter" format
was seen as trying to entertain. Those who found the program enjoyable highlighted the show's interesting and diverse guests, amusing rapport between
Regis and Kathie Lee, and commitment to "wholesome," "clean" material and
"good taste." People did find the show fairly educational, as it presented valuable information on health issues, cooking and "do-it-yourself" projects, "street
smarts," and current events, as well as Hollywood gossip and celebrity guests
like on *Letterman*. As one female student who had not watched the show "in
ages" wrote, "I picture them as one of the 'high-brow' shows." Fans of *Regis &
Kathie Lee* primarily emphasized the show's entertainment values, but many felt
that it was good for society, in promoting "values," including religious themes,
"portraying positive images," and informing people about events and issues. As
one female student wrote, "children can actually watch without worrying what
impression it will have on them." The show's strong detractors denied any educational and social value in the program, again primarily due to negative feelings toward the hosts, but many people who did not like the program seemed
more willing to grant that the show may be educational or socially valuable than
the common "just entertainment" refrain concerning *Letterman*.

The assumed audience for *Regis & Kathie Lee* was fairly homogenous —
most respondents suggested that viewers were "older," female, and middle-class.
Some (often derogatory) terms used to characterize the show's audience included "stay-at-home moms," "housewives," "soccer-mom types," the "soap
opera crowd," "middle aged or older," "retired persons," "my grandma," "maybe
some homosexual men," an "older more conservative audience," "people with
positive attitudes," "women involved deeply with religion," "single, middle-aged
Jewish women," "housewives over 180 lbs," and "lonely middle-aged women
who drink scotch in the morning." While many of the people who acknowledged that they enjoyed the program did not fit this profile, the surveys suggested that audiences imagine a narrowly-defined audience for this program,
far more so than for any of the other programs mentioned. Those who condemned the program questioned the taste of this presumed audience, wonder-
ing "who can tolerate" the hosts. Clearly both detractors and fans of this
program use markers of cultural identity concerning gender, class, age, education, and social values, to distinguish themselves from one another.

Even more than with *Regis & Kathie Lee*, *Larry King Live* prompted many
people, especially college students, to claim little or no knowledge of the

program. This was partly because it was the only nonbroadcast program on the survey — a number of responses mentioned they did not have access to cable or satellite. Additionally, although *King* often gets press when he features high-profile guests, the show is never activated within the discourses surrounding talk show controversies and thus rarely circulates outside the realm of CNN watchers. Most people who were familiar with the program felt it fit into the talk show genre, although some suggested that because the show did not actively incorporate an audience into the "talk" (not mentioning the call-in format), it was more of a strict "interview program." People suggested other generic terms, like "news," "journalism," "current events forum," "politics," and "call-in" show. Many participants noted a distinction between *King*'s mode of talk show from the more commonplace daytime form — one professional man favorably wrote, "Larry's show is the old school or first generation talk show where issues instead of personalities are important." Those who liked *King*, mostly older respondents, described the show as "intelligent," "informational," "relevant," "useful," and "respectable," while people who disliked the program complained about King's "self-serving" personality, "softball questions," "boring" topics and guests, and "biased" viewpoints.

Compared to the other talk shows discussed in the survey, fewer people found the program entertaining. Those who did highlight its entertainment value noted that this was primarily due to particular guests, especially when the show featured celebrities rather than political figures, although some felt "news and current events can be entertaining." Many people felt that the show provided an educational function, as it brought up "serious issues" and examined them carefully — as one female professional noted in comparing it to other talk shows, "he doesn't merely present an emotional response to an issue, but a more thoughtful, well-argued one." While some detractors condemned the show's educational effectiveness as "too facile and shallow" in presenting issues, almost all respondents who knew the show believed that *King* was at least trying to be informative in a journalistic tradition. In striving for informing viewers and debating issues, many participants thought the program was good for society, especially as compared with other talk shows — as one man noted, *King* "relays good, more reliable information and viewpoints than daytime talk shows."

The perceived audience for *King* fit with the perception of a "serious" program and, thus, was significantly different from the assumed average talk show audience. Many people noted that people who watched *King* were not talk show fans, but "news junkies," "political nerds," and "people who can't stand sitcoms." Terms used to describe this audience included "educated," "well-informed," "intellectual," "learned folk," "mature," "high-brow," "not concerned with being entertained," "more conservative," "people who like to hear truth," and "the opposite of a *Jerry Springer* viewer." Like with other programs, respondents who disliked the show castigated the perceived audience, using phrases like "the

Florida crowd that eats dinner at 4 p.m." and "boring people — probably golfers — golfers who talk about their golf scores." The cultural identity of this assumed audience was fairly homogenous — white, middle to upper-class, well-educated, middle-aged and older, and professional or retired. While respondents who liked the program were fairly gender balanced, the presumed audience was predominantly labeled male by many surveys. One male student, who admitted never seeing the show but respecting it nonetheless, characterized the audience quite baldly as "the doctor, the investment banker, the political analyst — the man. It is a show that involves politics, and women are not a part of that world." Thus, the cultural assumptions linked to *King* associated the program with a particularly respectable *habitus* — professional, educated, male, wealthy, white — and opposed this program with more entertainment-centered talk shows, from *Letterman* to *Springer*.

The two remaining programs on the survey represent the yin and yang of the daytime talk show, with *Oprah* culturally associated with almost all values that *Springer* is not — except high ratings, as the two programs were neck-in-neck in viewers at the time of the survey.[43] Nearly all respondents felt that *Springer* was in fact a talk show, with many suggesting that it was the epitome of the genre or "exactly what I think of as a 'talk show.'" Those who felt it was not a talk show accused the program of being "staged" or "fake," violating the impromptu authenticity that many noted as a core generic feature. Some people offered other generic labels, such as "trash show," "fighting show," "junk," "a white trash extravaganza," "a carnival show for weirdoes," "a circus of idiots," "the Christians and the lions," and "a comedy." Although most people labeled *Springer* as a talk show, most noted that it was a particularly extreme or troublesome variant of the genre; as one male student wrote, "I think Jerry Springer took the term 'talk show,' conquered it, and twisted it to his own ends." Thus, many respondents acknowledged that the program was both the "typical" talk show and at the low end of intrageneric hierarchies.

Not surprisingly, most of the respondents expressed extreme opinions about *Springer*. In offering their opinions about the program, people used terms such as "abominable," "awful," "despicable," "repugnant," "terrible," "revolting," "perverted," "crap," "tasteless," "absolutely hate it," "an insulting waste of time," "an embarrassment," "downright destructive," "crude and irresponsible," "I wish it were outlawed," and "the biggest piece of trash in the history of television." In contrast to these extreme condemnations, some respondents did admit that they enjoyed the program, primarily noting that it was entertaining, funny, outrageous, and "good wholesome, white-trash fun." Among those who liked *Springer*, nobody suggested that they read the program "straight," as a representation of real people solving real problems — a more typical pleasure was "it is funny watching people that are that dumb." Fans noted that they enjoyed watching the fights, people yelling at each other, and the ridiculousness of the situations, with no presumed educational or social value. Many participants, especially college students, mentioned that they used to find the program entertaining, but that it had gotten repetitive, predictable, and more "tame."

More than any other show in my survey, the values and audiences associated with *Springer* diverged based on participants' opinions about the program. Unlike the talk show genre as a whole, nearly nobody claimed that the show was intended to be educational or socially beneficial, although many respondents who condemned the program did take direct offense at its lack of social values. Many detractors felt that the show encouraged violence, poor morality, exploitation, and low cultural standards, explicitly labeling it as bad for society — much more so than the genre as a whole. People who hated *Springer* and castigated its demoralizing effects offered a particular vision of the show's audience which was distinctly unlike themselves — lower-class, uneducated, unemployed, racial minorities, "redneck trailer park trash from Arkansas," "wrestling fans," "idiots," "slobs," "sad sick puppies," and "people that eventually end up on the show." Interestingly, many people felt that the guests featured were actors and "fake," but also perceived that the guests typified the average audience member.

People who admitted to enjoying the program painted a different picture of its values and audience. Fans expressly denied that the show was attempting to do anything but entertain and shock audiences, suggesting that the producers were "in on the joke." While some fans noted that the show featured people not represented on other television programs, they claimed that *Springer* did not showcase these people to educate or promote diversity, but just for entertainment value. For people who enjoyed the program, the perceived audience was much more like themselves — college students, young, middle-class, and "people who have nothing better to do with their time, like me!!!" Thus, while detractors of the show thought the audience was uneducated, fans conceived of the audience as educated college students like themselves. The ways audiences watched the program were also divergent; one participant, who was "embarrassed" to admit he watched the show, suggested that the show's viewers fell into "two kinds — those that like to make fun of it and those that are genuinely entertained." But the responses from people who were "genuinely entertained" by the program also made fun of it, regarding their own enjoyment ironically and with a degree of camp. Some audiences might read the program more "straight" than the people accessed in this survey (possibly due to limitations in my sample), but within the audience discourses gathered, the only people who took the program seriously were those who condemned it, projecting this "sincere" spectatorship onto a hypothetical audience on the cultural margins.[44]

While *Springer* resided at the bottom of nearly all cultural hierarchies — even among fans who acknowledged the show as a "guilty pleasure" — *Oprah* was hailed as the generic exception. In the survey's first section, many participants decried the genre's "trashy" values and tone, with the common caveat of "aside from *Oprah.*" In discussing *Oprah* directly, these positive evaluations continued, as many participants offered comments like "the nonscummy daytime talk show" and "a breath of fresh air in the 'talk show' circuit!" Fans of the program, who predictably skewed more female in my survey, noted that it was "respectable," "informative," "not mindless," "upbeat," "classy," "truly inspiring," and "aimed at improving people's lives." Respondents who disliked the program called it "sappy," "too feminine," "manipulative," "bourgeois," "self-centered," and "over-commercialized," often castigating the "cult-like" worship Winfrey fostered in her audiences. Nearly everyone categorized *Oprah* as a talk show, although many noted that it was distinct from the genre as a whole in being less "trashy" and more "positive." A few people suggested that it had turned into more of a "self-help program," but many felt that it was the "prototype" or "avatar" of the talk show genre.

In assessing the values of the program, respondents seemed to be fairly balanced in viewing the program as entertaining, educational, and good for society. While those who disliked the program generally suggested that it was not entertaining, many detractors did find it educational and socially valuable, noting aspects like Oprah's book club promoting reading and Oprah calling attention to important social issues. As one male student wrote, "even though Oprah is not my bag, she is an avid promoter of education, self improvement, reading, etc." Another male student who did not like the show suggested that educationally, "as far as talk shows go it is pretty good." Some virulent opponents of the program claimed the show had negative social values, like one male student who claimed, "I feel she is being racist towards white men everywhere." Yet most people found the show to contribute positively to society in fostering education and literacy, addressing social issues, providing positive role models for minorities, and promoting and raising money for important causes. In trumpeting these particular values, many respondents explicitly suggested *Oprah*'s social good as an unusual and atypical feature for the rest of the talk show genre and television in general.

In constructing the typical audience for *Oprah*, respondents suggested that viewers were predominantly women (as a female student wrote, "It's a chick show without question"), middle-class, more African-American than most talk shows, and "a more literate group than the morons who watch *Jerry Springer.*" However, many participants noted that *Oprah* appealed to much broader demographics than most programs, offering qualitative assessments of the audience, like "goodhearted and emotional people," "what some might call *decent people*," or as one "male housewife" wrote, "anyone who wants to see the beauty that is still in this world." Those who disliked the program, especially younger men, questioned the show's audience, noting "she seems to have some sort of brainwashing ability on women" and typifying her audience as "fat old women." Most of the participants characterized *Oprah* as "higher quality" than other talk shows, suggesting that its appeals were more "legitimate" and socially worthwhile than the genre as a whole. In this way, audience usage of the talk show genre is similar to many of the dismissive public discourses, condemning the daytime talk show as a whole "except for *Oprah*."

What are we to make of the various discursive practices documented in this survey research? Certainly they "prove" nothing on their own — the comments gathered are neither representative of all audiences nor indicative of how generic categories operate within people's everyday lives. As actual discursive practices, this survey is admittedly suspect, both in its decontextualized posing of guiding generic questions and its representation of talk show audiences (and nonviewers). Yet in conjunction with other research analyzing talk show audiences, particularly more detailed ethnographic work and more broad contextual analyses, patterns and hierarchies of taste emerge that are formative of the talk show as a cultural category. We can see how people use broad generic categories, as well as subsets of a genre, to make sense of media texts, their assumed audiences, and perceived social impacts — respondents repeatedly tried to situate each individual program within the context of the talk show genre and its associated cultural assumptions. Within the genre, intrageneric hierarchies of value and definition help situate viewers' own preferences, linking people's taste to broader cultural values and assumptions.

Although I did not gather enough material to be able to map out the full cultural landscape of the talk show genre, per Bourdieu's own research, we can see how generic distinctions form a crucial component in differentiating people's tastes and locations within larger social structures of identity. While this research cannot offer definitive conclusions for the cultural operation of the talk show genre at large, a number of significant patterns may be instructive and provide correctives for the bulk of literature on the genre. Clearly, while many people did link a number of generic assumptions to the term "talk show," they did not equate the generic pronouncements with all types of programming categorized by the genre — most people who condemned the genre as a whole, made "exceptions" for one particular program or subgenre. Viewers actively mapped generic pleasures of programs they dislike onto presumed audiences of "others," whether they be lower-class *Springer* fans or female *Regis* viewers — audience members rarely condemned a program while describing its typical audience as people like themselves. Within the genre, numerous hierarchies of high versus low cultural value were used to justify both admiration and condemnation of most programs, as notions of entertainment seemed most variable with people's tastes. Of the programs mentioned, only *Springer* produced a "serious" level of concern for its social values and effects, although people who actually watched the show took it much less seriously than viewers who boycotted the program outright. Finally, viewers did not generally seem swayed by the publicized debates over the genre's social values, as they were reluctant to praise or condemn talk shows with similar vigor heard within high-profile discourses surrounding the genre's social value and appropriateness. Clearly a broad genre like the talk show enters into nearly every cultural *habitus* within American society, yet we need to study how the genre operates within people's lives much more specifically than through sweeping generic assessments or condemnations that typify the literature, both popular and scholarly, about the genre.

Methodologically, this study points to some important issues concerning media audience research. Being an audience member extends beyond the time spent in front of the television, as people use genre categories and other televisual concepts in many aspects of their everyday lives. The emphasis within media audience studies upon the specific act of reception limits the possible paths that audience analysis might take, particularly in the intersection between television and broader cultural practices. Looking at how genre categories circulate outside the act of watching television itself is one such way of broadening our conception of what it means to be media audience members and what methods are available to understand these complex social phenomena. While the turn toward the audience within media studies has produced important analyses and correctives, we are nowhere close to arriving at a complete or definitive methodology to explore the complex, diverse, and wide-ranging practices that fall under the rubric of television audiences. This survey is by no means a comprehensive or fully successful way to consider audiences — it has been a useful, but limited, tool for answering some of the particular questions I set out to address. Only by looking at the complex phenomenon of audiences from complementary angles using multiple methods can we envision a more robust and multidimensional picture of how people engage with media, both in the act of watching television and in the broader contexts of everyday life.

For the study of media genres, we must consider audiences not just as an afterthought, but as an integral site of media practice where genres operate as cultural categories, alongside and in conjunction with texts, industries, and broader historical contexts. Clearly, my survey demonstrates that at least some audience members use genre categories in diverse ways that directly contradict the assumptions made by the television industry, powerful critics, social institutions, and media scholars. Genres are an important facet of being an audience member, as genres form a "horizon of expectations" providing a framework for media reception. But audiences do not simply take genres as given — they engage in discursive practices that work to constitute the various assumptions of definition, interpretation, and evaluation that form genres as cultural categories. Only by studying these discursive practices themselves can we hope to understand the full scope of any given genre and appreciate the central role that audiences play within media culture. Of course, audience practices are not the singular defining site of media analysis — the practices constituting media genres run through industries, audiences, and finally texts, the site I turn to now in Chapter 5.

5
Policing Genres — *Dragnet*'s Texts and Generic Contexts

Thus far, I have explored how television genres operate in cultural sites atypical of most genre studies — policy decisions concerning quiz shows, scheduling and branding of cartoons, and audience discourses about talk shows. Additionally, these three genres necessitate a different approach than film-based models of narrative-driven genre analysis, either because their form lacks a narrative center (in the case of quiz shows and talk shows) or because their genre category is defined primarily by technology rather than narrative form or content (in the case of animation). Yet television texts remain important elements in the cultural practices of genres, and traditional narrative genres remain central for television. Thus, for the final two chapters, I turn to media texts as the anchoring site of genre analysis, looking at two genres that are more typical of narrative-driven media: police drama and situation comedy. As this chapter's case study of *Dragnet*'s generic practices looks to demonstrate, we can place the media text at the center of genre analysis without recreating the textualist assumption that marks traditional approaches to genre.

One of the unfortunate byproducts of the simultaneous development of television scholarship and cultural studies is that formal attributes of television texts have been given little scholarly attention. Part of this anti-formal shift stems from the particular emphasis placed on the decoding side of Stuart Hall's formative encoding/decoding model — while Hall emphasizes the importance of both encoding and decoding, scholars have adopted his model primarily by emphasizing the long-neglected latter part of the dyad.[1] Influential early explorations of television cultural studies, such as John Fiske's *Television Culture*, did explore issues of textual form and encoding processes, but the lasting influence of this work stemmed more from Fiske's innovative approaches to active audiences and decoding.[2] While cultural media scholars turned to both reception practices and cultural contexts in the 1990s, questions of textual structure were generally relegated to a formalist position within film studies. Although many formal analyses produced under this often-historical approach to film texts were quite productive, the neo-formalist school explicitly bracketed off the film text as object of study and eschewed larger political and cultural questions as outside its analytic purview.[3] Thus, the methodological divide between cultural and formal approaches clearly ceded the ground of textual form to formalists, with most television scholars abandoning questions of form in lieu of other concerns.[4]

Yet I believe we might examine form without being formalists — studying form does not have to be an end unto itself. Since cultural approaches to media studies have suggested that texts are one of the important sites in which meanings are made and political processes are played out, it behooves us to engage closely with textual practices to understand how texts are encoded, both industrially and formally. The formal analysis of media texts can — and should — be one of the most productive tools available to examine the processes that constitute our cultural field of analysis. We can move beyond formal analysis as a closed exercise without abandoning the insights that such examinations might provide. One such model, which has not received adequate consideration by cultural television scholars, is David Bordwell's approach of historical poetics, situating formal practices of media-making within explicit historical contexts of production and reception.[5] By looking at *Dragnet* via a historical poetic analysis to examine how cultural meanings and assumptions were encoded in the program, we can see how these textual elements fit into larger cultural and generic categories.

How might we integrate formal analysis into a cultural approach to genres? Formal techniques are often explicitly linked to the cultural categories of genres; for instance (as explored in Chapter 3), the limited animation techniques of the television cartoon were actively tied to the formation of the Saturday morning incarnation of the genre. The relationship of formal attributes to generic categories is not directly causal — the development of limited animation was not the primary stimulus in changing the genre's cultural value and definition. Yet, clearly, formal techniques are one of the potential practices incorporated into a generic cluster at a given historical moment. Thus, in looking at *Dragnet*, we can see how certain production techniques and visual elements that had been linked with the documentary film genre were explicitly activated and reincorporated into the context of the television police drama, highlighting these formal attributes as key elements of historical generic clustering.

The other common mode of textual genre analysis that has remained prevalent within media studies is interpretation. Often buttressed by a number of theoretical paradigms, such as psychoanalysis, Marxism, structuralism, and feminism, a common mode of television scholarship offers a detailed "reading" of a media text for the meanings that are encoded within the program.[6] Although I have argued against interpretation of genre texts as a mode of genre analysis, textual interpretations can play an important role in a larger project. Just as we might look at how various cultural practices circulate media meanings, from industrial memos to audience fan fiction, media texts themselves are clearly important sites where meanings are articulated and potentially activated into larger cultural circulation. Following contextually centered models of interpretation, like Stanley Fish's model of interpretive communities and Tony Bennett and Janet Woollacott's notion of reading formations, as discussed in Chapter 4, meaning can be viewed as formed through the culturally specific interplay of texts, audiences, producers, and contexts.[7] Thus, in turning to *Dragnet*, I consider what meanings are activated by the text, but only in context — textual interpretations are not close analyses produced through a theoretical lens, but discussions of meanings that circulated within both the texts and contexts constituting *Dragnet*. For instance, *Dragnet* points toward the importance of structuralist interpretation, not in embodying core dualities that are universally grounded in either American culture or the police genre, but as a specific activation of certain binary oppositions that had relevant historical meanings in 1950s America. Thus, interpreting a generic text need not be an end itself, but should be part of a more thorough analysis of how texts operate culturally and historically, activating larger circulating discourses and meanings using the categorical shorthand of genres.

Following my cultural approach to television genres, generic texts function as one important site in which we can see the active clustering of generic assumptions. One type of generic practice is the textual convention — formal attributes and patterns of meaning that are typical to the particular genre. But a genre is not simply the collection of these conventions. Genres are formed through the cultural activation of textual conventions, linking them to various assumptions of definition, interpretation, and evaluation, all under the categorical rubric of the given genre. Thus, we can find the narrative convention of "maverick cop bucking the system" as an active component of the police genre at specific historical moments, with particular texts, producers, audiences, and critics activating this convention with their generic practices. But this convention is neither a necessary nor causal factor in creating the genre — *Dragnet* works against this formulation in exemplifying an articulation of the police genre with no representations of systems getting bucked. All textual conventions are only contingently linked to a generic cluster, as changing contexts can alter the textual elements that are culturally assumed to be a component of the genre.

In examining the textual elements tied to a particular genre, we must also look to *how* they are generically linked, examining the discursive practices that serve to associate textual conventions to generic clusters. It is not enough to point out that particular police shows feature maverick cops, but we need to examine both the cultural processes by which this association came to be accepted as the common sense of the genre, and explore the repercussions of such associations for the cultural circulation of the genre category. This approach follows the model of generic genealogy explored in Chapter 2, tracing out the categorical continuities and discursive practices that are constitutive of the genre. Texts can be one site of this genealogical approach, examining how conventions are activated by drawing upon the various cultural assumptions that make up the generic category. Yet we cannot isolate generic texts, because it is only in the historical context of production and reception that genres have any cultural impact and coherence as categories. Thus, in examining media texts in context, I focus on examining not just the program in analytic isolation, but the larger *cultural life* of television texts, looking at how shows circulate in a range of spheres of practice. The text is certainly a nexus point, providing a clear boundary for analysis, but these boundaries are permeated by the larger processes by which the text is activated as a cultural object. By turning to the text, we must resist making textual boundaries too solid and separating texts from their contextual operation, for media only bear historical and social relevance through their larger cultural circulation.

In charting out any historical moment of a genre, texts can serve as a crucial site of generic practice. Similarly, considering the role of generic categories can expand our understanding of a specific program and its place in cultural history. Texts work as *sites of articulation*, in which certain cultural assumptions of definition, interpretation, and evaluation are linked to larger generic categories in a dynamic process. In this chapter, I examine *Dragnet* through this lens, exploring how the generic categories of police show, documentary, *film noir*, and radio crime drama were all activated within and around the program. *Dragnet* not only drew upon these categories in its textual conventions, formal properties, and encoded meanings, but also in its larger cultural circulation in the 1950s and 1960s, activating discourses of generic definition, interpretation, and evaluation. For the purposes of this chapter, I focus primarily on the text itself, limiting my contextualized analysis to moments when generic categories actively transect the permeable boundaries between text and context — in the next chapter, I explore the relationships between text and context more in depth in charting the cultural life of both *Soap* and *The Simpsons* as examples of genre parody. In turning to *Dragnet*, we can see how one of the most successful and interesting programs in media history both activated and altered generic categories, establishing the baseline cultural understanding of the police drama for years to come.

Stylized Authenticity/Authentic Style: *Dragnet*'s Generic Precedents and Legacies

There is an unfortunate gap between the importance of *Dragnet* within television history and the negligible attention it has been given by media historians. The program was one of the most successful and trailblazing shows of early television, setting vital industrial precedents in the popularization of telefilms, models of independent production, acceptance of reruns, and merchandizing of television programs. *Dragnet* stretched across media — originating on radio and spawning a feature theatrical film during its television run — and decades, with original programs spanning from 1949 to 1970 (not to mention a parodic 1987 film and two television remakes in 1989 and 2003). Generically, the show established most of the formal precedents for the police drama that programs still draw upon and react against today. *Dragnet* created a unique textual style and innovative use of telefilm, which were instantly recognizable and often imitated in early television.[8] Culturally, the program offered a distinctive vision of American social order and ideology, offering a rich terrain for media scholarship and analysis. But despite the program's historical and cultural importance, media scholars have treated the program with brief asides and casual mentions, with almost no close analysis of *Dragnet*'s array of historical facets.[9] This chapter is an admittedly partial remedy for this lack of attention, considering *Dragnet* as a site of genre practice.

To understand *Dragnet*'s role within genre history, I examine the multiple-media incarnations of the show, exploring how generic categories affected its cultural life and how the police genre as a cultural category was impacted by *Dragnet*'s long history of circulation. More than just an exemplary case of how to analyze texts within the framework of cultural genre theory, my consideration of *Dragnet*'s genre practices illuminates a crucial program within media history, explores the changing characteristics of generic categories over decades, and reflects on the impact of television programs on our understanding of social phenomena like crime, law, and the police. In charting out the cultural life of *Dragnet* and its activation of generic categories, we can see the assumptions linked to the documentary, semi-documentary, and crime genres all working to further the show's unique blend of stylized presentation and devout authenticity. Certainly, there is much more to be said about both *Dragnet* and the police genre than addressed in this chapter, but hopefully my examination serves as an entrance point to examining one of the more fascinating texts in the history of radio, television, and film.

When *Dragnet* debuted on NBC radio on June 3, 1949, it was slated for a quick demise. As recounted in a retrospective of creator/star Jack Webb:

> Network executives disliked everything about the new show — its underplaying, slow pace, attention to detail, lack of gun-play and violence — everything, in short, that Webb had painstakingly produced to make it different from all the other cops-and-robbers shows on the air.[10]

Positive critical reception and strong ratings changed these preconceptions, as the program quickly rose to the top of radio ratings. Webb had developed the program as an alternative to the postwar saturation of detective programs portraying hard-boiled loner gumshoes solving cases with gimmicks — including the show that had established him as a radio actor, *Pat Novak For Hire* (1946–49). In establishing a close working relationship with the Los Angeles Police Department (LAPD), Webb strove for a show steeped in authenticity and realism, showing a policeman who, "as in real life, was just one little cog in a great enforcement machine."[11] The show followed a clear pattern: as narrated by Webb's policeman Joe Friday, each episode dramatizes a case taken from the LAPD, with "the names changed to protect the innocent." Friday and his partner Ben Romero (played by Barton Yarborough) strictly follow police protocols in pursuing dead-end leads, interrogating witnesses, relying upon the crime lab and forensics, and eventually capturing the culprit. The audience never learns anything outside of Friday's perspective, discovering each plot development through his actions and narration. Similarly, we rarely encounter any story developments outside the realm of the specific case, apart from brief mentions of the two officers' personal lives; the characters are equated with their jobs, and their jobs are consumed with singular cases each episode. While cases change each week, the show hardly deviates from this basic formula throughout its many years on both radio and television.

As television began to loom as the inevitable future for radio drama, both Webb and NBC were eager to transfer this top-rated program to the small screen. While NBC wanted *Dragnet* to be produced live, following the traditions of culturally validated anthology dramas and other popular crime programs like *Man Against Crime* (1949–53) and *Martin Kane, Private Eye* (1949–54), Webb held out for telefilm. As discussed below, Webb's style and production techniques were so tied to film models that he took a financial risk, foregoing his own salary as star, producer, and director to convince NBC to fund thirteen episodes as telefilms. Webb's conviction turned profitable, as not only did *Dragnet* reign as NBC's highest-rated television program from 1952 to 1956, but the telefilm format proved to be vital in the lucrative rerun market. *Dragnet*'s television incarnation mimicked the basic formula of the radio version (which remained on the air simultaneously until 1955), only with Friday's new partner Frank Smith (played by Ben Alexander) taking over Ben Romero's radio role after Yarborough died suddenly after shooting only two telefilms. The program lasted on NBC until 1959, with reruns (entitled *Badge 714*) thriving simultaneously in syndication (and occasionally on NBC primetime as well). In 1954, Webb interrupted television production to make a feature-length theatrical release of *Dragnet*, which proved to be a cinematic hit for Warner Brothers. *Dragnet* returned to original television production for NBC from 1967 to 1970 with Harry Morgan as new partner Bill Gannon, but changes in the police genre and cultural context altered the mostly unchanged complexion of the program. The show lives on today in still common cultural references ("just the facts ma'am" and the now-clichéd theme song), continual syndication, and occasional parodies, like the Dan Ackroyd film *Dragnet* (1987), a Friday-clone library cop on *Seinfeld* (1989–98), Friday and Gannon's characters appearing on *The Simpsons* — and most recently a revival on ABC, as Dick Wolf, creator of the *Dragnet*-influenced *Law & Order* (1990–), recast Friday and Smith for 2003.

Dragnet was linked to a number of generic categories in its early emergence on television, with the program functioning as a site in which various generic assumptions were articulated together, detached from previous linkages, and activated in broader cultural circulation. These generic categories worked as cultural shorthand to activate a number of the ideological meanings that make *Dragnet* such a rich site of analysis, tying together discourses of authenticity and truth to buttress the show's conservative worldview.[12] Certainly, the primary genre active in this case is the police show, a generic category which *Dragnet* was instrumental in establishing on television. But as Rick Altman argues, genres rarely operate in "pure" form — multiple genres are strategically articulated by the industry, while audiences bring a range of generic frameworks to bear on their reception of texts.[13] I explore genre mixing more extensively in Chapter 6, but in examining *Dragnet*, it is vital to note that, even though most people would identify the show as a "core" example of the police show, other generic categories were activated by the text and its broader circulation, genres that are crucial to understanding the cultural life of *Dragnet*.

While *Dragnet* helped establish many textual and cultural precedents for the television police drama, it emerged on radio as part of a longer tradition of crime programs. According to J. Fred MacDonald's history of the genre, detective programs emerged in the early years of network radio of the late 1920s.[14] While the crime-solving detectives varied widely in occupation from policemen to mystery writers, private detectives to district attorneys, the narrative focus of all of these programs followed the hero's process in solving an episode's crime. MacDonald links two major generic trends tied to heroic types, suggesting that the "Realistic Detective" programs of the 1930s focused on mundane plot and procedures, while the "Glamorous Detective" shows of the 1940s featured more colorful characterization and settings. While, certainly, MacDonald's dualistic categorization is a reduction, it is useful in laying out the realm of radio crime programs preceding *Dragnet*. But it is doubtful that these diverse programs were experienced as a unified and coherent genre of *detective programs*. Certainly, other more specific categories such as *police show* and *mystery* had cultural relevance, as programs such as *Dragnet* received the Edgar Allen Poe award for Best Mystery Program, a categorization not dependent on the centrality of the detective. A more detailed genealogy of the generic terms and cultural circulation of radio crime drama falls outside the scope of this chapter, but clearly radio programs and cultural understandings of the detective genre had direct relevance on *Dragnet*.

Dragnet debuted in 1949 as part of what MacDonald terms the "Neo-Realistic Detective" phase of the genre, marked by a return to procedure over flashy characters, but with a new cynical attitude toward crime and society. MacDonald suggests this trend of the late 1940s parallels *film noir* through its presentation of crime as symptomatic of greater societal illness, the disillusioned and reluctant detective, resentment toward the wealthy, and the brutality and hopelessness of the criminal-detective cycle. MacDonald's characterization demonstrates the limitations of writing genre histories solely through textual interpretation and analysis. His account of both the genre and *Dragnet* relies on abstract trends, fitting examples into a neat historical lineage that breaks down upon closer examination. The programs he uses to exemplify the earlier trends of Realistic and Glamorous Detectives outlasted the dominant historical moments to which he ties them, with exemplars of all three trends airing side-by-side in the late 1940s. Additionally, while *Dragnet* certainly bears some markers of the Neo-Realistic model, it also fits features of the Realistic and Glamorous cycles enough to force us to question the relevance of these categories, especially without examination of how the genre operated culturally through broader production and reception. Kathleen Battles similarly questions MacDonald's genre progression, arguing that the early success of 1930s radio crime shows *Gang Busters* (1935–57) and *Calling All Cars* (1933–39) set the stage for the future development of the police procedural in a range of media.[15] While *Dragnet* certainly drew from the procedural tone and official authentication typical of these 1930s radio dramas, the show's low-key adult tone, avoidance of violence and sensationalism, and distinct stylistic markers came more directly from film sources.

Webb's radio resume primarily featured private detective roles in *Pat Novak For Hire* and *Johnny Modero, Pier 23* (1947), but it was a film role that led to Webb's inspiration for *Dragnet*. In 1948, Webb had a small part in the Alfred Wercker and Anthony Mann film, *He Walked By Night*.[16] This film belongs to a cycle of late 1940s films often termed "semi-documentaries," dramatizing true stories by combining authentic representations of "official procedures" (such as the workings of a police department) with *film noir* stylistic elements. For Webb, *He Walked By Night* served as both the textual touchstone and inspirational trigger for *Dragnet*. According to Webb, the film's technical advisor, LAPD Sergeant Marty Wynn, complained to Webb about the lack of realism in most radio crime dramas, suggesting that if Webb created a more authentic program, Wynn could provide him access to LAPD case files. Webb initially thought the idea was too out-of-touch with the radio genre's norms, which, despite the success of proto-procedurals of the 1930s, built a youth audience on sensationalist content. But as Webb became better acquainted with Wynn and the workings of the LAPD, he saw potential for authentic cases and procedures to capture an audience's ear as a change of pace.[17] While *Dragnet* may have been a generic innovation for radio, it fit well with the generic assumptions activated in late 1940s crime films.

The semi-documentary film cycle of the mid to late 1940s has not been addressed in much detail within film studies.[18] Often mentioned briefly within the context of *film noir*, crime films like *He Walked By Night* and *The Naked City* (1948) are held up as prototypical of both the semi-documentary cycle and *film noir* aesthetics.[19] With historical hindsight, this linkage is certainly valid — both types of films share textual conventions such as on-location shooting, urban crime narration, shadowy black-and-white photography, and a commitment to gritty realism. Yet *film noir* poses a particular problem for a cultural approach to genres. If we study genres as they operate as cultural categories, how can we grapple with a category that was devised by critics after most of the categorized films were produced and initially exhibited? One successful treatment of *film noir* as a cultural category, James Naremore's *More Than Night*, looks at how the generic term has been "projected onto the past" and how it operates as a contextualized facet of cultural circulation.[20] Yet since this chapter seeks to understand the generic categories that were activated by *Dragnet* at the time of its initial run, we cannot really argue that *Dragnet* drew upon *film noir* — even if we accept the contested position that *film noir* is a genre (rather than mode or style), *noir* did not function as a genre during the late 1940s and early 1950s origins of *Dragnet*. As Naremore explores, *film noir* does have a "generic function" as a cultural category, but not in the United States during the 1940s and 1950s, as the French critical work proposing the genre had barely crossed the Atlantic.

Does this mean that *Dragnet* is uninfluenced by the films of *film noir*? Certainly not, as a number of texts later understood as *noir*, most importantly *He Walked By Night* and *Naked City*, were direct and profound influences on Webb's creation. But he could not have drawn upon the genre of *film noir*, as it served no categorical shorthand at the time, linking cultural assumptions and textual conventions. Yet these films were not uncategorized, belonging to no genre. In looking for the relevant generic precedents formative of *Dragnet*, we should look at how two different, but linked, film genres were activated and drawn upon by Webb: the documentary and the crime film. These two genres mixed within the semi-documentary cycle in the late 1940s, a generic reference point that was explicitly taken up on 1950s television by *Dragnet* and its peers.[21] *Dragnet*'s semi-documentary lineage is its primary generic influence, as the show actively drew upon the clustered assumptions of authenticity and truthfulness from this filmic source to further its own ideological ends. Thus, to understand the generic precedents of *Dragnet*, we need to explore the dual influences of documentary and crime films.

The long history of documentary films is tangential at best to understand *Dragnet*. Most vital for this study, the 1940s saw a dramatic rise in both the production and exhibition of documentaries, as World War II justified both the financing of documentaries and their inclusion within film bills for communicating contemporary news of world affairs to audiences. British cinema saw the rise of a particular form of documentary filmmaking, in which factual events would be dramatized and occasionally fictionalized, but presented in the guise of documentaries — *semi-documentaries* as they were often termed. In the years following the war, the documentary genre was a much more publicized, viewed, and understood type of filmmaking than at any previous moment in film history. This rise in documentaries helped fuel a general shift toward realism within fictional films throughout world cinema, particularly in the Italian Neo-Realist movement, while British semi-documentary style became incorporated into a cycle of realist comedies produced by Ealing Studios following the war. American filmmaking was less influenced by this realist turn, although the impact of documentary themes and techniques were felt on social problem films, such as *The Lost Weekend* (1945) and *Home of the Brave* (1949), and "procedural dramas," like *Panic in the Streets* (1950), portraying a public health crisis, and *The Frogmen* (1951), detailing the training of Navy soldiers. But the most significant American incorporation of documentary style into dramatized film was within crime dramas.[22]

Most accounts of crime films of the 1940s use *film noir* as their focal point, exploring the stylistic and cultural features French critics isolated in their proposition of a theoretical genre in the late 1940s. Most of the films falling under the standard rubric of *noir* did have clearer generic ties to crime dramas of the time. Rather than tracing out a broader history of crime dramas in multiple media, I want to point to the emergence of a select few generic dominants in the 1940s, exploring how *Dragnet* fit into this matrix. Prior to the 1940s, the most common type of crime films and fiction were detective stories, focusing on a mystery solved through the rational skills of detectives like Sherlock Holmes; another vein of crime dramas were gangster pictures, which became quite popular in the 1930s.[23] But in the 1940s, two separate although linked variants of the crime drama emerged as generic dominants.

The first and most prevalent of these modes of crime drama was what Frank Krutnik terms the "tough thriller."[24] Following the rise of "hard-boiled" detective fiction in the 1930s, this brand of crime drama focuses on an independent male detective solving a crime relying more on his masculinity and physical endurance than deductive detection skills, while painting a cynical representation of urban America. The detective of the tough thriller might be part of the law enforcement establishment (such as the police), but he solves the crime by working outside social norms rather than following strict procedures, leading to the common political interpretation of the genre as critical of the establishment. For Krutnik, this tough thriller is the core of *film noir*, with all other variants peripheral and tangential to the *noir* genre. While Krutnik's approach is certainly textualist in focus (and theoretical assumptions), I believe that he is correct in noting that the central texts categorized as *film noir* most coherently fit this notion of the tough thriller and that theoretical explorations of *noir* are based on this particular dominant of the crime drama. Although most treatments of 1940s crime fiction and film are tied to this tough thriller dominant, it was not the primary influence on *Dragnet* and television crime dramas.

The second dominant of the crime drama of the 1940s was far more influential upon *Dragnet*: the semi-documentary police procedural. While this type of filmmaking had some parallels with the rise of the police procedural and true crime in novels, these literary forms did not fully establish themselves until the 1950s.[25] As discussed above, documentary forms proliferated during the war years and influenced traditional fictional films. The semi-documentary procedural was a distinctive film cycle in the latter half of the 1940s, commencing with *The House on 92nd Street* (1945). Produced by Louis de Rochemont, who had gained his fame as producer of the documentary film series *The March of Time* in the 1930s, *92nd Street* dramatizes the "true story" of the FBI preventing a German spy ring from learning of the American creation of the atomic bomb in the early 1940s. While the film is clearly a dramatic narrative "based on" the true story, numerous stylistic cues and overt signals foreground its claims to authenticity and linkage to documentary. The initial title cards emphasize that the film was shot on location and directly followed FBI files; the narrator signals that actual FBI surveillance footage was incorporated into the film. Additionally, a title card suggests that except for the "leading players,. . . all FBI personnel in the picture are members of the Federal Bureau of Investigation." While the narrative of the film is structured along fairly conventional espionage and mystery models, *92nd Street* carefully traces the procedures the FBI follows to solve crimes, marking the film's authenticating discourses and explicit ties to the official establishment of the FBI.

Other films followed *92nd Street*'s semi-documentary lead in carefully detailing the procedures used to solve crimes, including *Naked City* and *He Walked By Night*.[26] These two films had the most direct impact on *Dragnet* and the television police genre, as their accounts of urban police practices offer a semi-documentary model of the police procedural that *Dragnet* recast for the small screen. *Naked City* establishes its own authenticity similarly to *92nd Street* — through producer Mark Hellinger's voice-over narration, the audience is assured that all shots in the film were shot on location in New York City, using real New Yorkers as extras. The story traces the procedures police use to solve a murder case through legwork, crime scene analysis, and interviewing, as well as more traditional rational detection and piecing together of minor clues. While the city is portrayed as authentic, and the film uses actuality footage to establish a realist impulse, there is no indication that it was based upon a true story, and the plot twists and characterizations seem typical of the fictional genre.[27]

Despite the focus on procedures and realistic location, we also follow the personal lives of lead detectives Jimmy Halloran and Dan Muldoon, while Hellinger's omniscient narration takes the audience through the detection process, providing us information unavailable to the police.

Unlike *House on 92nd Street*, *Naked City* was not invested in presenting an authoritatively guaranteed vision of law and order, endorsed by the powers that be. Coscreenwriter Albert Maltz, who would later be indicted as one of the Hollywood Ten, and director Jules Dassin, a former Communist Party member, both viewed the film as an exercise in "social realism" designed to portray the inequities and harsh realities found in American cities.[28] They locate the criminal element in both the poor and the rich, offering more sympathy for the working-class murderer Garza than upper-class thieves Frank Niles and Dr. Stoneman. In filming on location and using actual New Yorkers, they strove to highlight poverty and social inequities as a left-leaning political statement, aspects of the film toned down by Universal Pictures in the final cut.[29] Even as the police succeed in solving the crime and apprehending the criminals, the film follows crime drama traditions by vesting the power to solve crimes in the individual detectives more than in the system itself. Thus in *Naked City*, realism and authenticity are motivated by social critique, rather than investment in the status quo and authoritative systems like in *House on 92nd Street*, making the film less consistent with the central assumptions of the semi-documentary cycle.

He Walked By Night is much more in line with the politics and tone of *House on 92nd Street* than *Naked City*, despite sharing an urban milieu and police procedural focus with the latter. The film opens with a title card that *Dragnet* would later copy nearly verbatim: "The record is set down here factually. . . as it happened. Only the names are changed. . . to protect the innocent."[30] Like *Naked City*, *He Walked By Night*'s voice-over narration sets the urban stage by painting a picture of Los Angeles marked by authenticity, assuring that "the facts are told here as they happened." The opening scenes portray the crime, in which a burglar shoots and kills a police officer to escape capture. The action then shifts to follow the police detectives in their pursuit of the killer, following the case history and investigative procedures used to capture the criminal, all rendered in authentic lingo and detail. As the narrator comments as the detectives search for leads, "police work is not all glamour and excitement and glory — there are days and days of routine, of tedious probing, of tireless searching." The detectives are seen only as part of a larger system, with few distinguishing markers between policemen, no glimpses into their private lives, and only minor characterization establishing anything beyond their roles as players in the larger criminal justice system.

While its narrative and characterization firmly locate *He Walked By Night* within the procedural semi-documentary tradition of *92nd Street*, aspects of the film's style and representations present more moral and political ambiguity than typical of this generic dominant. The visual style of chiaroscuro lighting and nighttime scenes are typical of the *noir* photography of cinematographer John Alton and codirector Anthony Mann, stylistic attributes more common to the "tough thriller" than the semi-documentary. Likewise, while the police are presented as interchangeable pieces of a law enforcement machine, the killer, Morgan is the most complex character in the film. Eventually revealed to be a former police radio technician, he is a technologically adept, cold-blooded opportunist whose only motivations seem to be survival and greed — a fully realized psychotic criminal presence who stands in stark opposition to the depersonalized set of procedural drones that typify the police detectives. As Krutnik argues, the scenes depicting Morgan are stylistically consistent with *film noir*, while the police segments are more in line with semi-documentary neutrality.[31] Thus, the moral ambiguity of Morgan's character is painted in the stark high-contrast black-and-white typical of *film noir*'s classics, whereas the black-and-white clarity of the police's ideological certitude is rendered in shades of dull gray.

The style, narrative, and characterizations of *Dragnet* all emerge out of this mixed bag of tendencies found in the crime films of the 1940s, as the show selectively drew upon the range of textual conventions and cultural assumptions linked to the genre during this era. Much like the semi-documentary dominant, *Dragnet* is adamant in asserting its own authenticity. The standard opening of the television program mimics *He Walked By Night*: "Ladies and gentlemen. . . the story you are about to see is true. Only the names have been changed to protect the innocent." The end credits highlight the technical advice provided by the LAPD, while the closing shots of the apprehended criminal character always note the criminal's sentence at an actual California penal institution. On-location exteriors throughout Los Angeles provide a clear sense of the urban milieu, while Webb strove to precisely reconstruct police headquarters for interior studio shooting; *Dragnet*'s televisual pilot was even shot on location at Los Angeles City Hall. Actual police lingo is used throughout the show without explanation, treating the audience as insiders to police procedures. Even the show's most recognized catch-phrase, "just the facts, ma'am," speaks to *Dragnet*'s unrelenting focus on objective truths. The show's style and authenticating tone were directly modeled upon documentary and semi-documentary filmmaking, drawing upon both textual conventions and cultural linkages to encode the text to resonate with realism and factuality.

Of course, notions of realism, authenticity, and fact are not objective modes of representation but rather communicative practices strategically evoked within texts for particular aims.[32] As mentioned before, *Naked City* used markers of realism to offer a critical left-leaning vision of the American city and its social problems. Similarly, the tough thrillers typifying *film noir* use gritty realism to present moral ambiguities and question the status of authority. The markers of authenticity within *He Walked By Night* are much more ambiguous, as detailed procedures and assertions of narrative accuracy situate the audience as allied with an intact criminal justice system. Yet the criminal's intelligence and complexity so outweighs the police's that the system does not receive a full endorsement — crime certainly does not pay, but it takes a few lucky breaks by the police to carry out justice. *92nd Street*, with the official imprimatur of the FBI, never questions the efficacy, motives, or morality of the fully functioning system, ensuring triumph over the ultimate unambiguous enemy, Nazi Germany. The politics of authenticity, as evoked by semi-documentary films, range in both political persuasion and efficacy, with the evocation of realism guaranteeing neither ideology nor its impact. The techniques *Dragnet* uses to communicate authenticity do not ensure its politics, but the elements it draws from semi-documentary films make specific and strategic linkages to ideological positions. The formal conventions linking *Dragnet* to semi-documentaries were not simply arbitrary stylistic choices, but politically motivated practices activating interpretative discourses tied to the crime film's generic cluster. By tracing out the various linkages made between *Dragnet* and its generic precedents, we can see how the program's textual and production practices did not emerge in a vacuum, but overtly drew upon assumptions to favor certain reading possibilities and frameworks of comprehension.

Dragnet most centrally draws upon the semi-documentary's claims to authenticity and officialdom. Like *92nd Street*, *Dragnet* foregrounds its own alliances with the official systems of crime fighting through its opening narration, credits, and access to true stories and locations. This alliance with the LAPD was more than in name alone — the police took an active role in shaping the stories and representational mode presented on *Dragnet*. While it seems that Webb and his writers never had direct access to actual case files, production personnel often shadowed police officers to get a procedural feel. LAPD Chief William Parker set up a system to provide stories and clear episodes of *Dragnet* to satisfy both Webb's yearning for authenticity and the LAPD's need for positive publicity. Police officers were encouraged to write up accounts of cases they felt would be of interest to television viewers; the LAPD Public Information Division would then channel appropriate cases to *Dragnet*'s producers, who would develop select stories into scripts. The scripts were vetted though the LAPD before shooting, making changes to ensure authenticity within the bounds of "positive images" of LAPD. Scripts were filtered for content as well, as the LAPD served both as a steward of its own image and also as a guardian of public morality, censoring topics like abortion and overt sexual content. Once the scripts were approved by the LAPD, a technical advisor from the relevant department (homicide, narcotics, etc.) would be assigned to the episode, maintaining a presence on set throughout the production process. Finally, the LAPD screened the completed episodes before airing, providing a last gateway of oversight before granting its mark of approval. Thus, the LAPD was an active partner throughout the production process, providing much more than just an official imprimatur; this relationship continued even into the exhibition realm as well, as the LAPD used *Dragnet* episodes in training its new officers.[33]

The active participation of official organizations like the LAPD was typical of documentary filmmaking, as many of the documentaries circulating during the 1930s and 1940s were produced for, or with the assistance of, government agencies. The establishment of the United States Film Service office in 1938 provided funding for filmmakers to produce documentaries and semi-documentaries for government agencies and programs, constituting a brief but important part of New Deal efforts to document the benefits of governmental programs. These alliances became more central during World War II, as the Office of War Information and U.S. Armed Services commissioned production of many films, ranging from documentaries of war efforts to fictional films aimed at raising morale.[34] Semi-documentary films of the late 1940s continued these collaborations, with governmental agencies actively endorsing *92ⁿᵈ Street*, the similar de Rochemont spy story *13 Rue Madeline* (1946), and LAPD's own representation in *He Walked By Night*. Thus, in the context of late 1940s America, the alliance between a dramatic media text and a governmental organization was well established as legitimating and a marker of quality — another instance of policy practices impacting genre categories. *Dragnet* drew this cultural assumption of authenticity and legitimization from the well-established generic linkages tied to documentaries and semi-documentaries of the 1940s.[35]

While *Dragnet* drew upon the officially sanctioned semi-documentary tradition of *92ⁿᵈ Street*, its mode of semi-documentary representation differs from this textual ancestor in one crucial respect. Films such as *92ⁿᵈ Street* and *13 Rue Madeline* dramatize actual historical events through careful reenactments and authenticating stamps of approval from the FBI. While these claims of authenticity parallel *Dragnet*'s in many ways, the semi-documentary model offered by *Dragnet* is distinctly *ahistorical*. The espionage tale of *92ⁿᵈ Street* takes place in a distinct time, explicitly referencing historical events, like the creation of the atomic bomb. For *Dragnet*, and its true crime inspiration *He Walked By Night*, changing the names did more than just protect the innocent. By removing any distinguishing markers of specific case histories, Webb was able to avoid libel lawsuits and misrepresenting innocent participants in cases. But this shift also changes the meanings of authenticity as encoded in the texts — whereas *92ⁿᵈ Street* portrays a specific historical event, *Dragnet* offers a universalizing and abstracted model of truth. The murders, frauds, and robberies found on *Dragnet* were authentic in general terms, but they had no explicit ties to recognizable events. *Dragnet* invites audience members to view each episode not just as a representation of an *actual case history*, but also as an authentic dramatization of *general truth*.

The combination of this generalized mode of ahistorical authenticity and *Dragnet*'s episodic repetition over many years on radio and television helped establish the meaning of the program, and the police show genre, as rooted in truth over history.[36] The historical veracity offered by *92ⁿᵈ Street* may have been a carefully rendered portrait of a specific instance of espionage, but the discursive authenticity that suffused *Dragnet* made every moment appear as both confirmed fact and generalizable truth. The representation of any particular crime, and subsequent capture by the police, exemplifies of a larger system of criminal justice, with little ties to a specific history which might limit universalizing the show's content as part of a greater reality. *Dragnet*'s anonymous, systemic, and repetitive practices become equated with an authentic rendering of "the way the world worked." The semi-documentary mode of *92ⁿᵈ Street* is more typical of what would later be termed *docudrama*, where specific historical cases are dramatized for film or television.[37] *Dragnet*'s mode of generalized realism draws upon assumptions of authenticity linked to the semi-documentary genre, but converts this authenticity into a more detachable and universalized ideological worldview, articulating factual discourses and truth value to the emergent television police genre.

This specific articulation of authenticity is, in many ways, *Dragnet*'s most lasting and interesting legacy. The program draws upon clear sources — crime films, documentaries, radio detective shows — to produce a thoroughly distinctive dramatic style which would be formative of the television police genre. The show's rearticulation of authenticity and drama was adopted by other 1950s police programs, such as *Highway Patrol* (1955–59), *The Man Behind the Badge* (1953–54), and *The Line-up* (1954–60), as well as spy programs like *I Led Three Lives* (1953–56) and medical shows like *Medic* (1954–56), which was created by *Dragnet* writer James Moser. In its rendering of authenticity, *Dragnet* also presents a specific vision of the world which, although certainly in line with the dominant ideology of the time, offers an unconventional picture of urban America, crime, and government. In charting out this particular style and vision, we can look at *Dragnet* as a site genre practice, drawing discourses of authenticity and ideology from its generic precedent of semi-documentary crime film and articulating them to the nascent category of television police show.

Dragnet's motivation was partly to present a realistic vision of police officers, eschewing the glamorized characterization typical of most film and radio crime dramas. One of the primary ways Webb accomplished this goal was to follow in the lead of *He Walked By Night*, avoiding the personal lives of officers, except through brief asides in the workplace. Thus while Friday's partners (Romero on radio, Smith on 1950s television, and Gannon on 1960s television) are all married and occasionally discuss their home life with Friday, the personal lives of the police serve only to render officers as everyday people with average lives. Personal relationships are nearly never incorporated into narratives, as the police are portrayed as fully able to separate between their personal and professional selves. Friday has nearly no personal life at all, as his partners all undertake a peripheral quest to find him a "nice girl" to settle down with. Webb did bring in a few girlfriends for Friday in the late 1950s, but none lasted beyond a few appearances, as the character's personal life conflicts with his functional role as the professional center of *Dragnet*'s authentic universe.

The acting style in *Dragnet* is also a crucial component of the show's unusual brand of authenticity, which became foundational for the police genre. Known — and frequently parodied — for his flat and monotone delivery, director Webb had other actors follow his lead for line readings, filtering out most emotional nuances and dramatic pauses. One of Webb's directorial tricks for achieving this effect (and cutting budgetary costs) was having actors work with minimal rehearsals, reading their lines off newly developed TelePrompTers rather than memorization.[38] This trick helped enforce one of *Dragnet*'s most noticeable stylistic quirks, an abundance of tight close-ups, but it also creates a strange sense of distance from the action. While the episodes are almost always made up of the material of high drama — murders and assaults, inquisitions and confessions — the acting style rarely taps into the emotional reservoirs more typical of contemporary police dramas. In the quest for realism, Webb's directorial style works against typical codes of naturalism via his approach to acting. Rather than indicating a failure of Webb's directorial or acting abilities (as has often been claimed), this odd feature of *Dragnet* points to the prioritization of *systemic* over *emotional* realism — the police are emotionally detached from the drama due to the proper and accurate functioning of the criminal justice system. In a certainly unintentional way — and with opposite political motives — Webb's style is almost Brechtian in its use of emotional distanciation to highlight the larger systems and universal trends at play within the drama. By making Friday, Smith, and the rest of the police little more than cardboard cutouts carrying out their duties, Webb denies audiences the ability to identify with fully realized characters. This emotional distance emphasizes that it is the police *system*, not the individual policeman as human being, that functions as the authentic agent of justice.

While the police on *Dragnet* are stripped of personalities and treated as functionaries, the various witnesses and victims they interview and encounter while carrying out proper procedures are more colorful. Friday and Smith meet drunk hotel clerks, confused shop owners, parents in denial, overly trusting senior citizens, and naïve teenagers, all with personalities more vivid than the ongoing police characters. Certainly these interesting side characters allow for narrative variety, humorous bits, and opportunities for Friday to offer moralistic enlightenment in monologue form; but the range of quirky people encountered by the police also paints a particular picture of the social order. The world of

Dragnet is inhabited by a wide range of unusual people with unusual problems, many of which were uncommon for 1950s television screens. This constellation of characters shows the sheer range of people whom the police must both serve and rely upon for information. Yet throughout this quagmire of difference, Friday and Smith maintain a neutral sameness for the entire run of the series. This juxtaposition between the heterogeneous social chaos and the homogeneous official police order promotes a belief that the police are simply better equipped to deal with social problems and urban chaos than its citizens, a position authenticated by the endorsement of the LAPD and articulated to the police genre.

While *Dragnet* shows emotionless police and quirky bystanders, the criminal targets of Friday and Smith's pursuit are often quite intriguing. As we are limited to Friday's perspective throughout the show, we do not get the full rendering of criminals as featured in *He Walked By Night* or *Naked City* — we only see the criminal from the official viewpoint of the police. This perspective is often limited to repeated denials, last-minute captures, and brief confessions. Yet *Dragnet* does present elements of criminals' psychology and characterization in more detail. In one of the more interesting episodes from the first season, a young Lee Marvin plays a serial killer whom Friday and interim partner Ed Jacobs capture, interrogate, and eventually get to confess to a string of unsolved seemingly random murders.[39] The entire episode unwinds as a conversation between these three men, as Friday and Jacobs peel back layers of denial to uncover the truth they suspected from the beginning. Finally, Marvin's character confesses to the killings, but insists that the police understand that he had no "real motives" — he killed people just because he could. His character expresses dismay at the inaccurate representations of murder in films and "phony mystery stories," noting that his own story and lack of motivation "wouldn't fly with a writer." His confession, along with Marvin's chilling portrayal, highlights *Dragnet*'s vision of the world counter to conventional generic traditions: crime is a force lacking explicable motivations, clear patterns, or even reason, but posing an omnipresent danger from which the police must constantly defend society.

This representation of the amoral and dispassionate killer draws from the crime films now known as *film noir*. Unlike traditional detective stories, *Dragnet*'s criminals usually lack discernable motives that must be combated by reason and deduction; the crimes that Friday and Smith fight often occur outside the realm of rationality and reason. Crime happens to, and is practiced by, all facets of society — rich and poor, young and old, cunningly brilliant or naively ignorant. In this way, *Dragnet* paints a cynical vision of the social order in which chaos is ever present, not to be escaped in the suburbs or overcome through wealth or education. Additionally, *Dragnet* brought a number of "social issues" to the screen that have been remembered as generally absent from 1950s television, such as drug use, pornography, adultery, and juvenile delinquency — although notably these social ills were presented in a typically low-key and nonsensational manner. Unlike many other programs of its era, *Dragnet* generally did not flinch from portraying society's many ills. This cynicism seems at odds with the conservative politics often tied to Webb and *Dragnet*, as the Los Angeles represented in the show is as dangerous as in the most gritty *film noir*, with no respites from the pervasive reach of crime. Yet unlike in *noir* films, the social order has a fully functional apparatus of justice, able to react to crime as it happens to stem its destructive tide. There is no sense that crime may be prevented in *Dragnet*, except in that specific criminals may be stopped from repeating their acts of lawlessness. The conservative ideology that *Dragnet* articulated to the police genre is not an idealized vision of society as presented in idyllic sitcoms, but the authenticated and unswerving belief in the system to continually discipline offenders and protect the innocent by reacting to ever-present threats and manifestations of crime.

Dragnet reassures audiences that the police system functions efficiently by positioning viewers as allied with the police, invisible observers of authentic procedures as they happen. The primary method *Dragnet* uses to situate viewers alongside the police is through limited narrative scope and Friday's first-person narration — everything we see, hear, and learn on *Dragnet* is from Friday's perspective. On radio, an announcer opens and closes the show to frame Friday's narration, explicitly situating the listener in the policeman's shoes. For example, one typical radio episode begins:

> You're a detective sergeant. You're assigned to Robbery Detail. For the past ten days, a gunman has been terrorizing the downtown area of your city. You know he's armed and dangerous. Your job: stop him! ... *Dragnet*, the documented drama of an actual crime. For the next 30 minutes, in cooperation with the Los Angeles Police Department, you will travel step by step on the side of the law through an actual case, transcribed from official police files. From beginning to end, from crime to punishment, *Dragnet* is the story of your police force in action.[40]

This opening use of second-person narration locates listeners alongside Friday and the LAPD, with claims of authenticity further cementing the audience into this ideologically circumscribed role. As the show became more routine in its production format, Friday took over narrating cases on the radio; the television program limits the role of additional narration even further, using "the story you are about to see is true" opening before handing off narrational duties to Webb's character.

This limited first-person narration is a break from semi-documentary and documentary traditions — films like *House on 92nd Street* and *Naked City* employ an omniscient third person voice-over, typical of documentary techniques. These films, as well as *He Walked By Night*, show events and scenes outside the knowledge of the protagonist, providing a mode of third-person omniscient narration typical of most fiction and films. Omniscient narration seems compatible with the factual authenticity rendered in semi-documentaries, as viewers are assured of complete and truthful knowledge of a dramatized reality. In *Naked City*, this omniscience is heightened by the narrator identifying himself as film producer Mark Hellinger — the film assures viewers that they will receive all the facts and knowledge at the disposal of the film's creator. Likewise, 1930s radio programs such as *Gang Busters* offer actual law enforcement personnel as narrators to authenticate the fictionalized accounts of crime.

Unlike the third-person voice-overs and narrative perspective common to semi-documentary film, *Dragnet* employs Friday's distinctive first-person narration and limits the action to his own experiences. In employing this device, *Dragnet* draws from generic traditions outside of the semi-documentary. In some ways, this is consistent with radio drama of the 1940s, as most shows were narrated by explicit voice-overs, often in the first person. The suspense dramas of the 1940s often employ first-person narration, but the tales are usually told from the perspective of the (potential) victim of a crime, not the detective.[41] Radio detective dramas are often narrated from a first-person perspective, similar to the tough thriller films of the 1940s — it is difficult to say which medium influenced the other in this regard, or if they both drew the device from hard-boiled detective fiction. Nevertheless, *Dragnet* clearly drew its mode of narration from the hard-boiled model common in film, radio, and fiction throughout the 1940s, as Webb had been the star of such radio detective dramas prior to *Dragnet*.[42] This link to the hard-boiled model is furthered through Webb's unusual tradition of naming all *Dragnet* episodes "The Big X," ranging from "The Big War" to "The Big Bird" — seemingly a reference to hard-boiled classics like *The Big Sleep* (1946) and *The Big Clock* (1948).[43] Yet *Dragnet*'s adoption of this hard-boiled tradition takes on new meanings and ramifications through its rearticulation to the semi-documentary crime genre.

Traditionally, the first-person narration of hard-boiled detectives is somewhat unreliable — we experience the fictional world through the perspective of a deeply flawed character whose perception colors our vision of the events and characters. Often in *film noir* thrillers, the voice-over is revealed to be the case's criminal, victim, or both.[44] Even when the narrator is the detective, his character traits are usually suspect at best — he might be more moral than the world he portrays, but not by much. Thus, in the hard-boiled thriller, the narration often renders narrators as complex characters, with the story experienced (often in flashback) as part of their borderline status as protagonist. *Dragnet* takes this narrational model of the hard-boiled thriller and relocates it within the world of the authenticated semi-documentary. While we experience everything via the limited perspective of Joe Friday, he is the most reliable of all possible first-person narrators, with no visible flaws, biases, or even emotions.

The hard-boiled thriller replaces an omniscient narrator with a morally-questionable character who is fully imbricated within the narrative, making the audience question the truth value of the narrated events. Webb reverses this relationship, taking the omniscient third-person "voice of God" of documentaries and placing him directly into the narrative, making the character of Friday as detached, objective, and reliable as Mark Hellinger in *Naked City*. Webb's well-known status as *Dragnet's* auteur — star, director, producer, and owner of production company — further cements his character's status as omniscient and reliable like Hellinger.[45] Thus while we experience everything from Friday's limited perspective, there is never any question that what we are being told is factual or accurate, effectively turning Friday, the *tabula rosa* of every policeman, into the site of authentic official knowledge in action.

Although Friday functions as supremely reliable, lacking the character flaws coloring the narration of hard-boiled detectives, his knowledge is distinctly limited — he does not know the solutions to the criminal mysteries encountered in each episode. While it is clear that Friday and Smith will solve every episode's featured crime before the final credits — neither Webb nor the LAPD would allow an unresolved case to raise doubts of police efficacy — Friday narrates each case without providing any information outside the moment-to-moment procedures undertaken to pursue justice. We get no clues as to a given suspect's actual guilt, whether a particular procedure will be effective, or when the criminal might strike again. *Dragnet's* documenting of authentic procedures relies upon this lack of future knowledge, as we are not following the deductive powers of a master detective like Sherlock Holmes. Rather, we are witnessing the powers embodied in the larger system of police procedure, embodied in the featureless "cog in a great enforcement machine," Joe Friday. Because we witness the machine in action, we pursue dead ends, follow leads that lead nowhere, and enact procedures that produce no results. As Webb described it, "the detective work, remote from the magical sleuthing of fictional private eyes, was the plodding, often dull kind of leg work it takes to solve real crimes."[46] Friday has no knowledge of which procedures will solve the crime, but he has ultimate faith in the system's ability to function, as the narration positions the audience as an active participant in the systemically guaranteed machinery of justice.

The limited scope of *Dragnet's* narration has significant effects for the ideological impact of the show and its generic legacy. Since we only ever see what Friday sees, we do not see the crimes themselves being committed. Cases come to the police via reports from victims or witnesses, and thus we are left to reconstruct the criminal acts along with the police. Because of this limited perspective, the social order is rarely witnessed in chaos — for a show centered around crime, there is a distinct lack of actual crime portrayed. We see the effects of crime upon victims, families, and criminals, as well as hearing these characters reconstruct crimes for the police, but crime itself is rarely seen in the level of detail reserved for police procedures — a direct contrast to the "blood and thunder" tone of 1930s radio procedurals.[47] Because of this limited vision of crime, we are denied the sensational thrill of witnessing antisocial behavior — we never view the countercultural behaviors that disrupt narrative equilibrium, consigned only to seeing the processes that restore the status quo.[48]

Another similar limitation further excises social disruption from the television screen — Webb kept gunplay and violence to a minimum on the show. While he claimed that this was part of his quest for authenticity, as violence was over-represented on crime dramas versus real police work, one effect of downplaying portrayals of violence and crime on *Dragnet* is to minimize moments in the text in which the social order upheld by the police is threatened, questioned, or undermined.[49] While the police on *Dragnet* often are unsure about the mystery at hand, they are rarely seen as vulnerable to the insidious forces of crime that almost always occur offscreen. Thus, as the foundation for the television police genre, *Dragnet* linked the textual conventions of downplaying violence and crimes occurring offscreen with cultural assumptions of ideological closure and authentic truth. Future crime programs, such as *Naked City* (1958–63) and *The Untouchables* (1959–63), would violate these conventions as a site of inno-vation, distinguishing themselves from Webb's textual model and disarticulating some of *Dragnet*'s generic assumptions of ideological closure.

Just as we never see crime represented in a way that might encourage viewers to identify with criminals, *Dragnet*'s mode of representing police procedures situates viewers as participants in the processes of police work. We hear Friday's narration complete with unexplained references to criminal code, police lingo, and forensic procedures. While the narrative usually clarifies vital procedural details, there is little attempt to explicate the terminology and techniques employed by police. In this way, the narration addresses an audience "in the know," with the illusion that Friday's voice-over could be read directly out of a po-lice report. By presenting the procedures without translation for a lay audience, *Dragnet* both further ensures its authenticity and helps position viewers as an ally of the police, a willing — and frequent — partner in the criminal justice system. This technique of procedural accuracy without explanation was viewed skeptically by NBC at first, thinking audiences would be lost among the lingo; *Dragnet*'s success in using authentic terminology has proven to be a staple of police shows as well as other genres, such as medical and legal dramas.

In transferring *Dragnet*'s radio success onto the television screen, Webb developed a distinctive visual style, both drawing from crime films and estab-lishing a unique look that would prove to be influential for the television police genre. Prior to *Dragnet*, most television crime dramas were shot in studios, broadcast live, and recorded via kinescope. The production values on programs like *Man Against Crime* and *Treasury Men in Action* (1950–54) were limited by their live format, with action confined to fourth-wall interior sets, camerawork privileging long takes and distant shots, and scripts requiring lengthy scenes to avoid set changes.[50] Webb's insistence on telefilm was partly driven by his desire to avoid such limitations, enabling him to continue the authenticated portrait of Los Angeles that had been a key part of the radio drama. *Dragnet's* radio origins directly impacted its televisual style, as Webb wanted to visualize his radio scripts, complete with frequent scene changes as necessitated by procedural authenticity, multiple characters, and exterior urban locations, all of which were easily rendered in the sound-only medium. But Webb was directly influenced by the stylistic possibilities of film as well, wanting to direct "a half-hour of motion pictures, not a half-hour of TV films."[51] Through his experiences appearing in Hollywood thrillers like *He Walked By Night* and *Sunset Boulevard* (1950), Webb found himself enamored of a visual style impossible to achieve in live broadcasting.

Webb's directorial style comprises a limited but complex assortment of tendencies and patterns that set vital precedents for the police genre. To establish the scene of Los Angeles, most episodes begin with an exterior shot of the city, accompanied by the well-known voice-over by Friday: "This is the city, Los Angeles, California. I work here — I'm a cop."[52] As the series progressed, opening segments become more complex, with full-fledged montage sequences portraying Los Angeles, people at work, suspicious activities, and police, all providing visual documentation of Friday's authenticating monologues following cues common to semi-documentary films. Montage sequences are important throughout *Dragnet*, as Webb uses them as bridges between dialogue scenes to condense a case's progress for the half-hour format. Underneath Friday's factual narration of procedures, Webb offers a montage of stock shots of Los Angeles, scenes of mundane police work (like sorting "card punch" records of fingerprints), and extreme close-ups of forensic photos and tests. These montage sequences expedite the narrative, as well as providing semi-documentary "visual evidence" of police at work to mark the show's authenticity.

The visual style of dialogue sequences adapts classic Hollywood techniques to create a style unique to *Dragnet*. Most scenes, such as interrogations, police discussions of procedures, and interviewing witnesses, follow a standard pattern: they begin with an establishing long shot locating Friday, Smith, and other characters in the given space. These establishing shots can be quite brief, lasting only a few moments to orient viewers, or quite lengthy, enduring over two minutes. Following this long shot, Webb shifts into a system of "line editing," cutting between tight close-ups of characters talking, with the rhythm of the edits always following the alternating dialogue.[53] In this highly unusual and strictly patterned mode of editing, Webb deviates from typical Hollywood style of invisible and varied edits between close-ups, with the camera lingering on actors for reaction shots and dramatic effect. On *Dragnet*, line editing continues until the end of the scene approaches, when Webb cuts back to the long shot before fading into another scene or montage via voice-over transitions.

Occasionally, an opening or closing long shot will begin or end with a dolly into or out from a close-up, but the majority of shots use minimal camera movement. Thus, the standard *Dragnet* sequence consists solely of line-edited tight close-ups, bookended by long shots, without the medium shots that conventionally mediate between these extremes within Hollywood film.

This peculiar style stemmed from Webb's directorial motivations as well as explorations in the nascent form of telefilm production. Webb clearly employed a number of techniques primarily for their cost-cutting capabilities — for instance, the tight close-ups and line editing enabled him to use TelePrompTers to save rehearsal time. Unlike most film set-ups, which shoot an entire sequence from a distance as a "master shot" to use for cutaways (known as coverage), Webb filmed the beginning and ending of scenes only in long shots, and the middle parts of scenes only in close-up, thus unusually limiting his footage to that which he planned on using. While these budgetary decisions informed his style, Webb's reported perfectionism in set details and acting style suggests that he would not have sacrificed any stylistic goals for cost or time concerns; his reported shooting ratio of 4:1 suggests that he was willing to overshoot to get the right shot.[54] Webb's fascination with tight close-ups grew after viewing the completed pilot episode and realizing that viewers would be seeing the show on small screens; he ordered two more days of shooting (at personal expense) to add close-ups and recut the show to play better on television.[55] Many of *Dragnet*'s television episodes were adapted from radio scripts with only minimal changes; thus, the rhythm of dialogue-driven radio episodes encouraged the pattern of line editing dialogue alternating with montage voice-over narration. Many dialogue scenes conclude with a "snappy" line from Friday moralistically judging a criminal's actions, followed by a musical cue underscoring the weight of Friday's line. This musical cue functions like an aural "reaction shot," providing the emotional impact of Webb's line without employing the standard visual reaction shot which would deviate from the line editing pattern and be unavailable for radio. But despite the origins of *Dragnet*'s stylistic peculiarities, clearly the show's unique style had an impact on the meanings offered by the program and the police genre.

Dragnet's visual style distinguishes it from nearly all of its contemporary television and film counterparts. It avoids the staged distance of live studio shooting, while deviating from the invisible editing and reaction shots of classical Hollywood filmmaking. While many reviewers, and Webb himself, label the program "realist," its stylistic quirks mark it as distinct from these two conventional modes of visual realism common to television and film screens in the 1950s, offering a visual tone that breaks from a "zero degree style" generally associated with conventional realist filmmaking. *Dragnet*'s style is not fully "anti-realist," as Webb's quirky conventions are not explicitly *avant-garde*, nor do they represent a radical break from the real world. Nevertheless, the stylistic difference between *Dragnet* and its contemporary texts is sufficient enough to suggest that viewers did see it as unusual, distinctive in its stylization.[56] While *Dragnet*'s style violates established codes of media realism, it does seem consistent with the model of semi-documentary authenticity it tenders through its stories, official endorsements, and attention to detail. As with characterizations and acting, *Dragnet* offers a distinctive combination of emotional distance and systemic authenticity, a juxtaposition continuing through the show's visual style. The long takes and distant shots keep audiences detached from characters, while the jarring staccato of line-edited close-ups deny characters' reactions and fracture typical invisible editing conventions emphasizing emotional naturalism. The primary effect of the show's style is again to highlight procedures over characters, facts over emotions, and rigid order over chaotic crime.

In this analysis of *Dragnet*'s textual conventions and practices, we can see how the show draws upon generic categories to further certain linkages and assumptions. By referencing the semi-documentary film, through procedural emphasis, montage sequences, and overt claims of authenticity and official endorsement, *Dragnet* solidifies its place as an articulation of true tales of the police. Through these devices, the show transcends its dramatized mode to draw upon the cultural assumptions of legitimacy, accuracy, and truth associated with documentary and semi-documentary films. The show also references hard-boiled detective dramas, with similar first-person narration and cynical visions of social problems, but through its mixture with semi-documentary authenticity, these assumptions often linked to *film noir* lose their association with *noir*'s moral ambiguity, becoming firmly ensconced within clear distinctions between right and wrong. Finally, the show is categorized by television crime dramas as its primary generic identification, serving as the foremost police show of its era; *Dragnet*'s textual ties to semi-documentaries through telefilm production practices recast most of the assumptions concerning the definitions and cultural meanings linked to this emergent television genre.

Just as *Dragnet* can be better understood by exploring its linkages to various generic categories, the textual features of *Dragnet* worked to articulate two important major assumptions to the larger categorical cluster of the police genre. First, the show's high production values helped legitimate its mode of production in an era when live television was assumed to be of higher cultural value than telefilm. As William Boddy discusses, the perceived "golden age of television" was predicated on the cultural valuation of liveness, which emerged on early television from theatrical and radio traditions.[57] Telefilms were shunned by critics as representing Hollywood's potential to "debase" the culturally validated genres of anthology dramas and variety programs. Webb faced resistance from NBC for wanting to shoot *Dragnet* on telefilm, as the network believed the show would be viewed as inferior if filmed. The popular and critical success of *Dragnet* on telefilm changed these cultural assumptions, especially as applied to crime dramas — by linking telefilm production to semi-documentary authenticity, *Dragnet* helped legitimate filmed television, overcoming negative associations with Hollywood sensationalism, artifice, and adulteration of truth. Instead of the scenic and narrative limitations of live crime shows, *Dragnet* offered endless possibilities of on-location shooting, multiple scenes, montage sequences, and occasional action sequences. While the stylized pace of Webb's line editing and staccato dialogue was often parodied (and is somewhat hard to take seriously today), *Dragnet* offers a rhythmic vibrancy distinguishing the show from its slow-paced live crime show peers. Within a few years of the show's televisual success, nearly all crime dramas shifted to telefilm, enjoying the production flexibility and potential for a lucrative rerun market that Webb had pioneered. *Dragnet* helped foster an important cultural assumption for the generic cluster of the crime show, starting the trend that police dramas would be stylistic innovators and feature high production values — a tradition that has continued through series like *Hill St. Blues* (1981–87) and *Homicide: Life on the Street* (1993–99).

Just as *Dragnet*'s textual practices linked certain discourses of definition — high production values, telefilm shooting, and action editing — and evaluation — legitimized telefilm and official institutional endorsement — to the cultural category of the police show, it also tied a number of interpretations to the generic cluster. *Dragnet*'s obsession with authenticity and representing the world from an "official" perspective gives the show a dominant ideological viewpoint. One of the representational strategies that *Dragnet* uses to solidify this worldview is the use of overt binary oppositions, such as law versus crime, order versus chaos, and efficient system versus rogue individualism. *Dragnet* invests these dualities with unambiguous difference, eschewing the gray area that might suggest that the lines between law and crime were anything less than crystal clear. Throughout *Dragnet*'s run, the show categorizes society into two distinct camps, with the police working to maintain the rigid boundary between chaos and order, the latter always triumphant in half-hour increments.

Discussing these binaries evokes structuralist theories of genre, in which social dualities are manifested in generic texts to play out cultural anxieties. Structuralist analysis has produced a number of cogent examinations of media texts, suggesting ways in which texts encode larger social structures through oppositions.[58] But structuralist approaches to genre operate on a more general and universalizing level than the cultural approach to genres that I have offered. Instead of following the typical structuralist path — examining texts and genres as symptomatic of social universals — we can look at texts as sites in which cultural notions like binary oppositions are specifically articulated to generic clusters. Obviously, binaries like law versus crime transcend *Dragnet* and the police genre, but they are not cultural universals waiting to be expressed by media texts. Rather than viewing the police genre as a site manifesting underlying social structures, we can see *Dragnet* furthering the cultural links between police dramas and the maintenance of these strict dualities. The specific articulation of these dualities within *Dragnet* is historically specific, situated within the context of 1950s cultural norms and traditions of media practice. The constant citation and maintenance of these dualistic boundaries on *Dragnet* helped solidify these ideologically charged binaries within the generic cluster, working to naturalize the notion that police dramas are assumed to uphold the status quo and warrant official endorsement.

One of the particular attributes of *Dragnet*'s use of these binaries was the lack of mediating figures. Structuralism often argues that to resolve strict oppositions, an anomalous category will "straddle" the binary to mediate between poles.[59] For crime dramas, this mediating figure is often the private detective — he enacts justice, but works outside the confines of the "official" bureaucratic justice system.[60] Within the police setting of crime stories, this figure is the "rogue cop," bucking the restrictive system to achieve society's ultimate ends.[61] But on *Dragnet*, the heroes are firmly ensconced within the systemic side of the binary, working as emissaries of the official judicial machine without violating the procedures that are held up as the guarantees of crime's ultimate punishment. Within the program's worldview, mediating figures are unnecessary, because the duality is reconcilable without reformulation — law overcomes crime, order trumps chaos, as unequivocally dramatized each episode. *Dragnet* linked this "hard dualism" to the police genre, as many programs throughout the 1950s followed its lead in dramatizing the official rhetoric of law enforcement. Webb thus established the basic model for the genre's assumed dominant meanings — which would be rebelled against in later years.

The ideological worldview represented by *Dragnet* was consistent with many threads of 1950s culture, where most media representations maintained a status quo that, although certainly not universally accepted, was still validated as a dominant myth of consensus and American contentment. The police were part of this social order, and that was not to be questioned — at least not on mainstream television. By the time Webb ended *Dragnet*'s first television run in 1958, the police genre had grown to be an established part of television schedules, although its popularity had dwindled significantly. In the late 1950s, the most watched televisual lawmen were found on another genre typified by its strict adherence to dualistic logic — the western. Like most genres, police shows and their generic category shifted with the times, as new programs were notable for their innovations over *Dragnet*'s generic baseline. Through the 1960s, changing cultural assumptions about police, law, and the social order helped contribute to divergent televisual representations of the police. But while these "after the fact" generic and cultural shifts are typical in any case study, they became central to *Dragnet*'s history, as Webb brought back the show for a new run on television in 1967. The resulting contextual clash demonstrates shifts in both generic and cultural history, as *Dragnet* found itself attempting to rigidly structure a world whose binary logic had undergone a cultural revolution.

A Black & White World. . . Now In Color! — *Dragnet's* Recontextualized Return

> "I don't know, Joe. When we were growing up, we saw things as black and white, right and wrong. Kids today just seem to look at everything as various shades of gray."
>
> — Bill Gannon, *Dragnet*, 1969

> "Brown. . . blue. . . yellow. . . green. . . lavender. . . pink. . . orange. . . red. . . red-red. . . and red. . . I can hear them. I can hear them all."
>
> — Blue Boy, *Dragnet*, 1967

When *Dragnet* returned to the airwaves in January 1967, the cultural meanings of the police had changed, both on television and in American society, during its nine-year absence. Whereas in the 1950s, the police were culturally represented — if not broadly accepted — as agents of social order and harmony, their status as "good guys" had been publicly questioned by the mid-1960s. The historical shorthand for understanding this era — equating the 1950s with content, social harmony and the 1960s with social turmoil and protest — is certainly a gross oversimplification.[62] America of the 1950s had numerous social problems, many of which were featured on the true stories of *Dragnet*, just as the majority of Americans were not protesting and rebelling in the 1960s. Nevertheless, by the time *Dragnet* returned to the airwaves in 1967, television viewers had seen Webb's own LAPD trying to quell the Watts uprising on the evening news, just one of many incidences of questionable police involvement in publicized events linked to the civil rights and anti-Vietnam movements. By mid-1960s, the LAPD had distinguished itself as a model of paramilitary structure with a controversial underbelly of racism and corruption.[63] Whereas viewers may have accepted the show's police-centered moral clarity in the 1950s, the changing role of the police as participants in social disorder had pushed the credibility limits of *Dragnet's* authenticated voice of authority.

The evolution of the police genre ran alongside this changing social history of the police. *Naked City's* television incarnation, based on the semi-documentary film, followed the tradition of *Dragnet* upon its late 1950s debut, but shifted its focus toward more psychological explorations and sympathetic characterizations of both criminals and the home lives of police. Like its source film, the show looked at crime as a social phenomenon, explored the urban milieu of New York as constitutive of criminality, and denied the black and white duality typical of *Dragnet*. *Naked City* also featured more violence, a trend maximized on shows like *M Squad* (1957–60) and *The Untouchables* as a way to draw in audiences. The latter program, like the era's popular westerns, placed crime into period dramas, linking clear dualistic justice to earlier moments in American history. While *Dragnet* had suffered through numerous one-shot parodies throughout its run, *Car 54, Where Are You?* (1961–63) linked the police genre with comedy explicitly, making the bumbling practices of police regular comedic fodder. While some police procedurals in *Dragnet*'s mold succeeded in the 1960s, like *The F.B.I.* (1965–74) and *The Felony Squad* (1966–69), the crime drama's popularity had been overtaken by the mid-1960s cycle of espionage programs like *I Spy* (1965–68) and *Mission: Impossible* (1966–73). Thus the assumptions in the generic cluster of police drama had changed during *Dragnet*'s absence, as increased violence, psychological explorations, periodization, and outright parody all destabilized the dualistic ideology favored by the 1950s dominant.

But despite the generic and cultural changes that *Dragnet* faced in returning to the airwaves, Webb refused to alter nearly any of the textual elements that had made *Dragnet* such a success in the 1950s. He returned with his ties to authenticity, exclusive focus on procedures over characters, and faith in clear ideological dualities fully intact. *Dragnet 1967*, as it was called upon its rebirth — to be relabeled *Dragnet 1968, 1969,* and *1970* as appropriate — made a few surface changes from the 1950s original. Since Ben Alexander was a regular on ABC's *Felony Squad*, Webb cast Harry Morgan as Friday's new partner, Bill Gannon. Webb produced *Dragnet 1967* in color, as was the era's technological norm, resulting in less emphasis on the gritty black-and-white visual style that marked the original's ties to *film noir*. Many of the cases Friday and Gannon investigated were topically tied to the 1960s milieu, especially as they busted hippies for marijuana and LSD use. But besides these slight shifts in appearance, *Dragnet* was still a product of the 1950s police genre and era, offering identical claims to authenticity, clear dualities of right and wrong, and unwavering systemic faith. Webb's directorial style changed only in degree, as the new version featured even faster line editing, even more monotonal line readings, even more dramatic musical cues, and an even more dour dedication to police work for Friday.

Dragnet returned to the airwaves as a made-for-TV movie in 1966; NBC liked the ratings results and encouraged Webb to revisit the series. Webb's own motivations for picking up Badge 714 again were both financial — his production efforts throughout the 1960s were a string of financial failures — and ideological. As he told *TV Guide*, "it's almost as if people were looking for this type of program. Judging by our ratings and our mail, there must be an enormous segment of the public which believes it's time that policemen no longer be misunderstood and maligned."[64] In the same interview, he dismisses the 1960s youth culture, suggesting that "there's a hell of a parallel between this generation and the decay of Roman civilization," expressing his well-publicized conservatism.[65] He saw *Dragnet* as a vehicle for presenting a restored vision of the social order, following the strict dualities that drove the show's original television run, with a new primary object of Webb's wrath: youth drug culture.

Narcotics have been a fairly frequent subject of *Dragnet* episodes dating back to the radio era, often investigating juvenile violations of narcotic laws and preaching to teenagers about the dangers of drugs. But in the 1960s, drugs on *Dragnet* serve as more than another criminal violation like murder or robbery — they become a metonymic stand-in for the radical changes to the social order that Friday and Gannon combated daily. More than any other crime in *Dragnet*'s late 1960s incarnation, Friday and Gannon fought against drugs and drug-related offenses.[66] The premiere episode of the series' new incarnation, "The LSD Story," demonstrates *Dragnet*'s approach to drugs, its awkward status within late 1960s culture, and dissonance with new assumptions of the police genre. Webb wrote the script, under the pseudonym John Randolph, chronicling Friday and Gannon's first encounters with LSD, as they busted Benjie "Blue Boy" Carver for public intoxication. The narrative posits the dangers of LSD, while the police must wait for the legislature to make the new drug officially illegal. By the time Friday and Gannon are given the right to bust "acid heads," they are too late, as Blue Boy is found dead from an overdose of multiple drugs. While the legal system was unable to save this one young addict, *Dragnet* dramatizes the systemic guarantee that future Blue Boys would be saved.[67]

Throughout this episode, as well as other treatments of 1960s drug culture on *Dragnet*, Friday and Gannon attempt to fit drugs and their users into the firm dualities they use to structure their fictional world — just as Webb attempted to locate youth drug culture into the binary logic of his vision of the police genre. But the dualities that resonated with audiences in the 1950s no longer held in the late-1960s, as the police procedures seemed incompatible with new forms of social disruption encountered by the LAPD. As the epigrammatic quotations beginning this section suggest, the police acknowledge that while they view the world as black and white, the new generation sees the gray areas between right and wrong. But Gannon and Friday cannot even discern the disjuncture between themselves and youth culture, as the tripping Blue Boy is much more enthralled by a range of *colors*, rather than shades of *gray*. The structuring dualities fostered by Webb and *Dragnet* cannot account for the experiences of youth culture — the counterculture was clearly operating on a different color spectrum than *Dragnet*'s black-and-white world. Even in switching to Technicolor production, Webb did not have the tools to contain the 1960s context within his representational palette. Although Webb had always offered a heavily stylized mode of realism, his inability to fit the countercultural object of his moralizing mission into his mode of authenticated police procedural helped lead *Dragnet* down the road of self-parody through excess, a sorry epilogue for the once-groundbreaking series.

The late-1960s was a transitional moment in the police genre. The semi-documentary dominant, popularized by *Dragnet* in the 1950s, was in the midst of its last hurrah, with *Dragnet 1967*, *Felony Squad*, *The F.B.I.*, *N.Y.P.D.* (1967–69), and Webb's own production *Adam 12* (1968–75). But the shifts in the genre's cultural meanings between *Dragnet*'s dual incarnations led to a different dominant for the 1970s. Drawing from the private detective and "rogue cop" traditions, this new mode of police show questions the efficacy of the system and procedures, focusing on the abilities of individualized police officers to work outside the official system which had been so revered on *Dragnet*. While *Ironside*'s (1967–75) main character is not a "rogue cop" per se, he is far from an anonymous cog in the machine — distinguished as both an exceptional detective and a disabled policeman in a wheelchair, he solves crimes idiosyncratically, rather than following anonymous procedures. Even more representative of this new mode is *The Mod Squad* (1968–73), focusing on three young ex-cons who embody that liminal space between law and crime.[68] With one foot in the counterculture and another in the police station, *Mod Squad* typifies the "maverick cop" dominant which would reign in the 1970s, with *The Streets of San Francisco* (1972–77), *Kojak* (1973–78), *Baretta* (1975–78), and *Starsky and Hutch* (1975–79) all pitting rogue heroes against both criminal chaos and bureaucratic systems.

Dragnet's legacy for the police genre did not die with the semi-documentary dominant in the 1960s. The show helped link assumptions of authenticity, procedural detail, and gritty urban realism to the cultural category of the police genre, associations that linger to this day. As the genre evolved in the 1980s, through *Hill St. Blues*' ensemble serialization and *Cagney & Lacey*'s (1982–88) gender reversals, *Dragnet*'s marks were still visible, even as a foundational baseline which these revisionist cop shows react against. The 1990s saw a return to *Dragnet*'s terrain even more, as *Law & Order*, *C.S.I.* (CBS, 2000–), and their spin-offs all display a fascination with procedure over characters, and *Homicide* and *NYPD Blue* (1993–) follow *Dragnet*'s lead in formal experimentation and heightened naturalism. Likewise, reality programs like *Cops* (1989–), *America's Most Wanted*, and *Unsolved Mysteries* mine *Dragnet*'s associations between crime and authenticity, documentary styles and ideological orthodoxy.

Dragnet's influence came full circle in 2003, when *Law & Order* producer Dick Wolf paid homage to his creative debts by remaking *Dragnet* for ABC. Yet again, *Dragnet*'s return offers a point of contrast to highlight the changing assumptions of the police genre and television. The new version features fewer procedural details, greater emotional realism, and an exchange of Webb's stylistic eccentricities for Wolf's established style of constantly moving hand-held cameras and intense performances. A telling change is in Friday's voice-overs — in the original, Webb's narration provided mainly dry procedural details and occasional judgmental commentary. In the new version, Friday often describes his opinions, hunches, and detecting strategies — off-limit elements for Webb's systemic realism. The new *Dragnet* marks the continued appeal of the police procedural, while reframing the show's style, tone, and politics for the contemporary genre that has been textually typified by *Law & Order* for over a decade. Despite the updates, the return of *Dragnet* was met with underwhelming reaction — even Wolf admitted that the experiment "didn't work," as he revised the show for its second season by renaming it *L.A. Dragnet* and decentered Friday from the first-person focus, before being cancelled after only five more episodes. The "new" new version promotes Friday to lieutenant, overseeing a stable of younger (and more attractive) detectives — transforming the remaining ties to the original into an even more typical generic program of today, like *C.S.I.* or *N.Y.P.D. Blue*.[69]

While today the original *Dragnet* may look stilted compared to its progeny, providing mostly camp pleasures on TV Land when it airs at all, it remains one of the landmark texts within media history, worthy of far more than the cursory analysis it has been accorded. In turning attention to the site of the generic text to consider *Dragnet*, the text functions as a site of categorical association, with assumptions from various genres being linked to *Dragnet* and new linkages forged with the nascent category of the police drama. By placing media texts at the center of my analysis, I am not suggesting that we can learn everything we might wish to know about *Dragnet* from the programs themselves — there are numerous questions left unasked that would need more detailed analysis of industrial, audience, policy, critical, and contextual practices to answer. Likewise, my textual analysis has tried to make clear ties to the cultural and historical contexts that are crucial to understanding the operation of genres as cultural categories. Even in its partiality, analyzing programs can demonstrate how texts work as sites of generic articulation, linking assumptions and conventions to and between genre categories within specific contextualized instances. In turning now to my final case studies, I draw upon the range of historiographic, industrial, audience, and textual issues raised in previous chapters to explore the vital practice of genre mixing.

6

Making Fun of Genres —
The Politics of Parody and Genre Mixing
in *Soap* and *The Simpsons*

Each chapter thus far has focused on singular genres. Although the genre practices examined have rarely been "pure" — genre mixing has played a role in each history, such as the incorporation of sitcoms into cartoons with *The Flintstones* and the blending of crime film and documentary for *Dragnet* — each chapter has been centered around one specific genre. This might suggest an erroneous (yet commonplace) assumption — generic practices are dependent on distinct, singular generic categories. But genre analysis must be able to account for the common practice of mixing genres, or what is commonly termed "hybridity," to be broadly applicable to how genres operate in television today. This chapter explores issues of generic mixing more directly, especially in the context of postmodernist theory, which often hails the blurring of genres as a paradigmatic element. My approach to mixed genres is more grounded in historical instances than postmodern theory, looking at the particular practices by which genres are culturally blended and the subsequent repercussions for genre scholars, especially concerning cultural politics. To provide a detailed account of mixing genres, I focus on one mode of generic combination — parody — through two specific historical moments of television genre blending tied to the situation comedy: *Soap* in the late 1970s and *The Simpsons* in the early 1990s.

Beyond Hybridity: The Cultural Practices of Generic Mixing

Hybridity has been a popular term within contemporary scholarship, used to discuss a variety of practices, from blurred identity categories to genre mixture.[1]

153

While hybridity may be quite useful in discussing cultural identity, I want to avoid the term "generic hybridity" because of its connotative associations. The term is based upon biological origins, suggesting the crossbreeding of two (or more) species; as argued in Chapter 1, biological metaphors are incompatible with a conception of genres as cultural categories. Since I contend that genres do not act like distinct biological species, the notion of hybridity does not correspond well to the more fluid process of generic mixing. Additionally, hybridity suggests a defined and bounded practice of crossbreeding — two species are combined, creating a hybrid. But generic practices are ongoing and disparate, not tied to a single act of combination to create a static hybrid. Thus, the term "genre mixing" is more indicative of an ongoing process of generic combination and interplay, not rooted in biological notions of taxonomic purity.

Since traditional definitional and interpretative approaches have treated genres as fairly distinct and bounded categories, discussions of generic mixture have tended to illustrate exceptional rather than common generic practices, especially as falling under the rubric of postmodernism. Postmodernism is, as might befit its theoretical pedigree, a slippery signifier, producing new meanings and implications practically every time the term is spoken or cited. I do not offer my own definition here, as I am more interested in how other scholars have looked at generic mixture using this theoretical lens, rather than attempting to provide my own take on so-called postmodern genres. For a number of postmodern theorists, the blurring of rigid generic boundaries is an axiomatic facet of postmodernist practice or a postmodern condition.[2] This postmodern tendency toward generic mixture is especially noted in regards to parody, or what is often termed "pastiche."[3] While useful analyses of cultural practices and conditions have emerged under the postmodernist masthead, I want to avoid grand pronouncements concerning generic tendencies and look more carefully at the processes of genre mixing that have been linked to postmodernity.

The postmodernist analysis of generic mixture contends that by blurring boundaries between genres, as demonstrated by texts confounding traditional generic analysis like *Twin Peaks* (1990–91) or *Pee Wee's Playhouse* (1986–91), genre categories are destabilized. This analysis is predicated on equating a genre with its distinct boundaries — the assumption is that, if a genre has overly permeable borders, it must not be a viable category, leading to generic dissolution. This assumption derives from traditional taxonomic approaches to generic categories, as biological categorization of species (and subsequent hybridity) would be indefensible without clear and distinct boundaries. But this approach is not grounded in how genres culturally operate — generic boundaries are permeable, fluid, historically contingent, and subject to change, while still offering categorical coherence at any given moment. If genres are viewed as cultural categories, the idea that generic mixing places firm boundaries in crisis does not necessarily suggest that genres are not still operative in important ways — in fact, as discussed below, the practice of generic mixture has the potential to foreground and activate generic categories in vital ways that "pure" generic texts rarely do.

Another questionable tenet of the postmodernist argument is that the type of generic blurring held up as paradigmatically postmodern is relatively new, tied to the cultural context of late capitalist society. But generic blending is not a new phenomenon — Rick Altman convincingly argues that the entire history of film genres have been predicated on processes of mixing.[4] While we cannot simply graft Altman's historical analysis of film genre onto television, certainly there are enough pre-postmodern examples of televised generic blurring to suggest that it is not an entirely recent phenomenon.[5] While recent "postmodern" television may exhibit generic blurring to a greater *degree* than typical of earlier television, it seems less than convincing to argue that there is a distinctive *mode* of postmodern generic practice, especially in how genres operate as cultural categories. I return to the question of postmodernism below in looking at *The Simpsons* as a case of generic mixing and parody often hailed as a postmodernist exemplar. But I am skeptical of a comprehensive account of postmodern generic dissolution, both on theoretical terms — genres are fluid enough to intermix without dissolving — and on historical terms — the practice of generic mixture has not radically transformed in recent years.

Instead of postmodern generalizations, I explore generic mixture in specific cultural practice. Genre mixing is potentially operative within all of the spheres of media practice I have discussed thus far in this project, including textual production, industrial decision making, regulatory policy formation, critical analysis, audience reception, and broader cultural circulation. Genres can be — and often are — mixed through the various discourses of generic definition, interpretation, and evaluation that constitute genres as cultural categories. Looking at the material ways that genre mixing plays out in cultural practice leads to distinctly different conclusions than have been asserted by both traditional genre critics and postmodernists — through the case studies below, I contend that generic mixing generally does not lead to the declining importance of genre, but actually reinforces and reasserts the role of genres in media practice.[6]

There are many distinct ways in which genres may be mixed; while not offering a comprehensive guide to generic "mixology," it is important to recognize other forms of genre mixing beyond the parodic mode explored below. The most standard form of generic mixing — genre fusion — works at the textual level primarily as a type of generic arithmetic: add one genre to another, allowing the associated assumptions to interplay. Fusion can occur at a variety of levels: individual episodes (sitcom *M*A*S*H* blends with the newsreel in the acclaimed 1976 episode "The Interview"), specific programs (*The Munsters* [1964–66] fuses horror and sitcoms), or emergent genres (the late 1980s rise of "dramedies" fusing dramas and sitcoms). Fusion can be fairly balanced, with both genres equally prominent in juxtaposition, such as *Law and Order*'s mix of police and legal dramas, or unbalanced, with one genre serving as the primary category while the other serves a secondary role — *Barney Miller* (1975–82) was primarily a sitcom, but drew upon some conventions and associations of the police show. Generic categorization can also shift over the life of programs as well — *M*A*S*H* began as a sitcom set during a war, but began emphasizing emotional realism more commensurate with a melodrama as the program evolved into a proto-dramedy.

This brief discussion of generic fusion might seem to counter my cultural approach to genres — aren't all the examples I just described textual in focus? Does generic mixing only occur within media texts? As argued in Chapter 1, genre definitions are not grounded in texts, but the cultural use of genres draws upon textual elements as the primary site of generic operation. While I would concede that generic mixing is most activated and manifest within the realm of the text, generic mixtures are defined, interpreted, and evaluated throughout all spheres of media within generic clusters. While the generic identity of *Win Ben Stein's Money* (1997–2002) might be textually more skewed toward game shows — and the pleasures that many fans take from the show might follow the assumptions of the game show genre as well — its production and exhibition by Comedy Central industrially works to foreground its comedic elements. As Henry Jenkins has examined, the practices of *Beauty and the Beast* (1987–90) fans defined the program's mixture of romance and action in quite different terms than the producers and network did, as fans refused to cede the terrain of genre to the text and its creators.[7] In both of these examples, the industry and audience might both cite the text as "proving" their particular generic definitions and interpretations, but it is only through the cultural circulation of these shows and their corresponding generic categories that genre mixture becomes an active cultural process. As I address with both *The Simpsons* and *Soap*, the cultural operation of generic mixing is neither guaranteed nor rooted in textual elements, although media texts contain the most common evidence for our everyday encounters with genres, especially in their mixed form.

According to traditional accounts of generic mixture, the process of blending two (or more) genres together results in a dilution of generic categories — as genres become less pure, they lose their distinction and their usefulness. Traditional critics have suggested that genre is most useful in either providing a distinct definition for textual categories or pointing to a core set of meanings contained within the genre's texts. Based on these assumptions, genre mixture confounds these clear categorical imperatives by diluting boundaries and core meanings. But if we look at genres as culturally operative categories, then genre mixing becomes a site of *heightened* genre discourse — industrial personnel, critics, and audience members spend more energy linking a mixed program like *Buffy the Vampire Slayer* (1997– 2003) to genre categories than more "pure" teen dramas like *Beverly Hills 90210* (1990–2000).[8] Even within texts themselves, mixed-genre programs like *Buffy* explicitly highlight and draw upon generic assumptions as they are placed in juxtaposition with other genres. For a narratively central instance, heroine Buffy's forbidden attraction for the brooding, older, and sexy outsider Angel is characteristic of a typical relationship within a teen drama. Angel's status as a cursed and remorseful vampire draws upon horror conventions of the highly sexualized monster both to amplify the taboos of their attraction and to highlight the artificiality of the typical brooding romance itself. By overlaying horror and teen drama, the conventions of both genres are made manifest and explicit, heightening generic assumptions and undercutting their illusion of naturalism through juxtaposition. Likewise, *Alias* (2001–) fuses the spy thriller with a family melodrama, allowing familial politics of divorce and betrayal to be filtered through double agents and hidden identities — the combination of generic assumptions makes each genre's norms richer and more vibrant through clever practices of fusion. Within more "pure" generic texts, such conventions are often downplayed or unspoken to avoid appearances of formula or repetition, making genre assumptions less manifest than on generically mixed programs.

Underlying many interpretative approaches to genres is the assumption that genre norms are most active when they are invisible — generic myths, rituals, and ideologies work on the level of the unconscious and can be "dispelled" when examined and brought to the surface. More recent work in a range of approaches to media scholarship, from cognitivism to cultural studies, has questioned the reliance of the unconscious as the primary site of interpretation.[9] Genres work primarily within cultural practices that are conscious and explicit, not beneath the surface. Given this shift in focus, genre mixing does not dilute the power of genres to perpetuate an unspoken myth, as some scholars contend. Rather, genre mixing brings generic practices to the surface, making the conventions and assumptions clustered within individual categories explicit through the juxtaposition of conflicting or complementary genres. While *90210* is probably a "purer" teen drama than *Buffy*, the latter program highlights the assumptions that are tied to teen dramas much more explicitly than on *90210*, activating the genre much more overtly in cultural practices. Lack of generic purity does not make any instance a less important site to explore the operation of genres — genre mixing can lead to more fruitful sites of generic analysis, as conventions and assumptions become more visible and therefore accessible for the genre historian.

Traditional accounts of genre mixing tend to be limited to the terrain of the text, ignoring sites of context, industry, and audience. For instance, a traditional analysis of *Sports Night* might try to define how the show exemplifies the "dramedy" mixture or interpret how the dramatic and serialized stories undercuts the sitcom's tradition of reinforcing the status quo.[10] I am more interested in exploring how a mixed program might exemplify the processes of genre mixture through a variety of sites within a generic cluster. We might look to the industrial struggle concerning the use of a laugh track, a traditional textual device of the sitcom, as an attempt of ABC to explicitly "genre" the program. This contrasts with creator Aaron Sorkin's own generic understanding, as he cites his background in theatrical writing:

> In theater you don't wrestle so much with the comedy-vs.-drama question. For centuries and centuries now we've been telling stories that employed as many elements as we could bring into it to create theater.... In the theater we have musicals and non-musicals, so *Sports Night* is a non-musical.[11]

While ABC categorizes *Sports Night* along the sitcom/drama axis, Sorkin rebuffs ABC's definitional practices by placing the show within the context of theatrical genres, just as viewers can refuse to cede ABC the power to define its programs for them. *Sports Night* fans on the Web site IMDB.com (which also covers television programs) complain about the laugh track and ABC's advertising strategies that try to lock the program into a simple category, preferring to celebrate the show's subtle blending of elements that transcend categorization.[12] Likewise, critics note how the show both fits into and diverges from the traditions of the sitcom, using terms like "dramedy" to provide viewers a framework for the program. In all of these sites, genres are activated, debated, redefined, and questioned, suggesting that generic categories are no less important to blended programs, but rather become quite salient when traditional boundaries are challenged or transgressed.

In charting out some of the ways in which genre mixture places generic categories in cultural operation, I have focused on generic fusion. Yet there are other ways in which genres may be mixed. For the rest of this chapter, I focus on generic parody as an important type of genre mixture.[13] While genre parody has been underexplored as an aspect of media genre analysis, most scholars who do discuss parody consider it a form of generic transformation or degradation, not genre mixing.[14] Steve Neale and Frank Krutnik explicitly address this issue, as they claim that generic parody should be distinguished from what they term "generic hybridization." They argue that "in contrast to genre hybrids, which combine generic conventions, parodies work by drawing upon such conventions in order to make us laugh. . . . The result is not the combination of generic elements, but the subordination of the conventions of one genre to those of another."[15] According to their definitional schema, parodies are always primarily comedies, because they work to make audiences laugh instead of eliciting generic effects tied to other genres — *Young Frankenstein* (1974) is not a horror film because it does not scare us. Their assumptions concerning parody seem to be widely held by most generic scholars — parody subsumes the genre functioning as the "parodic object" under the category of comedy because of the centrality of humor and lack of commitment to the other genre's core ideals.

This formulation of generic parody needs to be reconfigured for a model of cultural genre analysis. The cultural operation of genre is not an unconscious or "mythic" process, but rather an explicit and conscious one. A genre does not need to elicit its "underlying meaning structure" or "core definitional affect" to be categorically activated. Few could argue that the horror genre is irrelevant to *Young Frankenstein* — the film is clearly drawing upon the genre's cultural meanings and assumptions to motivate both humor and narrative suspense. In fact, genre parodies like *Young Frankenstein* rely upon and activate generic definitions, interpretations, and evaluations much more explicitly than "pure" cases of the genre being lampooned.[16] A text does not need to fit the core definitions of a genre to work as an important cultural site of that genre's artic- ulation and operation. Thus, we can look at parodic texts not as necessarily "belonging to" the genre which they parody, but as sites of generic operation, which makes the genre quite explicit and culturally active. As I discuss concerning *Soap*, parodic programs can also strategically draw upon elements from the genre and treat them seriously, eliciting pleasures and using defining elements of the genres being parodied.[17]

A common misconception tied to generic parody is that the parodic rendering of a genre is a symptom of the genre's decline and near-death.[18] This common tale regarding parody as the final stage in a genre's demise is predicated on the understanding of genre as a facet of media most active when unspoken and operating beneath the surface of texts. As genre conventions become coherent and accepted enough to become the topic of parody, the genre loses its power through its self-conscious articulation of conventions through parody or other transformations.[19] As the history of *Soap* aptly demonstrates, the soap opera did not perish from its parodic treatment. But if we avoid regarding genre as an un- spoken set of assumptions, then a genre being openly parodied and potentially undercut is not necessarily a sign of decline — in fact, the open explicit dis- course about genres within parodies can actually *affirm* rather than weaken generic categories. By highlighting the generic assumptions that often go un- spoken, the usefulness of the category is reiterated and made explicit through the practice of genre parody. In the specific historical instances of *Soap* and *The Simpsons*, generic categories became manifest and strengthened through par- ticipation in cultural debates via both genre mixing and parody.

To understand the cultural operation of genre parody, we can view parody as a particular mode of generic mixture between comedy and at least one other genre, which I call the "host genre."[20] When a host genre mixes parodically with comedy, some (but by no means all) of the resulting humor stems from ridi- culing the textual conventions and cultural associations of the host genre — *Police Squad!* (1982) catalogs the typical practices of police dramas, which are then undercut through excess or absurd juxtaposition. While the host genre is usually mocked within parodies, it can still provide more conventional associations and pleasures; just because a parody makes fun of a genre does not mean that the host genre must be subsumed by the parody. As *Soap* demonstrates, many of the cultural associations linked to soap operas remained intact and were explicitly activated by the program. Additionally, the conventions and assumptions of television comedy, most notably sitcoms, become central to the parodic practices offered in these two cases, as both shows function institutionally as sitcoms within the television schedule, framing audience responses and critical discourse.

In examining the cultural practices of genre parody in *Soap* and *The Simpsons*, I explore the "cultural lives" of these shows, charting their operation across the various spheres of industry, text, audience, and historical context. The processes of generic mixture and cultural circulation become manifest through the discursive practices situating the programs generically, bringing out the definitions, interpretations, and evaluations that constituted the categorical frameworks for these two shows. I draw upon trade press coverage, popular press commentaries and reviews, personal interviews, audience remnants, and textual analysis to chart out the constitutive processes of generic categorization relevant to our understanding these moments of media history. I first turn to *Soap*, where the dual categories of soap opera and situation comedy were parodically mixed in the late-1970s, entering into the midst of a highly publicized cultural controversy.

Serialized Parody: *Soap* and Cultural Controversy in the Late 1970s

> "I don't consider *Soap* a parody of a soap opera."
>
> — Susan Harris, *Soap* creator[21]

When *Soap* debuted on September 13, 1977, its cultural notoriety had probably already peaked. Starting with an inflammatory *Newsweek* article in June, *Soap* found itself at the center of a social maelstrom before it had even aired on ABC. Religious groups organized network boycotts and letter-writing campaigns to protest the as-yet-unseen show's salacious content, which had become exaggerated through well-publicized rumors. ABC launched a preemptive PR campaign to highlight its own dual commitment to social values and artistic integrity by assuring potential viewers that the show would neither violate social taboos, nor be toned down due to protests. Many affiliates made the unusual decision to drop the show or reschedule episodes to late-night timeslots. Press coverage focused on the show as the stand-in for the sexual revolution's emergence on primetime. Once the program debuted, the furor subsided, as the show proved to be both less culturally volatile and more popular with viewers than had been anticipated by its detractors. *Soap* broke ground for televisual representations of gays and female sexuality, yet the program was unceremoniously cancelled after four seasons because of ABC's inability to overcome continued threats of boycotts to draw sponsorship commensurate with the show's high ratings. The program has lived on, nonetheless, as a popular rerun in syndication, on Comedy Central, and through home-video sales — although it has been virtually ignored by media scholars.

In offering a history of *Soap*'s cultural life, I draw out the links between the program's tumultuous debut and its practices of genre mixing and parody. Two central questions motivate my analysis: how did genre mixture and parody operate within *Soap*'s cultural circulation, and what can *Soap* teach us about television genre mixture and parody? The generic clusters of comedy and soap opera operated around *Soap* in a variety of spheres, from industry to audience, text to context. By exploring the show's stormy history in terms of genre, I am not suggesting that the program should only be explored as a generic mixture; rather I look to how the program's generic status and processes contributed to its cultural understanding and controversy. Genres work as categorical conveniences, cultural "place holders" clustering a number of hierarchies and assumptions of value; in the case of *Soap*, the shorthand terms of "sitcom," "soap opera," and "parody" all came into play in the ensuing controversy. As argued in Chapter 2, this mode of "crisis historiography" lends itself to explore the discourses surrounding a program — because of *Soap*'s controversial reception, there are a wealth of accessible traces of cultural processes and assumptions that are usually ephemeral and unrecorded. The high degree of press coverage given to *Soap* offers the media historian a rare opportunity to access these traces of the past. This cultural history is then not to be seen as "typical" of genre mixtures or parodies, but as an exceptional case that may help us understand more typical examples.

Soap's generic practices were dependent on the industrial context of ABC in the late-1970s. Despite a few hits in the 1960s, ABC had long been the perennial third-place network, hampered by its second-tier set of affiliates and limited production partnerships dating back to the radio era. ABC brought in Fred Silverman from CBS to head its entertainment programming in the mid-1970s; Silverman's background in Saturday morning children's programming had schooled him in entertaining escapism over trying to educate or challenge viewers. Silverman led ABC past CBS and NBC by riding escapist programs like *Happy Days* and *The Six Million Dollar Man* (1973–78) to the top of the Nielsen ratings. Additionally, in the wake of governmental and public concerns about excessive violence on television, Silverman's ABC shifted its focus away from violent police shows like *Baretta* and *Starsky and Hutch*, turning to so-called "jiggle shows" like *Charlie's Angels* (1976–81) and *Wonder Woman* (1976–77), replacing controversial violence with more explicit sexual content. The two ABC sitcoms that best exemplify its model of sexual comedies aired back to back in 1977: *Three's Company* (1977–84) and *Soap*.[22]

Three's Company was generally viewed as a lowbrow sex farce, but ultimately harmless in its adolescent double-entendres and nonthreatening narratives of mistaken sexual identity. *Soap* had no such luxury of complacent acceptance; as soon as the show was slated to appear in ABC's fall 1977 schedule, critics and activists took up arms against the show's alleged indecencies. The controversy was set off by *Newsweek*'s preview article in June, in which writer Harry Waters painted the program as the most salacious and sexually explicit show yet to air on primetime television.[23] Waters highlighted the various sexual quirks of *Soap*'s characters, including impotence, homosexuality, cross-dressing, adultery, prudishness, and most controversially, the seduction of a priest in church (all of which were narratively born out except the in-church seduction — the priest character renounces his vows before he succumbs to lust). Waters noted negative reactions from various ABC affiliates who had screened the program, many of whom claimed that they would not air the show, especially in its 8:30 p.m. Central timeslot. Finally, he acknowledged that, despite the moral protests that he and other implied high-minded *Newsweek* readers might have with the show, many predicted that the show would be a hit and might "dirty" the airwaves for many years. Despite the claims of *Soap* creator Susan Harris that Waters had not actually seen the show when he wrote the article, this short piece of press ignited a firestorm of controversy concerning the show's suitability for primetime.[24]

In the wake of publicity triggered by Waters' article, a number of religious organizations issued broadsides against *Soap* and ABC. Catholic periodicals, the Christian Life Commission, the Southern California Board of Rabbis, the United Church of Christ, and the U.S. Catholic Conference all issued statements decrying *Soap* as "morally reprehensible."[25] Many of these groups had admittedly not viewed the show, basing their condemnations upon Waters' singular account of the program. Additionally, the National Gay Task Force took issue with the stereotypical representation of the character Jodie, threatening protests and taking out an ad in *Variety* calling Jodie a "gay Stepin' Fetchit."[26] Silverman responded to the controversy by pulling back advance publicity for the show and withholding screening requests from the press and interested groups, wanting to let the "public decide" the show's fate in the ratings. Silverman also attempted damage control with ABC's affiliates; in a July closed-circuit televised speech, Silverman argued that the press and interest groups had misrepresented the program. He claimed that not only would the show be cleaned up before airing, but that it would prove to be morally grounded and emotionally engaging, not just a long "dirty joke" as had been claimed.

By the time of *Soap*'s September 13 debut, nineteen ABC affiliates had refused to air the show and almost fifty others swapped *Soap*'s 8:30 Central timeslot with the hour-long drama *Family* (1976–80), placing *Soap* in the 9:30 Central slot.[27] ABC allegedly received over 22,000 letters protesting the program before it aired, although publicized protests nearly disappeared once the show debuted.[28] Despite the lack of support from some affiliates and threats of boycotts, the show was a ratings success, and the controversy soon dipped below the radar of publicity. However, threats of boycotts and protests impacted the program economically — sponsors were generally quite conservative when faced with controversy (especially during the 1970s), and thus ABC had trouble selling advertising slots at a rate commensurate with the show's ratings. As producer Paul Junger Witt remembers, ABC was never able to sell the show at its market value, making the show a financial loss for the network throughout its four-year run despite its high ratings.[29] Despite the declining publicity of the controversies, *Soap* never achieved acceptance with conservative groups, leading to a constant struggle between ABC, its affiliates, and sponsors, eventually ending with its premature cancellation in 1981.

While this tumultuous tale of *Soap* may be interesting media history, how is it tied to questions of genre? Generic categories became explicitly activated within the *Soap* controversy, serving as conceptual markers for a variety of values and assumptions central to the debated issues. The specific uses of generic categories and their cluster of assumptions within the discourses surrounding *Soap*'s premiere both provide a richer understanding of this moment in media history and offer us access to some generally unspoken facets of genres as cultural categories. The activation of multiple genre categories within the cultural circulation of *Soap* suggests that often generic mixing and parody can provide the spark for igniting controversies through the juxtaposition of conflicting clusters of generic assumptions.

To explore *Soap*'s generic history, we must understand the clusters of cultural discourses tied to the dual generic categories of sitcom and soap opera that were contextually active upon *Soap*'s debut. These brief generic accounts are necessarily reductive and over-simplified, but serve as backgrounds out of which *Soap*'s more complex history emerges. The soap opera has a lengthy history dating back to 1930s radio, but most relevantly in the late 1960s and 1970s, soap operas began to shift their focus toward emphasizing social issues like race relations, abortion, and women's health, as well as turning toward more bold depictions of sexuality. Its assumed generic definition was still linked to serialized narration and a focus on domestic life and romance, but the rise of social issue storylines and the dawning of the "action" plot, typified by late-1970s *General Hospital* (1963–), had somewhat broadened the genre's scope. While the genre was still culturally marginalized in daytime schedules with a predominantly female audience, soap operas were gaining in cultural cachet, exemplified by a fairly positive *Time* magazine cover story in 1976, and more support from male audiences. Thus, the soap opera was gaining in cultural recognition and legitimacy, even though the term still was seen as derogatory and used pejoratively when applied to other programs like primetime dramas.[30]

The situation comedy was also in a transitional phase in the late-1970s. After the "turn toward relevance" of early-1970s sitcoms like *All in the Family* and *M*A*S*H*, another vein of more escapist sitcoms emerged in the mid-1970s. Typified by ABC's hits *Happy Days* and *Laverne and Shirley* (1976–83), these programs offered an explicitly nostalgic emphasis on humor over social critique, reaching out to young audiences through physical humor and feel-good affirmation, instead of targeting quality audiences through relevant issues of the time or satire. Despite this shift among top-rated sitcoms, the genre clearly had dual identities in the mid-1970s, featuring both critical and reinforcing visions of American culture and families. While neither interpretation of the genre's norms was uniformly applicable, clearly the sitcom worked as a legitimate site of both social commentary and escapism during this era. Cultural operation of the sitcom as a generic cluster affirmed both of these aspects of the genre, often as tied to network identity — CBS sitcoms were generally relevant and socially critical, while ABC shows were typically escapist and aimed at younger audiences.[31]

Although *Soap* explicitly drew upon these dual categorical clusters, it was not the first parodic mix of the soap opera and the sitcom — an important precedent for the show was the syndicated hit *Mary Hartman, Mary Hartman* (1976–77). Norman Lear was the originating auteur behind *Mary Hartman*, although the episodes were written by a team of former soap opera writers led by Ann Marcus. *Mary Hartman* was truly an anomalous program, breaking many traditional rules of television programming, yet still intrinsically tied to genre categories. Lear had shopped the show to networks as a parodic take on daytime soap operas, focusing on the relationship woes and tawdry scandals of a working-class community in Fernwood, Ohio. All three networks passed on the program, suggesting that it was too unusual to succeed; Lear responded by syndicating the show to local stations himself, finding smaller stations to run the show stripped five days a week in either afternoon or late-night hours. Soon after the show debuted, it became the talk of the 1976 season, with an outpouring of positive criticism from highbrow sources usually dismissive of television, such *The Village Voice* and *The Nation*, as well as popular notoriety rare for a syndicated show. Like most of Lear's oeuvre, the show dealt with issues that had rarely been explicitly addressed humorously on mainstream television, from impotence to adultery, homosexuality to senility — all touchy topics featured in *Soap*'s contentious debut a year later. *Mary Hartman* did not attract the controversial reception of *Soap*, partly because it was a marginal addition to the television schedule, airing on minor stations in peripheral timeslots. Once most people knew about the show's controversial content, it had already been accorded a degree of hip cachet and hailed as another groundbreaking addition to Lear's canon.[32]

Mary Hartman not only set generic precedents for *Soap*, but also provided a framework for the cultural reception of the latter program. The press coverage of *Soap* nearly uniformly noted *Mary Hartman* as a reference point, often using Lear's program as a marker of high quality which was seen as lacking in *Soap*. Waters criticized the show by writing, "*Soap* cries out for Norman Lear's sophisticated artistry," while Frank Rich called the show "*Mary Hartman* without heart."[33] The press coverage before *Soap*'s debut focused nearly exclusively on the show's lasciviousness, pointing out how it lacked the social satire and subtlety of *Mary Hartman* and Lear's other shows. Lear himself was used as a stand-in for the entire category of socially relevant sitcoms, as many articles note that creator Harris had previously written for Lear's Tandem Productions, most notably authoring the infamous abortion episode of *Maude* (1972–78). Through comparisons to *Mary Hartman* and other Lear programs, critics often placed *Soap* on the low end of an intrageneric sitcom hierarchy.

In discussing *Soap* in the realm of the sitcom, the press drew upon culturally operative assumptions constituting the sitcom generic cluster at the time. *Soap* straddled the dual dominants of sitcoms in this era — socially relevant satires typified by Lear, and escapist, broad, and sexual comedies of ABC like *Three's Company*. Yet despite the presence of these two sitcom strains, the show was almost uniformly linked to the latter type of escapist sitcom. This was partly due to the emphasis on the early episodes of the program; as I discuss below, *Soap* turned toward more socially satirical comedy and human relationships throughout its run, de-emphasizing sexuality at least partly in response to the public controversies. The press regularly labeled the show as television's first sex farce or a "sexcom," furthering the linkage to ABC's other sexually driven programming.[34] Combined with the unfavorable comparisons to *Mary Hartman*, *Soap* was stigmatized as the worst the sitcom genre had to offer. While generally sitcoms had been seen as legitimate forms of entertainment and potentially sites of social commentary, some groups castigated the entire genre through their dismissal of *Soap*. The U.S. Catholic Conference called the sitcom "a traditionally mindless, escapist entertainment form," as Catholics had been adamantly opposed to some of the satirical assaults of Lear's programs as well.[35]

One crucial genre issue raised by the show's detractors concerned the treatment of sexual content comedically. Donald McGannon, head of a Baltimore ABC affiliate that rejected *Soap*, praised the show's quality, but noted, "it presents a variety of subject matter which I feel does not lend itself to comedic episodic comic [sic] form," suggesting that "such subject matter could be better handled in an adult manner in serious drama on television."[36] Many who protested *Soap*'s content claimed that the featured topics of homosexuality, adultery, and impotence were even more egregious because of their comedic framework. As one editorial in *Christianity Today* suggested, "the problem is not that *Soap* deals with sex but that it treats sex in an irresponsible manner. It irresponsibly laughs at and shamelessly exploits the tragedies of adultery, homosexuality, impotence, incest, crime, and senility."[37] This position was partially based on a textual component — by making these issues the subject of humor, the show was seen as making no moral judgments or condemnations of behaviors some felt to be troublesome. Additionally, these protests tapped into the cluster of cultural assumptions tied to television comedy — despite the rise of socially satirical sitcoms in the 1970s, the sitcom was still seen primarily as an escapist or affirmative genre reinforcing the status quo, rather than challenging audience preconceptions. This linkage was furthered by the specific ways that *Soap* drew upon its other generic category of the soap opera.

Critics and commentators often noted that the show was a parody of soap operas, using terms like "spoof," "satire," "takeoff," and "send up." Despite this parodic framework, the show was clearly understood as a "sexual soap opera" or "sex opera" as well.[38] Fred Silverman actually denied the parodic tie to the soap opera: "Despite its name, *Soap* is not a satire of daytime soap operas. It is perhaps best described as an adult character comedy, with a continuing story line."[39] Harris and Witt similarly denied the interpretation of the show as a soap opera parody, suggesting that they only drew the serial narration and title from the daytime genre, as discussed more below.[40] But whether or not *Soap* actually was intended as a soap opera parody, the soap opera genre was contextually activated, both as a parodic object and nonparodic influence for generic fusion.

One of the ways in which daytime soap operas were used within the *Soap* debates was a point of comparison concerning sexual content. Many critics noted that daytime soap operas had grown more permissive in representing sexual activities; as one writer noted, "throughout the afternoon on network soap operas, every permutation of copulation is permitted (off-camera)."[41] As more perceptive critics noted, sex itself is not the subject of either *Soap* or daytime soap operas, but rather the endless *discussion* of sex, as television's sexual explicitness had expanded just into the realm of innuendo, not action. Despite the prevalence of sexual material equal to or in excess of any of *Soap*'s perceived offenses within daytime soap operas, two major factors placed *Soap* at the center of the sexual controversy more than daytime programs. Due to comedic fusion, many detractors found *Soap*'s take on sexuality too glib and flippant, a characterization that could hardly be raised against soap operas — as one Catholic critic described the daytime representation of sex, soap operas turned even "the most secular, hedonist, libertine subjects into sacred fare."[42] While daytime programs did not necessarily frame adultery or sexual practices as "social problems" as critics might have wished, soap operas treating sex as dramatic subject matter seemed more palatable than the absurdist irreverence featured on *Soap*.

The second reason for the discrepancy between the controversy of *Soap* and the comparative acceptance of sex on daytime soap operas is more complex. *Soap*'s primetime slot fell within family viewing hours, especially in the Central time zone where it was scheduled to air at 8:30 p.m. Somewhat ironically, the nighttime schedule was defined as more accessible to constant threat of children's audiences than the daytime schedule — as one critic noted, "the blue lines are drawn around the primetime network hours."[43] This perception was less due to scheduling itself than to well-established linkages between the sitcom genre and family audiences. ABC countered this association by prefacing early episodes of *Soap* with a warning that the show was "an adult comedy program," yet the constant fear was that children would stumble onto this inappropriate program during primetime hours. Since the daytime schedule has traditionally been marginalized both by the industry and the groups who take time to attack the industry, similar content on soap operas fell under the radar of these protests — even though children were more likely to be able to stumble across afternoon programming without supervision. The daytime soap opera genre, with its long-perceived audience of housewives, seemed to have been begrudgingly accepted as a necessary but marginal media evil after decades of generic condemnation. *Soap* and its threat of being a primetime hit posed a larger threat because of its allegiance with the more mainstream genre of the sitcom.

One of the more interesting repercussions of *Soap*'s initial controversy involved how ABC attempted to assuage the fears of affiliates and religious groups. Via closed-circuit television, Silverman assured affiliates that the program would have a clear moral center in a statement reminiscent of the 1930s Hollywood Production Code:

> No character in *Soap* is ever rewarded for immoral behavior. And, in the final analysis, there will always be retribution for such behavior. This socially redeeming aspect of *Soap* becomes clear as the story unfolds from week to week.[44]

Another segment of Silverman's speech explained why the show had been so misrepresented in the press and interest group reactions:

> It is difficult, even unfair, to try to evaluate *Soap* on the basis of two half-hour episodes. . . . It is the unique nature of *Soap* that a conflict, attitude, moral dilemma or crisis set up in one episode may not see its resolution until 10 episodes later, a situation that parallels real life much more than the standard comedy series does.[45]

Silverman linked these two statements together by noting that, just as the serial form of *Soap* approximates real peoples' lives, the ongoing moral consequences of characters' actions will be true-to-life and result in well-rounded, human characters.[46]

While Silverman offered one particular interpretation of how the show's narrative form and generic traditions would impact the issues represented, one affiliate provided another reading of the show:

> Although bad behavior may be punished in the end, the *Soap* format is too many weeks in getting to the end of a situation, unlike *All in the Family*, *Maude*, and other serious sitcoms that wrap up at the end of each episode (or occasional two-parter).[47]

Here, Production Code-style moral guarantees conflict with serial narrative form; whereas typical sitcoms can reinforce morality and the status quo within a 30-minute frame, Silverman's promise that the guilty will be punished is undermined by the long-term storytelling model of the soap opera. A reader of the conservative magazine *Commonweal* made a cynical critique of Silverman's "sanctimonious assurance that, in the long run,. . . 'no one who did anything wrong would be shown to profit by it.' It just takes hanging in there for a few more episodes, while the ratings tick by."[48] *Christianity Today* criticized ABC's logic as "not very convincing since retribution for immoral behavior may not come for nine episodes and that even some regular viewers might miss the point since the crime and the punishment were separated by nine weeks."[49] For detractors of the program, the soap opera narrative form itself contributed to the questionable moral content of the program, as the ongoing storylines could never provide the ideological equilibrium that they desired from their sitcoms, furthering a linkage between the soap opera genre and assumed moral uncertainty.

One aspect of Silverman's morality guarantee receiving less mainstream attention was how the character of Jodie fit into his promise that "no character in *Soap* is ever rewarded for immoral behavior." As part of Silverman's speech to affiliates, he noted that many characters would learn from their initial mistakes, including that Jodie would not go through with his plans to get a sex-change operation and "eventually meets a girl and suddenly finds himself in the middle of an identity crisis."[50] The National Gay Task Force responded to this statement through an ad in *Variety*, which lambasted both Silverman's promised "straightening" of Jodie and his effeminate characterization in the first few episodes.[51] Certainly, the long-term development of Jodie's character did veer away from the initial stereotypes of cross-dressing and "swishy" behavior, making Jodie's character one of the most humane and appealing characters in the large ensemble. Yet the show also pushed him toward bisexuality (without ever using the term) — he had serious relationships with three different women (including one lesbian), and fathered a daughter, leading to a dramatic custody battle with a female lover who jilted him at the obligatory marriage altar. Although Harris and Witt suggested that, had the show been on for longer, Jodie would have had more lasting relationships with men, Jodie's characterization pacifying activists on both ideological extremes was as a sympathetic gay man who just happened to sleep mostly with women.[52]

The transformation of Jodie's character is indicative of *Soap*'s larger shift that Silverman signaled as part of his pre-debut defensive maneuvers. While assuring that the guilty will be punished and gain a greater moral perspective, he suggested that the show would raise its dramatic quotient, turning away from the broad farce typifying early episodes:

> I believe that *Soap* will present very positive models and will lead. I say that because I think that the underpinning of the show is the sanctity of the family unit — believe it or not. There is a scene between a mother and her daughter that will make you cry.[53]

A trade journal advertisement for the show offers a similar account of the show's appeals: "*Soap* takes the popular soap opera format and hurls it kicking and screaming into prime time. It plays mostly for laughs, sometimes sends darts and daggers instead of candy, comes close to being downright warm, and touches people close to home."[54] This account of the show's emotional tone seems fair — the show did expand its pallet to include more dramatic content, emotional resonance, and fully realized characterizations (along with more outrageous twists, like alien abduction and demonic possession). By incorporating more melodrama into *Soap*, the show played many of the conventions of the soap opera straight, contrasting the ways genre parodies have been characterized as dismissing and dismantling their host genres.

Notably, the creators of *Soap* denied that they had produced a work of genre parody. In a personal interview with producers Harris and Witt, they adamantly denied that *Soap* was a parody of soap operas. As Witt explained in comparing their program to *Mary Hartman*:

> We took the form and we called it *Soap*, we took the form of continuing story arcs, but... we were motivated not to do satire, but to have continuing stories, and not to have to tell an entire story in 23 minutes... So we weren't motivated by sending up soap operas, and I think *Mary Hartman* might have been.

When I asked him why they chose to call it *Soap*, he responded "originally it was to reference the type of storytelling we were using, and we didn't come up with anything better." Thus according to the producers' account of the show (with a caveat to the limitations of oral history and 20-year memory spans), *Soap* was not intended to be a work of genre parody — yet it still culturally functioned as one. By examining genre practices in their cultural operation more than textual incarnation, *Soap*'s cultural reception as a genre parody encourages us to analyze the program within the lenses of genre parody and fusion between sitcom and soap opera.

Harris suggested that the primary motivation behind *Soap* was the desire to write a serialized narrative. She noted that the typical structure of the sitcom, with its main and subplots resolving each episode, limited her options as a writer to develop the characters and stories she wanted to explore:

> If you want to write about other things, if you want to be able to broaden what you write about, it was a real luxury to not have to tell a story in 24 minutes. Then you can have scenes about nothing that moves the story forward. If you're going to tell a story in 24 minutes, everything has to count. You're really restricted as a writer, and as an actor.[55]

The result of this formal shift was the ability to feature scenes focusing only on character development and humor rather than plot — *Soap* frequently offered scenes featuring the female characters sitting around the kitchen table lamenting their troubles over ice cream, mining situations for humor and pathos without advancing narrative action. Additionally, Harris noted that the formal freedom gave her the "luxury. . . to do one scene that was complete lunacy, and then the next scene to make an audience cry," or as a critic described it, alternate between "broad farce" and "tragicomedy."[56]

Harris and Witt claimed that they only drew the serialized narrative format from the soap opera genre, denying all other stylistic, formal, and content linkages with the daytime genre. Additionally, they claimed never to have even seen any soap operas before creating the program, noting that the production values and content of the genre were "awful," furthering the standard cultural hierarchy devaluing daytime soap operas. But in turning to the textual practices of *Soap*, we can see that the program does draw explicitly upon the various conventions and assumptions of the soap opera, even if the linkages were as unintentional as the producers claimed. *Soap*'s textual practices exemplify the notion that, instead of dissolving and dismantling genres, parody can reaffirm generic categories by making their conventions and assumptions manifest. In looking at the program, I argue that, even if Harris and Witt's were not trying to satirize and comment upon soap operas, the show affirmed and championed many more aspects of soap opera genre than the producers may have even been aware of.

The show's basic formal characteristics signaled *Soap*'s allegiance to both sitcoms and soap operas. Shot in studio and on videotape, the production values are consistent with 1970s shows within both genres.[57] *Soap*'s taping before a live-audience and subsequent laugh track clearly fit into sitcom norms, as does the weekly half-hour primetime scheduling that ABC used to air *Soap*. The show's domestic situation, focusing on the romantic relationships and scandalous escapades of two sisters and their families, is certainly consistent with soap operas, as well as family sitcoms. The female-centered thrust of the program, focusing on the two sisters and looking more at traditionally feminized topics of romance, family, and gossip than workplace situations and action, draws directly upon soap opera assumptions. The large ensemble cast was also more typical of soap operas, with a shifting cast of over fifteen regular characters appearing in most episodes.

The differences between *Soap* and its sitcom/soap opera ancestor *Mary Hartman* are significant for how each show drew upon generic conventions and assumptions. *Mary Hartman* was more in line with soap opera form, with no laugh track, shaky production standards, daily episodes, and swelling orchestral music underscoring its (both sincere and parodic) melodrama. The humor of *Mary Hartman* was exceedingly dry, based upon unusual juxtapositions (such as Mary's equal concerns about a local mass murder and the waxy yellow buildup on her floors) and absurd characters and plots (like eight-year-old evangelist Jimmy Joe Jeeter getting electrocuted by a television falling into his bathtub). Without the cues of a laughing audience, the show's humor lurked beneath the slowly moving surface, as dramatic actions were played "straight" without punch lines or physical gags. *Mary Hartman* never invited audience members to laugh at the proceedings, as the pacing and tone worked against sitcom conventions of the era. *Soap*'s humor was much more in line with a traditional sitcom, with clearly laid-out gags, physical business, comedic misunderstandings, and frenetic pacing. While its narrative model and situational themes were pulled from daytime soap operas, *Soap*'s comedic mode fit well within the multiple modes of 1970s sitcoms.

Like Harris suggested, the convention most drawn from soap operas was the serialized narrative structure; *Soap*'s ongoing stories were rarely resolved, with cliffhangers left dangling for the next episode. Interestingly, *Soap* used an atypical convention to provide exposition and narrative summary for each episode — at the show's opening, announcer Rod Roddy summarizes significant plot points from previous episodes, while the show ends with Roddy posing pertinent questions about narrative loose ends. This convention was driven by a general fear that primetime programs could not retain enough of an audience to support serialized narratives; Harris and Witt recalled that this device was a quick way to summarize without wasting time on repetitive exposition.[58] While in many ways it was a unique device, we can see predecessors in radio serial dramas, which employed an announcer to narrate the dramatic action and provide continuity. Consistent with the comedic and parodic tone of *Soap*, however, Roddy's narration is generally tongue-in-cheek, offering jokes about the characters and undercutting the seriousness of the dramatic material he summarizes. As the show matured, the announcements use repetitive motifs, puns, and catch phrases to both provide exposition and humorously bewilder audiences; Roddy concludes each prologue by saying, "Confused? You won't be. . . after this episode of *Soap*." Despite the narrative impulse of the voice-overs drawing upon soap opera models, the device also drew from comedy traditions to form a generically mixed pattern typical of the series as a whole.

The narrative pattern and storylines of *Soap* are typical of soap operas much more than sitcoms. The only way to appreciate *Soap*'s convoluted plotting is to attempt to recap the narrative arc of one character over the show's four-year run. Thus, the lengthy and tragic story of Danny Dallas, son of Mary Campbell, one of the show's two central sisters: Danny, played by Ted Wass, broadly fits the common character type of the "dumb hunk," an object of female affection often undone by his naïve stupidity. Danny begins the series employed as a Mafia soldier, distraught about his father's suicide and angry with his mother's new husband, Burt. Danny tries to leave the mob, but the "Godfather" tells him he can only leave by killing the man who actually murdered his father; Danny agrees, but then learns that the killer is his stepfather Burt. Danny tries to kill Burt in a number of comedically mangled attempts, eventually realizing that he is not cut out to be a killer. He and Burt reconcile as Danny goes into hiding to avoid being killed by the mob for not carrying out his assignment. While on the run, he meets Elaine, irritating daughter of a high-ranking mobster, who agrees to have his name cleared if he marries her; Danny agrees, despite the fact that he cannot stand her. They marry, with Elaine annoying every member of the Campbell family after moving in with Mary and Burt. Eventually, Elaine softens her attitude as she and Danny fall in love; but just as they find happiness together, Elaine is kidnapped. Just before Danny delivers the ransom, Elaine escapes the kidnappers, but is shot running out the door, arriving at the Campbell's home only to die tragically in Danny's arms.

Danny becomes obsessed with seeking revenge on Elaine's kidnappers and killers. He eventually finds them, but is captured himself; he is soon freed by the main kidnapper's girlfriend Milly, who wants to date Danny as payback. Milly eventually breaks up with Danny because of his crazy family. Danny then meets Polly, a black woman, while visiting Elaine's grave, and they soon fall in love. In the course of their relationship and attempts to buy a house, they fight prejudices as an interracial couple. Meanwhile Burt is elected sheriff and appoints Danny as his deputy. Burt and Danny's attempts to bust a mobster are foiled when they are drugged and photographed at a staged orgy with a group of prostitutes. Polly turns down Danny's marriage proposal because of the stress caused by their interracial relationship, and the blackmail attempt is foiled when Danny convinces a hooker named Gwen to testify against the mobster Tibbs. Gwen and Danny soon fall in love, and Gwen gives up her job. Tibbs hires a hit man to stop the Campbells, successfully shooting Danny and damaging his kidney. To get a proper donor, Mary finally reveals that Danny's biological father is Chester Tate, estranged husband of Mary's sister Jessica. Chester donates a kidney to Danny and both recover, but Gwen leaves Danny because she's being blackmailed by Tibbs to spy on the Campbells. Danny finds solace in the arms of Annie, the young girlfriend of his biological father Chester; the last episode of the series concludes as Chester finds Danny and Annie in bed together, threatening to shoot them both.[59]

This fairly convoluted plot summary of just one of *Soap*'s many characters demonstrates narrative and formal patterns typical of both the show and the soap opera genre as a whole. Following Robert Allen's seminal analysis of the genre using "reader-oriented poetics," we can see how the program's form establishes norms and patterns by which audience members relate to *Soap*.[60] Allen explains both the genre's internal textual mechanics and the potential ways that audiences put soap opera texts to cultural use. *Soap* invited viewers to engage with the program using particular soap opera traditions and techniques identified by Allen. This argument runs counter to both the authorial insistence of Harris and Witt, who deny that the soap opera provided anything but a title and serialized narrative reference point, and traditional accounts of parody, which contend that genre parodies displace the host genre's pleasures and norms with those of comedy. But even though the show was certainly comedic and may not have intentionally employed soap opera conventions, *Soap*'s title, formal attributes, and cultural circulation encouraged viewers to engage with the show in ways parallel to Allen's account of the traditional daytime soap opera.

Most of the actions that take place within *Soap* are based upon interpersonal relationships rather than narrative events. Even with an action-oriented plot like Elaine's kidnapping, the motivating question of the storytelling is not "what will happen?" but "how will it impact the characters?" Thus, we see important narrative information relayed about events multiple times, redundantly providing exposition for audience members. Allen suggests that soap opera narratives are more paradigmatic than syntagmatic, focusing on associative choices of character interactions more than plot-driven combinations of new events. Based on this framework, it is less important what happens to a character than how characters react to events and how events are shared and communicated. For instance, the audience first learns that Burt killed Danny's father in the show's pilot, as Burt is talking to himself alone, a typical soap opera device. We then hear the same information repeated in subsequent episodes when the Godfather tells his associate that Danny must kill Burt, when the Godfather tells Danny to kill Burt, when Danny confronts Burt when he is going to kill him, when Burt talks about the issue to his therapist, in a flashback to the event, and when Burt finally confesses to Mary. Each time, narrative events are not pushed forward, but each retelling furthers repercussions across various relationships. As with soap operas, these communications provide a richer understanding of characters and their emotional histories;

unlike most soap operas, these communications are often played for laughs, puncturing the emotional weight of the event with humorous reactions and comedic side business. But even though the parodic mode of the show injects humor into narrative events, the emotional impact and character richness are still significant; soap opera conventions are still pleasurably "intact," even though they are parodied and mixed with comedy, as audiences care about these characters while they laugh at them.[61]

Like most soap operas, *Soap* features more outrageous and intricate plot development than sitcoms, but the actual amount of narrative action per episode is comparatively small. Actions occur in stops and starts, with some situations left ignored for numerous episodes at a time. Often a story is left dangling with just paradigmatic associations for weeks, and then resolved abruptly without significant repercussions. For instance, Danny goes into hiding once he decides not to kill Burt; for seven episodes, he is featured in a variety of comedic disguises briefly touching in with his family before going back on the run. No forward narrative progress occurs over this period (more than one quarter of the first season), but we view the evolving consequences of his situation upon his family. When he meets Elaine, his situation drastically changes, as she convinces her father to drop the contract on his life, and his story arc abruptly transforms from being a target of mob assassination into being forced into marriage, with the former scenario receiving almost no attention after the shift. This sudden change of plot direction is typical of *Soap* and soap operas — producers can both drag out a story indefinitely and end it with one quick twist. As Witt suggested to me, this provides great flexibility in terms of long-term commitments, allowing the producers to "pull audibles" in determining a character's future. While often the outrageousness of some of these developments (such as Danny's sudden love for his father's girlfriend Annie) can work to mock the conventions of the soap opera, the show's narrative suspense and complex character relationships are quite genuine and typical of other serialized narratives.

Another important facet of both *Soap* and soap operas is the centrality of melodrama. The term melodrama has been at the center of debates within media studies that do not need another rehashing. For my purposes, I am referring to melodrama following Linda Williams as a "mode" of media entertainment that foregrounds the sincere emotional response of pathos in response to on-screen events.[62] Many analysts of soap operas have considered the genre as a form of television melodrama, with shared centrality of emotional response and interpersonal relationships.[63] Yet parodic takes on the genre, such as *Soap* and *Mary Hartman*, are often considered outside the definition of the genre because they do not treat their subject matter seriously.[64] While certainly the melodramatic is not the primary emotional mode of *Soap*, it is difficult to serially watch the show and not experience sincere melodramatic engagement.

Possibly the best example of this melodramatic pull is the scene in which Elaine dies in Danny's arms; the show's quick pace and frenzied tone shifts abruptly to accommodate this moment of pure pathos, as the lovers reunite only to lose each other. This occurs at the end of an episode, which is typical of the program — instead of normal sitcom endings reinstating the status quo, the last scenes of *Soap* typically pose unresolved dramatic conflicts and elicit melodramatic emotional responses of suspense and pathos. The centrality of melodrama, narrative suspense, and the lack of plot resolution all draw upon soap opera conventions without any parodic undercutting — *Soap* invites viewers to watch the program as a sincere serial engagement as much as (if not more than) a parodic mockery.

Soap also engages with social issues in line with both its soap opera and sitcom forebears. Both genres saw a "turn toward relevance" in the 1970s, as issues like abortion, interracial relationships, and sexuality were incorporated into both daytime soap operas and primetime sitcoms. *Soap* followed in the steps of both of these genres, although the mode of social representation seen on the show was more consistent with the soap opera than the sitcom, as the two genres generally addressed social issues via differing tones. Sitcoms like *All in the Family* and *Maude* place a given issue within the social context of its era, creating debates between competing sides and often tying issues to contemporary political and cultural developments. Soap operas, befitting their general focus on interpersonal relationships, treat political issues almost solely as personal matters, focusing on how issues affect specific characters and their relationships more than society at large. For comparison, Erica's 1971 abortion on *All My Children* (1970–) was cast as a personal matter primarily reflecting her villainous character, while *Maude*'s 1972 abortion was framed as both political and personal, complete with in-depth discussions about the historical legacies tied to abortion.[65]

Soap's treatment of social issues draws more upon soap opera conventions than Lear's brand of social sitcoms. While issues of sexual discrimination are raised in Jodie's courtroom custody battle for his daughter, generally the politics of Jodie's sexual orientation are familial. Danny begins the series in denial of his brother's sexuality; Jodie's forthright coming out scene makes Danny accept him as a brother and man, not based on larger social or political issues beyond the family. Likewise Danny and Polly encounter larger societal resistance to their interracial coupling, but the issue is primarily played out within the realm of interpersonal relations between them and their families. This is not to condemn *Soap*'s personal treatment of issues — I don't wish to reiterate the hierarchy denigrating soap operas as compared to other cultural forms. But by pointing out how *Soap*'s patterns of representation of social issues and active sexuality fit more within soap opera norms, we can further understand why the program was met with such hostility. In importing the representational mode of daytime soap operas into primetime sitcoms, *Soap* instituted a categorical crisis that seemed to confound even its creators.

So what do we to make of Harris and Witt's claims that they were not parodying soap operas and that they were unfamiliar with the genre? On the one hand, we might doubt their assertions — they did name the program *Soap* after all! But there is an interesting implication for genre analysis at work here. They claim that besides the title, all they drew from soap operas was a serialized narrative format; as Harris told me, "the resemblance begins and ends with the [narrative] form." My analysis of the show suggests otherwise, noting that *Soap*'s use of melodrama, treatment of social issues, and focus on a large ensemble's interpersonal relationships surpass a simple adoption of serialized narrative — serial narratives of 1930s adventure films posit quite different assumptions within the same overall structure. Rather than attempting to definitively categorize the show to support or disprove their claims, we can look at Harris and Witt's denial of soap opera origins as a generic discourse, tapping into important assumptions clustered within the soap opera genre and tied to notions of parody. In disowning the soap opera influence, they reiterated common cultural hierarchies devaluing the visual look and narrative complexity of soap operas — they clearly felt that soap operas were neither enjoyable nor socially valuable, denying even having watched them. Despite this view, they also denied satirical intentions, as they seemed to feel that the soap opera itself was not necessarily worth parodying. We can also see their claims activating cultural assumptions tied to parody itself as a practice, assessing parodic goals as less worthy than more straightforward storytelling, which is common to derogatory dismissals of comedic films such as *Blazing Saddles* (1974) or *Airplane* (1980) as "just parodies" as compared to more "original" comedies. Harris and Witt understood their own practices within a set of cultural hierarchies that they reinforced, even if their own program seems to call those assumptions into question.

Possibly most interesting of all is how we might reconcile Harris and Witt's denial of *Soap*'s soap opera heritage with my analysis of the program's seemingly clear ties to the genre's conventions. Given their statements of intent — that they were not motivated by parodying soap operas, consciously drawing only serialized narratives and the title from the genre — how might we understand the other linkages that they do not account for? I would argue that the generic assumptions constituting the soap opera cluster were so entrenched and fixed by the late 1970s that it was impossible to detach the serialized narrative form from its generic associations. Even if they had never seen an episode of a soap opera, they had effectively absorbed these central assumptions and generic conventions by being part of a culture that uses the generic category broadly to demean anything that is seen as narratively drawn-out or excessively sentimental. If *Soap*'s producers did not create the show as a soap opera parody, it functioned as one because it emerged from a cultural context in which serial form and the soap opera genre were inextricably linked. For audiences and critics more versed in soap operas, the linkages became apparent and articulated within the discourses greeting the show's controversial debut. For the producers themselves, the genre was culturally active in unintentional ways — even if they just meant to borrow the narrative form, they ended up drawing upon many more cultural assumptions tied to the category than they had planned. This is not to suggest that soap operas bear unconscious myths, but rather that the connections between the genre and its narrative form were so culturally linked at this moment that serial narratives were impossible to view outside of the context of soap operas.

This categorical linkage between serial narrative and soap opera began to weaken following *Soap*'s debut. While this shift is not solely due to *Soap*, the show did set a number of precedents that soon became somewhat commonplace on primetime television. In the late 1970s and early 1980s, a rash of primetime serials emerged, rebelling against soap opera genre conventions. A number of primetime serial dramas like *Dallas* (1978–91) and *Dynasty* (1981–89) recast the potential audience for soap operas via flashy melodramatic style and excessive displays of wealth.[61] Likewise, the mixture of serialized narratives into other primetime genres, notably police shows such as *Hill St. Blues* and medical dramas such as *St. Elsewhere* (1982–88), redefined many of the central assumptions linked to the soap opera genre and denigrated notions of quality. Some of these were industrial assumptions — like the notions that audiences would never follow weekly continuing story arcs or that syndicators would be reluctant to embrace serials — while others were more widespread cultural beliefs, such as that serial narratives were only for female audiences. Regardless of whether it was a significant cause of this shift, *Soap* crested a wave drastically transforming the norms of both primetime narration and the marginalization of serial narrative form. The categorical crisis over *Soap* was a product of its place in television and cultural history; enough had changed by the time of the show's cancellation that a similarly controversial reception in the early 1980s would have been almost unthinkable.

Given this cultural analysis of *Soap*'s mode of generic mixture and parody, how are we to understand the role that genre played in the controversy? While the controversy was certainly caused by a range of different cultural factors, from widespread growth of sexual representations in television to the specific trigger of sex and the priesthood mentioned in Waters' inflammatory article, genre mixture and parody were significant contributing factors. Both the sitcom and soap opera genres formed a cluster of assumed associations at the time of *Soap*'s debut; the way *Soap* drew upon these associations and placed them in juxtaposition violated the norms by which these genres were culturally understood. Sitcoms were licensed to be socially satirical, following Lear's model, but the overlapping web of sexual relationships seen on *Soap* had previously been roped off into the marginal genre of daytime soap operas. Since *Soap* drew upon the narrative model (and title) of soap operas, the program was culturally understood as a violation of the strict division between these two genres. Thus sexuality, which had been tolerated in daytime soap operas, crossed over into the more puritanical category of the primetime sitcom; likewise, the treatment of sexuality as a serious matter within daytime soap operas was undercut through the shift to comedy. Not only did this shift in generic frameworks of comprehension impact the perception of *Soap*'s "problem," but it impacted the "cure" as well — Silverman's assurances of typical sitcom narrative resolutions and imposed morality came into conflict with the serialized ongoing structure of the soap opera.

Given that a component of *Soap*'s controversial history stemmed from the conflicting clusters of cultural assumptions making up its dual genres, might we suggest that generically blended and parodic programs have a tendency toward cultural controversy? I am reluctant to generalize based on one example, but certainly many programs which are generically mixed, either through parody or fusion, do face a particularly tumultuous cultural life, easily buffeted by competing contexts of reception. This is not an innate quality of parody or generic mixing that invites cultural controversy, but when different frameworks are juxtaposed, violating traditional norms and well-rooted assumptions, a cultural crisis is quite common. In turning to *The Simpsons*, comparable cultural processes at work in the program's practices of generic mixture and parody resulted in a similar moment of genre crisis.

Cartoon Realism: Genre Mixing, Parody, and the Cultural Life of *The Simpsons*

> It's an odd thing when a cartoon series is praised as one of the most trenchant and "realistic" programs on TV, but there you are.
>
> — Josh Ozersky, media critic[67]

> It's just a cartoon. People shouldn't pay that much attention to a cartoon.
>
> — Andy Schulze, 15-year-old[68]

Whereas *Soap* is a neglected moment in media history, *The Simpsons* is a canonized "valid object" of media studies, with numerous articles and books dedicated to its analysis.[69] The show fits perfectly into the dual niches of both quality and popularity that appeal to media scholars looking for an object of study acceptable to both academic colleagues and the general populace. Unlike *Soap*, *The Simpsons'* ongoing place in American popular culture needs no rescuing from the margins of history. But despite the wealth of materials available to the potential *Simpsons* scholar, few examine the show's generic practices, considering how the program's particular mixture of sitcom and cartoon has factored into its long success and initially controversial debut.

Many media scholars hail *The Simpsons* as the postmodernist exemplar, consistent with postmodernism's ties to genre mixture and parody. I wish to shift this ground somewhat, asking what does this paradigm offer *Simpsons* studies — how does labeling the show "postmodern" better our understanding of either the text, its generic practices, or its cultural context and circulation? Most critics who have lauded *The Simpsons'*s postmodernism call attention to its reflexivity. Jim Collins calls an instance of Bart watching his own Macy's Thanksgiving Parade float on television, "emblematic of a postmodern textuality."[70] Likewise, Matthew Henry points to the show's "shattering of the fictional illusion" as fulfilling one of postmodernism's "prerequisites," as exemplified by an episode's opening sequence in which the characters race into their living room, overshoot, and run off the frame of the "film" and into the realm of sprocket holes.[71] Yet to see these moments as indicators of a new postmodernism requires historical myopia. As John Caldwell suggests, *Simpsons*-style reflexivity and intertextuality have been features of television comedy since the medium's inception. Caldwell cites numerous examples, such as the oft-mentioned *Ernie Kovacs Show* (1951–56) and *Burns and Allen Show* (1950–58), but also less legendarily reflexive shows like *Texaco Star Theater* (1948–56), *Your Show of Shows* (1950–54), and *I Love Lucy* (1951–57).[72] Caldwell dismisses the postmodern label as descriptive of neither the medium's historical eras nor aesthetic movements, since textual practices said to typify postmodernism have run throughout television history.

However, the textual ancestry of *The Simpsons* predates even television, with a long tradition of animated film. Reflexivity has always been a defining component of animated shorts, dating back as early as 1914's *Gertie the Dinosaur* — definitely a pre-postmodern film. Donald Crafton argues that early animation was marked by "self-figuration, the tendency of the filmmaker to interject himself into his film," an aesthetic technique that has recently been hailed as typically postmodern, but clearly predates any moment of postmodernity.[73] Later animation in the 1930s and 1940s was well known for its reflexivity and self-awareness, regularly breaking down the medium's artifice and illusions; these techniques typify Tex Avery's work, but are found in films by nearly every animation studio in Hollywood.[74] Even the specific example Henry uses from *The Simpsons* to typify the show's postmodern tendencies is in itself a specific allusion to *Duck Amuck* (1953), Chuck Jones' virtuoso deconstruction of Daffy Duck's animated universe. Thus I am skeptical of these claims to *The Simpsons'* postmodern textual aesthetic, as the very same techniques hailed as typically postmodern have roots in the show's generic and medium precursors.

Another facet of postmodernism tied to *The Simpsons* and genre is the role of parody.[75] There is little doubt that parody is central to *The Simpsons*, but the scholarly implications of the parodic are less clear — does the show's use of parody make the program emblematically postmodern or a modernist relic? The scholarship concerning parody and postmodernism offers differing takes — compare Fredric Jameson's oft-cited nomination of pastiche as postmodern "blank parody" lacking the critical edge of modernist satire, to Linda Hutcheon's discussion of postmodernist "ambivalent parody" that both follows and ridicules a genre's conventions.[76] These definitions of postmodern parody might help us assess *The Simpsons*'s parodic tendencies and label them postmodern or not according to these (or other) schemas. But so what? How does this really better our understanding of the program or its cultural life?

This is not to suggest that parody is not a vital aspect of *The Simpsons*; however, I see little point in locating the program's use of parody within larger trends of postmodernism, as neither producers nor audiences generally use postmodernism as a category to make sense of the show. It is more productive to analyze media in actual cultural circulation than theoretical abstraction — does it help us understand the cultural life of *The Simpsons* whether the show is "postmodern" according to one definition? If "postmodern" were an active term that many critics, audiences, and producers used to make sense of the program, then it would be worth further inquiry. However, the only audience that uses this label to understand *The Simpsons* is academics (and just a small group of us at that). Unless we are interested in charting the discursive reception of the show within academic circles — which is not my project here — the postmodern label seems both unnecessary and a hindrance, given the argument that postmodern texts transcend genre definitions through radical eclecticism and boundary blurring.[77] Just as with *Soap*, mixed and parodic texts, while often labeled postmodern, can activate generic assumptions and conventions even more than so-called "pure" genre texts.

Not only have scholars followed the common linkage between parody and postmodernism regarding *The Simpsons*, but they have also looked at the show's parody as a sign of the decline of the sitcom genre. Parody is often hailed as the end of a given genre, like John Cawelti's suggestion that genre parodies are a sign of "generic exhaustion," the final stage before the disappearance of both genres and the "cultural myths they once embodied."[78] Some critics embrace this notion concerning *The Simpsons* — Henry suggests that the show's ratings success over *The Cosby Show* (1984–92) indicated that "the family sitcom in its traditional structure and conventional trappings was null and void," a claim in hindsight that seems to have misdiagnosed a cyclical illness as a terminal disease.[79] But since parodies do not seem to be particularly fatal to genres in most historical cases, we need to revise this common teleological narrative. Genre parody does not signal the demise or decline of a genre, but is a specific mode of generic practice that must be taken on its own terms, not as a final component in an overarching account of a genre's history. By figuring parody within larger generic processes, we can see how it can strengthen and reaffirm a genre, not lead to its demise.

To counter these claims about *The Simpsons*'s role within postmodernism and generic decline, we need to look at the show's cultural circulation, drawing upon genres as cultural categories. The program's early years are particularly instructive, as the show's initial novelty and controversial reception led to intense discussions and debates on how to make sense of this unusual program, similar to the model of crisis historiography used to study quiz shows and *Soap*. Examining a variety of discursive sites, including popular press reviews, commentaries, trade journal accounts, interviews with creative personnel, and academic critiques, I chart out the competing uses of generic terms such as sitcom, cartoon, animation, and parody, pointing to how notions of genre helped constitute a framework of understanding for this groundbreaking and controversial program.

It is obvious to even the most novice television viewer that *The Simpsons* is, on some level, a mixture of domestic sitcom and animated cartoon. It is hardly worth the effort to attempt to prove this categorical combination via either textual analysis or discursive examination. While it may be clear *what* genres the show draws upon, *how* the ramifications of this mixture might play out needs further discussion. How are these two genres culturally understood in tandem? What generic meanings are activated within the show's circulation? What historical predecessors are linked to the program within both genres? How do these genres establish a framework of understanding for *The Simpsons*, impacting how the show has been figured as a cultural object? By looking at these questions surrounding the show's emergence, we can explore the larger consequences of generic mixture in action, focusing on cultural hierarchies, implications of target audience, codes of realism, and notions of parody.

Critics regularly label *The Simpsons* first and foremost a sitcom. As advertising executive Betsy Frank suggests, "that's absolutely all that it is — a situation comedy that happens to be animated."[80] The press discourse surrounding the program regularly evokes the domestic family sitcom tradition: television critic Tom Shales calls the Simpson family "the flip, dark side of the Nelsons, the Andersons, the Bradys and all other sitcom families from the dawn of television."[81] A celebration of the program in *Time* magazine describes the family as "a typical sitcom family — the Honeymooners with kids, the Flintstones in suburbia — with typically outlandish dilemmas to face and resolve each week."[82] Another critic notes the antecedent of *The Simpsons*' hometown:

When *The Simpsons* first went on the air, viewers and critics alike were surprised that the show had exhumed one of television's hoariest formulas: a sitcom, albeit animated, about a blue-collar family living in a standard-brand American suburb, and not just any old suburb but a town called Springfield, just like the locale of *Father Knows Best*, the blithely Utopian sitcom of the 1950s.[83]

More contemporary sitcom examples also are held in opposition to *The Simpsons*: "The slightly skewed perspective of *The Simpsons* makes them a far more human and believable family than such carefully conceived, endlessly responsible TV facsimiles as the Huxtables, the Keatons, et al."[84]

This family sitcom ancestry is echoed by production personnel: creator Matt Groening notes, "at an early age I was most strongly affected by *Leave It to Beaver* and *Ozzie and Harriet*. [*The Simpsons*] is my skewed reaction to those shows." Even as he asserts the importance of these previous sources, Groening notes the show's violations of the genre's conventions: "The show has all the elements of its live-action family-oriented prototypes, with a twist."[85] Specifically, Groening notes that unlike sitcom conventions of small character ensembles and limited settings, the show's animated form gives the writers and animators freedom to open the genre outward from the typical domestic setting. Thus, he suggests that his "mutant *Ozzie and Harriet*" is "a hallucination of a sitcom" or "a sitcom, but there's no 'sit,'" suggesting a simultaneous investment in and disavowal of the generic category.[86]

Other critics link *The Simpsons* to a more recent trend within the domestic sitcom genre. Wholesome family programs like *The Cosby Show* and *Family Ties* (1982–89) were the most popular sitcoms in the 1980s, along with nondomestic successes such as *Cheers* (1982–93) and *Night Court* (1984–92), but successful new sitcoms of the late-1980s and early-1990s constituted a backlash against this vision of the happy American family. Typically critics point to the highly popular (and controversial) trinity of *Married. . .With Children* (1987–97), *Roseanne* (1988–97), and *The Simpsons* as representing "a new development of the situation comedy. Each program. . . focuses on a family marked by visual styles and characterization as bleak and miserable as those of former TV families had been handsome or cheerful."[87] One viewer's letter to *TV Guide* historicizes this phenomenon more aptly than any professional critic by suggesting that such "anti-family" backlash is typical whenever "there's an abundance of family sitcoms" — whether it's *Roseanne* as a response to *Growing Pains* (1985–92) in the 1980s or *The Addams Family* (1964–66) and *The Munsters* literally turning the perfect 1960s family into monsters.[88]

Critics also note *The Simpsons'* place within the genre of television animation. Even though critics regularly label *The Simpsons* as a cartoon, they often qualify it with additional markers of legitimacy or clarification. Hence, critics call the show a "half-hour adult cartoon series," "the most multi-layered cartoon since *Rocky & Bullwinkle*," and "more than a cartoon, it's TV's most intelligent comedy."[89] Clearly critics are working against dominant meanings of cartoons as just "kid's stuff" and unsophisticated entertainment by citing the show's intelligence and quality in the face of the low expectations of the animation genre. These hierarchies were central parts of the cartoon generic cluster at the time of the show's debut in 1990, as the decades of Saturday morning cartoons had established the genre as a lowbrow childish category. As discussed in Chapter 3, this transition from Saturday morning dominance to today's broader possibilities of adult animation hit its stride in the late-1980s, with the reemergence of Disney's animated features, the establishment of cable channels moving cartoons out of Saturday morning, and *The Simpsons*' debut as the first successful primetime cartoon since *The Flintstones*.

In the early-1990s, critics were quick to point to how the show successfully aspired to levels generally reserved for live-action programming, countering the traditional hierarchy that values live-action over animated, regardless of content. One critic labels the show "a prime-time cartoon series that's livelier and more vividly human than most live-action shows."[90] Another dismisses the question, "too much fuss over a cartoon show?" by citing the show's openness to "interpretive calisthenics," its high-level of "topical satire" and numerous "cultural references," legitimating the program in the face of cultural stigmas against animation.[91] Even an adolescent audience member asserts this hierarchy by denying the show's cartoonishness: "It's not really like a cartoon. . .but that makes it better."[92] However, the cartoon's pejorative qualities and low cultural status are never far from the surface, as one critic describes the show's wild success and ensuing controversy and notes, "the whole thing's totally improbable: we're talking about a half-hour cartoon."[93]

We do see an indication of these hierarchies' origins within press discourse as well. *USA Today* interviews animation historian Charles Solomon regarding the success of *The Simpsons* with all age groups:

> We tend to forget that what we think of as the great cartoons — the Warner Brothers cartoons of the '40s and '50s, the Disney cartoons of the '30s — were made for general audiences and could appeal to the most sophisticated member of the audience as well as the least. During the '60s and '70s, animation became stereotyped as a children's medium because of Saturday morning, which was a distortion. There's always been a big audience for animation, and this is one of the first projects that's been sophisticated enough in its approach to once again appeal to adults as well as to children.[94]

Solomon's argument has been borne out, as numerous other animated programs followed *The Simpsons* to succeed with an adult audience, including

Beavis & Butthead, *Dr. Katz, Professional Therapist* (1995–2000), *King of the Hill*, *South Park*, and the rise of Cartoon Network's adult audience discussed in Chapter 3.

The Simpsons is often explicitly contrasted with Saturday morning programming. One critic praises *The Simpsons* compared to a caricature of the genre: "Cartoons are either toy-oriented syndicated strips or huggable Saturday morning specials where a real crisis occurs when a bear loses his sweater."[95] Groening echoes these sentiments: "If there's anything this show has to overcome, it's adults considering it just another one of those crummy cartoons on TV."[96] Just as he cites *Ozzie & Harriet* (1952–66) as a formative text for *The Simpsons*, he names *Rocky & Bullwinkle* and other Jay Ward programs (like *George of the Jungle*) as the only previous examples of successful television cartoons to combine animated form and sophisticated humor.[97] *The Flintstones* and *The Jetsons* are often mentioned as key predecessors as primetime animated sitcoms, but *The Simpsons* is generally held up as more sophisticated and critical of both its sitcom and animated form, "an anti-*Flintstones* cartoon" distanced from the assumptions of the cartoon genre.[98]

The show's creators offer a number of textual instances of *The Simpsons* working against cartoon traditions. Executive producer James L. Brooks notes some of the benefits of the animated form, such as the ease of adding "locations" and new characters, but adds that "ducks won't talk... But little girls will play great blues on the saxophone! And women will have their money hidden in their hair."[99] While the world portrayed on *The Simpsons* adheres to certain codes of naturalism, its animated form allows for choices that a live-action show simply could not manage or afford. Groening further suggests, "there's a rule in drawing *The Simpsons* that they can never go cross-eyed, like all those cartoon characters on Saturday morning."[100] Elsewhere, he remarks, "we're the only cartoon show where, when people hit the ground, they actually get bruised and bloody."[101] Finally, he points to other typical genre conventions that *The Simpsons* violates: "The characters' heads do not get crushed by anvils. Their eyeballs do not pop out of their heads, and their jaws do not drop to the ground. Also, we have no laugh track," pointing to how the show breaks from conventions of both animation and sitcom genres.[102]

The key exception to Groening and Brooks's rules for animation is *The Simpsons'* cartoon within the cartoon, *The Itchy & Scratchy Show*. A direct parody of *Tom & Jerry*, as well as other classic chase cartoons, *Itchy & Scratchy* foregrounds the cartoon's assumed generic conventions, highlighting how *The Simpsons* as a whole abandons them. Paul Cantor offers a compelling explanation:

> If you are going to distinguish a cartoon within a cartoon, you must raise its cartoonicity to a higher power. In *Itchy & Scratchy*, anything

that is not pure cartoon has been ruthlessly stripped away to leave us facing the meaningless and gratuitous violence that is the quintessence of cartoon. . . . The total flatness of the cat-and-mouse world gives a rounded quality to the world of the Simpson family, and the humans no longer seem quite so cartoonish.[103]

Cantor's analysis points to the strategic use of generic conventions within *Itchy & Scratchy* that not only parody typical cartoons, but further separate *The Simpsons* as a whole from the cluster of assumptions tying the cartoon to mindless children's entertainment throughout decades of television.

The case of *Itchy & Scratchy* highlights the role of parody and genre mixing. As already suggested, critics often point to the show's dual generic identity, but typically the sitcom is noted more as the *object* or host genre of the show's parody, while the animated form becomes the *vehicle* for undermining the more typical sitcom genre. One critic called *The Simpsons* "the Antichrist of television sit-coms, with no surrender to tedious convention. The animated form unshackled the producers and opened the series to wild flights of irreverent fantasy."[104] Critics also note the simultaneous rebellion against typical animation techniques: "The script is wickedly anti-sitcom; the animation is viciously un-Disneylike."[105] Another critic notes its violation of both genres: "Sophisticated and satirical dialogue ensures that the humour [sic] is not typical of a cartoon series and unlike other cartoons, the characters are not cute and lovable. The producers deliberately avoided a 'sitcom' feel and the script has been described as, 'like Woody Allen writing for the Road Runner.'"[106]

One key effect of *The Simpsons*' use of generic blending was to broaden its target audience. Genres and target audiences are often explicitly and inextricably linked — genres are often defined (especially industrially) by an assumed audience segment, such as soap operas as dramas for housewives or sports as bait to catch men for advertisers. The sitcom audience has traditionally been seen as a mass, appealing to all demographic groupings, while the domestic sitcom has been specifically framed as entertainment "for the whole family." The genre has often been more targeted than this — think of the early 1970s rise of urban "quality" sitcoms (like *All in the Family* and *Mary Tyler Moore*) as part of the turn toward a younger, more urban, and more affluent audience than the rural fans of *Beverly Hillbillies* (1962–71) and *Green Acres* (1965–71).[107] However, the sitcom as a category has rarely been linked with narrow audience segments beyond general notions of "family entertainment." The cartoon has been far more bound to specific audiences in its history on television, with the genre clearly marked as children's programming — although, as argued in Chapter 3, this was a historical development, not a textual inevitability.

The Simpsons, as noted in nearly every mention of the program in 1990, was the first network primetime cartoon since *The Flintstones* was cancelled in 1966.

Groening often tells of the troubles getting a primetime cartoon on air, as network executives doubted that adults would watch a cartoon and were reluctant to only target kids. He was given his chance primarily because Brooks had a successful track record and Fox's fringe position in the late-1980s allowed them to take significant risks in hopes of unexpected payoffs. Groening introduced the characters in short segments on Fox's *The Tracey Ullman Show* in 1987, a program with a small but dedicated following among a sophisticated adult audience. *The Simpsons* debuted on Sunday nights at 8:30 Eastern, a time slot that Shales suggests is typically conducive to "family fare" more than any other night of the week.[108] *The Simpsons* succeeded beyond all expectations, providing Fox with its first Top Ten ratings hit and crossing demographic boundaries to reach "a huge and still-expanding audience of little kids, trend-wise teens and hip adults."[109] Articles note its large college student following and point to the show's success in merchandizing to children and adults alike.[110]

As is now clear, the show transcended the expectations of the cartoon genre, reaching the more broad-based audience of the sitcom.[111] But how did critics use genre categories to understand its target audience upon its debut? Most reviewers insisted that the show was intelligent, clever, and sophisticated, moving the program away from typical preconceptions about animation. As the show progressed, ratings and widespread merchandizing demonstrated that the program was drawing a significant audience of young children as well, prompting a jarring backlash. People who objected to the show's cynicism, satiric edge, or representations of Bart's mischief castigated Fox for targeting kids. A *Boston Globe* editorial argued, "*The Simpsons* is really an adult program whose cynical message appeals to people bored with conventional programs on other channels. Because the program is a cartoon and is broadcast early in the evening, it attracts many children."[112] Editorials such as these use generic assumptions of animation to critique the show's "adult" content like representations of disruptive children and troubled families, implying that cartoons should stick to their place — fringe timeslots and unchallenging content.

More enthusiastic critics like Howard Rosenberg offer differing views for the show's popularity with kids:

> *The Simpsons* is an unusual-for-TV, kid's-eye-view of the world, managing to tap genuine emotions and experiences, from violent video games to the euphoria of learning that school's been canceled by the season's first heavy snow. Yes, this is that rare series about kids that is written by people you can envision actually having been kids.[113]

Newsweek's Harry Waters similarly suggests, "there's little mystery to why the saga of the Simpsons enthralls the young. The series shamelessly panders to a kid's-eye view of the world: parents dispense dopey advice, school is a drag and happiness can be attained only by subverting the system."[114] He goes on to claim that children view the program as "real," a position juxtaposed with more adult hip and sophisticated views. Another critic summarily argues that the show "appeals to kids who like cartoons, to intellectuals who like satire. . . and to thugs who like a troublemaking hero."[115]

Even as critics look for ways to explain the show's appeal to diverse audiences, Groening constructs *The Simpsons* as designed for adults, not kids. He characterizes the appeal offered as "family entertainment in a new sense. . . . Adults are going to enjoy the witty dialogue and the funny story turns and kids are going to enjoy some of the wild sight gags."[116] Brooks similarly notes, "We finally found out what 'family entertainment' is, or should be. I've sat there watching the show with my folks and my young children and we all laughed at different things. I like that."[117] Clearly the producers conceived of a broad audience, even if they (at least initially) aimed for the adults and were happy to pick up the kids without effort.

But while Fox was certainly ecstatic to be able to reach such a broad audience, enabling the fledgling network to establish itself as a legitimate contender, the show's broad reach spurred a number of cultural repercussions, as *The Simpsons* found itself at the nexus point in a series of controversies. The program debuted to critical praise and high ratings, but soon became the target of critics and commentators who decried the show's "anti-family" content and questioned this prime-time cartoon's suitability for children. The show's success generated a wave of marketing and merchandizing, but just as Bart Simpson T-shirts became ubiquitous in elementary schools across the United States, new debates emerged as to whether "Underachiever and Proud of It" was an appropriate slogan for American youth, leading to school bans and public outcry.[118] Given these critical discussions, what are the linkages between these controversies, the program's assumed target audiences, and the cultural role of genre categories?

Notions of the "proper" audience for a given program, as often linked to generic clusters, are cited and mobilized in a variety of ways to further specific positions surrounding such cultural controversies. Thus, the previously quoted *Boston Globe* editorial cites the "cartoon-for-kids" assumption to criticize the show's rebellious characterizations and cynical attitude as inappropriate.[119] Another writer suggests that the program is primarily a satirical critique of family politics and that his kids "misinterpret" the show as a celebration of Bart's actions; thus their cartoon-centric appeals are "misplaced," even though the show's adult appeals are held up as admirable.[120] Finally, a mother of a child whose school banned Bart T-shirts directly criticizes the controversy in generic terms: "They're blowing it way out of proportion. It's only a cartoon. . . . To me, it's comical."[121] For this viewer, the show's genre serves to locate the program as both appropriate for children and not worthy of "serious" cultural consternation.

These three different viewers all activate the cartoon genre to defend their specific interpretations of the program and its "proper" cultural place — as inappropriate for children, as a "red herring" for audiences, and as a sign of cultural devaluation.

As these three divergent examples demonstrate, the cartoon genre has no inherent meanings, appeals to audiences, or even proper viewers apart from specific contexts, as each use the same claim to "cartoonishness" to further varying arguments. Since *The Simpsons* is often labeled a cartoon, and thus appropriate viewing for kids, viewers alternately use these assumptions to support both adult anxiety over the show's rebellious attitude and the perceived ridiculousness of fussing over an "insignificant" form of entertainment. Viewers and critics use the generic history of animation and its linkages with children's programming to situate the program within hierarchies of taste and cultural value. Just as some voices label *The Simpsons* a cartoon to call for greater industrial responsibility in targeting its assumed childish audience, others use the low cultural value of animation to dismiss moral concerns over such an inherently unrealistic and fantastic (and therefore culturally harmless) genre.[122] But this latter notion of "only a cartoon" is problematized by numerous claims for the show's realism — a trait that seems to directly contradict dismissive remarks about cartoon irrelevance — as one of the defining and pleasurable features of *The Simpsons* as a generic mixture.

As suggested in this section's epigrams, there is a certain ironic paradox in *The Simpsons*' "realistic" vision of the American family as achieved through the traditionally anti-realist mode of animation. In exploring the notion of realism in *The Simpsons*, we can see the term "realism" serving as a site of struggle which audiences, industries, and critics mobilize to further their points. Realism is no more stable or defined a concept than authenticity, as discussed in Chapter 5. Yet it is important to explore the ways discourses of realism became articulated to the cartoon genre surrounding *The Simpsons*, as critics point to this paradox as key to understanding this "all-too-real TV cartoon series."[123] Shales calls the family "funny-mirror reflections of what's weird and askew in American society, characters who have achieved a level of affection beyond that of most sitcoms performed by mere mortals."[124] Another critic suggests, "the animation disguises the fact that it consists of what we laughingly call in TV 'adult humor.' It is the most serious program we have about family relationships, the decline of education, the failure of parents, and the fact that kids today are no damn good."[125] Perhaps most interestingly of all, a survey of school children in Australia voted *The Simpsons* "the most realistic program on TV after the news."[126]

This paradox of animated realism is made even more explicit in comparison to live-action programs. One common contrast is to *The Cosby Show*, specifically motivated by Fox's decision to program *The Simpsons* directly opposite *Cosby* in the 1990 fall schedule. This clear juxtaposition — between a live-action family portraying idealized achievements with few real-life counterparts (especially among African-American families), and an animated family whose socioeconomic situation and emotional tenor looked more like themselves to viewers — provoked numerous commentaries. "Johnny Carson observed... that even though the idealized Huxtables on *The Cosby Show* are played by flesh-and-blood humans and the Simpsons are mere cartoon characters, *The Simpsons* seems more realistic. Family life at the Simpson home probably reminds more families of their own households than do the relatively homogenized antics of the Huxtable clan."[127] Similarly, one article quotes a street vendor selling bootlegged Bart T-shirts: "*Cosby* is the way it is supposed to be. *The Simpsons* is the way it really is — that's life."[128] This contradiction is even more heightened through the rise of "Black Bart" T-shirts, placing Bart within the framework of African-American culture; implicit in this move is that, for some viewers, the white Simpsons family may be even more representative of black culture than the African-American Huxtables. Even though cartoon life in Springfield might be unpredictable and unusual, to many the perfect family life of a black doctor and lawyer seemed even more inexplicable in contemporary American culture.

The Simpsons is also described as more realistic than its cohort of "anti-family" sitcoms. "Gross and funny in roughly equal measure, *Married...With Children* turns the TV family into a vicious cartoon. *The Simpsons*, a real cartoon, is actually much closer to recognizable human life."[129] Another critic similarly suggests that *Married*'s Bundys, "like all sitcom characters, aspire to the televisual purity of cartoon characters, but are stuck in rubbery bags of protoplasm with nothing but one-liners and a laugh track to hide behind. The Simpsons, oddly, are freer than other TV families to act human."[130] Groening himself points to *Married*'s more outrageous "cartoonish" take on the family, while claiming that *The Simpsons* moves away from outrageousness in exchange for "a family that is desperately trying to be normal."[131] Other critics compare *The Simpsons* to *Roseanne* to conclude that the animated family is more revealing and realistic than the Conners.[132] But how might we explain this seeming paradox of "cartoon realism," in spite of the genre's traditional assumptions privileging fantasy?

Groening highlights relevant production strategies: "I think the show delivers on our goal, which is to tell stories that people can connect to, that are funny and actually have some sort of emotional resonance you don't expect in a cartoon. We don't go for laughs for laughs' sake; we really are trying to tell stories that make you forget from time to time you're watching a cartoon."[133] Executive producer Sam Simon credits James Brooks for his "marching orders to do a show based on the emotional inner lives of its cartoon characters, and that's really never been done before."[134] Despite their animated form, the characters' personalities are more multifaceted and robust than most live-action sitcoms. But since they are "only cartoons," the writers can heap indignities and trauma upon them without making audiences feel too bad for the characters. As Solomon suggests, "if they were too real, you'd become too sympathetic and too sensitive about their feelings. But because they're obviously not real people, you can exaggerate and make things funnier without feeling any pain."[135] The iconic rendering of characters offered by animation simultaneously makes characters less "real" in terms of visual representation, and more "real" in their emotional resonance, a strategy extended even further with the low-key naturalism of *King of the Hill*.[136]

Dave Berkman furthers this argument, suggesting that, unlike *Roseanne*'s visual realism of working-class struggles, "there is an even more devastating reality to *The Simpsons*, one which succeeds only because, as a stylized cartoon, it is visually unreal."[137] He goes on to itemize the ways in which *The Simpsons* breaks the taboos of American television — portraying the threats of nuclear power, negative effects of excessive television viewing, and the "deceits perpetuated by American education" — aspects of reality that may only be seen on television when rendered by a team of cartoonists. Whereas the standard sitcom tradition-ally reaffirms the family through its weekly restoration of equilibrium, *The Simpsons* uses its cartoon form to pose problems, more akin to those of real life, that simply cannot be solved within a half-hour. The show then regularly solves these unsolvable problems in spite of itself, both parodying the artificial-ity of the sitcom tradition and demonstrating the power of animation to represent "realities" which cannot be captured in a three-camera studio or before a live audience.

One of many examples of this dual use and abuse of the sitcom narrative formula is the fairly typical episode "King-Size Homer."[138] In this episode's far-fetched premise, Homer discovers that to qualify for disability benefits, and thus get paid to stay home instead of going to work at the nuclear power plant, he needs to gain 61 pounds to become medically obese. Once this goal is achieved, Homer both revels in his governmentally enabled life of leisure and experiences discrimination as a "fat guy." Throughout the course of the episode, Homer's weight gains and subsequent treatment of his "disability" both violate the decorum of the normal sitcom and express the flexibility of the animated format to represent that which would be technically unfeasible for a live-action show.

The show's narrative resolution both highlights and undercuts sitcom conventions of restored equilibrium through parody. Homer's negligence in performing his job duties from home — he goes to a movie matinee, leaving the computer terminal monitoring the nuclear power plant's safety unattended — causes a potential meltdown, a typical mockery of the nuclear power industry that few live-action shows could politically sustain. Racing to the plant, he saves the day by falling to his seeming death into the exploding nuclear tank, but his enlarged size causes him to get stuck in the tank's vent, thus sealing the rupture and averting the crisis. As Lisa notes, "I think it's ironic that Dad saved the day while a slimmer man would have fallen to his death," highlighting the typical machinations of the sitcom's pat narrative resolution. Finally, in order to restore the show's situation to its beginning equilibrium, Mr. Burns agrees to pay for a liposuction to restore Homer to his normal 239-pound size in time for next week's episode. *The Simpsons* strategically employs the conventions of its sitcom genre while simultaneously parodying the assumptions of narration and episodic form linked to the generic cluster. This type of explicit generic parody and reference is typical of other episodes as well, with common allusions to the lack of continuity between episodes and the characters' loss of memory of past events. In another instance, when Principal Skinner is proved to be an imposter, the episode ends with the town judge decreeing, "Everything will be just like it was before all this happened! And no one will ever mention it again," ensuring an episodic return to equilibrium.[139]

This simultaneous denial and exaggeration of sitcom norms suggests the ways in which *The Simpsons* uses parody to position itself generically. Linda Hutcheon has argued that we should look to parody not just as a textual element or formal attribute, but as a "pragmatic" component of texts in their cultural encoding and decoding.[140] Thus the parodic tone of *The Simpsons* emerges not only in the text, but also in the interpretative insights of critics and audiences attempting to make sense of the show. One critic notes, "they are caricatures, not just of *us*, but of us in our national delusion that the life of the sitcom family is the way things are 'supposed' to be."[141] Similarly, another argues "*The Simpsons* is satire. Rather than engage in the pretentious misrepresentation of family life that one finds in the 'model family' shows (from *The Donna Reed Show* to *The Cosby Show*), this program admits that most parents aren't perfect."[142] The program's realism emerges not in its adherence to norms of naturalistic live-action programming, but from its parodic dismantling of unreal live-action sitcom conventions.

Issues of parody surface in debates surrounding the show's legitimacy for children as well. Peggy Charren, president of Action for Children's Television, defends the show on satirical grounds; she suggests that principals who banned Bart's image from school would probably interpret Jonathan Swift's classic satire "A Modest Proposal" as a legitimate cause to worry about child abuse.[143] On the other extreme, one writer describes how his children watched the show unaware that it was parody; after he intervened by teaching them the show's "proper" parodic framework, they stopped watching the show because they disliked satire, ultimately supporting his claim that it was not well suited for children.[144] *The Simpsons*' parody, and the audience's "failure" to interpret it as such, serves both to argue for the show's inappropriateness for kids and to refute such age-based condemnations of the program. But parody and satire are usually held up as legitimating traits, signs of *The Simpsons*' worth as more than just an average cartoon, as critics note the satirical edge to legitimate the adult pleasures of the text, even if kids (or other adults) miss them. Just as the program's animated form is often linked to its lack of cultural value, its parodic take on the sitcom (and nearly every other American cultural form) works to elevate *The Simpsons* as legitimate within established cultural hierarchies. This contrasts with the degraded understanding of "just parody" that the producers of *Soap* used to avoid devaluation in the different context of live-action programming of the late 1970s, suggesting that the shifting associations tied to the category of parody are subject to various interpretations across contexts.

Parody pervades *The Simpsons*, from the treatment of the sitcom genre discussed above, to the specific parodies of specific programs, films, and genres featured in particular episodes. Although the show has parodically mocked hundreds of references throughout its run, possibly the most extreme example of parody on *The Simpsons* is the unusual episode "The Simpsons Spin-Off Showcase."[145] The conceit of the episode is that Fox has asked the producers of *The Simpsons* to develop new shows to fill out the network's schedule. Host Troy McClure introduces pilots for three possible spin-offs from *The Simpsons* that Fox is allegedly considering, each a parody of a different genre: "Chief Wiggum P.I." places Springfield's police chief in New Orleans within a detective/action context, "The Love-Matic Grampa" spoofs fantasy sitcoms like *My Mother the Car* (1965–66) by reincarnating Abe Simpson as a love tester machine in Moe's Tavern, and "The Simpson Family Smile-Time Variety Hour" puts the family into a variety program, circa 1972. Whereas most episodes of *The Simpsons* situate parodies within the context of a sitcom narrative, this episode is more like annual Halloween episodes, which present a trio of short pieces that usually parody a common source, such as *The Shining* (1980) or *The Twilight Zone* (1959–64). Yet "Spin-Off Showcase" works against many of the conventions of the program's "realist" tendencies, highlighting the contrived and absurd traditions of most spin-offs. Whereas most parodies within *The Simpsons* relocate the host genre or text within the realm of comedy, this episode attempts to play each of the spin-offs more "straight" by making them extreme examples of what they parody without the modes of humor more common to the show at large.

Not surprisingly, fans of *The Simpsons* were quite mixed on how this episode played out. Within the fan reviews contributed online on The Simpsons Archive, regular viewers were split between finding the episode brilliantly subversive and tediously unfunny.[146] Notably, a number of enthusiastic viewers discussed the episode as "anti-funny," parodying the genres by making them as "lame" as possible. The middle segment, complete with excessive laugh-track and an inane theme song, "deftly shows the stark contrast between *The Simpsons* and the run-of-the-mill sitcom." More dismissive viewers found the episode's lack of humor atypical and disconcerting, especially in the final variety hour segment, where the jokes are purposefully unfunny and tired — as one viewer writes, "by parodying an awful show, it became near unwatchable." If any episode of *The Simpsons* deserves to be categorized as postmodern, this would be the one, with its lack of clearly identified spectatorial position and undefined critical relationship to the object of parody. But the fans' reactions suggests just how atypical this episode is — all acknowledged that whether they liked it or not, "Spin-Off Showcase" was among the most unusual entries in *The Simpsons* canon. Thus the application of postmodernism to understand *The Simpsons* use of parody is marginal at best, useful only for the show's most atypical moments, not the common practices of parody found in most episodes.

The cultural use of parody within the text and contexts of *The Simpsons* differs significantly from accounts of either postmodernist blank parody or generic dilution. Discourses of genre are parodically reiterated and foregrounded, not "flattened out" or terminated. Of course, these enunciations of genre are often framed critically, calling the assumptions of genre into question. Whether by undermining assumed sitcom realism by highlighting the genre's artificial narrative structure, or by exploding the assumptions of the cartoon through the hyperbolic violence of *Itchy & Scratchy*, *The Simpsons* does not destroy genres but highlights their cultural circulation and common currency among the show's media-saturated audience. By calling attention to these generic assumptions and mocking cultural conventions, the show tackles traditionally marginalized topics (from problematic nuclear power to problematic nuclear families) and questions the very media system circulating the show (as with "Spin-Off Showcase"). The animation of *The Simpsons* enables this oppositional take on the sitcom genre, probably the most conventional and mainstream television genre.

But just as our approach to genre necessitates examinations of the specificities of individual instances and contextual circulation, we need to avoid sweeping generalizations about parody "always" leading to opposition, co-optation, or postmodernism — parody must be regarded as a historical and contextual mode of production and reception, in addition to its more common textual conceptions. We must also recognize how parody can work to support more dominant and traditional notions of television culture. Jonathan Culler aptly points out how genre parody can work to further dominant meanings, even in the face of seeming "oppositional" content. He argues that "pseudo-parody" can create the illusion of resistant critique of the ideological conventions of a genre, providing readers an oppositional position toward the conventions of the form. But often this mode of parody serves only to "forestall a possible objection" for the reader, establishing a level of goodwill with an audience to create the sense of opposition, even as the text works to reassert the norms of the parodied genre.[147] Thus many viewers have commented that, while *The Simpsons* mocks the norms of the sitcom genre, ultimately the show contains the same level of sentimentality and "family values" of the shows it satirizes. I do not wish to resolve this debate between "real" or illusionary oppositional content and *The Simpsons*; rather I want to point to the problems with sweeping claims of a genre's (or genre parody's) inherently oppositional content or attitude — such generalizations are one of the reasons genre analysis has gotten a bad reputation within contemporary media studies.

I have not resolved the paradox of this section's epigrams — if *The Simpsons* is figured as quite "realistic," can it be "just a cartoon?" I think *The Simpsons* does work as both realistic animation and just a cartoon. By looking at how *The Simpsons* has been linked to generic codes of realism, notions of cultural validity, and assumptions of target audience, we can see how it is both discursively situated within already extant hierarchies of cultural norms and values, and works to further those systems of differentiation. *The Simpsons* was figured as "just a cartoon" by those wishing to dismiss its cultural value, or positioned as inappropriate to the cartoon genre in questioning its legitimacy for children. Other critics hailed the show's parodic take on the sitcom as realistic and therefore "quality" television, working against the normally held cultural conception of animation as children's programming. For these critics, animation was the generic addition that, ironically, enabled *The Simpsons* to be the era's most effective and realistic critique of the live-action sitcom. Thus even though cartoons have traditionally figured low on cultural hierarchies, in the case of *The Simpsons*, the animation genre raised the program above the ordinary sitcom to critique the host genre's vaunted place within American culture.

Assumptions about animation and family sitcoms situate the program within hierarchies and power relations impacting the show's reception and the ensuing controversies that emerged. But it would be a mistake to regard this generic framework as fixed or static. Just as the show is positioned within clusters of already extant generic discourses, *The Simpsons* and its long-term cultural life have worked to reconstitute and change the very generic notions that were partially formative of its initial cultural understanding. The success of the show with adults, partially overcoming the stigmas of animation's "childish" audience, have somewhat eroded these notions, along with other changing assumptions of cartoons detailed in Chapter 3. We can see the effects of this generic shift most dramatically in industrial practices, as numerous successful adult animated sitcoms have followed *The Simpsons*, from Fox's similar sitcoms *King of the Hill* and *Futurama*, to the even more adult-aimed cable programming of *Beavis & Butthead* and *South Park*.[148] But the generic assumptions of animation have not simply disappeared in the wake of *The Simpsons*, as both *Beavis & Butthead* and *South Park* have been embroiled in similar controversies surrounding their appropriateness for children who are assumed to be the "natural" target of animation. What these instances indicate most clearly is that an account of genre is necessary to understand how audiences and industries make sense of these generically mixed and parodic programs, and thus we cannot simply apply the rubric of the "postmodern" to deny the show's generic markers and subsequent cultural circulation through genre categories.

Genre mixing and parody are specific modes of generic practice that do not suggest the declining importance of genres, but rather foreground the role that genres as cultural categories play in situating texts within larger contexts. Genre mixing is not the exception that proves the rule of genre, as many genre critics have assumed. As Rick Altman has argued, mixing genres is the central process by which new genres emerge, old genres transform, and genre categories are put forward in common cultural practice.[149] Within texts, genre mixing often leads to greater foregrounding of generic practices, as the combination of different assumptions makes often unspoken genre conventions more manifest and explicit. The controversial receptions of *Soap* and *The Simpsons* were dependent upon generic mixture and parody, because conflicting clusters of assumptions collided. The generic processes running through these cases are not less important due to a lack of genre purity, but become even more crucial through their mixture and cultural crises. By looking at genre mixing in practice, media scholars can better understand the complex ways genres operate as cultural categories throughout media history, undoing the "purity bias" of most genre scholarship.

Conclusion
Some Reflections on Reality Television

So how do genres matter? They matter as cultural categories, discursive practices of definition, interpretation, and evaluation constituting generic clusters. They matter as historical processes, as the quiz show category accrues meanings through the radio era to forge the assumptions triggered in the crisis of the 1950s television scandals. They matter as industrial strategies, with scheduling and channel branding practices transforming the cartoon category across historical eras even when texts themselves remain unchanged. They matter as sites of audience practice, as the talk show category serves as a site of debate and judgment for a range of viewers, surpassing the moment of television viewing. They matter in creating texts, as *Dragnet*'s producers drew upon film, radio, and television genre categories to form the foundational set of assumptions for the police drama genre. They matter even when genre categories mix, as the discursive practices constituting multiple genres parodically collide through *Soap* and *The Simpsons* to create cultural controversies that ultimately reinforce the central role of genres in media.

Genres still matter in contemporary television, even as programs emerge that challenge traditional static genre definitions and point toward new generic clusters. Most notably since I began writing this book, the genre category of "reality TV" has emerged as a major site of international television production, audience engagement, industrial strategizing, genre mixing, and cultural controversy. In this conclusion, I point toward a number potential directions we might follow to understand this emergent genre. This is by no means a fully fleshed-out and researched case study like previous chapters; rather, it is an attempt to map the terrain for future study of this as yet underexplored generic landscape.[1] In exploring the possibilities for understanding reality TV, I consider how this new genre can be best understood as a cultural

196

category, looking to the connections between reality TV and the various case studies explored in this book.

So is reality TV a full-fledged television genre? Some textualist critics might hesitate, noting that reality TV draws upon other genres, including game shows, soap operas, dating shows, crime drama, talent shows, travel programs, and sports, to such a degree that reality TV lacks definitional coherence as a genre—what do all reality programs share that distinguishes them from other genres? I would argue that the core unifying feature of reality TV as a genre is not any textual element, but the broad circulation of the reality TV generic label as a category, allowing us to make sense of these programs and their cultural associations. Reality TV is a genre because we treat it as one, with regular iterations of the category in nearly every realm of media practice, from critics to networks, audiences to regulators. While perhaps other generic labels might be more accurate — "nonscripted programming," "gamedocs," and "docu-soaps" have been used by some — the broad cultural circulation of reality TV as a category is what makes it a genre, not any internal textual unity across programs.

Not to suggest that textual practices are irrelevant—obviously the ways reality TV programs function as *genre television* are important. One of the genre's central production strategies is genre mixing, recombinantly drawing conventions and assumptions from a range of genres in both innovative and derivative fashions. Reality TV's production norms were popularized with *The Real World* (1992–), establishing a number of editing and shooting conventions that meld serial narrative, verité camera style, and first-person confessional segments while making the apparatus of production as invisible as possible by downplaying the constructed nature of the program via appeals to the "real." These claims of realism draw upon generic precedents discussed in previous case studies, as quiz shows and *Dragnet* relied upon documentary style, unscripted action, and overt claims of authenticity to establish their legitimacy as more than fiction. The prevalent reality TV strain of "gamedocs" like *Survivor* (2000–), *The Amazing Race* (2001–), and *Fear Factor* (2001–) all are indebted to game show traditions, drawing upon the logic of humiliation and extreme behavior from radio's stunt dominant, as well as the high-stakes ongoing "characters" pioneered by 1950s television quizzes. Reality dramas such as *Real World*, *American High*, and *The Bachelor* (2002–) all rely on shorthand techniques of montage sequences, musical cues, and strategic casting of character types to maximize dramatic pleasures for audiences who are used to the pacing and style of fictional storytelling. Thus, a historical poetics of reality TV points to its texts as a site of complex narrative practice drawing upon traditions from a range of generic sources.

Just as reality TV shows use techniques from a range of generic precedents, these devices carry with them a set of assumptions and associations that are selectively drawn into the reality TV cluster. While game shows are a clear influence on a large number of reality shows, the discursive links to game shows are strategically activated and denied as needed. *Survivor* often downplays its game show roots to provide a greater sense of legitimacy, importance, and human drama to the show, while foregrounding that "it's only a game" as necessary to defuse both critics and overzealous fans looking to spoil the competition. These generic enunciations are encoded both in the text—*Survivor's* motto "Outwit, Outplay, Outlast" acknowledges its game roots, while the (almost literal) life-or-death stakes of the contest are heightened to a degree to undercut any residual game show frivolity—and in the discourses that surround the show, as producers, critics, audiences, and commentators all weigh in to debate its ethics, pleasures, and cultural meanings. Some of the cultural dissonance stemming from the questionable ethics of reality TV is tied to this dual adherence to and denial of genre assumptions. Dramatic pleasures are most engaging when conflicts and goals are extreme, while game show and sports contests promote their high stakes to entertain fans. Reality TV raises the stakes exponentially, while simultaneously assuring viewers that the situations are more risky, dangerous, and ultimately uncertain than game shows or sports. This may make shows like *Fear Factor* or *Temptation Island* (2001–) exciting, but many viewers squirm uncomfortably at the level of physical and emotional punishment people will undertake for a moment of television fame. The dramatic pleasures in action shows like *24* (2001–) or *Alias* rely upon the fictional frame to make their representational violence and anxiety palatable. Reality TV adopts this high-stakes emotional and physical action (without explicit violence—as of yet), but abandons the fictional frame; the result is an escalating series of programs exploring strategies of generic dissonance to press the boundaries of audience tolerance and pleasure.

The pleasures of reality TV raises another tie to previous case studies. In discussing talk shows, nonviewers of *Jerry Springer* assumed that the show's primary audience took the program seriously and mirrored the guests' demographics, while most fans claimed a different profile and ironic stance toward the show. A similar divergence applies for reality television—genre detractors may assume that, because a show gets high ratings, all viewers would be willing to participate in the ritual humiliation offered by a given program. While certainly many viewers are interested in crossing into the on-screen reality participation, the pleasures of viewing a reality show are no more dependent on wish-fulfilling than identification with characters in other genres like horror and gangster films. Just because a viewer enjoys watching a couple subject their relationship to the lures of lusty suitors on *Temptation Island* doesn't mean that she would like to join the party. The success of *Joe Millionaire* (2003) suggests that the pleasures of the romance reality show are not as simple as identification, as the program parodically invited viewers to mock contestants, judge their motives, and revel in the "twist" of the program's central deceit. The romance reality show, which like *Springer* has endured the wrath of cultural commentators decrying the demise of American culture, needs to be understood not just on its textual face, but as a site of cultural engagement for viewers to negotiate with the meanings it puts forward in the context of their own *habitus*. Thus to understand the pleasures and appeals of the genre, we need to go beyond textual constructs to examine audience voices and practices in constructing their own meanings and evaluations of the genre category.

Audiences must take what is given them from the television industry of course, and thus the industry's genre practices are formative of the category. Like with cartoons, television-specific practices like scheduling and branding move the industry's role beyond production of programs. For reality TV, scheduling played a key role in establishing the genre's early-twenty-first century boom—CBS debuted both *Survivor* and *Big Brother* during the summer of 2000, taking advantage of a typically dormant time for network television to experiment and hope for what proved to be a cultural sensation. Despite the general shift in contemporary television toward narrowcasting and audience segmentation, *Survivor* (and its quiz show predecessor *Who Wants to Be a Millionaire*) triggered a number of mass audience reality phenomena (followed by *American Idol* [2002–] and *Joe Millionaire*), highlighting the possibility of creating sensational hype out of reality programming. CBS likewise used scheduling practices to help define the reality audience by counterprogramming *Survivor* against *Friends* on Thursday nights, challenging NBC's domination of young-audiences with its Must See TV line-up. Post-*Survivor*, networks have been more creative in scheduling reality programming, taking advantage of summers, short-season program runs, and counterprogramming against established fictional hits like *The West Wing* (1999–) and *JAG* (1995–) to draw different demographics.

Channel identity and branding have been important practices in establishing the reality genre as well. As of this writing, Reality Central has yet to launch as a genre-delimited channel, yet branding among different established channels helps constitute genre categories. CBS established itself early as a reality forerunner, featuring both high-rated programs and more "respectable" shows like *Survivor* and *Amazing Race* while vocally critiquing the more "sordid" stunts featured on other networks. Fox reveled in the sordid, pushing the sexual envelope with *Temptation Island, Love Cruise* (2001), and the notorious special *Who Wants to Marry a Multi-Millionaire?* (2000), and drawing upon its branded history of sensationalism with *When Animals Attack* (1996) and *World's Wildest Police Videos* (1998)—although Fox clearly was willing to widen its brand, as its biggest hits have been the outrageous yet parodic *Joe Millionaire* and the comparatively wholesome *American Idol*. These competing brand identities certainly transcend the reality genre—CBS has long been the high-quality

"Tiffany network" for older "heartland" viewers, while Fox has cultivated a young lowbrow aesthetic from its debut—but the flexibility of the reality category is able to encompass a wide range of channel associations. Reality TV has not been limited to broadcast networks, as MTV pioneered the genre with youth-skewing *Real World* and *Road Rules* (1995–), and has continued to push the envelope by terrifying teenagers on *Fear* (2000–02) and celebrating college debauchery on *Sorority/Fraternity Life* (2002–). Bravo has drawn upon its artsy urbane reputation by highlighting young actors on *The It Factor* (2002–) and gay culture with *Queer Eye for the Straight Guy* (2003–) and *Boy Meets Boy* (2003–). Thus, even though reality TV has clustered a number of lowbrow disdainful associations, it can still serve as a site of quality and legitimization when linked to other culturally valid identities.

In considering the reality TV genre as a cultural category, academic discourses should be one active facet in its cluster of associations. Traditionally, critical media scholars have viewed television programming from a distance, commenting on that which has already been made. But the history of film genres like *film noir*, melodrama, and westerns suggests that academic analyses can filter into a broader cultural realm, altering the genre texts that are produced and the assumptions broadly constituting the category. Television scholars have publicly engaged with policy decisions, issues of representation, and debates on media violence, calling for shifts in regulation and production practices—although such interventions rarely come from critical and cultural scholars.[2] Reality TV provides an opportunity to participate in the public discourses shaping this nascent category along with journalistic critics and commentators. Public interventions into matters of taste and ethics can get dicey—one lesson of cultural studies is to respect and seek to understand popular tastes instead of condemning or "correcting" them—but just as we shouldn't cede our understanding of the talk show genre to the William Bennetts of the world, media scholars should take opportunities to bring our expert knowledge and opinions about hot-button media issues out of the classroom and academic journals. Personally, I would like to see more voices complicating the blanket condemnation of a homogenous notion of reality TV, noting the crucial cultural, political, and ethical differences between *Amazing Race* and *Fear Factor*. We can highlight historical continuities between contemporary reality TV and earlier precedents like *Truth or Consequences* and *Candid Camera* (1948–67),[3] discuss the political economic structures underlying *American Idol*, and consider how reality TV has functioned as a site of both heightened and problematic representation for gays and lesbians. Given the freshness of the generic category, reality TV is ripe for interventions by cultural scholars looking to reframe the tenor of public debates over media's social impacts.

These reflections on reality TV are admittedly brief and underdeveloped—more detailed mapping of the genre's discursive cluster is certainly needed to understand the specific shifts, cycles, and debates in reality TV that are constantly emerging. Yet hopefully future work on reality TV and other genres new and old will take up the challenge issued by this book: studying *television genres* is distinct from studying *genre television*. We need to invest our scholarly energies into understanding how genre categories emerge, change, and impact our broader cultural contexts. Studying genre texts is part of this process, but only as one part of a larger circuit of cultural practice, because genre discourses of definition, interpretation, and evaluation cross over realms of industry, audience, policy, criticism, and academia. By focusing on categorical processes, we can remind ourselves how genres matter—to networks, to critics, to producers, to viewers, to cultures, and hopefully to scholars as well.

Notes

Introduction: Genres That Matter

1. Most television scholars simply import film genre theory to their medium. The standard theoretical overview of television genres is Jane Feuer, "Genre Study and Television," in *Channels of Discourse, Reassembled*, ed. Robert C. Allen (Chapel Hill: University of North Carolina Press, 1992), 138–60. More recently, but still overly dependent on film theory, is Glen Creeber, *The Television Genre Book* (London: British Film Institute, 2001).
2. For instance, the entry on "genre" in Bernadette Casey et al., *Television Studies: The Key Concepts* (London: Routledge, 2002), 111, concludes, "classification into recognizable genres is becoming increasingly difficult, even on a common-sense level. As an academic tool of analysis, the genre approach may be finally losing its relevance."
3. The label of "woman's channel" is not solely a notion of target audience, as the label clearly indicates women's programming, often articulated to specific genres (such as made-for-TV movies); see Jackie Byars and Eileen R. Meehan, "Once in a Lifetime: Constructing 'The Working Woman' through Cable Narrowcasting," in *Television: The Critical View*, ed. Horace Newcomb (New York: Oxford University Press, 2000), 144-68.
4. Structuralist critics are especially tied to narrative syntax; see Will Wright, *Sixguns and Society: A Structural Study of the Western* (Berkeley: University of California Press, 1975), and Rick Altman, *The American Film Musical* (Bloomington: Indiana University Press, 1987), for two strong examples.
5. See Steve Neale, "Questions of Genre," in *Film Genre Reader II*, ed. Barry Keith Grant (Austin: University of Texas Press, 1995), 159–83, and Rick Altman, *Film/Genre* (London: BFI Publishing, 1999), for examples of genre analysis via film industry practices.
6. See Robert C. Allen, *Speaking of Soap Operas* (Chapel Hill: University of North Carolina Press, 1985), for a comprehensive history and analysis of the soap opera genre.
7. See Creeber, *Television Genre Book*, for the most recent example of such a handbook; Brian G. Rose, ed., *TV Genres: A Handbook and Reference Guide* (Westport, Conn.: Greenwood Press, 1985), and Stuart M. Kaminsky and Jeffrey H. Mahan, *American Television Genres* (Chicago: Nelson-Hall, 1985), are earlier examples.
8. I have purposely focused on entertainment genres over information genres like news, sports, and advertising, primarily to maintain consistency with literary and film genre theory; certainly, exploring television news as a cultural category would be quite illuminating, but would require a lengthy trip into the discipline of journalism studies.
9. Pierre Bourdieu, *Distinction: A Social Critique of the Judgement of Taste*, (Cambridge: Harvard University Press, 1984).

202

Chapter 1

1. *Jacobellis v. Ohio*, 378 U.S. 184 (1964).

2. Studies of genre within popular music studies have been more in line with my own cultural approach to genres, arguably because of music's lack of narrative basis forced critics to be more flexible in understanding the practices of genre. See Simon Frith, *Performing Rites: On the Value of Popular Music* (Cambridge: Harvard University Press, 1996), and Keith Negus, *Music Genres and Corporate Cultures* (London: Routledge, 1999).

3. Not all traditional approaches to genre abstained from questions of cultural power, because political questions motivated many ideological and structuralist accounts of film and television genres. Nonetheless, contemporary media studies has shifted toward more specific accounts of power and away from the broad macro-examinations that typify structuralism.

4. Jane Feuer, "Genre Study and Television," in *Channels of Discourse, Reassembled*, ed. Robert C. Allen (Chapel Hill: University of North Carolina Press, 1992), 138–60. Feuer's essay is certainly the most read overview of television genre analysis and has defined the field of genre studies for television for over a decade. Other contributions to television genre theory include Mimi White, "Television Genres: Intertextuality," *Journal of Film and Video* 37, no. 3 (1985); Gregory A. Waller, "Flow, Genre, and the Television Text," *Journal of Popular Film & Television* 16, no. 1 (1988), 6–11; and John Caughie, "Adorno's Reproach: Repetition, Difference and Television Genre," *Screen* 32, no. 2 (1991). See Glen Creeber, *The Television Genre Book* (London: British Film Institute, 2001), for recent (but not significantly different) overviews of television genre theory.

5. For one of the few definitional analyses of television genres (in conjunction with film), see Steve Neale and Frank Krutnik, *Popular Film and Television Comedy* (New York: Routledge, 1990); for a paradigmatic example of this approach within film studies, see Noël Carroll, *The Philosophy of Horror or Paradoxes of the Heart* (New York: Routledge, 1990).

6. For a particularly unsatisfying demonstration of these limitations, see "An Application of Northrup Frye's Analytical Methods to Quiz and Game Shows," in Stuart M. Kaminsky and Jeffrey H. Mahan, *American Television Genres* (Chicago: Nelson-Hall, 1985), 43–52.

7. See David J. Russell, "Monster Roundup: Reintegrating the Horror Genre," in *Refiguring American Film Genres*, ed. Nick Browne (Berkeley: University of California Press, 1998), 233–54, for a less troubling definition of the horror genre, though Russell's approach is no more suited to understanding how the genre fits into larger cultural contexts than Carroll's.

8. Note that some of these critical schools do not solely examine texts for meanings. This is especially true of cultural studies, the paradigm under which I most locate my own approach to genre. However, some work done in the name of cultural studies does interpret the core meanings of genres, even as they may deny the intrinsic and textual basis of these meanings.

9. For a range of typical interpretive accounts of television genres, see John Tulloch, *Television Drama: Agency, Audience and Myth* (London: Routledge, 1990); E. Ann Kaplan, *Rocking Around the Clock: Music Television, Postmodernism, and Consumer Culture* (New York: Methuen, 1987); David Marc, *Comic Visions: Television Comedy and American Culture*, 2nd ed. (London: Blackwell Press, 1997); Laura Stempel Mumford, *Love and Ideology in the Afternoon: Soap Opera, Women, and Television Genre* (Bloomington: Indiana University Press, 1995); and Horace Newcomb, *TV: The Most Popular Art* (Garden City, NY: Anchor Press, 1974). All of these projects look to interpret generic meanings, although they use varying theoretical assumptions and paradigms to do so. For the most influential film examples, see Will Wright, *Sixguns and Society: A Structural Study of the Western* (Berkeley: University of California Press, 1975); Thomas Schatz, *Hollywood Genres: Formulas, Filmmaking, and the Studio System* (Philadelphia: Temple University Press, 1981); and John G. Cawelti, *The Six-Gun Mystique*, 2nd ed. (Bowling Green, Ohio: Bowling Green State University Popular Press, 1984).

10. See Mumford, *Love and Ideology*, and John Fiske, *Television Culture* (New York: Routledge, 1987), 179–97, respectively.

11. Again, this ahistorical critique of interpretive approaches does not stem from their theoretical orthodoxy, but rather from the ways in which the approach has traditionally been practiced.

12. Robert C. Allen, *Speaking of Soap Operas* (Chapel Hill: University of North Carolina Press, 1985), and Robert C. Allen, "Bursting Bubbles: 'Soap Opera,' Audiences, and the Limits of Genre," in *Remote Control: Television, Audiences, and Cultural Power*, ed. Ellen Seiter, et al. (New York: Routledge, 1989), 44–55.

13. Another example of a historical account of television genres is Bernard Timberg, *Television Talk: A History of the TV Talk Show* (Austin, Tex.: University of Texas Press, 2002). A more developed and sophisticated history for film is Rick Altman, *The American Film Musical* (Bloomington: Indiana University Press, 1987). I won't discuss Altman's approach in depth here, as his book has not been very influential in television studies and because he revises a number of his positions in his more recent breakthrough work in genre theory, Rick Altman, *Film/Genre* (London: BFI Publishing, 1999). Steve Neale, *Genre and Hollywood* (New York: Routledge, 2000), also offers brief historical overviews of a range of genres.

14. Feuer, "Genre Study," 151.

15. E. D. Hirsch, Jr., *Validity in Interpretation* (New Haven, Conn.: Yale University Press, 1967), offers a theory of a singular "intrinsic genre" corresponding to an author's intended meaning.

16. For one typical example, see Graeme Turner, *Film as Social Practice*, 2nd ed. (New York: Routledge, 1993), 85–93. Turner places genre under the chapter of "Film Narrative," even though he defines genres as produced by texts, industries, and audiences. Another example is Leah R. Vande Berg, Lawrence A. Wenner, and Bruce E. Gronbeck, eds., *Critical Approaches to Television* (Boston: Houghton Mifflin, 1998), which places generic criticism under the chapter entitled "Text-Centered Approaches to Television Criticism."

17. Mumford, *Love and Ideology*, 17–18, argues against a definition of the soap opera based on audience pleasures or uses; she calls for a definition "that focuses instead on the specific characteristics of the genre itself" — namely the text.

18. Textual analysis is the nearly ubiquitous method for all approaches to genre.

19. Altman, *Film/Genre*, similarly suggests that genres have traditionally been viewed as equal to the corpus that they seem to identify, as defined by a common structure and topic (22–24). He considers Wittgenstein's concept of "family relations" concerning genres, but argues convincingly that genre definitions are contingent and historical, arriving through "use," not internal structures (96–99).

20. See Steve Neale, "Questions of Genre," in *Film Genre Reader II*, ed. Barry Keith Grant (Austin: University of Texas Press, 1995), 159–83, for his discussion of *The Great Train Robbery*'s reclassification from crime film into western, drawing on Charles Musser's research. Altman, *Film/Genre*, also addresses similar cases in the film genres of musicals and biopics. In Chapter 3, I discuss a similar instance concerning animated short films from the 1930s and 1940s, which became recategorized as children's cartoons in 1960s television.

21. For a detailed discussion of the role of the biological analogy in literary genre theory, see David Fishelov, *Metaphors of Genre: The Role of Analogies in Genre Theory* (University Park: Pennsylvania State University Press, 1993), especially Chapter 2. Altman, *Film/Genre*, 62–68, discusses the tradition of evolutionary models for film genres. This analytic approach and reliance on biological metaphors is evident in the title and methodology of Jeanine Basinger, *The World War II Combat Film: Anatomy of a Genre* (New York: Columbia University Press, 1986), for one example of many.

22. Altman, *Film/Genre* (especially Chapters 3–5), offers the most compelling and detailed account of the specific processes that film industries engage in to create and modify genres — in Chapter 3, I consider some television-specific practices.

23. Tom Magliozzi and Ray Magliozzi, *Car Talk Columns* [Web site] (May 1993 [cited 1 August 2003]); available from http://cartalk.cars.com/Columns/NEW_COLUMNS/Archive/1993/May/05.html.

24. This approach to media studies — examining the integrated relationships among industry, audience, text, and context — is drawn from Julie D'Acci, *Defining Women: Television and the Case of Cagney & Lacey* (Chapel Hill: University of North Carolina Press, 1994); see also Stuart Hall, "Encoding/Decoding," in *Culture, Media, Language*, ed. Stuart Hall (London: Hutchinson, 1980), 128–40; Richard Johnson, "What is Cultural Studies Anyway?" *Social Text* 6, no. 16 (1987); and Paul duGay et al., *Doing Cultural Studies: The Story of the Sony Walkman* (London: Sage Publications, 1997).

25. Allen, *Speaking of Soap Operas*, 8, discusses the origin of the term "soap opera." Altman, *Film/Genre*, offers a convincing account of the genrification process for films, as terms turn from adjectives tacked onto genres into full-fledged generic nouns.

26. This is not to say that industrially motivated terms do not get tied into genres. For instance, the industrial scheduling of Saturday morning cartoons or daytime talk shows seems to have become so ingrained into the genres that the scheduling terms have become specific subgenres themselves, as I discuss in Chapters 3 and 4. Altman, *Film/Genre*, 110–111, and Kevin S. Sandler, "Movie Ratings as Genre: The Incontestable R," in *Genre and Contemporary Hollywood*, ed. Steve Neale (London: BFI Publishing, 2002), 201–17, suggestively consider film ratings as generic categories; it is too soon to tell whether television ratings will become established as clear categorical markers as thoroughly as they have for film.

27. Altman, *American Film Musical*, addresses this specific case.

28. Andrew Tudor, "Genre," in *Film Genre Reader II*, ed. Barry Keith Grant (Austin: University of Texas Press, 1995), 3–10; the original piece was published in 1973, long before much of the genre criticism that Tudor effectively critiques in anticipation.

29. Unfortunately, Tudor himself fails to develop the most productive insights of his early essay. In Andrew Tudor, *Monsters and Mad Scientists: A Cultural History of the Horror Movie* (Cambridge, Mass: Blackwell, 1989), he offers what he cites as an expansion on his cultural approach to genre via a history of the horror genre, but his study is firmly textualist, focusing on narrative structure and story content over the cultural interplay between texts and other realms, like audiences and industries. Similarly the promise of Steve Neale's cultural work on genre theory [in Stephen Neale, *Genre* (London: BFI, 1980), and Neale, "Questions of Genre"] is not fulfilled in the actual generic analyses he undertakes (in Neale and Krutnik, *Popular Comedy* and Neale, *Genre and Hollywood*).

30. Foucault offers no singular theoretical piece outlining how discursive formations fit into cultural history. For the most relevant material, see Michel Foucault, *The Order of Things: An Archeology of the Human Sciences* (New York: Vintage Books, 1970); Michel Foucault, *The Archeology of Knowledge and the Discourse on Language* (New York: Pantheon Books, 1972); Michel Foucault, *The History of Sexuality: An Introduction* (New York: Vintage Books, 1978); and Michel Foucault, *Power/Knowledge: Selected Interviews and Other Writings, 1972–1977* (New York: Pantheon Books, 1980).

31. Carroll, *Philosophy of Horror*, 7, suggests the importance of this "check," even though his definition of horror contradicts more widespread notions of the genre.

32. See Altman, *Film/Genre*.

33. Michel Foucault, "What Is an Author?" in *The Foucault Reader*, ed. Paul Rabinow (New York: Pantheon Books, 1984), 101–20.

34. Tony Bennett and Janet Woollacott, *Bond and Beyond: The Political Career of a Popular Hero* (New York: Methuen, 1987), 46–47.

35. James Naremore, *More Than Night: Film Noir in Its Contexts* (Berkeley: University of California Press, 1998), 11, offers a similar link between Foucauldian theory and media genres in theorizing his "history of the idea" of *film noir*. Naremore's excellent work shows the rich possibilities of this approach, although he does not develop this theoretical idea explicitly.

36. In literary studies, see Tony Bennett, *Outside Literature* (New York: Routledge, 1990); Robert Hodge, *Literature as Discourse: Textual Strategies in English and History* (Baltimore: Johns Hopkins University Press, 1990); and Ralph Cohen, "History and Genre," *New Literary History* 17, no. 2 (1986); for film, see Neale, "Questions of Genre," Naremore, *More than Night*, and Neale, *Genre and Hollywood*. For television studies, only Allen, "Bursting Bubbles," has really pointed genre studies in this discursive direction.

37. Altman, *Film/Genre*. Neale, *Genre and Hollywood* engages with similar issues, but his take is much more synthetic of other work and sweeping in its attempt to account for every film genre. Altman offers a more philosophically nuanced and original set of arguments.

38. Other scholars drawing on Foucault's theory have used conceptual metaphors such as "sedimentation" [Judith Butler, "Performative Acts and Gender Constitution: An Essay in Phenomenology and Feminist Theory," in *Performing Feminisms*, ed. Sue-Ellen Case (Baltimore: Johns Hopkins University Press, 1990), 270–82] and "encrustation" (Bennett and Woollacott, *Bond & Beyond*), to describe how discourses accrue to create discursive formations. I have chosen "cluster" to suggest the fluid ongoing processes of genres, as these other terms evoke more permanent and hardened layering.

39. Tzvetan Todorov, *The Fantastic: A Structural Approach to a Literary Genre* (Ithaca: Cornell University Press, 1975), 13–14.

40. Altman, *Film/Genre*, 72–77; Neale, *Genre and Hollywood*, tackles these two theoretical genres as well.

41. An attempt to pose a theoretical television genre which falls short is Nina C. Leibman, *Living Room Lectures: The Fifties Family in Film & Television* (Austin: University of Texas Press, 1995); Leibman attempts to redefine the 1950s domestic sitcom as family melodrama, but in doing so neglects to account of the centrality of comedic form within both texts and, moreover, their cultural circulation.

42. For examples of psychoanalytic approaches, see Robin Wood, "Return of the Repressed," in *Planks of Reason: Essays on the Horror Film*, ed. Barry K. Grant (Metuchen, NJ: Scarecrow Press, 1984), 164–200; Margaret Tarratt, "Monsters from the Id," in *Film Genre Reader II*, ed. Barry Keith Grant (Austin: University of Texas Press, 1995), 330–49; and Kaplan, *Rocking Around the Clock*. For examples of cognitive approaches to genre, see Carroll, *Philosophy of Horror* (especially Chapter 4); Torben Grodal, *Moving Pictures: A New Theory of Film Genres, Feelings, and Cognition* (Oxford: Oxford University Press, 1997); and Noël Carroll, "Film, Emotion, and Genre," in *Passionate Views: Film, Cognition, and Emotion*, ed. Carl Plantinga and Greg M. Smith (Baltimore: Johns Hopkins University Press, 1999), 21–47.

43. Neale, *Genre and Hollywood*, 43.

44. Schatz, *Hollywood Genres*, 16.

45. The tendency for genres to both enable and sell out counter-cultural behaviors has been interpreted within many genres; Altman, *Film/Genre*, claims that this is an inherent property of genres themselves, a generalization of which I am dubious.

46. MTV debuted in 1981, but most commentators felt that cable did not have a significant impact until its debut on Manhattan and Los Angeles cable systems in September 1982. See Tom McGrath, *MTV: The Making of a Revolution* (Philadelphia: Running Press, 1996), 88–91.

47. Ibid.; see also Andrew Pollack, "Music on Cable TV Provoking a Debate," *New York Times*, 29 November 1982.

48. See Frith, *Performing Rites*, Chapter 4, for an excellent cultural analysis of musical genres.

49. MTV head Robert Pittman justified his station's "rock-only" policy via this generic code: "We hope to find more black musicians doing rock 'n' roll and new music. It's not a color barrier — it's a music barrier." Richard Gold, "Labels Limit Videos on Black Artists," *Variety*, 15 December 1982, 78.

50. See Lisa A. Lewis, *Gender Politics and MTV: Voicing the Difference* (Philadelphia: Temple University Press, 1990).

51. As of December 1999, *Thriller* was surpassed by *The Eagles Greatest Hits*; as of this writing, *Thriller* is #2 all-time.

52. For documentation of this chronology (with a few inconsistencies), see McGrath, *MTV*, 99–101; Steven Levy, "Ad Nauseum: How MTV Sells Out Rock & Roll," *Rolling Stone*, 8 December 1983, 37; J. Randy Taraborrelli, *Michael Jackson: The Magic and the Madness* (New York: Birch Lane Press, 1991), 322; Christopher Andersen, *Michael Jackson Unauthorized* (New York: Simon & Schuster, 1994), 108–9; and Dave Marsh, *Trapped: Michael Jackson and the Crossover Dream* (New York: Bantam Books, 1985), 216–20.

53. This aspect of MTV's policy is difficult to research — I have found no documentation of MTV's practices involving *Beat It* and the opening prologue. My discussion of this is based on my own recollection as reported on MTV when first featuring the *Beat It* video. Whether or not this was a serious concern of MTV's or just an excuse to continue to exclude Jackson's videos (I would guess the latter), this moment serves as an example of how conceptions of a genre's definition are culturally operative with material results.

54. Some similar film practices include differentiated film bills in the 1930s and 1940s (with separate newsreel, animation, A feature, and B feature slots), genre-defined theaters (such as art houses or porn theaters), and generically delimited film festivals or screenings. Yet film genre analysis mostly ignores issues such as these as well, and any attempt to translate between these practices and television scheduling and channel-delineation would need to be rethought significantly.

55. The exceptions to this difference include film series, such as *Star Wars*, but certainly television serializations are far more common than film ones.

56. Feuer, "Genre Study," 140.

57. Neale, *Genre and Hollywood*, 41–42 critiques Altman's work on the musical on similar grounds.

58. See Pierre Bourdieu, *Distinction: A Social Critique of the Judgement of Taste* (Cambridge: Harvard University Press, 1984); and Pierre Bourdieu, *The Field of Cultural Production: Essays on Art and Literature* (New York: Columbia University Press, 1993).

Chapter 2

1. For a representative set of examples, all examining sitcom history, see Jane Feuer, "Genre Study and Television," in *Channels of Discourse, Reassembled*, ed. Robert C. Allen (Chapel Hill: University of North Carolina Press, 1992), 138–60; David Marc, *Comic Visions: Television Comedy and American Culture*, 2nd ed. (London: Blackwell Press, 1997); and Ella Taylor, *Prime-Time Families: Television Culture in Postwar America* (Berkeley: University of California Press, 1989).

2. Marc, *Comic Visions*. See Rick Altman, *Film/Genre* (London: BFI Publishing, 1999), especially 22–24, for a discussion of the generic corpus.

3. See Michel Foucault, *The Archeology of Knowledge and the Discourse on Language* (New York: Pantheon Books, 1972); Michel Foucault, *Power/Knowledge: Selected Interviews & Other Writings, 1972–1977* (New York: Pantheon Books, 1980), 78–108; and Michel Foucault, *The Foucault Reader* (New York: Pantheon Books, 1984), 76–100.

4. See Hayden White, *Tropics of Discourse: Essays in Cultural Criticism* (Baltimore: Johns Hopkins University Press, 1978), and Hayden White, *The Content of the Form: Narrative Discourse and Historical Representation* (Baltimore: Johns Hopkins University Press, 1987), for an illuminating discussion of narrative strategies and historiography.

5. Thomas Schatz, *Hollywood Genres: Formulas, Filmmaking, and the Studio System* (Philadelphia: Temple University Press, 1981), offers this narrative schematic to a number of film genres; J. Fred MacDonald, *Who Shot the Sheriff?: The Rise and Fall of the Television Western* (New York: Praeger Press, 1987), offers a similar account of the television western.

6. Altman, *Film/Genre*, especially 30–68.

7. Although I offer a television-specific approach to genre, this case study focused primarily on radio, not TV. While acknowledging the crucial medium differences between radio and television, a television-specific approach can account for radio genres, especially in the early radio period which preceded television. Given that commercial television in the United States drew its industrial structures, corporate hierarchies, established audience, and many specific programs directly from radio, television historians must acknowledge the central role radio has played in constituting the norms for TV. The same holds true for genre history as well— nearly every genre that emerged on television in the 1950s had a direct predecessor on radio. Certainly these genres transformed when emerging on television, especially with the visual influence of film. While we cannot assume that genre operates identically for radio and television, we should be able to account for the ways radio established TV's generic traditions without any major methodological overhauls. Because my primary analytic question motivating this study is what generic precedents set the stage for the television quiz show scandals, my exploration of radio is done in the name of understanding television—I make a similar move in Chapter 5, looking at both film and radio to understand *Dragnet*'s televisual incarnation.

8. Kent Anderson, *Television Fraud: The History and Implications of the Quiz Show Scandals* (Westport, Conn.: Greenwood Press, 1978); Joseph Stone and Tim Yohn, *Prime Time and Misdemeanors: Investigating the 1950s Quiz Scandal* (New Brunswick, N.J.: Rutgers University Press, 1992). One of the best accounts of the scandals is William Boddy, "The Seven Dwarfs & the Money Grubbers: The Public Relations Crisis of U.S. Television in the Late 1950s," in *Logics of Television*, ed. Patricia Mellencamp (Bloomington: Indiana University Press, 1990), 98–116, which places the controversy within the context of 1950s television; given the short length of Boddy's article, not addressing radio predecessors is understandable.

9. Thomas A. DeLong, *Quiz Craze: America's Infatuation with Game Shows* (New York: Praeger Publishers, 1991).

10. See J. Fred MacDonald, *Don't Touch That Dial!: Radio Programming in American Life from 1920 to 1960* (Chicago: Nelson-Hall, 1979), for brief mentions of the genre, surrounded by detailed discussions of more "legitimate" genres like detective shows, westerns, comedy, and news; Susan J. Douglas, *Listening In : Radio and the American Imagination, from Amos 'n' Andy and Edward R. Murrow to Wolfman Jack and Howard Stern* (New York: Times Books, 1999), focuses on radio quiz shows as the topic of audience analysis, as explored by Herta Herzog in Paul Felix Lazarsfeld, *Radio and the Printed Page* (New York,: Duell Sloan and Pearce, 1940).

11. DeLong, *Quiz Craze,* 6.

12. Ibid., 1–3; Norm Blumenthal, *The TV Game Shows* (New York: Pyramid Books, 1975), 13. For more on the rise and fall of movie giveaways and games, see Douglas Gomery, *Shared Pleasures: A History of Movie Presentation in the United States* (Madison: University of Wisconsin Press, 1992), 69–73.

13. DeLong, *Quiz Craze,* 10.

14. Airdates of radio programs come from Harrison B. Summers, *A Thirty-Year History of Programs Carried on National Radio Networks in the United States, 1926–1956* (New York: Arno Press, 1971).

15. "Bowes Inc.," *Time,* 22 June 1936, 63; DeLong, *Quiz Craze,* 11.

16. "Ether Bees," *Literary Digest,* 13 March 1937, 32–34.

17. "Stop the Money," *Business Week,* 21 August 1948, 22.

18. Don Eddy, "Daffy Dollars," *American Magazine,* December 1946, 38–39+.

19. Ibid., 39.

20. The crucial term here is "giveaway," as the FCC was referring to programs which gave prizes to the listening audience more than studio-contained contests.

21. DeLong, *Quiz Craze,* 141–42.

22. Notably the term "game show" did not appear throughout my research. According to Olaf Hoerschelmann, "Quiz and Game Shows," in *Encyclopedia of Television,* ed. Horace Newcomb (Chicago: Fitzroy Dearborn, 1997), this term emerged as the dominant label for the post-scandal television genre, but had no role in the radio era genre.

23. See Hans Robert Jauss, *Toward an Aesthetic of Reception* (Minneapolis: University of Minnesota Press, 1982), for a consideration of dominants for literary genres; Steve Neale, "Questions of Genre," in *Film Genre Reader II,* ed. Barry Keith Grant (Austin: University of Texas Press, 1995), 159–83 offers a similar account for film genres.

24. Henry F. Pringle, "Wise Guys of the Air," *Saturday Evening Post,* 11 May 1946, 18–19+.

25. In Lazarsfeld, *Radio and the Printed Page,* 64–93; see also Douglas, *Listening In,* 144–48.

26. Dorothy T. Hayes, "Quiz Kids," *Parents' Magazine,* April 1941, 71.

27. NBC Collection, State Historical Society of Wisconsin (SHSW), Madison, Radio Scripts, Box 483, Folder 3, "*Quiz Kids,* 1/1/41."

28. Norman Cousins, "S.R.L. Award to *Information Please,*" *Saturday Review of Literature,* 6 April 1940, 12.

29. FCC Collection, National Archives, College Park, Maryland, Letter from Mrs. Ivan Bishop, Grand Rapids, Mich., 8/7/48, Docket #9113, Box 3877. Numerous other letters in this file offer similar testimonies.

30. "Bright Quiz," *Time,* 10 March 1941, 41.

31. Maurice Zolotow, "Quiz Queen," *Saturday Evening Post,* 27 July 1946, 89.

32. Edwin O'Connor, "It's Spontaneous!" *Atlantic Monthly,* January 1951, 88–90.

33. FCC Collection, Anonymous letter, 8/11/48, Docket #9113, Box 3877.

34. For examples of articles emphasizing the genre's authenticity, see Henry Morton Robinson, "Information Please," *Reader's Digest,* January 1939, 65–69; and Pringle, "Wise Guys of the Air."

35. Michel Foucault, *The History of Sexuality: An Introduction* (New York: Vintage Books, 1978).

36. NBC SHSW, Letter from Mrs. A. J. Smith, 8/19/40, Central Correspondence, Box 78, Folder 55, "Miles Laboratories, 1940."

37. See J. P. McEvoy, "The Quiz Kids," *Reader's Digest,* October 1940, 23–2; Hayes, "Quiz Kids;" John K. Hutchens, "Who Thought Up the Quiz Show?" *New York Times Magazine,* 23 August 1942, 31; and Jerome Beatty, "Baby Miracle," *American Magazine,* August 1943, 140.

38. Jerome Beatty, "Master Mind," *American Magazine,* February 1941, 56.

39. Pringle, "Wise Guys of the Air," 146.

40. Ira Peck, "Quiz Shows Are No Clue to the I.Q.," *New York Times Magazine*, 7 October 1951, 25.
41. Jerome Beatty, "Backstage at the Give-Aways," *American Magazine*, July 1949, 61. Scripts found in the NBC collection confirm this claim.
42. Altman, *Film/Genre*. Todd Gitlin, *Inside Prime Time* (New York: Pantheon Books, 1985), also discusses the role of "recombinant culture" in creating new programs and genres.
43. Beatrice Schapper, "Daffy Truth or Crazy Consequences," *Reader's Digest*, April 1943, 106.
44. John Lear, "Part-Time Lunatic," *Saturday Evening Post*, 4 August 1945, 14.
45. See "To the Top With Mistakes: *Truth or Consequences* Leads Quiz Shows as a Yearling," *Newsweek*, 24 March 1941, 62; and Hutchens, "Who Thought Up the Quiz Show?", 31.
46. Schapper, "Daffy Truth or Crazy Consequences," 108.
47. Eddy, "Daffy Dollars," 133.
48. "Shindig," *Time*, 27 November 1939, 39–40.
49. "Speaking of Pictures," *Life*, 17 January 1949, 14–16; Eddy, "Daffy Dollars," 134.
50. "Quizzing Bee," *Newsweek*, 15 March 1948, 62.
51. Jerome Beatty, "Have You a $100,000 Idea?" *American Magazine*, March 1947, 45.
52. "This Family Knows the Answers," *American Magazine*, September 1946, 146.
53. Edwin O'Connor, "Prove You're Human!" *Atlantic Monthly*, February 1947, 113.
54. Hutchens, "Who Thought Up the Quiz Show?", 31.
55. Beatty, "Have You a $100,000 Idea?" 93.
56. Peck, "Quiz Shows Are No Clue to the I.Q."
57. O'Connor, "Prove You're Human!", 113.
58. Albert Crews, *Radio Production Directing* (Boston: Houghton Mifflin, 1944), 258.
59. Hutchens, "Who Thought Up the Quiz Show?", 12.
60. Zolotow, "Quiz Queen," 18.
61. Quoted in ibid., 90.
62. *Champagne for Caesar* (United Artists, 1950), dir. Richard Whorf.
63. Peck, "Quiz Shows Are No Clue to the I.Q."
64. Quoted in "River of Gold," *Newsweek*, 2 August 1948, 51.
65. Peck, "Quiz Shows Are No Clue to the I.Q.," Crews, *Radio Production Directing*, 260.
66. Hayes, "Quiz Kids," 27.
67. Robinson, "Information Please," 68–69.
68. Crews, *Radio Production Directing*, 258.
69. "Shindig." The only example mentioned of a *Truth or Consequences* contestant who would not fulfill his stunt for a prize was a diehard Brooklyn Dodgers fan who refused to defame his team on the radio to win World Series tickets; he was given the tickets for his loyalty nevertheless.
70. NBC SHSW, *Pot o' Gold* Script, Central Correspondence, Box 78, Folder 28, "Lewis-Howe Co., 1940."
71. *Pot o' Gold* (United Artists, 1941), dir. George Marshall.
72. DeLong, *Quiz Craze*, 32–37.
73. See Kenneth Thompson, ed., *Media and Cultural Regulation* (London: Sage Publications, 1997), and Justin Lewis and Toby Miller, eds., *Critical Cultural Policy Studies: A Reader* (Malden, MA: Blackwell, 2003), for overviews of this field.
74. See Heather Hendershot, *Saturday Morning Censors: Television Regulation before the V-Chip* (Durham, NC: Duke University Press, 1998), and Laurie Ouellette, *Viewers Like You?: How Public TV Failed the People* (New York: Columbia University Press, 2002), for the former; see William Boddy, "Senator Dodd Goes to Hollywood: Investigating Video Violence," in *The Revolution Wasn't Televised*, ed. Lynn Spigel and Michael Curtin (New York: Routledge, 1997), 161–83 for the latter.
75. Mandated by Section 326 of the Communications Act of 1934; see Walter B. Emery, *Broadcasting and Government: Responsibilities and Regulations* (Lansing: Michigan State University Press, 1961), 212.
76. Originally the lottery mandate was part of Section 316 of the Communications Act. In 1948, this portion of the act was repealed, and a nearly identical ban of broadcast lotteries was incorporated into the U.S. Criminal Code. In 1954, the U.S. Supreme Court held that enforcing this code was a component of the FCC's jurisdiction. See ibid., 224–26.
77. Numerous memos to this effect can be found in FCC Collection, Box 151, Folder 21–3 (1935–46).
78. "Justice Dept. Clears *Pot o' Gold* Program," *Broadcasting*, 15 April 1940, 13.
79. "Stop the Money."

80. John McNulty, "The Jackpot," *New Yorker*, 19 February 1949, 36–57; *The Jackpot* (Twentieth Century Fox, 1950), dir. Walter Lang.

81. See Erik Barnouw, *A History of Broadcasting in the United States: The Golden Web* (New York: Oxford University Press, 1968), 227–36, for a discussion of the Blue Book and the regulatory climate of the late 1940s.

82. "Threat to Radio Gift Shows," *U.S. News & World Report*, 20 August 1948, 19.

83. Quoted in "No Chance," *Time*, 29 August 1949, 60.

84. "Giveaway Front," *Newsweek*, 5 September 1949, 44.

85. Quoted in Beatty, "Backstage at the Give-Aways," 61.

86. Memo from James Lawrence Fly, Chairman, to Harry Bannister, General Manager of WWJ Detroit, FCC Collection, 3/27/44, Box 151, Folder 21–3 (1935–46).

87. Quoted in "Goodbye, Easy Money," *Time*, 16 August 1948, 65.

88. "Time's Almost Up," *Newsweek*, 16 August 1948, 53.

89. Brief by Louis Cowan Productions, FCC Collection, Docket 9113, Box 3877.

90. Quoted in "No Chance."

91. Beatty, "Backstage at the Give-Aways," 61.

92. Jack Gould, "Jack Benny or Jackpot?" *New York Times Magazine*, 15 August 1948, 16, 39.

93. "Public Favors FCC Giveaway Proposal," *Broadcasting*, 23 August 1948. Letters held in FCC Collection, Docket 9113, Boxes 3877–3879. Of course archived audience letters should not be interpreted as a stand-in for general audience sentiments, as letter writers are a self-selected group marked by strong opinions and belief in prioritizing feedback to larger institutions. They do, however, offer a range of discourses that audiences used to discuss the genre in nonarchived sites and practices.

94. Card from Mrs. C. W. Creely, Bronx NY, 9/27/48, Docket 9113, Box 3877, FCC Collection.

95. Letter from Theodore Badgley, Montclair N.J., 11/15/48, Docket 9113, Box 3877, ibid.

96. See various letters in Docket #9113, Boxes 3877–3878, ibid.

97. Letter from Mrs. Ivan Bishop, Grand Rapids MI, 8/7/48, Docket #9113, Box 3877, ibid.

98. Letter from R. Stuart Hume, Middletown NY, 8/7/48, Docket #9113, Box 3877, ibid.

99. Letter from William Potter, Schenectady NY, 9/25/48, Docket #9113, Boxes 3877, ibid.; other letters in this box offer similar assertions.

100. Robert C. Allen, *Speaking of Soap Operas* (Chapel Hill: University of North Carolina Press, 1985), and Michele Hilmes, *Radio Voices: American Broadcasting, 1922–1952* (Minneapolis: University of Minnesota Press, 1997), discuss the cultural value of radio soap operas. Barnouw, *Golden Web*, 109–110 and 216–18, addresses the anti-recording stigma on early radio.

101. See Leonard H. Marks, "Legality of Radio Giveaway Programs," *Georgetown Law Journal* 37 (1949), for a detailed discussion of the legal definitions of lotteries and giveaways.

102. FCC Ruling, "Broadcast of Lottery Information," in Docket 9113, Box 3877, FCC Collection. The disputed license renewal of WARL, concerning their giveaway *Dollars for Answers*, set the precedent for this broad reading of consideration; see Docket #8559, Box 3423 — Northern Virginia Broadcasters, Inc., WARL, FCC Collection. See also Marks, "Legality of Radio Giveaway Programs," 328–33.

103. Quoted in *Federal Communications Commission v. American Broadcasting Company*, 347 U.S. 284; 74 S. Ct. 593; 1954 U.S. LEXIS 2674; 98 L. Ed. 699 (1954).

104. Marks, "Legality of Radio Giveaway Programs," 333–37.

105. Various briefs, Docket 9113, Boxes 3877–3879, FCC Collection.

106. *FCC v ABC*.

107. Ibid. §1304 refers to the United States Criminal Code containing the anti-lottery statute.

108. "Decline and Fall," *Newsweek*, 31 October 1949, 43.

Chapter 3

1. Thomas Schatz, *Hollywood Genres: Formulas, Filmmaking, and the Studio System* (Philadelphia: Temple University Press, 1981).

2. See Thomas Elsaesser, "Vincente Minnelli," in *Genre: The Musical*, ed. Rick Altman (London: Routledge & Kegan Paul, 1981), 8–27, and Charles Musser, "Divorce, DeMille and the Comedy of Remarriage," in *Classical Hollywood Comedy*, ed. Kristine Brunovska Karnick and Henry Jenkins (New York: Routledge, 1995), 282–313.

3. See Jane Feuer, *The Hollywood Musical*, 2nd ed. (Bloomington: Indiana University Press, 1993), and Kevin S. Sandler, ed., *Reading the Rabbit: Explorations in Warner Bros. Animation* (New Brunswick, N.J.: Rutgers University Press, 1998).

4. See Jim Leach, "North of Pittsburgh: Genre and National Cinema from a Canadian Perspective," in *Film Genre Reader II*, ed. Barry Keith Grant (Austin: University of Texas Press, 1995), 474–93.

5. The primary theoretical accounts of these diverse industrial practices are Steve Neale, "Questions of Genre," in *Film Genre Reader II*, ed. Barry Keith Grant (Austin: University of Texas Press, 1995), 159–83, and Rick Altman, *Film/Genre* (London: BFI Publishing, 1999). For a rare example of a genre analysis accounting for more than just production practices in considering the industry, see Eric Smoodin, *Animating Culture: Hollywood Cartoons from the Sound Era* (New Brunswick, N.J.: Rutgers University Press, 1993).

6. This is further complicated with programs coexisting in reruns and first-run — audiences are confronted with the "same" program from different historical moments, creating certain contradictions and ruptures that cannot be resolved by conceiving of a singular "moment of production."

7. See Todd Gitlin, *Inside Prime Time* (New York: Pantheon Books, 1985), 56–62, for a detailed discussion of both of these aspects of television industrial practice in the three-network era.

8. See Ann Gray, *Video Playtime: The Gendering of a Leisure Technology* (London: Routledge, 1992), for an account of these practices.

9. Susan Murray, "'I Think We Need a New Name for It': The Meeting of Documentary and Reality Television," in *Reality TV: Remaking of Television Culture*, ed. Susan Murray and Laurie Ouellette (New York: New York University Press, 2004).

10. I use the terms "cartoon" and "animation" somewhat interchangeably throughout this chapter. While not identical in connotation — cartoons have been tied more to children's audiences and short format, while animation is a more neutral formal delineator — I draw the use of these terms from the press discourses I use as my research material. Cartoon is certainly the more specific generic label for both Saturday morning and Cartoon Network, and thus I try to use it to stand in for the genre as a whole.

11. Leonard Maltin, *Of Mice and Magic: A History of American Animated Cartoons* (New York: Plume Books, 1987), 343.

12. For an overview textual chronicle of television animation, see the Introduction to Hal Erickson, *Television Cartoon Shows* (Jefferson, N.C.: McFarland & Co., 1995), 5–46. Jeremy G. Butler, *Television: Critical Methods and Applications* (Belmont, Calif.: Wadsworth Publishing, 1994), 261–86, addresses the formal evolution and construction of television animation. Heather Hendershot, *Saturday Morning Censors: Television Regulation before the V-Chip* (Durham, N.C.: Duke University Press, 1998), looks at how the categories of cartoons and children's television were impacted by production and regulatory practices in the 1970s. Carol Stabile and Mark Harrison, eds., *Prime Time Animation: Television Animation and American Culture* (London: Routledge, 2003), collects a number of essays primarily on contemporary television animation. Paul Wells, *Animation and America* (New Brunswick, N.J.: Rutgers University Press, 2002), offers a frustratingly incomplete account of the rise of television animation.

13. Gary Grossman, *Saturday Morning TV* (New York: Dell Publishing, 1981), 5–6.

14. See Tino Balio, ed., *Hollywood in the Age of Television* (Boston: Unwin Hyman, 1990), especially pages 4–9.

15. The direct results of the Paramount decision on exhibition and film bills has not been sufficiently researched. This account is drawn from Jeff Lemberg, *Encyclopedia of Animated Cartoons* (New York: Facts on File, 1991), 9; while not a scholarly source, the argument is consistent with most work on the film industry in the 1950s.

16. See Maltin, *Of Mice and Magic*, for accounts of these studios. Both MGM and Warner reopened animation units in the 1960s, primarily to supply television animation.

17. Christopher Anderson, *Hollywood TV: The Studio System in the Fifties* (Austin: University of Texas Press, 1994), 133–55.

18. Erickson, *Television Cartoon Shows*, 13–16.

19. Information about specific programs is primarily drawn from Erickson, *Television Cartoon Shows*; Lemberg, *Encyclopedia of Animated Cartoons*; Stuart Fischer, *Kids' TV: The First 25 Years* (New York: Facts on File, 1983); and Alex McNeil, *Total Television: A Comprehensive Guide to Programming from 1948 to the Present*, 3rd ed. (New York: Penguin Books, 1991).

20. The film industry reached an agreement with the Screen Actors Guild, Writers Guild of America, and Directors Guild of America to pay residuals for television sales for all films made post-1948, effectively privileging pre-1948 product because of larger profit margins for studios. See Balio, ed., *Hollywood*, 30–31.

21. The process of censoring cartoons is difficult to trace, as centralized standards and practices documentation does not exist, especially for syndication. Walter Lantz suggests that none of his cartoons with black characters made it to television in Danny Peary and Gerald Peary, eds., *The American Animated Cartoon: A Critical Anthology* (New York: E.P. Dutton, 1980), 196, and as quoted in Maltin, *Of Mice and Magic*, 182.

22. See Patrick Brion, *Tom and Jerry: The Definitive Guide to their Animated Adventures* (New York: Harmony Books, 1990), 29.

23. Lists of edited scenes and cartoons appear on Jon Cooke, *The Censored Cartoons Page* [Web site] (10 September 2001 [cited 7 August 2003]); available from http://looney.toonzone.net/ltcuts/.

24. J. Fred MacDonald, *Blacks and White TV: Afro-Americans in Television Since 1948* (Chicago: Nelson-Hall Publishers, 1983).

25. See Karl F. Cohen, *Forbidden Animation: Censored Cartoons and Blacklisted Animators in America* (Jefferson, N.C.: McFarland & Co., 1997), for the most extended, although frustratingly anecdotal and incomplete, account of cartoon censorship.

26. Michael Mallory, *Hanna-Barbera Cartoons* (New York: Hugh Lauter Levin Associates, 1998), 24; Anderson, *Hollywood TV*, 59.

27. Butler, *Television*, 272–73.

28. Erickson, *Television Cartoon Shows*, 10.

29. Ibid., 21.

30. Butler, *Television*, 277–81.

31. Quoted in Smoodin, *Animating Culture*, 12.

32. "*The Boing Boing Show,*" *Variety*, 19 December 1956; McCandlish Phillips, "Without Lisping Pigs," *New York Times*, 17 March 1957, II: 3.

33. Memo from Fred Wile Jr. to Mike Dunn, dated September 15, 1954. In NBC Collection, State Historical Society of Wisconsin (SHSW), Madison, Box 374, Folder 57, "Programming, Children's."

34. Promotional brochure, in ibid., Box 374, Folder 57, "Programming, Children's."

35. Cy Schneider, *Children's Television: The Art, the Business, and How It Works* (Chicago: NTC Business Books, 1987), offers an insider account of Mattel's advertising history.

36. Maltin, *Of Mice and Magic*, 147.

37. Erickson, *Television Cartoon Shows*, 19.

38. Ien Ang, *Desperately Seeking the Audience* (New York: Routledge, 1990).

39. Eliot Hyman, "Cartoons: Child's Best TV Friend," *Variety*, 30 July 1958, 43.

40. NBC SHSW, Box 369, Folder 6 — Charles Barry, *Howdy Doody*. In letter from Adrian Sarnish to Barry, August 6, 1953.

41. "Cartons of Cartoons for TV," *Variety*, 31 July 1957, 33+.

42. "*Woody Woodpecker,*" *Variety*, 9 October 1957.

43. "*Top Cat,*" *Variety*, 4 October 1961.

44. See Erickson, *Television Cartoon Shows*, 21.

45. "*King Leonardo and his Short Subjects,*" *Variety*, 2 November 1960; Sonny Fox, "TV Versus Children," *Television Quarterly* 1, no. 3 (1962), 40–44.

46. "The Blue-Blooded Hound Who's in the Black," *TV Guide*, 10 January 1959, 28–29; "Satire from the Animal Kingdom," *TV Guide*, 23 January 1960, 20–22.

47. Quoted in Peary and Peary, eds., *American Animated Cartoon*, 140–41.

48. Quoted in ibid., 165.

49. See Norman Klein, *Seven Minutes: The Life and Death of the American Animated Cartoon* (London: Verso, 1993), for an example of such a narrative.

50. Rebecca Farley, "From Fred and Wilma to Ren and Stimpy: What Makes a Cartoon 'Prime Time?'" in *Prime Time Animation*, 147–64, argues that this "double-coding" practice is a mistaken interpretation of animation's mass appeals, suggesting that the role of animated play and pleasure has been critically understated. Regardless of this interpretation, the producers and critics of this era did clearly view dual appeals in cartoons as the key to their success.

51. Quoted in Thomas J. Fleming, "TV's Most Unexpected Hit," *Saturday Evening Post*, 2 December 1961, 62–66.

52. "Review: *Huckleberry Hound*," *TV Guide*, 25 June 1960, 23.

53. Jane Kesner Ardmore, "TV Without Terror," *Parent's*, July 1962, 42–43+.

54. James Snead, *White Screens/Black Images: Hollywood from the Dark Side* (New York: Routledge, 1994), 84–85. See also Hendershot, *Saturday Morning Censors*, 216.

55. Lynn Spigel, "Seducing the Innocent: Childhood and Television in Postwar America," in *Ruthless Criticism: New Perspectives in U.S. Communication History*, ed. William S. Solomon and Robert W. McChesney (Minneapolis: University of Minnesota Press, 1993), 259–90.

56. "Cartoons Endure for UAA," *Broadcasting*, 10 August 1959, 74–75.

57. The airdates listed for this and other primetime cartoons refer to their primetime runs; as I discuss below, these shows were rescheduled and rerun on Saturday mornings, usually without generating new episodes.

58. See Anderson, *Hollywood TV*, for a detailed account of ABC's studio partnerships.

59. Schneider, *Children's Television*, 24 and 112.

60. "Animation Scores a Breakthrough," *Sponsor*, 27 June 1960, 43–45.

61. For negative reviews, see "*The Flintstones*," *Variety*, 5 October 1960; Gilbert Seides, "Review: *The Flintstones*," *TV Guide*, 18 March 1961, 15; and Jack Gould, "TV: Animated Cartoon," *New York Times*, 1 October 1960, 39. Most positive reviews came in subsequent years after the show's release — see "Stone Age Hero's Smash Hit," *Life*, 21 November 1960, 57–60; Fleming, 1961; "*The Flintstones*," *Variety*, 20 September 1961; "*The Flintstones*," *Variety*, 19 September 1962; and Brooks Atkinson, "Critic at Large," *New York Times*, 4 October 1963, 32.

62. See Chapter 6 on genre mixing and *The Simpsons* for more on this process.

63. See Michael Curtin, *Redeeming the Wasteland: Television Documentary and Cold War Politics* (New Brunswick, N.J.: Rutgers University Press, 1995), 248, for a discussion of the innovation–imitation–saturation cycle and documentaries. Jason Mittell, "Classic Network System," in *The Television History Book*, ed. Michele Hilmes (London: BFI Publishing, 2003), offers an overview of this industrial technique.

64. See J. Fred MacDonald, *Who Shot the Sheriff?: The Rise and Fall of the Television Western* (New York: Praeger Press, 1987), on westerns; Curtin, *Redeeming the Wasteland*, on documentaries; Michael Kackman, "Secret Agents, Civil Subjects: Espionage, Television, and Cold War Nationalism" (dissertation, University of Wisconsin, 2000), on spy programs; Lynn Spigel, *Welcome to the Dreamhouse: Popular Media and Postwar Suburbs* (Durham, N.C.: Duke University Press, 2001), on fantasy sitcoms.

65. Fleming, "TV's Most Unexpected Hit."

66. "*The Alvin Show*," *Variety*, 11 October 1961.

67. "*The Jetsons*," *Variety*, 26 September 1962.

68. Richard K. Doan, "Where Did All the People Go?" *TV Guide*, 11 February 1967, 10–13.

69. NBC SHSW, "Children's TV Viewing Patterns," April 19, 1962, in Box 184 (NBC Research Bulletins), Folder 23. While I am not able to judge the accuracy of the numbers represented in this graph, they certainly were considered "real" and accurate by networks making programming decisions. This numerical evidence is not proof of actual audience composition, but of the ways in which networks understood and constructed their audience, and therefore is useful information to reconstruct the reasons networks shifted cartoons to Saturday morning.

70. See Joseph Turow, *Breaking Up America: Advertisers and the New Media World* (Chicago: University of Chicago Press, 1997).

71. Joseph Turow, *Entertainment, Education, and the Hard Sell: Three Decades of Network Children's Television* (New York: Praeger Publishers, 1981), 72–73.

72. See Hendershot, *Saturday Morning Censors*, and Ellen Seiter, *Sold Separately: Children and Parents in Consumer Culture* (New Brunswick, N.J.: Rutgers University Press, 1993), for more on cartoon controversies.

73. Newton N. Minow, *Equal Time: The Private Broadcaster and The Public Interest* (New York: Atheneum, 1964), 52 and 54.

74. See Turow, *Entertainment, Education*, 50–52, and Mary Ann Watson, *The Expanding Vista: American Television in the Kennedy Years* (New York: Oxford University Press, 1990), Chapter 7, for more on this era in children's programming and government influence.

75. See Derek Kompare, "Rerun Nation: The Regime of Repetition on American Television" (dissertation, University of Wisconsin, 1999), 79–80, on color's effects on syndication. Maltin, *Of Mice and Magic*, 229, discusses how Warner Brothers "colorized" black and white Looney Tunes in the 1970s for the television market.

76. See Henry Jenkins, *The Children's Culture Reader* (New York: New York University Press, 1998), and David Buckingham, *After the Death of Childhood: Growing Up in the Age of Electronic Media* (Malden, MA: Polity Press, 2000), for exemplary work in this area.

77. Quoted in Jeffry Scott, "Turner tooning in Cartoon Network," *Atlanta Journal and Constitution*, 29 September 1992, D1.

78. NBC withdrew from Saturday morning cartoons in 1992, shifting to teen-centric sitcoms like *Saved by the Bell* and more recently, extending its daily *Today* show to weekends; see Jim McFarlin, "'Toons Are Still on the Saturday Schedule," *Detroit News*, 17 September 1992. CBS has incorporated more sports programming on its Saturday morning lineup.

79. Gerard Raiti, "The Disappearance of Saturday Morning" [Web journal] (*Animation World Magazine*, 30 April 2003 [cited 11 August 2003]); available from http://mag.awn.com/index.php3?ltype=pageone&article_no=1751, offers an analysis of these causes, focusing more on children's psychology and family dynamics than industrial transformations.

80. See Susan Napier, *Anime from Akira to Princess Mononoke* (New York: Palgrave, 2001), for the best scholarly account of anime, including a discussion of American fandom.

81. More fringe animation emerged on cable as well, including MTV's *Liquid Television* (1991–93) and *Aeon Flux* (1995–96), and Independent Film Channel's experimental animation programs.

82. See Maltin, *Of Mice and Magic*, and Klein, *Seven Minutes*, for examples of such "classic" discourses.

83. Timothy Burke and Kevin Burke, *Saturday Morning Fever: Growing Up with Cartoon Culture* (New York: St. Martin's Griffin, 1999), 1. See also 92–97 for a discussion of the cultural cachet of Saturday morning among Gen-Xers.

84. For another industrial account of Cartoon Network, see Kevin S. Sandler, "Synergy Nirvana: Brand Equity, Television Animation, and Cartoon Network," in *Prime Time Animation*, 89–109.

85. Balio, ed., *Hollywood*, 285–86.

86. This assumption was challenged throughout the run of *Ren & Stimpy*, as detailed in Mark Langer, "Animatophilia, Cultural Production and Corporate Interests: The Case of Ren & Stimpy," in *A Reader in Animation Studies*, ed. Jayne Pilling (Sydney: John Libbey, 1997), 143–62.

87. "Turner Broadcasting System Has the World 'Talkin' Toon,'" *PR Newswire*, 1 October 1992.

88. Linda Simensky, Senior Vice President of Original Animation, Cartoon Network, personal interview with author, August and September 1999.

89. Jeff Jensen, "Cartoon Net Is Off to Quick Start," *Advertising Age*, 12 October 1992, 27.

90. Chris Kaltenbach, "Old Enough to Sing the Praises of 'Toons," *Los Angeles Times*, 29 December 1994, F10; Simensky, personal interview.

91. Note that in 2000, Turner launched a Cartoon Network spinoff channel called Boomerang, featuring primarily Hanna-Barbera cartoons of the 1960s and 1970s that are less featured on Cartoon Network. Three years later, the channel is still quite marginal, lacking significant penetration on cable systems — as of June 2003, it reaches only 9 million households, compared to Cartoon Network's 82.6 million.

92. Simensky, personal interview.

93. Turow, *Breaking Up America*.

94. According to Simensky, personal interview, children reportedly appreciate these ironic promos as well.

95. See Turow, *Breaking Up America*, for a discussion of branding and contemporary television; Sandler, "Synergy Nirvana," discusses Cartoon Network's branding strategies.

96. Simensky, personal interview.

97. Steve Weinstein, "Hanging Out with Yogi and Huckleberry," *Los Angeles Times*, 1 August 1994, F1.

98. Simensky, personal interview; see also Sandler, "Synergy Nirvana".

99. See Sandler, ed., *Reading the Rabbit*, for examples of this dichotomy in action.

100. See Altman, *Film/Genre*, 23–24.

101. See http://home.nc.rr.com/tuco/looney/50greatest.html for a Web site discussing these specials and one fan's take on the canon.

102. Jerry Beck, *The Fifty Greatest Cartoons as Selected by 1,000 Animation Professionals* (Atlanta: Turner Publishing, 1994).

103. Note that in 1994, Turner did not own the post-1948 Warner library, including most of Jones' classic works.

104. Cartoon Network generally does not feature the type of experimental shorts seen on channels like Independent Film Channel, as Simensky suggests they simply do not fit the "psychographic" of the Cartoon Network audience. The furthest that Cartoon Network strays in the experimental direction is through their Sunday night program, *O Canada*, which features more nonmainstream National Film Board of Canada shorts, although Simensky notes that their choices of Canadian material are still the most "cartoony" of the bunch.

105. See Hendershot, *Saturday Morning Censors*, for an account of these controversies.

Chapter 4

1. Ien Ang, *Desperately Seeking the Audience* (New York: Routledge, 1990). See also James A. Anderson, "The Pragmatics of Audience in Research and Theory," in *The Audience and Its Landscape*, ed. James Hay, Lawrence Grossberg, and Ellen Wartella (Boulder, CO.: Westview Press, 1996), 75–93; and Joli Jensen and John J. Pauly, "Imagining the Audience: Losses and Gains in Cultural Studies," in *Cultural Studies in Question*, ed. Marjorie Ferguson and Peter Golding (London: Sage Publications, 1997), 155–69.

2. For typical accounts of this ideological position toward genre reception, see Thomas Schatz, *Hollywood Genres: Formulas, Filmmaking, and the Studio System* (Philadelphia: Temple University Press, 1981); Robin Wood, "Return of the Repressed," in *Planks of Reason: Essays on the Horror Film*, ed. Barry K. Grant (Metuchen, N.J.: Scarecrow Press, 1984), 164–200; and Laura Stempel Mumford, *Love and Ideology in the Afternoon: Soap Opera, Women, and Television Genre* (Bloomington: Indiana University Press, 1995).

3. See Torben Grodal, *Moving Pictures: A New Theory of Film Genres, Feelings, and Cognition* (Oxford: Oxford University Press, 1997), and Noël Carroll, "Film, Emotion, and Genre," in *Passionate Views: Film, Cognition, and Emotion*, ed. Carl Plantinga and Greg M. Smith (Baltimore: Johns Hopkins University Press, 1999), 21–47.

4. A common problem within examples of media scholarship is claiming to study audiences, when the analysis rarely treads beyond the realm of the text. For instance, in Rick Altman, *Film/Genre* (London: BFI Publishing, 1999), 144–65, Chapter 9 accounts for the role of genres in viewing processes through textual analysis, never looking at actual audiences. Likewise, John Thornton Caldwell, *Televisuality: Style, Crisis, and Authority in American Television* (New Brunswick, N.J.: Rutgers University Press, 1995), 249–83, claims to examine the televisual audience, but does so only through industrial and textual accounts.

5. Stuart Hall, "Encoding/Decoding," in *Culture, Media, Language*, ed. Stuart Hall (London: Hutchinson, 1980), 128–40.

6. Christine Gledhill, "Pleasurable Negotiations," in *Female Spectators: Looking at Film and Television*, ed. E. Deidre Pribram (New York: Verso, 1988), 64–89, p. 74.

7. Tony Bennett and Janet Woollacott, *Bond and Beyond: The Political Career of a Popular Hero* (New York: Methuen, 1987), 60–69. See also Tony Bennett, *Outside Literature* (New York: Routledge, 1990), 78–114, for more on reading formations and genre.

8. Bennett and Woollacott, *Bond & Beyond*, 81; see also Stephen Neale, *Genre* (London: BFI, 1980). This position is also similar to the reader-reception literary theory of Hans Robert Jauss, *Toward an Aesthetic of Reception* (Minneapolis: University of Minnesota Press, 1982), especially the notion of genres providing "horizons of expectations" for audiences.

9. See Chad Edward Dell, "Researching Historical Broadcast Audiences: Female Fandom of Professional Wrestling, 1945–1960" (dissertation, University of Wisconsin, 1997).

10. Stanley Fish, *Is There a Text in This Class? The Authority of Interpretive Communities* (Cambridge: Harvard University Press, 1980).

11. See Jacqueline Bobo, *Black Women as Cultural Readers* (New York: Columbia University Press, 1995), and John Tulloch and Henry Jenkins, *Science Fiction Audiences: Watching Doctor Who and Star Trek* (New York: Routledge, 1995), for examples of interpretive community studies.

12. Janice A. Radway, *Reading the Romance: Women, Patriarchy, and Popular Literature*, revised ed. (Chapel Hill: University of North Carolina Press, 1991).

13. For a similar analysis of struggles over television genre categories, see Henry Jenkins, *Textual Poachers: Television Fans and Participatory Culture* (New York: Routledge, 1992), 120–51, for a discussion of industry versus fan struggles of the genre(s) of *Beauty and the Beast*.

14. See Constance Penley, "Brownian Motion: Women, Tactics, and Technology," in *Technoculture*, ed. Constance Penley and Andrew Ross (Minneapolis: University of Minnesota Press, 1991), 135–61; Lisa A. Lewis, ed., *The Adoring Audience: Fan Culture and Popular Media* (New York: Routledge, 1992); and Jenkins, *Textual Poachers* for the crucial works in fan studies.

15. The term "ethnographic" is quite slippery, as argued in Andrea L. Press, "Toward a Qualitative Methodology of Audience Study: Using Ethnography to Study the Popular Culture Audience," in *The Audience and Its Landscape*, ed. James Hay, Lawrence Grossberg, and Ellen Wartella (Boulder, Colo.: Westview Press, 1996), 113–30, and David Gauntlett and Annette Hill, *TV Living: Television, Culture, and Everyday Life* (London: Routledge, 1999), 8. I will keep with the tendencies within cultural studies to use ethnography to mean any qualitative research in which scholars interact with their subjects to generate some sort of "data," whether through interviews or longer-term participant-observation as in anthropological traditions.

16. David Morley, *Television, Audiences and Cultural Studies* (New York: Routledge, 1992), provides an overview and discussion of this pioneering methodology; see Ellen Seiter et al., eds., *Remote Control: Television, Audiences, and Cultural Power* (New York: Routledge, 1989), and Sut Jhally and Justin Lewis, *Enlightened Racism: The Cosby Show, Audiences, and the Myth of the American Dream* (Boulder: Westview Press, 1992), for American iterations.

17. For an elaboration of this critique, see Ien Ang, *Living Room Wars: Rethinking Media Audiences for a Postmodern World* (New York: Routledge, 1996), 47.

18. See Jane Feuer, "Reading Dynasty: Television and Reception Theory," *South Atlantic Quarterly* 88, no. 2 (1989).

19. See Karen E. Riggs, *Mature Audiences: Television in the Lives of Elders* (New Brunswick, N.J.: Rutgers University Press, 1998), for the former; for examples of genre-delimited ethnographies, see Radway, *Reading the Romance*; Ellen Seiter et al., "Don't Treat Us Like We're So Stupid and Naïve: Toward an Ethnography of Soap Opera Viewers," in *Remote Control* 223–47; and Tulloch and Jenkins, *Science Fiction Audiences*.

20. The model developed by Hall and Morley emphasized nonnarrative public affairs programming, considering decoding more in terms of political beliefs than narrative interpretation. Cultural media scholars have adapted this model for fictional narrative programming, following John Fiske, *Television Culture* (New York: Routledge, 1987); the specific issues involved in switching the framework of interpretation and decoding for this model seem to have been underexamined.

21. Elana Levine, "Re-Viewing Ethnography: Media Audiences, Cultural Studies, and the Limitations of Knowledge" (paper presented at the National Communication Association, Chicago, Ill., 4 November 1999), makes this argument for more fully incorporating practices of everyday life and "context" into audience studies; see also Gauntlett and Hill, *TV Living*.

22. For examples of audience analysis focused on talk show texts, see Julie Engel Manga, *Talking Trash: The Cultural Politics of Daytime TV Talk Shows* (New York: New York University Press, 2003); Jane Shattuc, *The Talking Cure: TV Talk Shows and Women* (New York: Routledge, 1997); and Sonia M. Livingston and Peter Lunt, *Talk on Television: Audience Participation & Public Debate* (New York: Routledge, 1994).

23. See Robert C. Allen, *Speaking of Soap Operas* (Chapel Hill: University of North Carolina Press, 1985), and Robert C. Allen, "Bursting Bubbles: 'Soap Opera,' Audiences, and the Limits of Genre," in *Remote Control: Television, Audiences, and Cultural Power*, ed. Ellen Seiter, et al. (New York: Routledge, 1989), 44–55.

24. See Lawrence W. Levine, *Highbrow/Lowbrow* (Cambridge: Harvard University Press, 1988), and Peter Stallybrass and Allon White, *The Politics and Poetics of Transgression* (Ithaca: Cornell University Press, 1986).

25. Pierre Bourdieu, *Distinction: A Social Critique of the Judgement of Taste* (Cambridge: Harvard University Press, 1984). See Kim Christian Schrøder, "Cultural Quality: Search for a Phantom?" in *Media Cultures: Reappraising Transnational Media*, ed. Michael Skovmand and Kim Christian Schrøder (London: Routledge, 1992), 199–219 for the connection of Bourdieu to television audience analysis.

26. Radway, *Reading the Romance*, 53.

27. Bourdieu, *Distinction*, 88, 169–175.

28. See John Fiske, "Popular Discrimination," in *Modernity and Mass Culture*, ed. James Naremore and Patrick Brantlinger (Bloomington: Indiana University Press, 1991), 103–16.

29. See Jennifer Hyland Wang, "'Everything's Coming Up *Rosie*': Empower America, Rosie O'Donnell, and the Construction of Daytime Reality," *The Velvet Light Trap*, no. 45 (2000), and Shattuc, *Talking Cure*, for accounts of these cultural debates.

30. I have specifically excluded radio talk shows, such as *The Howard Stern Show* and *The Rush Limbaugh Show*, to ensure medium specificity in asking people to define the genre.

31. For the central literature on television talk shows (focusing on daytime talk), see Shattuc, *Talking Cure*; Livingston and Lunt, *Talk on Television*; Patricia Joyner Priest, *Public Intimacies: Talk Show Participants and Tell-All TV* (Cresskill, NJ: Hampton Press, 1995); Vicki Abt and Leonard Mustazza, *Coming After Oprah: Cultural Fallout in the Age of the TV Talk Show* (Bowling Green, OH: Bowling Green State University Popular Press, 1997); Joshua Gamson, *Freaks Talk Back: Tabloid Talk Shows & Sexual Nonconformity* (Chicago: University of Chicago Press, 1998); Andrew Tolson, *Television Talk Shows: Discourse, Performance, Spectacle* (Mahwah, N.J.: Erlbaum, 2001); Kevin Glynn, *Tabloid Culture: Trash Taste, Popular Power, and the Transformation of American Television* (Durham: Duke University Press, 2000); Laura Grindstaff, *The Money Shot: Trash, Class, and the Making of TV Talk Shows* (Chicago: University of Chicago Press, 2002); and Manga, *Talking Trash*. For a rare instance of a more inclusive approach to the genre's corpus, see Bernard Timberg, *Television Talk: A History of the TV Talk Show* (Austin, Tex.: University of Texas Press, 2002).

32. All of these programs, and dozens more, are categorized as "talk shows" by print sources like *TV Guide* and online resources like *Yahoo! TV* (http://tv.yahoo.com), sites of genre definition far more influential and widespread than scholarly analyses. At the time of this analysis (1999), *Live with Regis and Kathie Lee* had not been changed to *Live with Regis and Kelly*.

33. See Manga, *Talking Trash* for an example of this type of audience research.

34. Of course, access to the Internet is itself a significant limitation, excluding many people via class, education, and skill-related barriers; despite these limitations, my survey was accessible enough to reach a sufficiently broad segment of talk show audiences, with a broad range of age, geographical, and cultural differences. See Shattuc, *Talking Cure*, for an attempt to access a broad range of viewers in a hospital setting with admittedly mixed results.

35. Offering extra-credit points on their final exam, I e-mailed students in the large lecture course Survey of Radio-Television-Film as Mass Media in the Communication Arts Department at the University of Wisconsin–Madison in the Fall of 1999. I was not an instructor for this course during this semester — thanks to Ron Becker for allowing me to use his course for such research.

36. Of the 221 students in the course, 164 participated in the survey, with 85 female and 79 male respondents. Four identified as Asian or Asian-American, two as Mexican-American, one as African-American, three as mixed race, and the rest as White or Caucasian. Concerning sexual orientation, three self-identified as bisexual (two female, one male), two as gay males, and the rest as either heterosexual or straight.

37. alt.tv.talkshows.daytime and alt.tv.talkshows.late. Neither of these were particularly active newsgroups; thus participation from these links was low.

38. Amongst the 76 respondents gathered from e-mail and USENET, 48 were female, and ages ranged from 15 to 79, with most between 30 and 50. Two identified as Asian, one as Hispanic, one as African-American, with the rest providing variations on White, European, Jewish, and Caucasian. Occupations varied greatly, most commonly students of various levels, educators, "housewives," and various professional careers. Geographically, there was certainly a Midwestern emphasis, along with a strong Northeast presence, but surveys came from a broad variety of states, with entries from Canada and the United Kigdom. Concerning sexual orientation, four people self-identified as bisexual (three female, one male), four as gay (three male, one female), one as "undefined," and the rest were variations on straight or heterosexual, or left blank.

39. Other types of issues that could have elicited evaluative responses include "truthfulness," "public debate," "community," and "access to diverse voices"; for time considerations, I limited myself to just three broad topics.

40. Of the 240 responses I received, only 4 (1.67%) explicitly claimed that talk shows were "bad for society," while 23 others (9.58%) discussed harmful social effects for the genre. I believe these numbers would have been higher had I asked "Do you think talk shows are bad for society?" as many people noted that they felt the genre was not "good for society" without discussing any

harmful opinions. Nevertheless, explicitly negative condemnations were quite marginal among respondents. I offer these quantified results not to suggest any representative percentages, but to highlight how marginal this seemingly prevalent discourse was within my survey; to truly quantify these results, I would certainly need different methodological and theoretical models.

41. See Shattuc, *Talking Cure*; Gamson, *Freaks Talk Back*; Glynn, *Tabloid Culture*. Although I certainly did not ask participants explicitly "Do you think talk shows foster democracy and public participation?" the answers to the "good for society" question suggest that this is not how most viewers conceptualize the genre.

42. I am not suggesting that these audiences must be apolitical in their engagement with talk shows — this one survey question is insufficient to evaluate such an issue. Yet it definitely points out that, while most cultural studies analyses have examined the politics of media consumption, pleasures of "entertainment" are seemingly more central to audience practice, a facet that has been under-explored within much ethnographic work.

43. I purposely did not place these two programs next to another in my survey, as I wanted to vary between typical daytime issue-oriented shows and other types of talk shows. I am dealing with them together here because they are the most noted programs within the public discourses about daytime talk shows, and they provide good counterpoint to one another.

44. Manga, *Talking Trash*, 121–31, offers an example of one viewer who both enjoys and takes *Springer* seriously, although Manga notes this as an exception to the normal mode of viewing the show (and Springer's own claims).

Chapter 5

1. Stuart Hall, "Encoding/Decoding," in *Culture, Media, Language*, ed. Stuart Hall (London: Hutchinson, 1980), 128–40.

2. John Fiske, *Television Culture* (New York: Routledge, 1987).

3. See David Bordwell and Noël Carroll, eds., *Post-Theory: Reconstructing Film Studies* (Madison: University of Wisconsin Press, 1996), for something of a "manifesto" outlining this school of film studies.

4. One of the few close analyses of televisual form is John Thornton Caldwell, *Televisuality: Style, Crisis, and Authority in American Television* (New Brunswick, N.J.: Rutgers University Press, 1995), in which Caldwell clearly makes style an important site of analysis for political and cultural issues—although the promise of Caldwell's book exceeds its eventual results.

5. See David Bordwell, "Historical Poetics of Cinema," in *The Cinematic Text: Methods and Approaches*, ed. R. Barton Palmer (New York: AMS Press, 1989), 369–98, and Henry Jenkins, "Historical Poetics and the Popular Cinema," in *Approaches to the Popular Cinema*, ed. Joanne Hollows and Mark Jancovich (Manchester: Manchester University Press, 1995).

6. For a dismissive yet important critique of interpretative criticism, see David Bordwell, *Making Meaning: Inference & Rhetoric in the Interpretation of Cinema* (Cambridge: Harvard University Press, 1989).

7. Stanley Fish, Is *There a Text in This Class? The Authority of Interpretive Communities* (Cambridge: Harvard University Press, 1980); Tony Bennett and Janet Woollacott, *Bond and Beyond: The Political Career of a Popular Hero* (New York: Methuen, 1987).

8. Although *Dragnet's* stylistic innovations seem to be quite influential, they have been ignored by the few stylistic histories of TV. Most notably Caldwell, *Televisuality*, 45–52, offers a stylistic chronology of television's shift from live to telefilm in the 1950s without a single mention of *Dragnet*. Likewise, the most recent overview of the police genre, in Glen Creeber, *The Television Genre Book* (London: British Film Institute, 2001), has no mention of *Dragnet* at all.

9. The only contemporary examination of the show I was able to find is Eric Schaefer, "'This is the City': *Dragnet* and the Discourse of the Postwar Metropolis" (paper presented at the Society for Cinema Studies, Dallas, Tex., 10 March 1996). The rest of the scholarly material on *Dragnet* consists of a few minor theses: Richard Arlo Sanderson, "An Investigation into the Elements of Documentary Film and Their Use in the Production of the Television Film Series, *Dragnet*" (masters thesis, University of Southern California, 1958); Charles A. Varni, "Images of Police Work and Mass-Media Propaganda: The Case of *Dragnet*" (dissertation, Washington State University, 1974); and Karen Connolly-Lane, "More than 'Just the Facts': *Dragnet* as Reactionary Mythology" (masters thesis, San Diego State University, 1997).

Two popular biographies of Jack Webb deal with the show extensively, but in a less-than-scholarly fashion: Daniel Moyer and Eugene Alvarez, *Just the Facts, Ma'am: The Authorized Biography of Jack Webb* (Santa Ana, Calif.: Seven Locks Press, 2001), and Michael J. Hayde, *My Name's Friday: The Unauthorized but True Story of* Dragnet *and the Films of Jack Webb* (Nashville, Tenn.: Cumberland House, 2001).

10. Leslie Raddatz, "Jack Webb Revisited," *TV Guide*, 2 February 1963, 16.

11. Jack Webb, "The Facts About Me, Part II," *Saturday Evening Post*, 12 September 1959, 86.

12. My use of the term "ideology" in this chapter follow's Stuart Hall's notion of a dominant "ideological effect" produced discursively rather than a structural top-down imposition; see Stuart Hall, "On Postmodernism and Articulation (edited by Lawrence Grossberg)," in *Stuart Hall: Critical Dialogues in Cultural Studies*, ed. David Morley and Kuan-Hsing Chen (New York: Routledge, 1996), 131–50.

13. Rick Altman, *Film/Genre* (London: BFI Publishing, 1999).

14. J. Fred MacDonald, *Don't Touch That Dial!: Radio Programming in American Life from 1920 to 1960* (Chicago: Nelson-Hall, 1979), especially Chapter 3 — "Detective Programming and the Search for Law and Order," 155–94. I rely upon MacDonald's account of the radio genre somewhat reluctantly, as his historical account of radio has been questioned by more recent scholarship—see Michele Hilmes, *Radio Voices: American Broadcasting, 1922–1952* (Minneapolis: University of Minnesota Press, 1997), 111–13. Kathleen Battles, "Calling All Cars: Radio Crime Dramas and the Construction of Policing During the Depression Era" (dissertation, University of Iowa, 2002), develops a revisionist account of the early years of radio crime drama that should supplant MacDonald's account.

15. Battles, "Calling All Cars."

16. The film credits Wercker as sole director, but critical accounts point to Mann as an important collaborator given codirecting credit after the fact.

17. See Hayde, *My Name's Friday*, and Moyer and Alvarez, *Just the Facts, Ma'am*, for slightly differing accounts of these origins.

18. The best account of this cycle from an institutional perspective is William Lafferty, "A Reappraisal of the Semi-Documentary in Hollywood, 1945–1948," *The Velvet Light Trap* 20 (1983). See also Thomas Schatz, *Boom and Bust: The American Cinema in the 1940s* (New York: Scribner, 1997), 378–86, and Jack C. Ellis, *The Documentary Idea: A Critical History of English-Language Documentary Film and Video* (Englewood Cliffs, N.J.: Prentice Hall, 1989).

19. For treatments of semi-documentaries as part of *film noir*, see J. P. Telotte, *Voices in the Dark: The Narrative Patterns of Film Noir* (Urbana: University of Illinois Press, 1989); Ellis, *Documentary Idea*; Frank Krutnik, *In a Lonely Street: Film Noir, Genre, Masculinity* (New York: Routledge, 1991), 202–208; Paul Schrader, "Notes on Film Noir," in *Film Genre Reader II*, ed. Barry Keith Grant (Austin: University of Texas Press, 1995), 213–26; and especially Carl Richardson, *Autopsy: An Element of Realism in Film Noir* (Metuchen, NJ: Scarecrow Press, 1992).

20. James Naremore, *More Than Night: Film Noir in Its Contexts* (Berkeley: University of California Press, 1998), 11.

21. It is difficult without more detailed research to know whether the semi-documentary functioned as a coherent cultural category used by industrial personnel, critics, and audiences in the late 1940s; Lafferty, "Reappraisal of Semi-Documentary," suggests that it did not, although his evidence is unclear. It is certain, however, that both documentaries and crime films were operative generic terms that bore direct relevance both to *Dragnet* and its semi-documentary film influences.

22. This documentary and semi-documentary history is drawn from Ellis, *Documentary Idea*, especially 106–64. Lafferty, "Reappraisal of Semi-Documentary," suggests that we must attribute much of the rise in semi-documentary production to cost-cutting and economic efficiency of Hollywood in peril.

23. See Carlos Clarens, *Crime Movies: From Griffith to the Godfather and Beyond* (New York: W.W. Norton and Company, 1980), for a typical textual chronology of the genre.

24. Krutnik, *In a Lonely Street*, 24–44.

25. See George N. Dove, *The Police Procedural* (Bowling Green, Ohio: Bowling Green University Popular Press, 1982), and Christopher P. Wilson, *Cop Knowledge: Police Power and Cultural Narrative in Twentieth-Century America* (Chicago: University of Chicago Press, 2000).

26. Other important films in the semi-documentary cycle include *13 Rue Madeline* (1946), *Boomerang* (1947), *Kiss of Death* (1947), *T-Men* (1947), and *Call Northside 777* (1948).

27. Richardson, *Autopsy*, suggests that the film was actually based on a true story, but that the filmmakers shied away from publicizing this element for fears of lawsuits.

28. For a detailed production history and analysis of *Naked City*, see ibid., 76–116.

29. Schatz, *Boom and Bust*, 392, contends that *Naked City* is markedly conservative in its politics, avoiding "social problem" explorations. I agree more with Richardson's reading of the film's more contradictory and ambivalent politics.

30. These ellipses are in the original title card.

31. Krutnik, *In a Lonely Street*, 206–207.

32. For a still-relevant discussion of realism and its ideological ramifications, see Fiske, *Television Culture*, 21–47.

33. This account of the LAPD's involvement in *Dragnet* comes from Sanderson, "Investigation into Documentary Film," and Joe Domanick, *To Protect and To Serve: The LAPD's Century of War in the City of Dreams* (New York: Pocket Books, 1994), 117–34.

34. Ellis, *Documentary Idea*, discusses these governmental efforts in filmmaking. Battles, "Calling All Cars", notes that official involvement in radio production dates back to 1930s crime dramas, which drew upon a general documentary impulse of the era.

35. The ties between official authoritative endorsement and fictional programming would continue in television, with spy programs like *I Led 3 Lives*, as explored by Michael Kackman, "Citizen, Communist, Counterspy: *I Led 3 Lives* and Television's Masculine Agent of History," *Cinema Journal* 38, no. 1 (1998); NASA's endorsement of the short-lived space program *Men Into Space* (1959–60); and the American Medical Association's involvement in medical dramas of the 1960s, as discussed in Joseph Turow, "James Dean in a Surgical Gown: Making TV's Medical Formula," in *The Revolution Wasn't Televised*, ed. Lynn Spigel and Michael Curtin (New York: Routledge, 1997), 185–99.

36. Compare *Dragnet*'s generalized truth claims with *I Led 3 Lives*' historically grounded discourse; see Kackman, "Citizen, Communist, Counterspy."

37. See Alan Rosenthal, ed., *Why Docudrama? Fact-Fiction on Film and TV* (Carbondale: Southern Illinois University Press, 1999).

38. See Jerry Buck, "Just the Facts: The Secret of *Dragnet*'s–and Webb's–Success," *Emmy Magazine*, January/February 1987, 38–47+, and Hayde, *My Name's Friday*, 61–62; Webb actually was an early investor in TelePrompTer technology, advocating the use of the technology across genres.

39. "The Big Cast," originally aired February 14, 1952. As a historiographic note, it has been quite difficult to view many episodes of *Dragnet* from the 1950s. While the 1960s version has been recently syndicated on Nick at Nite and TV Land, the black-and-white episodes have been off-the-air for many years. As they are mostly in the public domain, a number of low-budget video companies have released videos of selected episodes; through collector sources, I have obtained copies of approximately 20 episodes on tape. Additionally, other episodes are available in archival collections and museums. Nevertheless, I have only seen about 25 of the 276 episodes produced in the 1950s. As I have argued in Jason Mittell, "Invisible Footage: Television Historiography and the Case of *Industry on Parade*," *Film History* 9, no. 2 (1997), 200–18, issues of access and visibility are directly constitutive of the histories that may be written; the lack of availability of 1950s *Dragnet* episodes is certainly a large component in the program's conspicuous absence from media history.

40. Radio script from episode "The Big Token." Jack Webb Collection, University of California Special Collections, Los Angeles. My research suggests that *Dragnet*'s producers did not have direct access to "official police files"—I presume this authenticating claim on radio referred to the practice of the LAPD providing descriptions of cases for writers and answering production questions.

41. See Allison McCracken, "Scary Women and Scarred Men: Radio Suspense Drama, Gender Trouble, and Postwar Change (1943–1948)," in *Radio Reader: Essays in the Cultural History of Radio*, ed. Michele Hilmes and Jason Lovignio (New York: Routledge, 2002), 183–207.

42. Webb also had a small part in *Sunset Boulevard*, which employed innovative first-person narration from beyond the grave.

43. All 1950s episodes of *Dragnet* follow the "Big" pattern except the pilot, "The Human Bomb." This quirky phrasing even found its way into *Dragnet* scripts, as often shots are referred to as "BIG CLOSEUP"—see Webb UCLA Collection.

44. See Karen Hollinger, "*Film Noir*, Voice-Over, and the Femme Fatale," in *Film Noir Reader*, ed. Alain Silver and James Ursini (New York: Limelight Editions, 1996), 243–59.

45. *Dragnet*'s press coverage highlighted Webb's multiple jobs in producing the program, suggesting that many audience members saw him as the show's creator as well as star.

46. Jack Webb, "The Facts About Me, Part III," *Saturday Evening Post*, 19 September 1959, 144.

47. See Battles, "Calling All Cars."

48. Altman, *Film/Genre*, argues that most genres are predicated on representing countercultural behaviors and pleasures, with the narrative thrust working to restore equilibrium.

49. John Fiske, *Power Plays Power Works* (New York: Verso, 1993), 124–37, argues that representations of violence allow disenfranchised viewers to resist hegemonic messages within popular entertainment, a pleasure that is all but absent from *Dragnet*.

50. See Erik Barnouw, *A History of Broadcasting in the United States: The Image Empire* (New York: Oxford University Press, 1970), 22–24, on *Man Against Crime*, and Michael Kackman, "Secret Agents, Civil Subjects: Espionage, Television, and Cold War Nationalism" (dissertation, University of Wisconsin, 2000), 33–38, on *Treasury Men in Action*.

51. Quoted in Patrick Lucanio and Gary Coville, "Behind Badge 714: The Story of Jack Webb and *Dragnet*, Part II," *Filmfax*, October/November 1993, 41.

52. This final phrase met with protest from the LAPD, who objected to the term "cop." After the first few seasons of *Dragnet*, the LAPD convinced Webb to change the phrase to "I work here—I carry a badge." See Domanick, *To Protect and To Serve*, 125–29.

53. See Gary Coville and Patrick Lucanio, "Behind Badge 714: The Story of Jack Webb and *Dragnet*, Part I," *Filmfax*, August/September 1993, 53, for a discussion of Webb's line editing.

54. Richard G. Hubler, "Jack Webb: The Man Who Makes *Dragnet*," *Coronet* (September 1953), 29.

55. Hayde, *My Name's Friday*, 43. The pilot, "The Human Bomb," (airdate 12/16/51), is less distinctive in its visual style than later episodes, as clearly Webb was still a novice director and had yet to devise his distinctive look.

56. As more evidence of the show's distinctiveness, *Dragnet* was one of the most parodied programs in 1950s television, with Milton Berle, Stan Freberg, *Mad Magazine*, and Johnny Carson all producing notable parodies of the program's style and tone.

57. William Boddy, *Fifties Television* (Urbana: University of Illinois Press, 1990).

58. See Will Wright, *Sixguns and Society: A Structural Study of the Western* (Berkeley: University of California Press, 1975), and Thomas Schatz, *Hollywood Genres: Formulas, Filmmaking, and the Studio System* (Philadelphia: Temple University Press, 1981), for the most fully realized structuralist analyses of film genres. Geoffrey Hurd, "The Television Presentation of the Police," in *Popular Television and Film*, ed. Tony Bennett, et al. (London: BFI Publishing, 1981), 53–70, and Dennis Giles, "A Structural Analysis of the Police Story," in *American Television Genres*, ed. Stuart M. Kaminsky and Jeffrey H. Mahan (Chicago: Nelson-Hall, 1985), 67–84 present structuralist analyses of the television police genre.

59. John Fiske, *Introduction to Communication Studies*, 2nd ed. (New York: Routledge, 1990), 118.

60. See John G. Cawelti, *Adventure, Mystery, and Romance: Formulas as Art & Popular Culture* (Chicago: University of Chicago Press, 1976).

61. See Krutnik, *In a Lonely Street*, 191–93.

62. See Daniel Marcus, *Happy Days and Wonder Years: The Fifties and the Sixties in Contemporary Cultural Politics* (New Brunswick: Rutgers University Press, 2004), for an analysis of this trope of cultural memory.

63. See Wilson, *Cop Knowledge*, and Domanick, *To Protect and To Serve*.

64. Quoted in Richard Warren Lewis, "Happiness is a Return to the Good Old Days," *TV Guide*, 19 October 1968, 39.

65. Ibid., 42.

66. Varni, "Images of Police Work," offers a content analysis to show that the 1960s *Dragnet* featured narcotics crimes more than any other criminal topic.

67. For a brief account of this episode in relation to representations of youth culture on 1960s television, see Aniko Bodroghkozy, *Groove Tube: Sixies Television and the Youth Rebellion* (Durham, N.C.: Duke University Press, 2000), 76–80.

68. See ibid. for a strong account of *Mod Squad*.

69. Rick Porter, *L.A. Dragnet Widens for Second Season* [Web site] (Zap2it.com, 15 July 2003 [cited 16 July 2003]); available from http://tv.zap2it.com/tveditorial/tve_main/1,1002,271%7C82314%7C1%7C,00.html.

Chapter 6

1. See Steve Neale and Frank Krutnik, *Popular Film and Television Comedy* (New York: Routledge, 1990), 18; Alastair Fowler, *Kinds of Literature: An Introduction to the Theory of Genres and Modes* (Cambridge: Harvard University Press, 1982), 183–88; and Matt Hills, "Reading Formation Theory and the Rising Stakes of Generic Hybridity," in *Red Noise: Buffy the Vampire Slayer and Critical Television Studies*, ed. Lisa Parks and Elana Levine (Durham, N.C.: Duke University Press, forthcoming), for a representative range of examples from many using hybridity as a term for genre mixing.

2. See Ralph Cohen, "Do Postmodern Genres Exist?" in *Postmodern Genres*, ed. Marjorie Perloff (Norman: University of Oklahoma Press, 1988), 11–27; Linda Hutcheon, *A Poetics of Postmodernism* (New York: Routledge, 1988); Jim Collins, "Genericity in the Nineties: Eclectic Irony and the New Sincerity," in *Film Theory Goes to the Movies*, ed. Jim Collins, Hilary Radner, and Ava Preacher Collins (New York: Routledge, 1993), 242–63; and Ihab Hassan, *The Postmodern Turn* (Columbus: Ohio State University Press, 1987).

3. See Fredric Jameson, *Postmodernism or, the Cultural Logic of Late Capitalism* (Durham, N.C.: Duke University Press, 1991).

4. Rick Altman, *Film/Genre* (London: BFI Publishing, 1999).

5. In this project alone, I have pointed to early generic mixtures like *You Bet Your Life* as a comedy/quiz, *The Flintstones* as a cartoon/sitcom, and *Dragnet* as a cop show/documentary. See John Thornton Caldwell, *Televisuality: Style, Crisis, and Authority in American Television* (New Brunswick, N.J.: Rutgers University Press, 1995), 22–24, for another discussion on this topic.

6. Toby Miller, *The Avengers* (London: BFI Publishing, 1997), 96, makes a similar argument in discussing the genre mixing of *The Avengers*: "Such texts do not imply that genres no longer exist; on the contrary, they demonstrate the centrality of genre as a sounding-board and point of resistance against which originality can be measured."

7. Henry Jenkins, *Textual Poachers: Television Fans and Participatory Culture* (New York: Routledge, 1992), 120–51.

8. See Hills, "Reading Formation Theory."

9. See David Bordwell, *Making Meaning: Inference & Rhetoric in the Interpretation of Cinema* (Cambridge: Harvard University Press, 1989), and David Morley, *Television, Audiences and Cultural Studies* (New York: Routledge, 1992), for similar critiques from quite different approaches.

10. See Leah R. Ekdom Vande Berg, "Dramedy: *Moonlighting* as an Emergent Generic Hybrid," *Communication Studies* 40, no. 1 (1989), for a similar approach to an earlier example.

11. Quoted in Mike Dennis, *Interview with Aaron Sorkin* [Web site] (Zap2it.com, 1999 [cited 9 November 1999]); available from tv.zap2it.com/shows/features/tvbiz/p/a/99/05/17sorkin.html.

12. See http://us.imdb.com/CommentsShow?0165961.

13. For accounts of parody within film studies, see Dan Harries, *Film Parody* (London: BFI Publishing, 2000), and Wes D. Gehring, *Parody as Film Genre* (Westport, CT: Greenwood Press, 1999). Television parody has been all but ignored; see Michael Kackman, "Secret Agents, Civil Subjects: Espionage, Television, and Cold War Nationalism" (dissertation, University of Wisconsin, 2000), for a specific account of television spy parodies like *Get Smart*.

14. See John G. Cawelti, "*Chinatown* and Generic Transformation in Recent American Films," in *Film Genre Reader II*, ed. Barry Keith Grant (Austin: University of Texas Press, 1995), 227–45, and Thomas Schatz, *Hollywood Genres: Formulas, Filmmaking, and the Studio System* (Philadelphia: Temple University Press, 1981), for influential examples.

15. Neale and Krutnik, *Popular Comedy*, 18–19.

16. Harries, *Film Parody*, and Dan Harries, "Film Parody and the Resuscitation of Genre," in *Genre and Contemporary Hollywood*, ed. Steve Neale (London: BFI Publishing, 2002), 281–93, develops this point more fully.

17. Heather Dubrow, *Genre* (New York: Methuen, 1982), 24–25, argues, "the decision to parody a genre at the very least indicates some involvement with its values, not a 'radical' dismissal of the particular genre," a position echoed by Harries, *Film Parody*, and Harries, "Resuscitation of Genre."

18. See Schatz, *Hollywood Genres*, 36–41. Harries, *Film Parody*, employs and explores Schatz's arguments without clearly weighing in on whether this general tendency is an accurate account of a genre's life cycle.

19. Cawelti, "*Chinatown*," details some of the ways in which genres transform besides parody (which he terms "burlesque").

20. Much work on parody, especially under the rubric of postmodernism, suggests that parody need not be humorous – see Hutcheon, *A Poetics of Postmodernism*, 26. While much contemporary parody might be the more ironic "signaling of difference" that Hutcheon calls for, genre parody on television uses humor as its central ingredient. The self-conscious dismantling of generic conventions, typical of postmodern aesthetics, is rarely operative on television; when it is, such as on *Twin Peaks*, parody is not the most useful framework to understand its practices.

21. Susan Harris and Paul Junger Witt, Personal Interview with Author, 11 November 1999.

22. This history of ABC and 1970s sexual television is drawn from Elana Levine, "Wallowing in Sex: American Television and Everyday Life in the 1970s" (dissertation, University of Wisconsin, 2002).

23. Harry F. Waters, "99 and 44/100% Impure," *Newsweek*, 13 June 1977, 92.

24. In Harris and Witt, personal interview, Harris noted, "The man was entitled to his opinion. . . if he *had seen* the show!. . .He hadn't seen the show, and he talked about things that simply didn't exist." Press accounts claim that Waters had seen the program in an early-June press screening.

25. For an overview of the protests, see Geoffrey Cowan, *See No Evil: The Backstage Battle over Sex and Violence on Television* (New York: Simon & Schuster, 1979); Arthur Lubow, "Soap Hits the Fan," *New Times*, 2 September 1977, 29–40; and Dwight Whitney, "What Uproar Over *Soap?*" *TV Guide*, 26 November 1977, 4–10.

26. Quoted in Kathryn C. Montgomery, *Target: Prime Time: Advocacy Groups and the Struggle over Entertainment Television* (New York: Oxford University Press, 1989), 98.

27. "*Soap* Creators Counter-Attack: 'Why No Support From Others?'" *Variety*, 12 October 1977, 52.

28. Montgomery, *Target*, 96.

29. Harris and Witt, personal interview.

30. See Carol T. Williams, *"It's Time for My Story": Soap Opera Sources, Structure and Response* (Westport, Conn.: Praeger Press, 1992), 29–32; Levine, "Wallowing in Sex."

31. NBC featured far fewer sitcoms in this era, and most were unsuccessful, with the exception of *Sanford and Son*, produced by CBS auteur Norman Lear. As with any broad generalization like this, there are numerous exceptions that belie this generalized claim. See Todd Gitlin, *Inside Prime Time* (New York: Pantheon Books, 1985), and Levine, "Wallowing in Sex" for discussions of the cultural politics of 1970s sitcoms.

32. See Levine, "Wallowing in Sex" and Diane Alters, ""We hardly watch that rude, crude show": Class and Taste in *The Simpsons*," in *Prime Time Animation: Television Animation and American Culture*, ed. Carol Stabile and Mark Harrison (New York: Routledge, 2003), 165–84.

33. Waters, "99 and 44/100% Impure;" Frank Rich, "Viewpoint: *Soap*," *Time*, 12 September 1977, 72–74.

34. See Lubow, "Soap Hits the Fan," 30.

35. Frank Beermann, "U.S. Catholic Hierarchy Hammers *Soap*," *Variety*, 17 August 1977, 33.

36. "Group W in Lather Over *Soap* as 'Sex Opera' Critics Snipe," *Variety*, 13 July 1977, 34.

37. "Memo to Networks: 'Clean Up TV!'" *Christianity Today*, 30 December 1977, 42.

38. "The Man with the Golden Gut," *Time*, 5 September 1977, 46–50; "Group W in Lather."

39. "ABC Fights For Its *Soap* Under Shower of Criticism," *Variety*, 20 July 1977.

40. Harris and Witt, personal interview.

41. Lubow, "Soap Hits the Fan," 30. See also Rich, "Viewpoint: *Soap*;" Whitney, "What Uproar."

42. Joan Vail Thorne, "The Tubular Family," *New Catholic World* 221, no. 1322 (1978), 60.

43. Lubow, "Soap Hits the Fan," 30.

44. Quoted in ibid., 37.

45. Quoted in "ABC Fights."

46. Witt suggested to me that Silverman's assurances about *Soap*'s morality were not imposed by the network but rather stemmed from concerns that a "deeply religious" cast member had expressed about the program. The producers had told the cast and network that characters "who commit acts, who harm others or are morally reprehensible would suffer for it." Harris and Witt, personal interview.

47. Quoted in "Dope on *Soap*: Pull Some Ads, 15 Affils Scram," *Variety*, 31 August 1977, 57.

48. Josephine Jacobsen, "Soap Bubbles," *Commonweal*, 25 November 1977, 739.

49. "Memo to Networks."
50. Quoted in Lubow, "Soap Hits the Fan," 38.
51. Montgomery, *Target*, 98.
52. Harris and Witt, personal interview.
53. Quoted in "Golden Gut."
54. Columbia Pictures Television advertisement, *Television/Radio Age*, 26 September 1977, 9.
55. Harris and Witt, personal interview; Harris makes similar comments in Wayne Walley, "Golden Girl of Sitcoms: Susan Harris Helps TV Catch Up to Real Life," *Advertising Age*, 30 January 1986, 4.
56. Harris and Witt, personal interview; Robert Sklar, "Jay Sandrich: The Best There Is," *American Film*, May 1978, 19.
57. Sitcoms in the 1970s had started employing videotape over telefilm, especially through Lear's Tandem programs, although many production houses including MTM continued to use telefilm, leading to the dual production mode employed for the genre to this day.
58. Harris and Witt, personal interview.
59. *Soap* was cancelled in 1981 after four seasons; the final episode aired on 20 April 1981, with no narrative resolutions, leaving at least five characters in jeopardy via life-or-death cliffhangers.
60. Robert C. Allen, *Speaking of Soap Operas* (Chapel Hill: University of North Carolina Press, 1985).
61. I have informally interviewed many fans of *Soap* from the show's original run, and nearly all celebrate the show's rich characters, relationships, and sincere pathos — often more than its sexual comedy and outrageous parodic characters and plot developments.
62. Linda Williams, "Melodrama Revised," in *Refiguring American Film Genres*, ed. Nick Browne (Berkeley: University of California Press, 1998), 42–88. Like Williams, I reject the notion of melodrama as "excess," as based on a narrow sample of particular melodramatic films.
63. See Laura Stempel Mumford, *Love and Ideology in the Afternoon: Soap Opera, Women, and Television Genre* (Bloomington: Indiana University Press, 1995); Christine Geraghty, *Women and Soap Opera: A Study of Prime Time Soaps* (Cambridge, U.K.: Polity Press, 1991); and Jane Feuer, *Seeing Through the Eighties: Television and Reaganism* (Durham, N.C.: Duke University Press, 1995).
64. Mumford, *Love and Ideology*, 32, makes this argument.
65. See Williams, *It's Time for My Story*, and Montgomery, *Target*, for discussions on these two differently genred abortions.
66. See Feuer, *Seeing Through the Eighties*.
67. Josh Ozersky, "TV's Anti-Families: Married. . . with Malaise," *Tikkun* 6, no. 1 (1991), 11.
68. Quoted in Sharon Shahid, "Hey, dude, what do you think about *Simpsons?*" *USA Today*, 14 June 1990, 11A.
69. John Alberti, *Leaving Springfield: The Simpsons and the Possibilities of Oppositional Culture* (Detroit: Wayne State University Press, 2003); William Irwin, Mark T. Conard, and Aeon J. Skoble, *The Simpsons and Philosophy: the D'oh! of Homer* (Chicago, Ill.: Open Court, 2001); Matthew Henry, "The Triumph of Popular Culture: Situation Comedy, Postmodernism and *The Simpsons*," *Studies in Popular Culture* 17 (1994), 85–99; Kevin Glynn, "Bartmania: The Social Reception of an Unruly Image," *Camera Obscura* 38 (1996), 60–91; Alters, "Class & Taste."
70. Jim Collins, "Postmodernism and Television," in *Channels of Discourse, Reassembled*, ed. Robert C. Allen (Chapel Hill: University of North Carolina Press, 1992), 327–53, 335–336.
71. Henry, "Triumph of Popular Culture," 95.
72. Caldwell, *Televisuality*, 23.
73. Donald Crafton, *Before Mickey: The Animated Film, 1898–1928*, revised ed. (Chicago: University of Chicago Press, 1993), 11.
74. See Paul Wells, *Understanding Animation* (London: Routledge, 1998).
75. Note that parody is another hallmark of animated cartoons. For further discussion on parody in animation, see Donald Crafton, "The View from Termite Terrace: Caricature and Parody in Warner Bros. Animation," *Film History* 5, no. 2 (1993), 204–30.
76. Jameson, *Postmodernism*, 16–19; Hutcheon, *A Poetics of Postmodernism*.
77. Collins, "Postmodernism and Television," implicitly suggests this in his discussion of *Twin Peaks*; see Cohen, "Do Postmodern Genres Exist?" for a compelling discussion and refutation of this argument.

78. Cawelti, "*Chinatown*," 244. Schatz, *Hollywood Genres*, offers a similar account of the role of parody as the nadir of genre; see Tag Gallagher, "Shoot-Out at the Genre Corral: Problems in the "Evolution" of the Western," in *Film Genre Reader II*, ed. Barry Keith Grant (Austin: University of Texas Press, 1995), 246–60 for a strong and convincing rebuke to this position.

79. Henry, "Triumph of Popular Culture," 93; the family sitcom continues to thrive today, with traditional examples like *Everybody Loves Raymond* (1996–) and *The King of Queens* (1998–) peacefully coexisting alongside more revisionist shows like *Malcolm in the Middle* (2000–) and *The Bernie Mac Show* (2001–).

80. Quoted in Scott Williams, "Move Over, Flintstones, *The Simpsons* Have Arrived," *Associated Press*, 7 February 1990.

81. Tom Shales, "The Primest Time: Sunday Night Television, from *The Ed Sullivan Show* to *The Simpsons*," *Washington Post*, 11 March 1990, G1. Shales' quote refers to *Ozzie & Harriet* Nelson, *Father Knows Best*'s Anderson family, and *The Brady Bunch* as *The Simpsons*' sitcom fore-families from the 1950s and 1960s.

82. "Simpsons Forever!" *Time*, 2 May 1994, 77.

83. Joe Morgenstern, "Bart Simpson's Real Father," *Los Angeles Times*, 29 April 1990, 12.

84. Randy Lewis, "Let's Give the Kids a Break on the Bart Simpson T-Shirts, OK?" *Los Angeles Times*, 13 May 1990, 55D. The Huxtables inhabited *The Cosby Show* and the Keatons were on *Family Ties*, two highly successful 1980s family sitcoms.

85. Quoted in Ozersky, "TV's Anti-Families," 11; M.S. Mason, "*Simpsons* Creator on Poking Fun," *Christian Science Monitor*, 17 April 1998, B7.

86. Quoted in John J. O'Connor, "Prime-Time Cartoon of Unbeautiful People," *New York Times*, 21 February 1990, C18, and Kenneth R. Clark, "*The Simpsons* Proves Cartoons Not Just for Kids," *Chicago Tribune TV Week*, 14 January 1990, 3.

87. Ozersky, "TV's Anti-Families," 11. See also Dave Berkman, "Sitcom Reality," *Television Quarterly* 1993, 63–69.

88. W. Pierce, "Letter: Leave It to Bart," *TV Guide*, 14 April 1990, 41.

89. Richard Zoglin, "The Fox Trots Faster," *Time*, 27 August 1990, 64–67; Hugh David, "Cartoon Kickback on the Sidewalk," *The Independent*, 29 July 1990, 17; "From Toddlers to Teens. . .," *TV Guide*, 2 March 1991, 6–15; Ed Siegel, "Hey, Dudes! They're Back!" *Boston Globe*, 11 October 1990, 57.

90. Morgenstern, "Real Father."

91. Tom Shales, "*The Simpsons*: They're Scrapping Again — But This Time It's a Ratings Fight," *Washington Post*, 11 October 1990, C1.

92. Quoted in John Anderson, "Cool Cartoon Causes Kooky Craze," *Newsday*, 5 March 1990, II: 4.

93. Harry F. Waters, "Family Feuds," *Newsweek*, 23 April 1990, 58–63.

94. Quoted in Sharon Shahid, "*The Simpsons*: Kids Like to be Gross, Shock Their Parents," *USA Today*, 14 June 1990, 11A.

95. John Horn, "*The Simpsons*, From the Maker of *Life In Hell*, Offers a Twist on Cartoons," *Associated Press*, 10 January 1990.

96. Quoted in Dan Schefelman, "Mutants Make His Nuclear Family Funny," *Newsday*, 1 February 1990, 69.

97. Anderson, "Cool Cartoon."

98. Michael Reese, "A Mutant *Ozzie and Harriet*," *Newsweek*, 25 December 1989, 70. As discussed in Chapter 3, *The Flintstones* was not thought of as mundane children's entertainment in the 1960s.

99. Quoted in Shales, "Primest Time."

100. Quoted in Morgenstern, "Real Father."

101. Quoted in Bill Brioux, "Keeping Up with *The Simpsons*," *TV Guide*, 29 March 1997. Note that exceptions to this do emerge, such as Homer's noted trait of being nearly impervious to phys-ical harm, especially head injuries.

102. Quoted in Schefelman, "Mutants." The lack of laugh track is notable, as previous primetime cartoons, such as *The Flintstones* and *The Jetsons*, had adopted the sitcom convention of the laugh track, even though they were clearly not "filmed before a live studio audience."

103. Paul A. Cantor, "In Praise of Television: The Greatest TV Show Ever," *American Enterprise*, September 1997, 34–37.

104. John Carman, "Don't Have a Cow! TV Hit Few Highs," *San Francisco Chronicle*, 30 December 1990, 46.

105. John Lichfield, "Giving New Meaning to Family Viewing," *The Independent*, 8 July 1990, 11.
106. Lesley Hetherington, "Here Comes *The Simpsons*," *Green Guide*, February 1991.
107. See Gitlin, *Inside Prime Time.*
108. Shales, "Primest Time."
109. Morgenstern, "Real Father."
110. Alice Cary, "Big Fans on Campus," *TV Guide*, 18 April 1992, 26–31; Ozersky, "TV's Anti-Families," 11.
111. Note that many articles suggest that the show did have an unusually high following among children as compared to other family sitcoms.
112. "Bad Bart," *Boston Globe*, 17 October 1990, 18.
113. Howard Rosenberg, "Bart & Family Try to Make the Grade," *Los Angeles Times*, 11 October 1990, F1.
114. Waters, "Family Feuds."
115. Mike Hughes, "Groening: Life in the Big Leagues," *Gannett News Service*, 29 July 1990.
116. Clark, "*Simpsons* Proves."
117. Quoted in Shales, "*The Simpsons*."
118. For accounts on these controversies, see Glynn, "Bartmania," and John Fiske, *Media Matters: Everyday Culture and Political Change* (Minneapolis: University of Minnesota Press, 1994).
119. "Bad Bart."
120. Tommy Denton, quoted in Glynn, "Bartmania," 66–67.
121. Quoted in "Principal Expels Bart Simpson," *Associated Press*, 28 April 1990.
122. See James Snead, *White Screens/Black Images: Hollywood from the Dark Side* (New York: Routledge, 1994), 84–85, for an account of animation's "rhetoric of harmlessness."
123. Donnie Radcliffe, "Marge to Barb; Don't Have a Cow, Ma'am," *Washington Post*, 12 October 1990, B1.
124. Shales, "*The Simpsons*."
125. Marvin Kitman, "That Quirky Simpsons Spark *The Simpsons*," *Newsday*, 6 December 1990, 85.
126. Terry Flew, "*The Simpsons*: Culture, Class and Popular TV," *Metro Magazine*, no. 97 (1994), 19.
127. Shales, "*The Simpsons*."
128. Laurel Shaper Walters, "'In' T-Shirts of Bart Simpson Are Out at Some Schools," *Christian Science Monitor*, 27 September 1990, 14.
129. Richard Zoglin, "Home Is Where the Venom Is," *Time*, 16 April 1990, 86.
130. Ozersky, "TV's Anti-Families," 14.
131. Quoted in Jim Sullivan, "Animation's Answer to the Bundys," *Boston Globe*, 14 January 1990, A1.
132. See Joanna Elm, "Are the Simpsons America's TV Family of the '90s?" *TV Guide*, 17 March 1990, 7–8; Berkman, "Sitcom Reality," 68–69.
133. Quoted in Rip Rense, "The Mainstreaming of Matt Groening," *Emmy*, August 1990, 106.
134. Jim Schembri, "Bart's Blues," *The Age*, November 1991.
135. Quoted in Shahid, "*The Simpsons*."
136. See Scott McCloud, *Understanding Comics: The Invisible Art* (New York: HarperPerennial, 1993), for a discussion of iconic versus photo-realist representation in comics.
137. Berkman, "Sitcom Reality," 69.
138. "King-Size Homer," originally aired 5 November 1995.
139. "The Principal and the Pauper," originally aired 28 September Skinner's 1997. This edict was violated in "I, D'oh-bot" (11 January 2004), as Lisa brings up Sleinner's secret to convince him to overlook the death of her cats, thus again denying narrative change in lieu of sitcom equilibrium.
140. Linda Hutcheon, *A Theory of Parody: The Teachings of 20th-Century Art Forms* (New York: Methuen, 1985).
141. Frank McConnell, "'Real' Cartoon Characters," *Commonweal*, 15 June 1990, 390.
142. Victoria A. Rebeck, "Recognizing Ourselves in the Simpsons," *The Christian Century*, 27 June 1990, 622.
143. David Arnold, "Bart a Class Act?" *Boston Globe*, 13 October 1990, 1.
144. Quoted in Glynn, "Bartmania," 67.
145. "The Simpsons Spin-Off Showcase," originally aired 11 May 1997.
146. See htpp://www.snpp.com/episodes/4F20, accessed 15 January 2004.

147. Jonathan Culler, *Structuralist Poetics: Structuralism, Linguistics, and the Study of Literature* (Ithaca, N.Y.: Cornell University Press, 1975), 148–52.
148. See Carol Stabile and Mark Harrison, eds., *Prime Time Animation: Television Animation and American Culture* (London: Routledge, 2003), for more accounts of these transformations.
149. Altman, *Film/Genre.*

Conclusion

1. Reality television has just recently received scholarly attention. Most notably, see Susan Murray and Laurie Ouellette, eds., *Reality TV: Remaking of Television Culture* (New York: New York University Press, 2004); James Friedman, ed., *Reality Squared: Televisual Discourses on the Real* (New Brunswick, N.J.: Rutgers University Press, 2002); Sam Brenton and Reuben Cohen, *Shooting People: Adventures in Reality TV* (London: Verso, 2003); and the special issue of *Television & New Media* on *Big Brother*, 3:3, August 2002.
2. See Henry Jenkins, "Professor Jenkins Goes to Washington," *Harper's*, July 1999, as a rare exception.
3. See Anna McCarthy, ""Stanley Milgram, Allen Funt, and Me": Cold War Social Science and the Roots of Reality TV," in *Reality TV* Eds. Murray and Ouellette, for the latter.

Appendix A
Cartoon Network's Greatest
50 Cartoons, aired 3/20/99

1. *Duck Amuck* (WB: Jones, 1953)
2. *One Froggy Evening* (WB: Jones, 1955)
3. *What's Opera, Doc?* (WB: Jones, 1957)
4. *Feed the Kitty* (WB: Jones, 1952)
5. *The Cat Came Back* (National Film Board of Canada, 1988)
6. *Gerald McBoing Boing* (UPA: Cannon, 1951)
7. *Rabbit Seasoning* (WB: Jones, 1952)
8. *I Love to Singa* (WB: Avery, 1936)
9. *A Pest in the House* (*Daffy*) (WB: Jones, 1947)
10. *The Great Piggy Bank Robbery* (*Daffy*) (WB: Clampett, 1946)
11. *Hair Raising Hare* (WB: Jones, 1946)
12. *Draftee Daffy* (WB: Clampett, 1945)
13. *King Size Canary* (MGM: Avery, 1947)
14. *Red Hot Riding Hood* (MGM: Avery, 1943)
15. *Bad Luck Blackie* (MGM: Avery, 1949)
16. *Porky in Wackyland* (WB: Clampett, 1938)
17. *The Big Snooze* (*Bugs*) (WB: Clampett, 1946)
18. *A Dream Walking* (*Popeye*) (Fleischer, 1934)
19. *Ventriloquist* Cat (MGM: Avery, 1950)
20. *Rabbit of Seville* (WB: Jones, 1950)
21. *Little Red Riding Rabbit* (WB: Freleng, 1941)
22. *Little Rural Riding Hood* (MGM: Avery, 1949)
23. *The Cat Concerto* (*Tom & Jerry*) (MGM: Hanna-Barbera, 1947)

24. *A Wild Hare* (WB: Avery, 1940)
25. *Quackor–Dexter's Laboratory* (Cartoon Network)
26. *Wossamotta U.* (*Bullwinkle*)
27. *Northwest Hounded Police* (MGM: Avery, 1946)
28. *Gee Whiz* (*Road Runner*) (WB: Jones, 1956)
29. *The Cat that Hated People* (MGM: Avery, 1948)
30. *Duck Dodgers in the 24-1/2 Century* (WB: Jones, 1953)
31. *Popeye the Sailor Meets Sinbad the Sailor* (Fleischer, 1936)
32. *Corny Concerto* (WB: Clampett, 1943)
33. *The Dot and the Line* (MGM: Jones, 1965)
34. *Deputy Droopy* (MGM: Avery, 1955)
35. *Puss Gets the Boot* (*Tom & Jerry*) (MGM: Hanna-Barbera, 1940)
36. *Swooner Crooner* (*Porky Pig*) (WB: Tashlin, 1944)
37. *Screwball Squirrel* (MGM: Avery, 1944)
38. *Little Johnny Jet* (MGM: Avery, 1953)
39. *Betty in Blunderland* (Fleischer, 1934)
40. *Superman* (Fleischer, 1941)
41. *Spud Dud* (*Huckleberry Hound*) (Hanna-Barbera, 1960)
42. *Walky Talky Hawky* (WB: McKimson, 1946)
43. *Tweetie Pie* (WB: Freleng, 1947)
44. *The Two Mouseketeers* (*Tom & Jerry*) (MGM: Hanna-Barbera, 1952)
45. *The Pink Phink* (UA: Freleng, 1964)
46. *Ghost with the Most* (*Pixie & Dixie*) (Hanna-Barbera, 1958)
47. *Goonland* (*Popeye*) (Fleischer, 1938)
48. *Drag-A-Long Droopy* (MGM: Avery, 1954)
49. *The Chicken from Outer Space* (Cartoon Network)
50. *Billy Boy* (MGM: Avery, 1954)

Appendix B

Jerry Beck, *The Fifty Greatest Cartoons as Selected by 1,000 Animation Professionals* (Atlanta: Turner Publishing, 1994).

1. *What's Opera, Doc?* (WB: Jones, 1957)
2. *Duck Amuck* (WB: Jones, 1953)
3. *The Band Concert* (Disney, 1935)
4. *Duck Dodgers in the 24-1/2 Century* (WB: Jones, 1953)
5. *One Froggy Evening* (WB: Jones, 1955)
6. *Gertie the Dinosaur* (Winsor McCay, 1914)
7. *Red Hot Riding Hood* (MGM: Avery, 1943)
8. *Porky in Wackyland* (WB: Clampett, 1938)
9. *Gerald McBoing Boing* (UPA: Cannon, 1951)
10. *King Size Canary* (MGM: Avery, 1947)
11. *Three Little Pigs* (Disney, 1933)
12. *Rabbit of Seville* (WB: Jones, 1950)
13. *Steamboat Willie* (Disney, 1928)
14. *The Old Mill* (Disney, 1937)
15. *Bad Luck Blackie* (MGM: Avery, 1949
16. *The Great Piggy Bank Robbery* (*Daffy*) (WB: Clampett, 1946)
17. *Popeye the Sailor Meets Sinbad the Sailor* (Fleischer, 1936)
18. *The Skeleton Dance* (Disney, 1929)
19. *Snow White* (*Betty Boop*) (Fleischer, 1933)
20. *Minnie the Moocher* (*Betty Boop*) (Fleischer, 1932)
21. *Coal Black and de Sebben Dwarfs* (WB: Clampett, 1943)

22. *Der Fuehrer's Face* (Disney, 1943)
23. *Little Rural Riding Hood* (MGM: Avery, 1949)
24. *The Tell-Tale Heart* (UPA, 1953)
25. *The Big Snit* (National Film Board of Canada, 1985)
26. *Brave Little Tailor* (Disney, 1938)
27. *Clock Cleaners* (Disney, 1937)
28. *Northwest Hounded Police* (MGM: Avery, 1946)
29. *Toot, Whistle, Plunk and Boom* (Disney, 1953)
30. *Rabbit Seasoning* (WB: Jones, 1952)
31. *The Scarlet Pumpernickel* (WB: Jones, 1950)
32. *The Cat Came Back* (National Film Board of Canada, 1988)
33. *Superman* (Fleischer, 1941)
34. *You Ought to Be in Pictures* (WB: Freleng, 1940)
35. *Ali Baba Bunny* (WB: Jones, 1957)
36. *Feed the Kitty* (WB: Jones, 1952)
37. *Bimbo's Initiation* (Fleischer, 1931)
38. *Bambi Meets Godzilla* (Marv Newland, 1969)
39. *Little Red Riding Rabbit* (WB: Freleng, 1941)
40. *Peace on Earth* (MGM: Harman, 1939)
41. *Rooty Toot Toot* (UPA: Hubley, 1952)
42. *The Cat Concerto* (*Tom & Jerry*) (MGM: Hanna-Barbera, 1947)
43. *The Barber of Seville* (*Woody Woodpecker*) (Lantz: Culhane, 1944)
44. *The Man Who Planted Trees* (Frederic Back, 1987)
45. *Book Revue* (*Daffy*) (WB: Clampett, 1946)
46. *Quasi at the Quackadero* (Sally Cruikshank, 1975)
47. *Corny Concerto* (WB: Clampett, 1943)
48. *A Unicorn in the Garden* (UPA: Hurtz, 1953)
49. *The Dover Boys* (WB: Jones, 1942)
50. *Felix in Hollywood* (Winkler, 1923)

Index